WARSAW TESTAMENT

WARSAW TESTAMENT

By Rokhl Auerbach

Translated by Samuel Kassow

Warsaw Testament
By Rokhl Auerbach
Translated by Samuel Kassow

White Goat Press, the Yiddish Book Center's imprint
Yiddish Book Center
Amherst, MA 01002
whitegoatpress.org

© 2024 by White Goat Press
Printed in the United States of America at The Studley Press, Dalton, MA
10 9 8 7 6 5 4 3 2

Paperback ISBN 979-8-9886773-8-3
Hardcover ISBN 979-8-9886773-9-0
Ebook ISBN 979-8-9894524-0-8

Library of Congress Control Number: 2023922649

Book and cover design by Michael Grinley

Cover photograph from the United States Holocaust Memorial Museum,
courtesy of Rafael Scharf

This book has been made possible
with generous support from
Larry and Muriel Gillick
and
Rosa E. Rosenberg

Table of Contents

Introduction

By Samuel Kassow

OF THE SIXTY PEOPLE that historian Emanuel Ringelblum invited to work on his secret Warsaw Ghetto archive, the Oyneg Shabes,[1] only three survived. One of them was Hersh Wasser, a historian, secretary of the archive, and one of Ringelblum's closest collaborators. Another was his wife, Bluma Wasser (née Kirszenfeld), a teacher who helped catalog the archive's collections and was among the first to document the use of gas vans to murder Jews in the Chelmno death camp. Rokhl Auerbach, a writer and journalist, was the third.

During the war Auerbach kept a secret diary, which she later published along with several other books describing her life in the Warsaw Ghetto and on the Aryan side of the city. Few memoirists told the story of the Warsaw ghetto with as much passion and insight as Auerbach did; few worked more diligently to persuade historians, lawyers, and the wider public to listen—really listen—to the testimony of survivors and to remember not just the famous names but also the ordinary people who went to their deaths. She urged her listeners not to forget their names, their foibles, their hopes and dreams, the little worlds that were destroyed along with them. She asked her readers to remember aspects of the Warsaw Ghetto that tended to fade into obscurity: the soup kitchens, children's libraries, house committee fundraisers, chamber concerts, choir rehearsals, young teenagers flirting at work and finding first love.

At a time when the Warsaw Ghetto Uprising emerged as *the* symbol of Jewish resistance and heroism during the Holocaust, it was Auerbach who pleaded with the wider public to remember the writers and poets along with the fighters, to respect the importance of cultural and spiritual resistance, and to ponder not just the trauma of mass murder but also the deep wound of cultural genocide.[2] The Germans committed a double murder: the physical destruction of the Jews and the erasure of their Yiddish speech and cultural legacy.

By all accounts Auerbach was not a happy person, nor was she easy to get along with.[3] Whether in prewar Warsaw literary circles or in Israel where she settled in 1950, Auerbach remained the outsider, often valued for her hard work and dedication but rarely regarded as a leader, an authority, or a decision maker. In a Jewish milieu dominated by political parties and ideological passions, Auerbach was a loner, belonging to no party and therefore lacking protectors and promoters to defend her and publicize her writings. Being a woman did not help either.

What Auerbach did have, to the day she died in Israel on May 31, 1976, was a mission: to protect and continue the legacy of the man who became her most important mentor, Dr. Emanuel Ringelblum, and that of his secret archive in the Warsaw Ghetto, the Oyneg Shabes.

>——◄

Ringelblum, a historian of Polish Jewry and a social activist, started the archive because he understood that one could resist with pen and paper as well as with guns. The Germans believed that they would win the war and that they would determine how, or if, the world would remember the Jews. The stakes were high. Just before he was killed in Majdanek, Ignacy Schiper, another leading Jewish historian in Poland and one of Ringelblum's teachers, told a fellow inmate: "What we know about murdered peoples is usually what their killers choose to say about them."[4] Ringelblum imbued all of his co-workers, including Auerbach, with the firm belief that even if they did not survive themselves, they would first gather and bury documents to ensure that even from beyond the grave *they* would write their own history, not the Germans. Thanks to those time capsules, they hoped, posterity would remember the murdered Jews as individuals with names and faces rather than as anonymous victims.

Had this archive disappeared forever, historians would have been dependent on German documents, Polish sources, and a few survivors' memoirs. Scholars could have investigated the development of German occupation policy, and they might have traced Polish attitudes toward the Jews. But they could have written little about the inner life of the Warsaw Ghetto. The religious writings of the Piaseczner Rebbe, Kalonymus Kalman Shapira; the thousands of pages of the underground press; the diaries of Ringelblum and Abraham Lewin; children's essays; escapees' accounts of Chelmno and Treblinka; hundreds of essays on small towns under German occupation, and much more—all would have vanished forever.

Of course, survivors would have written their memoirs and given their testimonies. But those accounts would have reflected what they knew after the event, not Jewish voices in real time. The testimony of those who survived mass murder was quite different from the words of those who did not know the final outcome, who were living in communities that were not yet destroyed. Survivor accounts recalled the ghetto as a holding pen for the camps rather than as a living community. The blazing anger and rage against other Jews, so common in contemporaneous writing, was much less evident in postwar testimonies. Indeed, certain striking differences between Auerbach's contemporaneous writings and her postwar revisions underscore this point, as she herself acknowledged.

Beginning in the 1970s, many superb studies have appeared about Warsaw Jewry during World War II. One need only cite the works of Ruta Sakowska, Israel Gutman, Havi Dreifuss, Jacek Leociak, Barbara Engelking, Katarzyna Person, Leah Preiss, or the more controversial but important monograph of Gunnar S. Paulsson.[5] Without the Ringelblum archive, it is hard to see how most of the books by these scholars could have been written. Without the archive, what could we have known about social conflict, folklore, Jewish reactions to the tightening Nazi vise, the attitudes of intellectuals, religious life, economic conditions, and resistance?

The determination to carry on Ringelblum's legacy began as soon as Auerbach left the ghetto, in March 1943. When the war ended, she buttonholed everyone she could find and demanded that Jewish organizations do everything possible to locate the buried caches of the Oyneg Shabes archive. The Yiddish writer Mendel Mann recalled Auerbach's talk at the third anniversary commemoration of the ghetto uprising, held in Warsaw in April 1946. After many tiresome speeches full of political posturing, Auerbach, the only woman on the podium, got up to speak.

She did not make any speeches, she did not "explain the meaning" of the uprising. She implored! With a stubbornness that deeply affected me, she demanded, she exhorted: "Remember," she cried out, "there is a national treasure under the ruins . . . Even if there are five stories of ruins, we must find the archive. I'm not making this up. I know what I'm talking about! This isn't just talk! This is coming from my heart. I will not rest, and I will not let you rest. We must rescue the Ringelblum archive!"[6]

Mann remembered that Auerbach's talk was met with a cool reception. People had their own troubles; they didn't need an archive to tell them what they had gone through.

Auerbach disagreed. More than ever before, survivors had to organize a systematic and collective effort to record the past and continue the work of the Oyneg Shabes. The traditions of the Ringelblum archive could counteract disturbing trends she had already noticed in early postwar memoirs of the Warsaw Ghetto. Some survivors—converts like the eminent biologist Ludwik Herszfeld or Polonized Jews like the pianist Wladyslaw Szpilman—presented, she believed, a skewed and distorted picture of the ghetto, "othering" the Yiddish-speaking Jewish masses. What could one expect, she asked, from individuals who had been so distant from Jewish society before the war?[7] Auerbach also complained about how political parties rushed to instrumentalize the memory of the ghetto and of Jewish resistance to claim credit and burnish their own roles.

Instead, Auerbach held up the model of the Oyneg Shabes, in which, she felt, a shared sense of national mission had trumped political differences. In the aftermath of the catastrophe a wounded nation had to look at its record, the good as well as the bad. To tell the whole truth, to add and subtract nothing, was a debt owed not just to the victims who had died but to the nation that had to recover and rebuild. Auerbach hallowed the exploits of the ghetto fighters and the partisans, but she did not want their story to overshadow and diminish the memory of the 99 percent who had no weapons.[8] As she wrote in 1958, "An entire people, clutching pens, in ghettos, in hiding places, in the face of gas chambers and machine gun muzzles, found the strength to write—for the sole reason that at some time the world should know."[9]

Her sense of mission led her to encourage survivors to record their experiences and to make sure that their voices were heard. After Auerbach left Poland for Israel in 1950, she established the witness testimony department of Yad Vashem.[10] What Annette Wieviorka called the "era of the witness"—the Eichmann trial being a key example—came about in no small measure thanks to the unstinting efforts of people like Auerbach to highlight the importance of survivor testimony.[11] At a time when scholars like Raul Hilberg argued that documents were better sources than survivor accounts, Auerbach countered that yes, documents were well and good, but they were a source that usually had more to say about perpetrators than victims. Long before eminent scholars like Saul Friedlander and Jan Tomasz Gross argued for the importance of victim narratives, Auerbach insisted that scholars and jurists take that testimony seriously, focusing not just on content but also on nuances of body language, phrasing, and affect. So what if those giving testimony got some names and dates wrong? Their authority as witnesses, the legitimacy gained from having been there, far outweighed mistaken details.[12]

Since so few of her writings have been translated into English, Auerbach remains relatively unknown outside a small circle of scholars.[13] Hopefully this present translation of her memoirs of the destruction of Warsaw Jewry, Jewish cultural resistance, and her own struggle to survive the war will give English-language readers a chance to appreciate the life and insights of an extraordinary woman.

>—<

Auerbach's wartime writings were divided into two periods: her two-and-a-half years in the Warsaw Ghetto, from 1940 to 1943, and the time she lived on the Aryan side of the conquered Polish capital, from March 1943 until the Polish uprising in August 1944. The ghetto writings, done on assignment for the Oyneg Shabes, were buried in tin boxes and milk cans along with the rest of the archive. After Auerbach left the ghetto, the clandestine Jewish National Committee, which tried to continue the work of the Oyneg Shabes, asked her to keep writing.[14] In 1943 and 1944 Auerbach composed two long essays: *They Called It Resettlement* and *Together with the People*. Polish friends helped her bury those materials in the Warsaw Zoo and the Mokotow fields in the south part of Warsaw.

Auerbach handed over the first cache of her ghetto writings to the Oyneg Shabes under harrowing circumstances. On July 22, 1942, the Germans began the liquidation of the Warsaw Ghetto. Each day seven to ten thousand Jews were rounded up and sent to the gas chambers of Treblinka. A few days later, on July 26, Ringelblum called an emergency meeting of the Oyneg Shabes executive committee and ordered everyone to hand over all their writings, notes, and essays—finished or unfinished—for immediate burial.[15] By then the Germans had already deported 30,000 Jews using the Jewish police as bloodhounds. They assured the policemen that if they handed over a daily quota of Jews for deportation, they and their families would be spared.

As Auerbach handed over her ghetto writings to the Oyneg Shabes on July 26, she attached a note in Yiddish that exposed her feelings: fear, anger, despair.

> I am handing over this unfinished essay to the archive. The fifth day of the "aktion." Perhaps such horrors have occurred before in Jewish history. But such shame, never. Jews as tools [of the killers]. I want to stay alive. I am ready to kiss the boots of the worst scoundrel just to see the moment of revenge. REVENGE REVENGE remember.[16]

In that same note she wondered whether her writings would share the same fate as the scribblings of a coal miner trapped in a cave-in whose body would never be found. Would anyone read them; would anyone care? Besides, she could no longer write coherently. If she survived, what good would she be to anybody?

That note might also be read as a last will and testament. How could Auerbach be sure that she would survive another day or another week? But against all odds Auerbach survived that summer, in part because of good hideouts, in part because of sheer luck. When the first phase of the deportation ended on September 12, and with the ranks of the Oyneg Shabes severely diminished, Ringelblum regrouped and refocused his efforts. He had Auerbach move to a new address in the central ghetto and set her up in a fictitious job so she could work full time for the archive.

When she took up her writing again on the Aryan side, she no longer had any doubts about her reasons for doing so. By mid-1943 the Warsaw Ghetto was nothing but burned rubble, its Jews murdered, a few harried survivors still holding on to life in hideouts or using false Polish papers. Of course, she had to write. She owed that to the dead and to Ringelblum, who was still alive and expecting her to continue. So late at night, in a room on Smolna Street, she would write until the early hours of the morning. After a few hours of sleep, she would then get up to make her rounds of the city, carrying money and messages to Jews in hiding and working as an assistant to a Polish manufacturer of paper bags.

Those nocturnal sessions, when she put her raw memories and emotions on paper, were not easy. How could she find the words to describe what she had seen? In late 1943, she wrote:

> The mass murder, the murder of millions of Jews by the Germans, is a fact that speaks for itself. It is very dangerous to add interpretations or analyses to this subject. Anything that is said can quickly turn into hopeless hysteria or endless sobs. One must approach this subject with the greatest caution, in a restrained and factual manner . . . this has been my intention: not to express but to transmit, to note only facts but not to interpret.[17]

As she quickly realized, however, this mandate was impossible, even for herself.

>——<

When the Germans fled Warsaw in January 1945, Auerbach retrieved *They Called It Resettlement* and *Together with the People,* her writings from the Aryan side. After the discovery of the first and second caches of the Ringelblum archive in September 1946 and December 1950, Auerbach also gained limited access to her ghetto writings, which included an important diary, an essay on the soup kitchen that she directed at Leszno 40, and the testimony of Treblinka escapee Avrom Yankev Krzepicki, whom she interviewed in late 1942. As she surveyed those bits of paper plucked from the ruins, Auerbach mordantly remarked that she had better luck saving documents than people.[18]

When she left Poland for Israel in 1950, Auerbach did not let those precious papers out of her sight. "These manuscripts have endured much hardship," she wrote.

> They were buried in the ground, and I, by myself, agonized and suffered to bring them once again into the light of day. I succeeded in getting them out of Poland and they came to Israel with me. I brought them in a special box. I never parted with them, either on the train or on the boat.[19]

After the war, first in Poland and then in Israel, Auerbach rewrote and edited all these writings. The differences between what she wrote during the war and what she published later reflect both a personal journey of survival and an ever-evolving search for the meaning of Holocaust memory. These writings—revised and rewritten—appeared in numerous newspaper articles as well as in three books published in Israel: *Behutsot Varsha* (*In Warsaw Courtyards*), *Varshever tsavoes* (*Warsaw Testaments*), and *Baym letstn veg* (*The Last Journey*).[20] This volume presents the reader with a full translation of *Varshever tsavoes* along with selections from *Baym letstn veg*. Both books are largely based on her 1943–44 writings, while also including lengthy excerpts from her ghetto diary and notes. *Varshever tsavoes* was published in 1974, two years before Auerbach died of cancer. She personally edited the book and added footnotes, most of which are reproduced in this translation. *Baym letstn veg* appeared one year after Auerbach's death. She clearly had no chance to edit the manuscript and did not add explanatory or reference notes. *Baym letstn veg* also contained many repetitions that Auerbach doubtless would have spotted had she lived to finish the final editing. However tempting it was to create a fully edited version of these writings for the present volume, this translator believes that he does not have the right to do so, although the order of some entries has been changed.

After the war, when she had recovered her wartime manuscripts, Auerbach's writing took on another purpose: to ensure that the Jewish people not only kept faith with the dead, but also used the lessons of the Holocaust to strengthen the Jewish state and tighten the bonds between Israel and the Diaspora. The breathtaking solidarity that world Jewry exhibited in the weeks before the outbreak of the Six-Day War in 1967, when the very existence of Israel seemed to be in doubt, convinced her more than ever that the lessons of the Holocaust remained vital for the future of the Jewish people.[21]

ROKHL AUERBACH'S LIFE encompassed many touchstones of the twentieth-century East European Jewish experience. She was born in 1899[22] in Jewish Galicia and spent her youth first in rural Podolia and later in Lemberg, its cultural hub.[23] In 1932 she moved to Warsaw, the prewar Jewish metropolis, and spent some of the most significant years of her life moving in the city's journalistic and literary circles. During the war she was imprisoned in the Warsaw Ghetto, where she was recruited into the Oyneg Shabes archive. After escaping the ghetto, she posed as a Polish woman in the German-occupied city and served as a courier for the Jewish underground. In postwar Poland she emerged as a pioneer of Holocaust research through the Central Jewish Historical Commission, along with Philip Friedman, Michal Borwicz, Joseph Kermish, and others. After immigrating to the State of Israel she organized the survivor testimony division at Yad Vashem and played an important behind-the-scenes role during the Eichmann trial, urging the prosecution to present a wide-ranging story of Jewish suffering based on survivor testimony rather than a narrow focus on Eichmann's particular activities in the Nazi bureaucracy. Through it all she had to contend with many personal setbacks and suffer many frustrations and slights.

Like her fellow Oyneg Shabes collaborator Peretz Opoczynski, Auerbach was a superb observer of the everyday. She had a fine sense for the behavior and speech of different classes of Polish Jews, whether they lived in small towns or in urban centers like Warsaw. Like Ringelblum, she was a native of that part of southeast Galicia known as Podolia, with towns that were Jewish and Polish and a countryside that was largely Ukrainian. Before moving with her family to Lwow, she spent her childhood in a remote village—not a shtetl—called Lanowitz, where she acquired a love of Jewish folklore and the Yiddish language. The pioneering Jewish folklorist and ethnographer Shmuel Lehman interviewed her many times about the folk songs and customs of the rural Jews of Podolia. She devotes a long chapter to Lehman in this book.

Living cheek by jowl with Polish and Ukrainian neighbors, she also came to feel an unmistakable bond with her Slavic environment. That complex relationship between Jews and non-Jews in the Polish and Ukrainian borderlands, marked by a nuanced interplay of intimacy and alienation, sympathy and enmity, neighborly tranquility and bouts of sudden violence, left a permanent imprint on her personality. She believed that her childhood surroundings later helped save her life:

> How did I survive on the Aryan side when hundreds of other Jews perished? It certainly was not because I was smarter. What helped me were my early years growing up in a village. Those close ties with non-Jews left a mark on my personality. What rubbed off on me was that rural Slavic temperament . . . [24]

Much of the power of Auerbach's reportage stemmed from her ability to navigate cultural boundaries and from a life that straddled different worlds: village, shtetl, and city; Yiddish and Polish; Ukrainians, Poles, and Jews; Galicia and Warsaw; religious and secular; Diaspora nationalists and Zionists; the Jewish literary elite and the Jewish masses.

><

Like many other Galician Jews, Auerbach combined a deep Jewish identity with a first-class Polish education and cultural sensibility.[25] At Lwow University in the early 1920s Auerbach befriended the young poet Debora Vogel and the budding writer and painter Bruno Schulz. She urged them to start writing in Yiddish, and Vogel indeed did so.[26] In 1929 she helped found *Tsushtayer*, a literary journal that tried to bring the Polish speaking Galician Jewish intelligentsia closer to Yiddish. In large part thanks to Auerbach and Vogel, *Tsushtayer* published many women writers in Yiddish as well as critical discussions of their work.[27]

Auerbach would go on to have many interests, but one of the

most salient was her devotion to Yiddish and Yiddish secular culture. Her vision of that culture was inclusive rather than exclusive, one that united Jews and transcended political differences, a culture whose creativity would silence the mockers who regarded Yiddish as nothing more than low class *zhargon*.[28]

In the end *Tsushtayer* could not achieve its ambitions. It folded in 1932 after three issues, unable to overcome financial difficulties and disagreements over politics. For Auerbach, Yiddish culture came first and politics second, but others disagreed. As she edited the journal, she had to endure some condescending and misogynistic sniping aimed at her and at Vogel.[29] Such incidents continued when she left for Warsaw and strove to win respect as a writer. In the late 1930s she earned the nickname "Di Literarishe Baylage" (The Literary Supplement), a snide reference to her relationship with the brilliant Yiddish poet Itsik Manger, with whom she lived and who was at the height of his literary powers.[30] Later she wondered if her path in Yad Vashem would have been easier had she not been a woman. But such difficulties only encouraged Auerbach to redouble her efforts to highlight the critical contributions of women to Yiddish literature.

Despite her love of Galicia and of Lwow, Auerbach realized that Yiddish high culture faced a bleak future there.[31] In 1932 she moved to Warsaw, the biggest Jewish community in Europe and the center of the Yiddish press and theater. Above all, Warsaw was home to the legendary Tlomackie 13, headquarters of the Association of Jewish Writers and Journalists. At any hour, day or night, the lights were on in Tlomackie 13: there you could find fierce political rivals hunched over a game of chess, Friday night dances, holiday balls, lectures and debates, Jews from distant shtetls showing up to invite famous Yiddish writers and journalists for weekend lectures. Visitors to Tlomackie 13 always remembered that the "shed" (the building was referred to as the "buda," or "shed") was full of music and song. At any moment they might hear spontaneous renditions of Yiddish folk songs or the tango tunes popularized by Artur Gold and J. Peterburski. The writers also loved to sing the songs of the Jewish underworld, which were collected by the folklorist Shmuel Lehman. Cantors like Gershon Sirota would stop by and trade stories with Menakhem Kipnis, who collected Jewish folk music, edited the journal *Cantor's World,* and wrote articles on music for the Yiddish press. This was also a time when Yiddish films became popular in Poland. Movies such as *The Dybbuk*, *Yidl mitn fidl* (*A Jew with a Fiddle*), and *A brivele der mamen* (*A Letter to Mother*) attracted large audiences on both sides of the Atlantic. Tlomackie hosted many pioneers of the Yiddish cinema, including Joseph Green, Leo Forbert, Michał Waszyński, and others.[32] The saga of Tlomackie 13 figures prominently in these memoirs.

But beneath the surface not all was well with Yiddish culture in Poland. By the late 1930s increasing numbers of Jews were speaking Polish as their first language and attending Polish schools. While the Jewish dailies in the Polish language were becoming more widely read, the Yiddish press was losing circulation. Many of the movers and shakers who had graced Yiddish Warsaw with their presence in the 1920s—Perets Markish, Uri Tsevi Grinberg, Israel Joshua Singer, and Auerbach's close friend Melech Ravitch—had left Poland for the Soviet Union, Mandatory Palestine, the United States, or Australia. It seemed as if Yiddish culture was in decline, and for every well-paid journalist and successful writer, there were dozens who were dependent on part time jobs and measly honoraria. Many deeply resented the lucky few and nurtured their grievances. Adding to the feeling of malaise were destructive political tensions and intrigues.

After a brief marriage to the poet Ber Shnaper failed, and after she became the partner of the brilliant and tempestuous Yiddish poet Itsik Manger, Auerbach supported herself, precariously, by translation and by writing articles and reviews for the Jewish press in Yiddish and Polish. When Manger was sober he wrote brilliant poetry and prose; when he was drunk, which was often, he would turn quite nasty, with Auerbach often the target of his anger. Her relationship with Manger, never easy, faced new hurdles when Poland refused to renew his residence visa in 1938 (he was a Romanian citizen) and forced him to leave the country. Their next—and last—meeting, in 1946, was a traumatic experience for Auerbach. Manger hoped that Auerbach would return to him. She made it clear that her main purpose now was to continue the legacy of the Oyneg Shabes and that she no longer had the emotional strength to deal with him. At a reception in London in 1946, where Auerbach was attending the World Jewish Congress as a member of the Polish Jewish delegation, Manger came drunk, accused Auerbach of exploiting the tragedy of Polish Jewry for her personal gain, and called her a prostitute. They never met again.[33]

Like so many of her compatriots, Poles and Jews alike, Auerbach watched with mounting dread as German threats against Poland escalated during the spring and summer of 1939. Right up until the Friday morning of September 1, when German bombers appeared over Warsaw, Auerbach and her friends hoped that somehow Hitler might flinch. As Polish resistance collapsed, German forces encircled Warsaw; Auerbach was trapped inside the city as it endured German artillery fire and daily air raids. By the time the Poles surrendered the city, at the end of September 1939, thousands of civilians had been killed and about a quarter of Warsaw's buildings suffered serious damage.

After Poland's capitulation Auerbach was about to flee to Lwow when she received an unexpected summons from Emanuel Ringelblum asking her to stay in Warsaw and run a soup kitchen. Most of the Jewish elite had run away, but Ringelblum reminded Auerbach that not everyone had the right to flee.

>——<

Ringelblum thus brought Auerbach into the far-flung network of the Aleynhilf, the "Self Help" of the Warsaw Ghetto, with its 1,200 house committees, dozens of soup kitchens, and day care centers for children, all of which served as venues for clandestine cultural activity. The leaders of the Aleynhilf saw the organization as the conscience of Warsaw Jewry, a counterweight to the German-imposed Judenrat.[34] For Auerbach, the Aleynhilf was a revelation, a sterling example of how prewar political opponents could put aside their differences and work together for the common good.[35]

During World War I the great Yiddish writer I. L. Peretz had stressed the interdependence of relief efforts and *zamling*, the gathering of documents to enable Jews to write the history of their experiences. In the Second World War, by the same token, the Aleynhilf made the functioning of the Oyneg Shabes archive possible. Ringelblum used the soup kitchens and refugee centers to gather information and find writers, as well as to save the members of the Jewish intelligentsia by giving them jobs. In 1941 he recruited Auerbach to the Oyneg Shabes by asking her to write an essay about her soup kitchen. Auerbach's soup kitchen at Leszno 40, which fed two thousand Jews a day, offered her a unique vantage point to get to know and observe a large number of "customers." In a telling coincidence, that kitchen was in the same building where Peretz had directed relief efforts for Jewish refugees in 1914 and 1915. As Auerbach would stress after the war, had it not been for Ringelblum she would not have written a thing.

The story that Auerbach wrote for the Oyneg Shabes provided a gripping, behind-the-scenes look at the desperate battle that the ghetto was fighting against hunger. Auerbach investigated the "social history" of hunger, using the story of a soup kitchen as a microcosm of human relationships and choices. The dead who ended up in the pits of the Gęsia cemetery were not an undifferentiated mass but individuals whose idiosyncrasies Auerbach recorded. She deftly caught the phrases or habits that made them memorable: the young mother, expelled from her shtetl, who arrived at the soup kitchen with four children in tow and a tot suckling at her breast; a family of solid, rugged Jewish boys from a country farm who had also been expelled into the ghetto. Each day they would take a bowl of soup for their aged father. When they mentioned him, they never failed to add "may he live until 120." These were solid members of the Jewish middle class, now reduced to desperate poverty.

Auerbach, as the director of the soup kitchen, confronted serious psychological pressures and moral challenges. Like other figures in the Aleynhilf she had seen herself as an honest public servant imbued with the moral code of the progressive Jewish intelligentsia. Very quickly, however, she discovered that for the masses of starving desperate people who came to the kitchen each day she represented authority and power. In their eyes she had become an arbiter of life and death. Like Ringelblum, she had come from a milieu that was imbued with love for the "Jewish masses." Now these masses, these ordinary Jews, stormed her office, blocked her in the corridors, and begged for extra soup tickets. They looked at Auerbach as someone who could save them. Some confronted her in silent supplication, others yelled and reminded Auerbach loudly of their former status. Then there were the children, who would come in packs and cajole her in Yiddish-accented Polish, "plosze, pani"—"please, ma'am"—for some extra food.

It seemed to her then as if the kitchen only prolonged their agony and saved no one. Should she favor a chosen few or dole out equal rations and save none of them? Ringelblum asked the same question.[36] Increasingly frustrated, Auerbach singled out a chosen few for special care: the religious poet Yisroel Shtern for instance, or a German-speaking refugee from the Sudetenland, Brocksmeier, who had survived Dachau and whom Ringelblum wanted to keep alive as a witness. This former athlete, the "Datch" as he was called in Warsaw Yiddish, won Auerbach over with his impeccable manners, good nature, and spry sense of humor. For Auerbach Brocksmeier became a litmus test and a challenge. She bent her rules and gave him extra food. When he began to become apathetic, a common sign of starvation, she would yell at him that she could feed him but that he had to summon the will to live. It was important, Auerbach felt, to win at least one victory. But here too she failed. In her diary entry of August 4, 1941, she noted, "What is the use of all of our work if we can't save even one person from death by hunger?"[37] In the face of her mounting frustrations, Auerbach also had to deal with the growing terror that engulfed the ghetto. In 1942 the Germans began a wave of nocturnal shootings, and ominous reports reached the ghetto of mass killings in the provinces.[38]

Impressed with her essay on the soup kitchen, Ringelblum gave her new assignments. In September 1942, Ringelblum and Shmuel Winter, a sympathetic member of the Judenrat, asked Auerbach to interview Abraham Krzepicki, who had escaped from Treblinka. Auerbach's debriefing of Krzepicki became one of the most important documents of the Oyneg Shabes, and many of its details were included in a report that the archive sent to London in November 1942 using the channels of the Polish underground. Those interviews with Krzepicki were another emotional ordeal for Auerbach. She knew that she was doing something important by preparing a document that would reveal German crimes to the world. The experience also gave Auerbach a special bond with Treblinka survivors, about whom she wrote in the late 1940s and whose honor she defended in the 1960s during the controversy over Jean-Francois Steiner's book *Treblinka: The Revolt of an Extermination Camp*.[39] At the same time, Krzepicki's descriptions of the brutality of the camp and the agonizing mass death in the gas chambers deepened her own terror of what probably seemed like her own fate.

FOR AUERBACH, MEMORY and mourning demanded a painful return to the intense, vibrant world of prewar Jewish Warsaw. It was a world that one of her mentors, the Yiddish poet Melech Ravitch, had described as a sprawling mosaic of different Jewish tribes and subcultures; a mosaic of hundreds of thousands of Hasidim, of Polish-speaking middle class Jews; of Litvaks, Bundists and many more.[40] Auerbach took its shattered bits and pieces and reconstructed a mosaic of memory based on dozens of individual vignettes. Thus she spoke for those who had no one to remember them: the ordinary Jews she came to know in the ghetto as she ran the soup kitchen at Leszno 40 and the Jewish writers, artists, and actors whose milieu she had shared since the 1930s. The more one knew about what and whom the Germans had murdered, the more one could grasp the enormity of the national devastation. And as Auerbach struggled to describe the destruction of Warsaw Jewry, her story shifted into an argument for Warsaw's particular place in the history of Polish Jewry.

In 1945 Auerbach recalled that she first came to Warsaw, exactly twenty years before, during the intermediate days of Passover, as tens of thousands of Jews were streaming to the Gęsia cemetery to dedicate the Peretz Mausoleum, the Ohel Peretz.

> ... That was the first time I had seen such a thing, and I was astonished and deeply moved. Organized and spontaneous delegations swept through the mass of Jews of all walks of life wearing caps and hats and yarmulkes; businessmen and workers, young and old: a mobile forest of people. To my eyes it looked like something out of Asia. I could never have seen such a thing among Jews in Lemberg ... This was Jewish Warsaw and this was how it expressed its feelings for one of its spiritual leaders. As many Jews as were then gathered in the Gensher cemetery are not now to be found in all of Poland.[41]

In a similar vein, and around the same time, the writer Leo Finkelshteyn, a good friend of Auerbach's, also tried to grasp what Jewish Warsaw had meant. As it did for Auerbach, what Warsaw conjured up for Finkelshteyn were the huge crowds: the masses of Jews who came to Peretz's funeral; to the May Day demonstrations;

to greet Hasidic rebbes. Unlike Vilna, whose place in Jewish life rested on its heritage and historical tradition, Warsaw's prominence derived from its sheer mass and power. Unencumbered by encrusted traditions, Warsaw was the great pathbreaker in the modernization of Jewish life.[42]

Just weeks before he perished, Abraham Lewin, a key member of the Oyneg Shabes, also tried to describe the special place of Warsaw. Writing in late 1942, he emphasized that Warsaw was the nerve center of Polish Jewry, which was in turn the cultural heart of the Jewish people. How, he asked, would the Jewish nation survive this unprecedented disaster?[43] Lewin would soon be murdered, probably in Treblinka. But his question underscores the special agony felt by Holocaust victims who had to witness the destruction of their families, their people, their city, and their Yiddish language without the consolation of knowing—for example—that a Jewish state would arise after the war. If Auerbach could do nothing else, she could at least ensure that posterity remembered what this great Jewish metropolis once meant.

Before the war Auerbach confessed a certain ambivalence toward Jewish Warsaw. On the one hand she was quick to defend the Jewish masses from accusations leveled by condescending outsiders.[44] Yet she freely admitted that she shared the widespread pessimism about the future of Warsaw as a Jewish, and more specifically Yiddish, cultural center, especially considering the rampant acculturation and economic woes of Polish Jewry. After the war she revised her previous skepticism. It would be easy to dismiss Auerbach's change of heart—her belief that before the war she had underestimated Jewish Warsaw's true potential and promise—as a post-Holocaust need to sanctify what had been destroyed. But that would not be accurate.

In her postwar writings Auerbach explained that she had doubted the prospects for Yiddish culture in Poland because she had underestimated the vitality of the Jewish masses. It was her work for the Aleynhilf, in the soup kitchens, that brought her into close contact not only with ordinary Jews but also with impressive leaders of the religious world that she never would have come to know otherwise. It was then that she understood Jewish life to be so deeply rooted, and Jews so numerous, that the nation could have counted on the cultural capital of Polish Jewry for generations to come.

... Yet we were in the middle of a powerful, dynamic, and large Jewish folk community ... those same masses were too numerous and too concentrated to lose the essential core of their national identity. The religious strata . . . comprised such an enormous reservoir of spiritual energy and human resources that they more than compensated for all we lost through assimilation.

We writers thought that we had come too late and all that remained was a wilted garden. We did not realize that the garden was about to offer a rich new harvest of fruit—had the cataclysm not engulfed us all.[45]

What she saw in the ghetto represented a flowering of Jewish genius, a bright flame just before the final destruction. On the Aryan side, Auerbach devoted a large part of her wartime and postwar writings to the Warsaw Jewish intelligentsia that had been murdered: writers Kalman Lis, Yosef Kirman, and Yoshue Perle; actresses like Miriam Orleska; painters and sculptors Abraham Ostrzega and Roman Kramsztyk; composers and choir directors such as David Eisenstadt; and singers such as Eisenstadt's daughter Marysia. She described Shiye Broyde, her boss in the Aleynhilf, who had translated Plato's dialogues into Yiddish and who, had he survived, would have enriched the Yiddish language; Yankev Glatshteyn, who led a choir of impoverished, working-class children; Yisroel Shtern, who wrote his best poetry, Auerbach believed, just months before his death; Rosa Simchowicz, a saintly pedagogue who had dedicated her life to working in the secular Yiddish school system; and Leyb Shur, a devotee of Yiddish books and libraries. As Auerbach traced the broad reach of Yiddish culture, which embraced music and the arts as well as literature, she underscored the depth of a German murder machine that destroyed a language and culture along with a people. As she notes in the present volume, the Romans had at least respected the cultures of their conquered foes. Not so the Germans.

One of the greatest of Auerbach's wartime works, and one of the very few translated into English, was *Yizkor*,[46] first written, she said, in late 1943 and devoted to the memory of Jewish Warsaw.[47] While sitting in a trolley car in November 1943, she had seen a Polish woman weeping over her son, whom the Germans had shot. At least the woman, whose lips moved like the biblical Hannah's, could mourn her son in public, Auerbach thought, while she did not dare betray her grief over the destruction of her entire people. That night, as she tells the story, she went to her room at Smolna 24 and began to write her elegy for Warsaw Jewry.

> I may neither groan nor weep. I may not draw attention to myself in the street. And I need to groan; I need to weep. Not four times a year. I feel the need to say *Yizkor* four times a day.

She poured out her soul as she tried to describe the murder of her people: the children whom she remembered from ghetto schools, tough Jewish workers, hardened women shopkeepers, young scouts, courting couples, intellectuals—all gone. Even if a few individuals survived, the vibrant, raucous, and diverse mosaic of Warsaw Jewry had been destroyed. *Yizkor* humanized the victims by recalling not only their individuality but also their city, the specific urban milieu that shaped them and that made them "Varshever."

Auerbach began the essay by describing a natural catastrophe she remembered from her childhood: a flood that swept everything before it.

> . . . At a distance one could see mouths gaping, but one could not hear the cries because the roar of the waters drowned out everything.
>
> And that's how the Jewish masses flowed to their destruction at the time of the deportations. Sinking as helplessly into the deluge of destruction.
>
> And if, for even one of the days of my life, I should forget how I saw you then, my people, desperate and confused, delivered over to extinction, may all knowledge of me be forgotten and my name be cursed like that of those traitors who are unworthy to share your pain.

In other essays, Auerbach regretted the lack of armed resistance before January 1943. *Yizkor* was different. Unlike the works of other Oyneg Shabes writers who observed the deportation, such as Shiye Perle, Israel Lichtenstein, or Peretz Opoczynski, Auerbach's *Yizkor* projected empathy rather than anger. As David Roskies has pointed out, by using the imagery of a flood, of a natural disaster, she anticipated future questions that those who were not there might pose.[48]

No, the mass murder was not a metahistorical event. But its enormity was too horrible and too unprecedented to allow for glib theories and facile questions that might compromise the memory of the Jewish masses she cherished so deeply. How does one resist a flood or an earthquake? What befell the Jews was so unthinkable and so calamitous that they were psychologically unprepared. Implicitly, Auerbach was anticipating the invidious distinctions that many would make after the war between the few who fought back with weapons and the many who had allegedly died without resistance. It was the entire people she wrote about in *Yizkor*, not just the fighters who had risen up a few months before.

In the end this secular writer could only repeat the words of the traditional *Yizkor* prayer. For Auerbach, *Yizkor* was a return not to religion but to the murdered world of her birth, to a community that did not have to invent new words to describe pain and loss. They were already there, in the prayers. Like her murdered friends, Auerbach was *tsuzamen mitn folk*—together with the people.

>—◄

In *Yizkor*, as in so much of her other work, Auerbach tried to explain how brilliantly the Germans exploited mass psychology to fool the Jews and make it easier to murder them. By the same token, drawing on her prewar interest in psychology, Auerbach explored how Jews reacted to their individual and national tragedy: the mechanisms of self-defense, delusion, misplaced hope, and the struggle for life.

Auerbach's sensitivity to the psychological dimension of Jewish responses to the Holocaust was a natural continuation of her prewar university study of psychology and phenomenology. Her involvement with the YIVO (Yiddish Scientific Institute), whose Warsaw branch included Emanuel Ringelblum, also played a role. YIVO director Max Weinreich had made special efforts to incorporate the insights of Sigmund Freud and social psychology into the study of Polish Jewish youth. In the highly politicized and divided world of interwar Polish Jewry, where so many thinkers stressed the primacy of the collective over the individual, Weinreich—in his "Youth Studies" (*yungforshung*) project, for instance—argued that one could not understand "Klal Yisroel" (the collective) without grasping the aspirations, drives, obsessions, and hopes of "Reb Yisroel"—that is, the many individuals who made up the Jewish mass in Poland.[49]

Similarly, Auerbach in her Holocaust writings highlights the complex interplay of psychological factors within individuals, families, and entire social groups. She told a complicated story of resilience, vitality, and self-sacrifice on the one hand and of corruption and moral collapse on the other. She had brilliant insights—resulting from conversations with folklorist Shmuel Lehman in the ghetto—about how rumors, jokes, and street songs could serve as a defensive reflex, a poignant but powerful sign of instinctive resistance.

Auerbach stressed the Germans' skillful use of psychology to effect the destruction of Warsaw Jewry and to use the Jews' strengths against them. The Germans played with the Jews and with their natural instincts for self-preservation and hope. In her brilliant observations of the mass hysteria that gripped the ghetto in the summer of 1942, Auerbach described how the very qualities that had served Jews so well in the past—practicality, pragmatism, hard headedness, and natural optimism—now accelerated their plunge into the abyss.

> And still other Jews. Broad shouldered, deep voiced, with powerful hands and hearts. Artisans, workers. Wagon drivers, porters, Jews who, with a blow of their fists, could floor any hooligan who dared enter their neighborhoods.
>
> Where were you when your wives and children, when your old fathers and mothers, were taken away? What happened to make you run off like cattle stampeded by fire? Was there no one to give you some purpose in the confusion? You were swept away by the flood, together with those who were weak.
>
> And you sly cunning merchants, philanthropists in your short fur coats and caps. How was it that you didn't catch on to the murderous swindle?[50]

Would other peoples, confronted with a similar assault, have acted better? Auerbach did not think so. Did Warsaw Jewry eventually recover from the shock and fight back? Yes. Should one blame the Jewish masses for not having fought back earlier? Only those who had not been there, Auerbach implied, would do so. Was armed resistance the only way the Jews stood up to the Germans? Absolutely not.

>—◄

One of the more striking features of Auerbach's writings from this period is her portrayal of Poland and the Poles. As Havi Dreyfuss has shown, the cautiously positive image that many Polish Jews had of their Polish compatriots at the beginning of the war and the occupation became sharply negative after the beginning of the mass murder in 1942.[51] But after Auerbach reached the Aryan side and became a courier who distributed money and aid to hidden Jews, she was in constant contact with a group of Poles most Jews never encountered: the liberal, intellectual elite. Her descriptions of individuals such as Jan and Antonina Żabiński are particularly instructive and insightful. Jan Żabiński had been the director of the Warsaw Zoo, as well as an officer in the Polish underground. During the war he and his wife helped many Jews, including Auerbach herself.

Auerbach's devotion to the memory of Jewish Warsaw in no way diminished her empathy for Polish Warsaw and its sufferings. In *Varshever tsavoes* she penned a sympathetic portrayal of Warsaw's mayor, Stefan Starzyński, who called on his fellow citizens to resist the Germans and who led the city during the terrible siege in September 1939. Right after a bombardment of Jewish neighborhoods, Starzyński paid a visit and stroked the heads of Jewish children. Perhaps, Auerbach speculated, as he walked through those Jewish streets Starzyński thought about how Poland had treated its Jews as second-class citizens before the war. Perhaps the terror of the siege had a silver lining. For a brief moment the fight against a common enemy brought Poles and Jews together and offered a glimpse of what might have been.[52] Before the war Starzyński had not been known as a philosemite. But like so many others, Auerbach speculated, perhaps the war caused him to "grow beyond himself."

Many people would naturally wonder, Auerbach noted, why Starzyński and his fellow Poles defended Warsaw at all. It was a hopeless fight that led to many needless civilian casualties. Another

Warsaw Jewish diarist, Chaim Kaplan, had nothing but contempt for a doomed battle that caused so much suffering. But Auerbach, nurtured on Polish romanticism, was full of admiration:

> Romanticism? Idealism? Let the cynics scoff all they want. I scorn them. Other European peoples didn't fight like the Poles. We Polish Jews understood their fight, we fought alongside them, and we understand it even now.[53]

>——<

When the war ended Auerbach played a key role in establishing a Jewish Historical Institute in Poland, collecting survivor testimonies and publishing monographs and eyewitness accounts. During those years Auerbach published books about Treblinka and about the Warsaw Ghetto Uprising.[54] She became interested in film as a medium for conveying the story of the Holocaust and helped write the screenplay of the Yiddish film *Undzere kinder* (*Our Children*), which appeared in 1948. In postwar Poland she worked closely with scholars like Philip Friedman, Joseph Kermish, and Nachman Blumenthal, who had a significant impact on her work in the years to come.

However promising her work was, it soon became apparent that she had no place in a Poland that was quickly becoming a Stalinist dictatorship. Ber Mark, who became the director of the Jewish Historical Institute, imposed a new regime and toed the Communist line. Most of the scholars who worked there, including Michal Borwicz, Friedman, Kermish, and Isaiah Trunk, packed their bags and left.

Although Auerbach had a chance to go to the United States, she chose to settle in Israel, convinced that the new state was where the Jewish people could recover and thrive. She arrived in 1950, and after a six-month intensive Hebrew course (which produced mixed results) she redoubled her efforts to promote the gathering of witness testimony and protect the memory of the Holocaust. Her major opportunity came in 1953, with the founding of Yad Vashem.

The fifteen years that Auerbach worked at Yad Vashem brought her both gratification and bitter disappointment. When Yad Vashem began its work it seemed as if Auerbach finally had the chance to fulfill her life's mission and continue Ringelblum's legacy. In March

1954 Auerbach was appointed the head of the department of survivor testimony. The department was located in Tel Aviv and suffered from cramped quarters and an inadequate budget. Nonetheless, Auerbach began a relentless drive to track down survivors and collect their accounts.[55] Thus, she hoped, Yad Vashem would carry on the work of collecting documents and writing history that had begun before the war in the YIVO, continued in the ghettos and camps, and after the war expanded to include efforts by survivors to publish memorial books.

At Yad Vashem Auerbach crafted detailed guidelines to help interviewers question survivors. She stressed the importance of letting survivors talk, with a minimum of interference and commentary. To that end, tape recorders and video recorders, rather than interviewers' notes, were essential.[56] While there was a widespread belief that encouraging survivors to speak about the past only deepened their pain, Auerbach believed that the opposite was the case, and that delving into their experiences, especially with an interlocutor who was also a survivor, had therapeutic value.

Unfortunately, the proper approach to survivor interviews wasn't the only point of contention within the organization. Simmering tensions between Yad Vashem president Ben-Zion Dinur and Auerbach, along with other survivor-scholars working there, turned into a nasty public fight. Dinur, a respected historian, believed that Yad Vashem should work closely with the Hebrew University, engage trained academics, and devote its resources to studying the history of Jewish communities in Europe and the development of modern antisemitism. As a dyed-in-the-wool Zionist, Dinur regarded the Holocaust as the culmination of a long process and a terrible reminder that Jews never had, and never would have, a stable future in the Diaspora. What actually happened in the ghettos and the camps, however sad, poignant, or compelling, did not change the wider historical picture. People like Auerbach lacked the proper academic training and were too close to the event, too emotional, to approach it with proper perspective. Her emphasis on the phenomenology of the mass murder—the fear, the horrors of the death trains, the humiliations of the victims even as they were herded into the gas chambers—stood in stark contrast to Dinur's preference for a wide-ranging study of relations between Jews and non-Jews in Europe. Under his leadership Yad Vashem focused on procuring documents from European archives and preparing a massive multivolume history of Jewish communities in Europe (*Pinkas Ha-Kehillot*). Dinur allocated a great deal of space in Yad Vashem's main building to the Jewish history department of the Hebrew University.

Tensions within Yad Vashem escalated in 1958 when the directorate tried to curtail the authority of Auerbach and other survivors in the institution, including Joseph Kermish, Nachman Blumenthal, and Nathan Eck. In October 1958 Auerbach published a withering attack on the Yad Vashem leadership. In it, she accused the organization of having failed in its mission. It had published little and had little contact with the survivor community. Dinur totally failed to understand the importance of Holocaust research. Yad Vashem, she believed, owed it to the survivors, and to the Jewish state, to remain true to the legacy of the Oyneg Shabes and to the movement during and after the war to write and bear witness. Instead, Dinur had turned Yad Vashem into a desiccated academic institution with little interest in, or connection with, the survivors. In response, Dinur attempted to have Auerbach removed from her post, a move that quickly backfired. After a storm of public protest forced Yad Vashem to reinstate her, Dinur himself resigned.

>——≺

Auerbach saw the Eichmann trial, which began in April 1961, as a major turning point in the memory of the Holocaust. Trials of Nazi war criminals after the war in various European countries did not put the Jewish story front and center. Now a Jewish state, speaking in the name of the living and the dead, would seek justice and tell the truth. To do this, she believed, it was vitally important for the prosecution to use survivor testimony and focus on the entire process of mass murder, not just Eichmann's actual deeds. Auerbach scored a major victory when she convinced Gideon Hausner, the chief prosecutor, to foreground survivor testimony and to tell the wider story.[57]

Yet her own testimony at the trial turned out to be a bitter disappointment. Under the impression that she would be given ample time to testify, she had planned to talk about Emanuel Ringelblum and about cultural and spiritual resistance in the ghetto. But at the last minute the prosecution scheduled two heroes of the Warsaw Ghetto Uprising, Antek Zuckerman and Zivia Lubetkin, to testify in what she had thought would be her morning slot. These living icons of Jewish valor were a hard act to follow, and when Auerbach finally got to the witness stand in the afternoon, her remarks about Ringelblum, the Aleynhilf, and the soup kitchens fell flat. She did not help her case by testifying in Hebrew, a language she had not fully mastered. Making no attempt to hide their impatience with what they considered to be somewhat irrelevant testimony, the judges cut her off after forty-five minutes. Adding insult to injury, for unknown reasons the film of her testimony vanished and never appeared in the video record of the trial. The experience left her embittered. She wrote to Aryeh Kubovy, "I am very hurt and I will not recover easily or quickly from this."[58]

>——<

In 1968, when Auerbach turned 65 (according to her self-reported age), Yad Vashem insisted on her retirement. As she wrote to Jacob Robinson, it was a relief to be freed from what she regarded as the "burdens and the humiliations" of working at Yad Vashem. But she worried about the future of the department she had built up with so much effort. If she had someone to protect her, she told Katz—a husband, or a political party—she might have gotten better treatment from the Yad Vashem directorate. But she was alone.[59]

Her last years brought her no happiness or relief. Now working to publish *Varshever tsavoes*, she received a diagnosis of breast cancer in 1972, and in December 1975 her condition took a turn for the worse. Yad Vashem, Yiddish writers, and others asked Kupat Holim (Israel's state-sanctioned health insurance fund) to place Auerbach in a special hospital for chronic diseases and old age. Benjamin Armon, chair of the board of Yad Vashem employees, wrote that "Rachel is a lonely and forlorn woman. Her family was killed in the Holocaust and there is no one to take care of her."[60]

One of her few consolations was the publication of *Varshever tsavoes* in 1974. She had hoped to live long enough to publish the second volume, *Baym letstn veg*. It appeared in 1977, a year after she died. Hopefully these volumes, now translated into English, will serve to recognize and further the mission to which she dedicated her life.

Editor's Note

Rokhl Auerbach's *Warsaw Testament*, while written in an accessible style, presents several challenges to contemporary readers. It is a hybrid text, combining Auerbach's wartime writings and her later reflections. It is structured in a thematic, rather than strictly chronological, order, and often presents itself as a collage of memories and anecdotes rather than a continuous narrative. It also presumes that the reader has some cultural and historical knowledge about prewar Yiddish and Jewish culture.

In some ways, the present translation compounds these difficulties. In addition to *Warsaw Testament*, this volume includes selections from Auerbach's later work, *The Last Journey*, adding to the hybridity and collage-like nature of the text. (See the Introduction for more information on these two books.) It also incorporates two sets of notes: Auerbach's own, as well as those of the translator.

For the sake of clarity and transparency, selections from *The Last Journey* are printed on shaded pages and placed where they are thematically most appropriate. This volume also includes a number of supplementary resources to help the reader navigate the text. Notes provide necessary background information, and there is a collection of short biographies of the people who appear in Auerbach's narrative. A chronology of events either mentioned in the text or concerning Auerbach's own biography help compensate for the nonchronological nature of the book. It is our hope that these resources will allow the reader to better appreciate Auerbach's vivid and vital descriptions of her experiences, and those of her friends and colleagues, in Nazi-occupied Warsaw.

Foreword

"Together with the People: A Tragic Chronicle of the Murder of Jewish Writers and Artists in Warsaw." In 1943 that was the first title I chose for this book. It was originally meant to be a chapter in a Polish publication about the destruction of Warsaw Jewry, and I was asked to write it by someone in the Jewish underground on Warsaw's Aryan side.

But as I began to write that one chapter kept getting longer and longer, filling one notebook after another. I wrote then that,

> So few Jewish writers, scholars, and artists are still alive that we can count them on the fingers of both hands. And since we can't be sure that they will survive in the end, I feel a sacred obligation to describe their fate. It's only right that their colleagues and friends, as well as admirers and ordinary Jews throughout the world, should know what happened to them. They should find out who died earlier and who later; who was killed by a bullet and who was struck down in an epidemic; who perished in the flames of the burning ghetto; who died in Treblinka, Chelmno, or simply on the familiar streets of his native city.
>
> Here, a few names; there, a list of addresses pulled from a mass grave. And a few rays of light shining on a few faces from the anonymous multitudes of the murdered.
>
> As long as I keep on going, though lost in a vast void, engulfed in a fog of unwept tears, I will remember, and I will record.

I am not the only one on the Aryan side who wrote memoirs of the destruction. But we found ourselves in different situations. Some authors were being hidden by Poles and did not have to conceal their identities. There were those who had to fear that a random scrap of paper might betray them to their Polish landlords and lead to certain death. I belonged to this second category.

Driven by an uncontrollable impulse, I wrote in secrecy and solitude. I was living in a small detached room in an apartment inhabited by Germans and Poles at Smolna 24. It belonged to a woman named Krauze. In the autumn of 1943 and during the winter of 1943–44, working between midnight and 5 a.m., I wrote two works: *They Called It Resettlement*, on the Great Deportation of 1942, and what became, as I kept adding more material, an early draft of this book. In the daytime I would hide my notebooks at the bottom of a drawer and cover them with the apples, pears, dark flour, and barley cereal bought with the ration cards. Just before Easter 1944 Mrs. Krauze's *Volksdeutsche*[1] maid spied on me through the keyhole of an adjoining room before I had a chance to turn out the light. This could have had terrible consequences. But thanks to a warning from a Polish tenant, I got rid of the contraband and did not write any more until the outbreak of the Polish uprising on August 1 and the subsequent evacuation of Warsaw.

As the Soviets got closer to Warsaw, I took all of my notebooks (which a Jew in a hideout had recopied in the meantime) and gave them to the former director of the Warsaw zoo, Doctor Jan Żabiński. He put them in a large, hermetically sealed glass jar and buried them under a rock on the grounds of the zoo in Praga. During the Polish uprising of 1944, Żabiński's villa was heavily damaged. Żabiński himself was wounded and became a POW. The other residents were driven out and dispersed.

In April 1945 I dug up my notebooks. They were undamaged and complete. A second copy of the notebooks, along with the testimony of a Jew from Lwow named Elisha Landau, were buried in the Mokotow fields.[2] These fields were mined and saw heavy combat in January 1945, when the Soviets attacked and drove out the Germans. But this second cache of writings survived as well. Unfortunately, I had better luck saving documents than saving people.

This winter, 1973–1974, marks thirty years since those nightly writing séances at Smolna 24. In 1954 Am Oved published *In the Courtyards of Warsaw* in Hebrew. Many of its chapters, and especially many passages suffused with lyric pathos, were first written in Mrs. Krauze's apartment. I should add that in 1946 an unedited version of the second wartime manuscript, written in 1943–1944, appeared in the original Polish in *Nasze Słowo*, the bimonthly journal of the Right Labor Zionists.

I did not lack opportunities to publish these and other works in Yiddish. My book about the murder of writers and artists was listed for publication in a book series published in Argentina.[3] And I was busy with other projects, other books, other troubles and worries. For example, together with Hersh Wasser I was trying to organize the search for the Ringelblum archive.[4] During my work in the Jewish Historical Commission in Lodz I documented and published a book about Treblinka as well as one about the Warsaw Ghetto Uprising. I worked in dramatic productions about the Holocaust and on the only film about the Warsaw Ghetto Uprising, *Ulica Graniczna*.[5] After my return from working on this project in Czechoslovakia I lost two years until I was able to leave Poland and emigrate to Israel in 1950.

Books have their own fates. In the original text of the Smolna notebooks there is a passage that sheds light on the difficulties I would later face in publishing this book.

> I regard what I'm writing now as a draft. If I manage to stay alive, I will have to return to this text, correct it, and provide more information, re-read the works of the murdered writers, compare facts, rethink some conclusions. In short, I'll have to complete the project.

And, strange as it may be, the most important and the most thoroughly justified explanation for the delay in finishing this book is precisely that agenda and those obligations that I took on more than thirty years ago.

If I wronged anyone by the delay it was first and foremost myself. It took me so much time, after I arrived in Israel, to track down the prewar works of the murdered authors and above all to comb through every last line of their ghetto writings, some of which were discovered in the two parts of the underground Ringelblum archive and subsequently published.[6] I pored through the memorial books of their hometowns. I found out biographical details from relatives and former neighbors who settled in Israel. Whenever possible I compared my own memory of dates and facts with those I learned from relatives and friends from their youth. In some cases I was able to correct erroneous information in biographies compiled by people who had not been in Warsaw.

And still I want to emphasize that my book is not meant to be an authoritative list of the murdered writers who were in the Warsaw Ghetto, and much less so the murdered artists. Emanuel Ringelblum assumed that task many years ago. In 1944 he wrote about the fate of community activists, teachers, and well-known public figures who perished in the deportations. Jonas Turkow also wrote a detailed and authoritative account of these people, and especially about the fate of Jewish actors.

Here the reader will find descriptions of encounters with associates and friends who for the most part I knew before the war and who I would meet again during the war years. My recollections of them describe not only their fates but also their literary legacies. I tried, as much as possible, to verify the information about the former, disregarding the fabricated stories that often surfaced later.

>——<

Sometimes a writer does not grasp the deeper meaning of what he wants to say. For many years I regarded my writings about the murdered writers and artists as a memorial and requiem for a world that was hurled into the abyss. Only as I rethought and reshaped my account did I realize that memorialization was neither my sole purpose nor the only theme of my work. I shifted my focus away from their final journeys and toward the last period of their lives, which was marked by a profound degree of insight that shaped their understanding of the catastrophe. For a long time I wanted to call these essays "Creativity and Destruction." These writers, artists, and public figures were starving; they were barely surviving. But what became increasingly apparent to me as I looked back was the burning dedication with which they threw themselves into their creative work and cultural activity.

In the past I had written that a retrospective moral appraisal of Jewish life in the ghetto would regard only the armed resistance movement as more important than this upsurge of the life of the spirit, of cultural creativity. Now I realize that armed resistance and cultural activism were not distinct from one another but two sides of the same coin: an affirmation of life in the face of death and a part of our struggle for human dignity, beauty, wisdom, strength, and spirit.

Our colleagues, the Jewish writers and artists, neither abandoned this struggle nor did they suffer defeat. They wrote, they sang, they hoped, and they believed. They have not left us. They are still here: in their legacy, in how we remember them, in their last poems. They are still with us: our brothers who were murdered, the archives that were burned, the pages that were soaked in tears.

This book is consecrated to the memory of the new generation of Jewish heroes and martyrs, the dearest and most precious sons of the Jewish people, who fell so that the Jewish people could have a future.

— Rokhl Auerbach, Tel Aviv, Hanukkah 5734

Part 1: Warsaw Fought

1. BLADES IN THE SKY

In the summer of 1939 I was unemployed. Like many other journalists just starting out in the Jewish press, I had to support myself from the honoraria I received for occasional articles in the Yiddish- and Polish-language Jewish newspapers. Only during vacation time, when the regular employees were gone, was I able to land a temporary job on this or that newspaper. During the last two weeks of August I worked the night shift in the printing shop of *Nasz Przegląd*,[1] making final corrections for the next day's edition. Stanislaw Filozof was the night editor.

Until late into the night the Polish Press Agency was transmitting alarming bulletins about incidents on the Polish-German border. So both of us, along with the printers, had to endure the excruciating tension on the eve of the war, literally until the last minute.

On the night of August 31 we left our jobs at the print shop after twelve. It wasn't far from Nowolipki 7 to my apartment at Przejazd 1. But the city was blacked out, and Filozof decided to walk me as far as the gate of my building.

As we passed the Mostowski Palace, in the wide triangle formed by Przejazd, Nowolipie, and Mylna Streets, we saw just one soldier, a rifle on his shoulder, standing guard in front of that building, the headquarters of the mobilization department of the north Warsaw military region. Having just printed such alarming news in tomorrow's newspaper, we were taken aback by the idyllic tranquillity we saw in front of this important military installation.

"I already reported here with my military identification papers,"

Filozof responded to a remark of mine in a tone of bitter irony. "They told me to wait for a call-up letter. There was no hurry." Many people who had reported in response to the order for general mobilization were still waiting to be sent to their units.

"I saw them," I exclaimed, happy that I could add something. "There are thousands of called-up men. They're crowding the trains together with the vacationers returning from summer holidays. The trains are full of refugees from Poznan and Silesia. Men, women, children—crowds of civilians are lying on the train platforms with their baggage. Children are crying, the trains are jam-packed, you can't find a connection in any direction. As you go down the stairs in the stations you crash into crowds of people coming up from the lower platforms. The two groups collide, and nobody can move. There are cries, screams. People come to blows. I saw men with cudgels, the police are helpless, everything is jammed, blocked."

"Jammed, blocked." Filozof repeated my words. "Men? What kind of men? Where were they going?" In his tone I detected a note of anger, suspicion, innuendo . . .

I told him why I was at the train station. I had gone there to accompany a brother-in-law of my late brother. He was one of the "Polish citizens" who spent nearly a year in Zbąszyn because Poland did not want to let them enter the country.[2] It was only now that they stamped their papers and admitted them, even without train tickets.

Until 1933 this Emil Geles had a shoe factory in Essen in the Ruhr. Now he wanted to get to Lwow but couldn't find a place on a train. I waited with him for three hours but finally had to go to work. I still hadn't absorbed everything that he told me.

"This state has no right to exist," he told me in German. This Jew from Essen, whom they robbed of everything and expelled, also learned from refugees who arrived later about the "Night of Broken Glass."[3] But in his eyes, the guilty state was not Germany but, amazingly, Poland. This humiliated, spat on, injured Jew still thought in terms of Nazi propaganda.

"And what do you expect, my kind lady?" Filozof answered. "The psychological techniques of German propaganda are more developed than ours. Even in this they are better equipped. And as far as military technique goes, what is there to say?"

"So that means . . ." I asked, and I had a terrible feeling inside.

"Unfortunately there's no use fooling ourselves," he answered. It's a matter of days, perhaps hours."

We had almost reached the gate of my building. In the sky one could see the searchlights of the Polish air force. Were they really looking for German planes over Warsaw?

We walked by the Fama cinema. On the side street that connected Przejazd and Nalewki we could see the old building of the Arsenal Museum of Antique Weapons. The clock on some church tower chimed one. The first hour of the first of September, 1939.

A light autumn rain began to fall and the lightly moistened dust on the street smelled of earth, of upturned earth in the middle of the city.

I felt very tired and rang for the janitor to let me in.

>——<

Four hours later people suddenly awoke to the noise coming from above the city. Strange whistles echoed from the sky, and from a distance one could hear the sound of explosions. Soon after the wailings of the Polish air raid sirens filled the air.

Some of the early risers, who had to get up to go to work, tried to convince their wives that this was just an air raid drill of the Polish civil defense—the OPL.[4]

The first bombs of the Second World War fell on a Jewish institution for children with special needs in Otwock. A few dozen people were killed or wounded. Among the wounded was the director, Yiddish poet Kalman Lis.

Later, in the early days of the occupation, I ran into Filozof in the Jewish writers' kitchen, where he was working as a director. It was located in a courtyard of Tlomackie 13, the former home of the Association of Jewish Writers and Journalists.[5] I remember that particular meeting well and described it in the notebooks that I wrote on the Aryan side. Did I speak to him after that? Maybe. I can't remember. Maybe I met him at the funeral of some writer? I think I ran into him for a few moments during the first week of the Great Deportation. That must have been very early in the morning, before the daily manhunts began, when we were both running along Leszno Street in opposite directions. We nodded to each other and kept running. This was a devil's game in which we were all chasing a mirage, the lure of

3

work papers that would supposedly save us and our colleagues from deportation. That was the last time I saw the colleague with whom I worked those last two weeks before the war. I heard nothing more about him, although I made many inquiries. Why didn't he join his colleagues Szwalbe and Wagman and cross the Bug River to the Soviet zone of occupation?[6] Did "Stach"—the Polish speakers at the paper called him that—try to hide on the Aryan side? Or if he didn't, why not? To this day I haven't found anybody who can explain what happened to him.

>—<

As for Emil, the refugee from "Essen an der Ruhr," I heard from his sister (my sister-in-law Lonia) in a letter I received from Soviet-occupied Lwow that the Soviets deported him "to an unknown place."

That much we know. Perhaps that was the fate of the majority of the Zbąszyn refugees who had the "luck" to reach the territories occupied by the Soviets after September 17, 1939. After all, many Polish Jews who fled the Germans were arrested and murdered by the Soviets as "German spies" as soon as they reached Soviet territory.

I kept getting postcards from my sister-in-law for about a year after the Germans occupied Lwow.[7] Toward the end of our correspondence in the summer of 1942, the phrase "an unknown place" began to appear when she mentioned friends and neighbors we had both known. Then in November I got a postcard that informed me that Lonia and the 15-year-old Lusia, Lonia's and my late brother's daughter, were also sent to "an unknown destination."

That postcard was sent by my late brother's 19-year-old son Mundek, a graduate of the Abraham Karkis vocational school in Lwow. The postcard was dated August 13, 1942, but since I had already moved to a new place, and because the Germans in Warsaw were also busy in those summer months sending people to "an unknown destination," the postcard gathered dust for a few months until by some miracle it finally reached me.

After that there were no more miracles. Nor did I hear any more from Mundek. During the war and for thirty years after I inquired and searched and wrote, but I still know nothing about what happened to my dearest and only nephew. I don't know whether they sent him to

Belzec or murdered him in the Janowska camp after they exploited every ounce of strength his young body could give for the needs of the German war machine.

>——<

Light beams in the Warsaw skies on the night of August 31–September 1, 1939.

A new era had begun, a hallmark of the Second World War: the murder and total extirpation of civilian populations. The Jews were the first targets and proportionally the greatest victims.

2. CANDLES AT TWILIGHT

It seemed as if we, the last prewar generation of Jewish writers in Poland, came onto the scene just when it was all going downhill.

The heady intellectual *Sturm und Drang* that had convulsed Yiddish literature in the 1920s with new names, new genres, and new themes, and which had pulled it out of its old nineteenth-century provincialism, was now just a memory. The most prominent figures of that pleiad—Perets Markish, Moyshe Kulbak, I. J. Singer, Uri Tsevi Grinberg, Melech Ravitch, Isaac Bashevis, and others—had already left Poland. Some went to Russia, some to America, some to Palestine. Those who stayed suffered from inner and external conflicts; they were dissatisfied with everything and everybody. At every turn people complained about the "decline." The newspapers were controlled by insiders—party or family cliques—and we newcomers who arrived in the capital from all over Poland had to fight hard to find our way, for a small foot in the door, for a tiny salary.

"Warsaw, Moscow, or New York?" In those days the Yiddish press debated the true center of Yiddish literature. We newcomers were least likely to believe that it was Warsaw. We were too close to it and we lacked perspective. And all of us, young and old, were full of resentment against the Association of Jewish Writers and Journalists at Tlomackie 13.

Yet we were in the middle of a powerful, dynamic, and large Jewish folk community. A great cadre of political, economic, and social activists worked nonstop. The Jewish masses were going through a spontaneous process of emancipation and acculturation.[1] But those same masses were too numerous and too concentrated to lose the essential core of their national identity. The religious strata, the enormous "black forest of Jewish Orthodoxy," comprised such an enormous reservoir of spiritual energy and human resources that they more than compensated for all we lost through assimilation.

We writers thought that we had come too late and all that remained was a wilted garden. We did not realize that the garden was about to offer a rich new harvest of fruit—had the cataclysm not engulfed us all.

>——<

Even though many writers left Warsaw to settle in places both Jewish and non-Jewish, and even though many of the more assimilated writers moved over to the Polish press and the Polish cultural orbit, Yiddish culture nonetheless benefited from a large influx of new talent.

Some writers had more talent than others. Some were blessed with originality and creativity. There were mediocrities who made a living by writing to suit popular tastes. There were unhappy specimens with frustrated ambitions who simply hung around. But there were also dazzling writers endowed with genius who basked in the adoration and devotion of the Yiddish reading public.

There were five—and just before the war, six—Yiddish dailies along with two afternoon editions, as well as weekly and professional journals and photographic supplements. There were two Jewish dailies in Polish. Each of these newspapers had a circulation in the tens of thousands on weekdays—and the weekend and holiday editions had double that. The Association of Jewish Writers and Journalists had over four hundred members and the Jewish section of the Polish Journalists Association two hundred.

In Warsaw there were two full-time Yiddish theaters and several traveling troupes. There was an actors union at Leszno 2, at the corner of Przejazd, almost directly across from Tlomackie 13.

There was an association of Jewish sculptors with dozens of members, several music organizations, and many choirs and orchestras, some of which were connected with various political, trade, and youth organizations. There were publishing houses, libraries, and all sorts of circles, clubs, and theatrical studios.

This is not the place to describe the varied and vibrant network of Jewish schools, or the many local and national communal organizations and institutions, banks, and free loan societies, or the Jewish public health apparatus. And what about the political parties, the

sport clubs, the Jewish Landkentenish Society?[2] Or the many synagogues, prayer houses, study halls, and Hasidic *shtibls*, many of them
hundreds of years old?

Polish antisemites would gnash their teeth and fulminate about
a separate Jewish "state" within Poland. Well, they were not entirely
wrong, especially in the cultural sphere.

To be sure, that Jewish "state" limped along. It got little support
from the central government or from town councils. It depended on
voluntary "taxes" offered by Polish Jews, on the help of Jewish organizations from abroad, and on the donations and moral support
of ordinary Jews who, poor as they were, had a strong Jewish consciousness.

Yes, that Jewish "state" struggled to get by—but it was still a real
presence in Jewish life. This was Jewish autonomy in a modern, secular sense. As long as the Jewish masses survived, it functioned, and
it made an impact. It accompanied those masses until the last step on
the road to destruction.

>——<

Outside of Warsaw there were smaller centers with their own newspapers, periodicals, theaters, and literary groups: Lodz, Krakow,
Lwow; larger provincial towns like Radom, Lublin, Częstochowa; and
above all, Vilna.

Vilna, long a center of rabbinic learning, showed that in the new
era of modern Jewish culture she still fully deserved her traditional
title of "The Jerusalem of Lithuania." Thanks to her firm determination to ground Jewish life in Yiddish and in a Jewish cultural context,
Vilna became home to the YIVO[3] and the citadel of Jewish secular
schools, where gymnasia and special seminars prepared cadres of
teachers. Vilna became the breeding ground for a new kind of Jewish
intellectual.

After Germany attacked the Soviet Union in 1941, Jewish Vilna
became one of the first victims of the German murder campaign.
Those writers who had not emigrated or who had not managed to flee
into the Soviet interior shared the fate of Vilna Jewry and were murdered in the Ponary forest.[4]

While I'm at it, what should I say about Lemberg, my Lemberg, the Jewish capital of old Austrian Galicia?⁵ Recently I read through some old issues of *Chwila*.⁶ Lwow was acculturated and it was Zionist. But what really mattered was that this provincial center, with its many different movements and intellectual currents, was Jewish to the marrow. Names changed, but the essence of these different movements in Galicia—the inner fire, the essential vitality—did not.

There was the Baal Shem Tov, and—no comparison intended—Shabetai Tsevi, and, to add another thousand degrees of separation, Jacob Frank. Hasidism and the Enlightenment, Zionism and assimilation, Communism and modern Yiddish poetry, Moyshe-Leyb Sassover⁷ and Moyshe-Leyb Halpern.

Not a stone has remained of the old Jewish Lemberg. Not even the graves or the tombstones, which they used to pave the streets.

When I turned the pages of *Chwila,* I felt as if blood was dripping from my fingers. This rich creative milieu disappeared into the abyss, along with the names and books. Who will inscribe them in the memory of our people? Who will rescue their works from oblivion?

Lemberg—my Lemberg!

And what has happened to Jewish Krakow, a city where I did not live? Or Przemysl, Stanislawow, Tarnopol, Kolomej, Buczacz?

But that is not what this book is about. It's not a historical discussion about this or that Jewish center. I am writing what I remember about personal encounters, conversations, observations, and ordeals; only what I saw myself, with my own eyes, what I experienced on my own and sealed with my own fate.

3. MY LAST TIME AT TLOMACKIE 13

September 5, 1939. I was living at Przejazd 1; the poet Nokhum Bomze and the painter Mendel Reif were living in the same apartment. It was now the fifth day of the air raid sirens and the bombing of the city. It just so happened that on Tuesday, the fifth of September, there were fewer alarms than on the days before. That evening Bomze ran in with the still top-secret, terrible news that Warsaw was being evacuated; the army was going to withdraw to new lines of defense and the government was going to leave the capital. Hitler would march in tomorrow, maybe the day after tomorrow.

It was a terrible blow.

Despite the optimistic headlines in the newspaper, we knew that the military situation was bad. Evidently the Germans were using a new kind of technique. They drove deep wedges behind the lines and then used a hurricane of fire and steel to destroy even the most heroic defensive efforts. We knew about the work of the fifth column, which hampered the mobilization and military movement. But still, none of us thought that things were as bad as they were.

We still nursed the fear that Poland—and the other European nations—would seek a new compromise with Hitler.

For years Hitler had blamed the Jews for inciting war, and he warned that they would pay the price. Today we realize that his threats were horribly real. There was a certain truth in his charge that the Jews wanted war. More than anything we were against making peace and giving him concessions. When we saw that war was unavoidable and that there would be no new peace agreement, we all felt a great sense of relief. But we believed too much in the power of the "just war"; we exaggerated its strength.

Jewish soldiers responded to the call of the Polish government and went off to fight with conviction and enthusiasm. We were ready to make the greatest sacrifices. We did not reckon with the danger of a Polish rout and of a German invasion and occupation.

Such a shock could well have broken us, but we did not break. They say that imminent danger sparks the release of a hormone that dulls sensitivity and sharpens the instinct for self-defense.

>———<

Someone once remarked that one can think about the Second World War in terms of massive population movements. The immediate reaction to danger is to flee! I saw this during the war, both with the Poles and the Jews. The Germans made it a factor in their military tactics, since a mass flight of refugees blocked major roads and paralyzed the movements of the defending army.

To my great surprise I discovered that I almost totally lacked this instinct to run.

When Bomze delivered his bitter news, he also reported that some room had been reserved for Jewish journalists in the press car of the evacuation train that would leave Warsaw that night. Places would go to those journalists who had the most to fear from the Germans, like political commentators and chief editors.

That night, for the only time during the whole war, I packed a bag and was almost ready to run with the others. Bomze said that there were fifteen places reserved for Jewish journalists, and I naively thought that if there was room for fifteen men, there would certainly be space for a sixteenth journalist—a woman. That's probably what would have happened had I gotten to that train. Or had I really wanted to run.

>———<

It was fated that the Association of Jewish Writers and Journalists would not die in its own bed, in its longtime headquarters at Tlomackie 13.

It all happened about a year or a year and a half before the war. A dispute broke out between the owner of the building and the "impresario" of the association, David Ribayzn. To stir the pot there was the writer Henekh Ash, a member of the governing board. Around that time, after a personal misfortune, Ash tried to distract himself by channeling his energies into the internal affairs of the association. In the event, his maniacal energy earned him the enmity of both Ribayzn and the landlord.

Ash found a very unsuitable building at Graniczna 11. Gala events had been the association's main source of income, and in this new building the small hall was on the third floor. The building required a lot of work, which cost a fortune. But Ash persevered. He had the walls upholstered with brownish-gold brocaded fabric, installed pretty lights in the windows, and organized a housewarming. Everything was moved to Graniczna, including the priceless archive of literary manuscripts; the collection of portraits, including the large oil paintings of I. L. Peretz and Sholem Asch; and other paintings by Jewish artists that had graced the walls of Tlomackie 13.

The new location on Graniczna was close to the railroad station and to the electric plant on Zielna, obvious targets for German pilots. During the second week of the war Graniczna 11 suffered a direct hit and was totally destroyed, along with the archives and every other trace of the association.

A month later, after Warsaw capitulated and the Germans marched in, people realized what had been lost and bitterly regretted that ill-fated move.

Tlomackie 13 had been synonymous with the association, and that old building emerged unscathed. But even before Graniczna 11 went up in smoke, the bombs had started to fall on Warsaw's Jewish quarter.

>——◄

That Tuesday evening, September 5, Graniczna 11 was still standing. I can still remember my visit that evening.

When I showed up with my satchel, the whole building was dark except for two offices. Ber Rozen, the secretary of the literary union, and Y. L. Levinstein, the secretary of the journalists syndicate, were preparing to leave. Using flashlights masked by a blue filter, they were combing through documents and letters. Someone had urged them to make sure that the Germans didn't get their hands on the lists of members' names and addresses.

That same night certain colleagues burned books and journals containing anti-Nazi material. Despite the tragic situation, the poet Reyzl Zychlinski could not suppress a laugh when she told me about a certain young poet who, on the night of September 5–6, ripped out each page of his first published book of poems and tossed them one by one into the oven. He thought that as soon as the Germans took the city their first priority would be to barge into his rented room and grab the little book with his anti-Nazi poems.

A group of journalists was standing in the two large rooms, ready to leave. Only members of the journalists syndicate were entitled to a place on the train. Now, as always, "mere authors" were second class. Even among the journalists and editors only fifteen would be able to leave. Yes, there was a list, but many whose names were not on the list turned up with suitcases. Some of them were shouting and became hysterical.

This was the first Jewish "selection." A bit diffidently, not really sure of myself, I suggested that as the only woman I should latch on to the group. Maybe, once everyone got to the station, there would be room for me too. Now I believe that I was right. In the end more than fifteen journalists left. But my suggestion was brushed aside. A member of the executive committee fobbed me off by saying that "women were in no danger." Those most threatened should have priority. As the assembled group fought and argued about who should go and who shouldn't, a few people decided to take their names off the list. The first to do so was Moshe Indelman, who was the head of the journalists syndicate and a co-editor of *Haynt*.[1] Like the captain of a sinking ship, he did not want to save himself at someone else's expense. Another *Haynt* writer, Aaron Einhorn, also thought it over and decided not to leave. The squabbling gave him a sense of what he could expect in the future. Perhaps his elitist sensibility dissuaded him from becoming a refugee.

I also remember Zusman Segalovitsh. He came carrying only a small briefcase. No knapsack, he said; he would leave with only the briefcase. That gesture soon came back to haunt him. I remember the letters he sent from Bialystok to Ruth Karlinska, imploring her to send him some clothes.

With whom else did I exchange final goodbyes? Somehow, I can't remember exactly.

The windows of the writers headquarters were wide open, the rooms were pitch black, and the light of an early autumn moon lit up the faces of those leaving and those staying with a deathly, greenish-silvery hue.

>—<

The journalists who were going to the train dispersed to say goodbye to friends or to pack some more things. They had to be at the train station at midnight.

Aaron Einhorn's decision to stay very much affected me. I resolved that I would also stay behind; after all, I would be in good company.

As if on purpose, those who were leaving all gathered together, while Einhorn, his wife, Bracha, and I left the building.

We left at about 10 p.m. It was eerily quiet and the air was fresh and clear. There were no air raids at night. The blacked-out city, the full moon shining over the trees of the Saxon Garden, the lack of traffic—all these combined to create a sense of peace and quiet. The nightmare of our new reality had receded, at least for a while.

I left the Einhorns when we reached Zelazna Brama gate. The Einhorns lived on Mirowska, I at Przejazd 1. On that moonlit night we said goodbye to each other with a sense of relief. We had just experienced a shock and were about to go through new traumas. The deluge was coming closer and closer, but the three of us had just made a decision. We all went to sleep in our own beds. We were tired, and some of the tension was gone. It's as if our bodies gathered new strength to allow us to live through what awaited us the next day.

The evacuation train was bombed that same night. The writers reached Lublin but then, like birds roused from their nest, scattered in different directions. In the coming days, after the arrival of the Germans in Warsaw, other Jewish writers and journalists followed their lead and left.

Some reached safety—or what seemed like safety. Others failed to find any refuge or safe corner until their dying day.

Meanwhile, those of us who remained would now experience the siege and defense of Warsaw—a prelude to ever more horrible days ahead.

4. September Neighbors

There is a prologue to this story. About a year before the war Joseph Kamien and his wife and stage partner Nadia Kareny moved into the same building where I lived at Przejazd 1. I was subletting on the sixth floor and they moved into a rented room on the fourth. Kamien's landlord had a telephone I would use from time to time, so we had an opportunity to meet. Of course I knew of them earlier, Kamien as an actor in the Vilna Troupe and Kareny from Ararat and Azazel.[1]

Joseph Kamien was the younger brother of Alex Stein, who was the star of the Vilna Troupe and who partnered with Miriam Orleska in most of the performances I saw in Lemberg. Later on Kamien also joined the ensemble. Since two Steins on the theater placards might be confusing, they turned the younger brother into a Kamien, the Slavic version of Stein. Although he played minor roles in those days, he was so good that he enthralled his audiences.

I remember one of those minor roles, in Henning Berger's *The Deluge*. He played a sprightly little black man, a Piccolo in a luxury hotel on some island. Tray in hand he flitted to the rhythm of some catchy tune, whistled and sang as he served drinks, and took orders from the doomed, wealthy guests who were trapped by a volcanic eruption and who awaited their fates as the waves rose higher and higher.

He seemed to be totally carefree and childishly happy, yet at the same his jocosity was spooky. It was as if he were the outrider of those dark forces that were dragging this tiny, isolated enclave into the abyss. As I write this, I don't have the text of that play in front of me. And I don't know what's in the text, so I can't guess the actual intentions of the playwright and director. But I do remember the way this young beginner played that role and the delightful surprise it was for devotees of Yiddish theater.

15

Kamien got better and better and displayed his great talent in ever more demanding roles. I remember his acting, makeup, and costume in the main role of Moshe Lipshitz's comedy *A Tale of Hershele Ostropolyer*. He revealed himself to be much more than a mere comedian; he emerged as an engaging, spontaneous comic actor who could summon the demonic layers that lurked beneath the droll surface.

>—◄

A few years after I saw Kamien perform in Lemberg I got to know him personally, in Warsaw, at Tlomackie 13. In the late 1930s he would appear in special performances accompanied by the Vilna singer Lubochka Levitska. At any rate that's how he would introduce her after he finished his own routine and called her to the stage.

By that time he had already suffered a calamity. He was diagnosed with Buerger's disease and lost his leg. Now wearing a prosthesis, he switched to solo recitals. He was not the kind of actor who lingered over the lyric nuance of a text, highlighting the rhythm and beauty of each word. No, he chose a repertory that played to his sense of drama and his ability to interpret diverse characters.

During this new period of personal agony, this dynamic and vigorous artist, who used to throw himself into each role with every ounce of energy he had, now had to contend with a disability that hampered his ability to express himself onstage. But he didn't give up. He fought back against his fate and did not want anyone's pity. He was angry about his disability but also resented anyone who treated him like an invalid. I think that after a time he began to cope successfully. Even with one leg he was more talented than other actors. He didn't just play roles. He was an entire one-man theater. Stage acting was just a tiny part of the vast reservoir of dramatic energy that surged inside of him.

Kamien's entire milieu came to life in his acting. He was an amazing observer who had a genius for mimicking the speech and gestures of other people. He had the makings of a first-rate novelist or playwright. I think that this was where he was headed. He was on the cusp of revealing a great talent defined not by material success nor by this or that role but by the creative challenge of impersonation. He knew how to skillfully improvise monologues and sketches that caught the traits and foibles of people he met. At first glance these sketches seemed to be mere caricatures. But they were much more than that. His acting caught the essential features of the people he imitated, and that included virtually anybody he came in close contact with. In the literary club on Tlomackie, people called this kind of improvisation "making a film." It demanded a high level of acting talent, a rare gift granted only to a chosen few. Kamien was not the only actor who could do this, but he lifted this genre to perfection. Spontaneously and impromptu he would "work over" the expressions and sayings of his "victim"—the voice, the tone—and create a new text, a super-text that revealed the problems and hidden complexes of his subject. He could be a real devil, but he improvised with such charm and good humor that his "victim" would laugh along with everybody else. And besides, what choice did he have?

Kamien's "victims" were the different personalities of Tlomackie 13—writers, newspaper editors, actors, impresarios. People fell off their chairs laughing when he showed up—early evening was his best time—and chose a target. I remember to this day his portrait of his good friend the impresario Miss Garielov. Today instead of parody we have only elegy.

His targets were not just the personalities of Tlomackie 13. He also imitated his landlady of the fourth floor of Przejazd 1. He gave lifelike impersonations of a cat. There was a routine he would perform for children about two tomcats. The tomcats would threaten each other in the corner of a courtyard, challenging each other with threatening hisses and meows, but in fact they were scared to death of one another.

That was Kamien. And he was a character in his own right, who was not so easy to get along with—a jokester who could act like a capricious child. That's what I observed about him during the bombardment of Warsaw, in the worst days of September 1939, when I was his neighbor.

>—<

Before I start describing those days, I should say something about Nadia Kareny, Kamien's wife at the time. I would see her when she came to act in Lemberg with the Azazel or Ararat. She was a dazzling blond and was blessed with a flawless soprano voice. When she sang impish, mischievous songs by Gebirtig and Broderzon, or duets with Joseph Strugacz, she added a special Jewish twist that warmed the heart.

In Warsaw I would see her perform from time to time in oper- ettas and "tragedies set to music and dance," as they were then called. In the middle of the action she would come out, right to the edge of the stage. Then she would hit some high notes, belt out a song, or do a little dance number. Her phenomenal memory for texts and tunes amazed me. She was full of music, a walking encyclopedia of Jewish theater tunes and Russian and Jewish folk songs.

In the last days of August 1939 Miriam Orleska and I saved Nadia from serious danger when we took her to the hospital for an urgent operation. At the time Kamien was not in Warsaw. He was stuck in western Galicia where he had been on tour, and he got back to War- saw only after the war had begun.

It took him two or three days to get from Krakow to Warsaw, sur- rounded by crowds of desperate refugees with baggage and children all trying to flee to the center of the country. Hobbling on his good leg, he struggled to squeeze into crowded trains. Other passengers, moved by the gruesome sight of Kamien forced to hold his prosthe- sis aloft, helped him climb through a window into the jam-packed compartment. Even today I shudder when I think of what he went through, just as I shuddered back then when, surrounded by snoring neighbors in the air raid shelter, I listened to him describe that event- ful journey from Krakow to Warsaw on August 30 and 31.

>——<

From the first hours of the German invasion of Poland, the Polish military and the civilian population were practically defenseless from German air assault. Polish airspace was captured by the Ger- mans even before they grabbed Polish territory. Most of the planes of the Polish air force were destroyed on the ground by German bombs before they had a chance to take off.[2] During the first week of the war Polish anti-aircraft guns were able to shoot down a few German planes, but this in no way affected the total German control of air- space over Warsaw and the whole country.

Here and there, along the large rivers, the Poles fought desperate battles aided by suicidal charges of the Polish cavalry, as the Polish generals tried to stop the advance of the motorized teutonic monster.[3] Here and there lieutenants and sergeants swore to stop the German advance with their own bodies, to fight to the last man and bullet. They kept their promise. At the same time they sacrificed not only themselves but also the towns where they fought, on which the vengeful Germans vented their anger.

These acts of heroism made no difference. The diabolically rapid German advance pushed its pincers deep into Poland, creating isolated pockets and moving ever closer to the center of the country.

The government left the capital in overloaded trains; armored railroad cars moved along the bombed railway lines carrying the country's gold reserves and archives. The commander of the army and the general staff still hoped to organize a line of defense along the Bug River. But as soon as the Soviets invaded eastern Poland on September 17, the high command, the president, and the government crossed the Romanian border to avoid falling into Soviet captivity.

>——<

Warsaw was left to defend itself. The radio was still broadcasting, announcing alarms and all-clears between bars of Chopin's "Military Polonaise." In between it also played a song that had not been heard for many years on Polish radio: the socialist hymn "Red Flag."

Both stations, Warsaw 1 and Warsaw 2, were broadcasting. Around midnight on Thursday September 7 the city's loudspeakers carried a bizarre speech by Colonel Roman Umiastowski, the propaganda chief of the Polish general staff. He issued an order that "all men who are capable of bearing arms should leave the city and follow the army east, where they will be mobilized."

As if that weren't enough, Prime Minister Sławoj Składkowski made a short farewell speech to the people and declared that "because of the danger that threatens Warsaw, the government must leave the capital with the firm resolve to return after the victorious end of the war."

These two speeches caused indescribable panic and confusion among the population. It seemed as if everybody was leaving the nest, preparing to flee from their homes, from the city, from the air raids. It looked like a herd of cattle stampeding away from a fire.

The flight of young Jews had already begun when the rumors started about the evacuation. A day earlier I had said goodbye to two friends and neighbors from Przejazd 1—Nokhum Bomze and Mendel Reif. But the panic and flight that started after Umiastowski's speech was something else entirely, hard to describe, impossible to compare to anything else.

That night I didn't sleep in my room at Przejazd 1. The walls and furniture were already scratched and dented from the explosions. The glass of the window panes, which we had so carefully "protected" with paper tape, lay shattered all over the floor. The air was thick with the smell of fire and smoke, a smell that would stay with Warsaw's inhabitants long after that first month of the war.

In keeping with the new unwritten rules of wartime, I slept on the floor of a downstairs apartment. I took my best dress and my new coat. For a pillow I used a bag that contained my personal possessions on top of a pair of sturdy shoes. As soon as it got light out, I went to the gate to see what was happening.

The street looked like a swollen river that had overflowed its banks. The exodus of men had been going on all night, and now in the pre-dawn hours it reached its peak. Young men and women were marching from the western and southern districts of the city toward the major roads that led east. The crowd of people filled up all of Przejazd from end to end, a mass of heads, marching feet, backs saddled with rucksacks. Here and there one could see someone marching with a tall broomstick held high, like a flag bearer in a May Day demonstration. Perhaps people thought they'd come in handy on the long march ahead. They tied bundles to the sticks and rested them on their shoulders. Now and then one could spot young couples with children on their backs moving with the crowd, pushing strollers loaded with possessions.

That's exactly what the Germans were trying to accomplish with their blitzkrieg tactics, which they used first in Poland and then in other countries. The aim was to force huge crowds of civilian refugees to leave the cities and take to the roads where they would be terrorized with bombs and machine guns. The congestion would make it impossible for the army to move, intensify the panic, paralyze the government, and bring down entire countries in a matter of days.

There were also those who marched east carrying nothing. Perhaps they saw it all as a lark. They didn't understand that they were leaving Warsaw for many years, maybe for good. They didn't realize that they might never again see the people they had just left.

Many of those who stayed suddenly experienced—after their husbands, sons, or fiancés had left—a need to rush out, as if they felt a sharp jolt inside, as if a snake had suddenly bitten their heart. There was a sense of regret, a realization that important words had not been said. Along the edges of the shoving crowds that filled the entire width of the streets one could see them push forward, shouting names, moving along with those who were "following the army." Maybe they remembered that they had forgotten to tell or give them something important. Maybe they wanted to persuade somebody to return, or perhaps they decided to leave with them after all. Carried along by an uncanny sense of dread, they shuffled along, here and there waving a package of food, a coin, or a note with the addresses of relatives.

As I looked on in amazement, I too felt a pang of regret. Was I right to have stayed? Shouldn't I have joined Bomze and Reif and gone to Lemberg?

Suddenly I realized that somebody was standing beside me at the gate. It was Joseph Kamien, leaning on his cane. He was totally mesmerized as he absorbed the scene playing out before him: people are leaving the city, men of military age!

Some magical impulse urged him to run along after them on his one leg. Finally he noticed me and yanked me by the arm. "I need my old crutches. Come upstairs with me and help me pack! I don't want to be here when the Germans come. I have to go!"

I stared at him and saw a glint of madness in his eyes. I understood that appealing to reason would get me nowhere.

"Panie Osiu," I said to him in Polish, "how can you do such a thing to Nadia? What will she say when she comes back from the hospital and finds out that you were here for a while and then left Warsaw and didn't even say goodbye?"

That argument worked. He turned around and went up in the elevator "to rest a bit."

That day the elevator was still working.

>—<

After the government evacuated and after the departure of many young men who followed Umiastowski's appeal, a new civilian and military leadership, headed by two generals, emerged to organize the defense of the city. They mobilized labor battalions to work on fortifications. The air defense committees in each district and each building were reorganized and reinforced.

Stefan Starzyński, the mayor of Warsaw and the commissar of civil defense, solemnly declared that Warsaw would be defended. He spoke nonstop to the population. Even after his voice gave out he kept talking. Starzyński called for calm and for civic responsibility. He gave lectures on how to deal with the incendiary bombs that landed on rooftops. Despite the fact that the Germans had already occupied much of Poland, the defense of Warsaw became his rallying cry—even though with his military background he knew full well that there was no hope of either help or victory.

Starzyński, the old veteran of Pilsudski's legions, worked hand in hand with the elderly socialist leader Niedziałkowski. They knew that this was all about going down fighting—a battle for the "last fortress." It was a fight inspired by what the great Polish poets had written after the loss of independence, words that had been read for 150 years. It was as if the twenty years of Polish independence had totally disappeared and what mattered now was the old determination to sacrifice everything for the honor of the people and the right to their own state.

Romanticism? Idealism? Let the cynics scoff all they want. I scorn them. Other European peoples didn't fight like the Poles. We Polish Jews understood their fight, we fought alongside them, and we understand it even now.

So that first doomed fight began, the first of what became three defiant battles waged by the city against the colossal satanic power. The second would begin three and a half years later behind the ghetto walls.

>——<

It went on for ten more days. The city was totally surrounded; German patrols had already entered the suburbs and outlying areas. The water system and electrical grid worked only sporadically. Gas supplies had already been cut off to avert the danger of explosions. Water to put out the numerous fires, and even to wash wounds, was becoming scarce.

People would spend all night in lines outside the few working bakeries and many would return home with nothing. If they were able to reach home at all.

Dead people and dead horses lay in the streets of Warsaw, the "open city."[4]

The million civilians, together with the 100,000 soldiers surviving from the defeated and largely disarmed army, continued with a tragic determination and stubbornness to fight a war the military leadership had already given up for lost.

Temporary cemeteries were dug in all squares and public gardens for soldiers who were killed and for the far greater number of civilians who were buried alive or suffocated in bombed-out buildings.

Wave after wave of Stuka bombers took off from newly captured Polish airfields and dropped their explosives and incendiary bombs before returning for a new load. Every now and then a puny Polish anti-aircraft gun would get off a few shots, but unlike during the first days of the war you no longer heard any talk of shot-down German airplanes. Sometimes white leaflets would rain down that called on the population to reject the "Polish and English deceivers" and to end it all.

But the inhabitants of the city kept on suffering and did not demand surrender. There were no demonstrations calling for an end to the fighting, no protests about unnecessary casualties or the destruction of the city.

Those who had jobs left their families every day and went to their posts. It was expected that each person would do his duty and meet his obligations.

Jews also formed labor battalions. They served as watchmen on rooftops and smothered incendiary bombs with sand. They saved houses from burning down and obeyed Starzyński's instructions and the orders of the air defense.

The eve of the Jewish New Year came on September 13, and the Wehrmacht high command marked that day with a special air raid on the Jewish section of Warsaw.

That same evening I heard an eyewitness account of Starzyński's visit to the Nalewki and Franciszkanska area, which suffered the most in that air attack. He walked out of his car and could barely take a step because of the thick crowd of Jews packing the street. Many houses were still burning, while others had been blocked off by firemen. Here and there desperate attempts were being made to rescue people trapped under collapsed buildings. Starzyński spoke with the victims, patted the heads of children, shook the hand of a young man who ran along the rooftops with a shovel and sand and kept two buildings from burning down. He comforted and encouraged the people on those Jewish streets. Maybe in this time of his profound and tragic exaltation he remembered how before the war, in this very city, in this very country, Jews had been insulted and harmed. Maybe he believed that just now they needed his words of encouragement even more than others.

Jews should remember and recognize this wonderful and tragic person who, during those frightful and momentous days, achieved a stature he never had before.

Starzyński was also thinking about the Jewish population on the eve of the Germans' entry into the city. In his last proclamation, written just after the formal capitulation was posted all over the city on either September 28 or 29, he added a special paragraph. It stipulated that all ordinances are equally binding on the Jewish population and that no special measures may be issued specifically against Jews.

By that time there was not very much that he could do, but he remembered to direct one last word of encouragement to the Jewish population.

Everyone knows what happened next. The promise made by the German generals turned out to be worth no more than their other promises. The restrictions began on the very first day, when vats of food appeared on the streets to feed the hungry inhabitants. Starzyński was powerless to do anything. In the very first days of the occupation he was sent to the Pawiak prison as a hostage and never emerged from German captivity.[5]

But we're getting ahead of ourselves. Let's go back to Joseph Kamien and Nadia Kareny.

This happened sometime in the third week of the war. Maybe some of those who left Warsaw reached their destination and saw the Soviets march into Poland. Meanwhile Warsaw was still not occupied, either by the Germans or the Russians. But it suffered from the double blows of aerial bombing and artillery shelling. Surrounded on all sides, with flames everywhere, the city burned and bled and refused to surrender.

People who were then going to and from work through the devastated city would see groups of nuns in long habits and white hoods carrying the wounded on stretchers from hospitals and first aid stations that had been bombed. Either there were no other means of transportation or they simply weren't available. The nuns carried the wounded to other hospitals, but it often turned out that by the time they got there those places had been bombed as well. Or that shrapnel killed both the nuns and the wounded they were carrying.

Hospitals and first aid stations began to display white sheets with a red cross on their roofs, large enough to be easily seen from above. They hoped that their buildings would be spared. But it quickly became apparent that instead of protecting the buildings, the sheets and red crosses made them special targets. On one of those days a group of bombers attacked the large group of buildings that housed The Child Jesus Hospital.

The radio was still making limited broadcasts. We heard the news: the Germans had bombed the hospital; the city command had protested the Soviet invasion of eastern Poland. Our group huddled around the radio in the first-floor apartment in the rear left wing of Przejazd 1, discussing this sensational news, when we suddenly heard somebody ask in Polish: Is Joseph Kamien here? And who should appear in the open door but Nadia Kareny, looking like a prima donna beginning the last act of an opera. She was dressed in a silk sleeping gown and wore silk house slippers on her bloody feet. Her disheveled blonde hair flowed over her shoulders; her eyes seemed distended from fear and suffering.

A Polish scout had brought her. He was a member of the scout brigades that were rescuing people from burning buildings and doing other such tasks in the besieged city. As the neighboring part of the hospital had started to burn and as the windows in her hospital room shattered, she only had time to grab a nightgown and run out. The scout found her half conscious in the garden and carried her. She asked him to take her to the Jewish section—a distance of several kilometers through rubble, bomb craters in the sidewalks, and wooden boards hastily placed over trenches in the middle of the city. The journey took a couple of hours. No sooner had the scout delivered Nadia than he disappeared, even before we could offer him a drink of water.

The Germans were not bombing at night, and the intense artillery shelling of the center of the city had not yet begun. There was a room on the first floor to the right of the stairs that was being used as a shelter. The people staying there gave Nadia a space in a corner on the right side of the kitchen, through which one had to pass to get to the other rooms. They fixed up a kind of cot for her and put together some chairs for the invalid Kamien so he could stretch out and sleep.

There was no way they could return to their place on the fourth floor. By that time the elevator had not been working for over a week, and the fourth floor itself was no longer habitable.

>——<

For ten more days we bedded down in the first-floor rooms and in the annex at Przejazd 1. I don't want to describe that time in any more detail, although I clearly remember particular conversations, incidents, and vignettes from that most terrible phase of the siege, when we no longer had water, lighting, or the radio.

"Go up on the roof and look at how Warsaw is burning," somebody said as he urged me to go with him, but I didn't go. I even avoided going to the gate to look at the flames that surrounded us on all sides—boulevards of burning houses.

The city was in its death throes. On its streets, bloody and exhausted, the Polish state was collapsing.

One of the first pieces I wrote for the Ringelblum archive was a description of walking the streets of the city on the first afternoon after the beginning of the cease-fire. I went with two neighbors of mine from Przejazd, Ruth Karlinska and Hela Herman, whom I had befriended during the bombings. I had spent some time in the first-floor room on their landing. It had also served as an air raid shelter and as a refuge for those who had become homeless after they were forced to flee their own apartments. They too had to leave their place on a higher floor, and we would often meet each other in that shelter, where they stood out for their exemplary behavior during the air raids. Kamien and Nadia were in a first-floor room across the hall. I had first met Ruth at Tlomackie 13, and Hela was a niece of Professor Moses Schorr.

As we were walking we saw burning buildings with nobody trying to put out the fire. We somehow clambered, climbed, and managed to get as far as the figure of the Madonna on Krakowskie Przedmiescie. It was undamaged, something that the Christian population regarded as a miracle. Before the image of the Mother and Child a group of women were crossing themselves. They lay with their faces to the ground in order not to see what was happening around them. We heard people whispering nearby: "It's like an earthquake, it's as if no human hand could have done this."

Kamien also took his crutches to see what was going on outside. But no sooner did he leave than he was forced to go back. A few days later he was able to hobble some two or three hundred meters down the middle of Leszno and Tlomackie, streets where the Germans ordered people to remove rubble and clear a way for their military units. He ran into some theater people and came back encouraged that there were people like himself who were trying to find a way out of this dire predicament.

One could see people trudging along the cluttered streets carrying pails, pots, buckets, and kettles to get water from the Vistula River. Others lugged sacks full of canned food and sugar salvaged from the unguarded and pillaged military warehouses. I saw long lines of Polish soldiers, their uniforms unbuttoned, without leather belts or insignia. They were marching toward Krasinski Square to lay down their weapons, as stipulated by the cease-fire terms. Their faces were remarkably expressive.

As I was standing in line by the Vistula to get some water, I noticed from afar a few soldiers marching along the riverbank. They tore off their military overcoats, crumpled them up, and with a lot of gusto hurled them into the river. When I returned, my description of what I saw moved Kamien greatly. He was fascinated by that scene where the victors and the vanquished met face to face. That evening he acted it out for those of us who had already returned to our damaged apartments; another one of his "films." Maybe someone told him about the negotiations that were going on between German and Polish generals in some undamaged palace. Maybe at some point he had seen Rodin's sculpture *The Burghers of Calais*, where the citizens of a fallen city walk along their own road to Calvary to give the keys of the city to the victorious commander.

His imagination carried him over the ruins of Warsaw to where the last act of the great tragedy was taking place.

He played the part of the Poles. His face darkened with intense anguish, his eyebrows furrowed close together, angry, mournful. They maintained a stance of heroic silence. They were proud, prepared to undergo any sacrifice, to shoulder the burden of disaster that befell them.

Suddenly he turned into a victorious general, angry but also contemptuous, puffed up with pride and scorn, the yearning for revenge now satisfied. He turned his back on the imaginary Polish officers, made a show of not wanting to look at them. A short bark, a backward jerk of the head. He threw words over his shoulder, refused to listen to what they had to say. He dictated terms . . .

I'm not at all sure that's how the meeting between the Polish and German generals really went. Or that the Prussian Junkers who had hitched themselves to Hitler's wagon had indeed disregarded the rules of military etiquette that normally marked such encounters.

But Kamien saw the scene with all the instincts of his artistic imagination. He grasped its elemental essence. This was Kamien: the very personification of the dramatic craft, a playwright, an actor, the stage etched into his very being.

>——<

Here is yet another example of personal experience intersecting with unfolding historical events.

This happened one month after the Germans marched in. People were hitting the road and getting out of Warsaw—Kamien and Nadia too.

I see them now as if they're right in front of me. He was clean shaven, with a *narciarka* on his head, the latest fashion among Warsaw Jews.[6] Nadia was in her coat lined with seal fur, ready to travel, her hair nicely done. There was a whiff of perfume. She tied a lace shawl around her blonde hair, probably something left over from a play.

It was a frosty morning. Along with someone else they had hired a horse and wagon, which was waiting out front. They were heading to Bialystok and from there hoped to take a train to Vilna. We all kissed goodbye. They left me a memento from their home, a small pot to boil milk. We parted as if we were characters in a historical novel.

That was the last time I ever saw Kamien.

>—<

As the war dragged on I got some news about them. After the Germans attacked the Soviet Union in 1941, I heard that he was one of the first Jews who were murdered in Vilna.

But I only heard the truth about Kamien after Nadia returned to Poland in 1946. It turned out that when the Soviet-German war began, they were on tour in Soviet Belarus. They had been doing the same programs of monologues and songs that they had presented in Poland. They managed to evacuate into the Russian interior, finally landing in Uzbekistan. Then came the end. The terrible sickness that had ravaged Kamien's bones returned, and they had to amputate his other leg. This happened in a hospital in Karaganda. Kamien's talented daughter Lea Koenig—one of Israel's best actresses—managed to find out what happened to him. He died in the hospital in January 1942. While he was lying on his deathbed he still entertained everybody on his ward with skits and improvisations, including impersonations of wounded soldiers, doctors, nurses, and other sick patients.

Until his last moment he remained true to himself.

5. Sunday "Five o'Clocks" at Mrs. Cecilia Slepak's

Cecilia Slepak was the first of our circle to realize that we had to do something to drive away despair.

It must have been sometime around the end of November or beginning of December 1939, on one of the shortest, darkest days. The city was beginning to emerge from the chaotic heaps of stones, bricks, and ruins of houses that were smashed by bombs and shells. The antitank ditches had been filled in and the barricades taken down. Not all the gravesites—mounds of yellow clay with four-sided military hats placed on the temporary crosses—had been removed. On all the squares, in each small plot of soft earth, one saw either graves or open pits from which bodies had been exhumed, including the Polish and Jewish victims from September. The corpses buried underneath collapsed houses filled the air with the stench of death that, combined with the smell of smoke, hung over Warsaw during all the years of the occupation. The foredoomed battles to come would cause more fires and more deaths; the smell of smoke and corpses would never abate.

In a way it was fortunate that life had become so tough. The hunger, bitter cold, and constant danger of being kidnapped by the occupiers for forced labor—all this forced you to be alert, to keep your guard up, and not to sink into apathy and depression.

At the beginning of the occupation one could stay outside only until 6 p.m. Later on the curfew began at 7 or 8 p.m.

Cecilia Slepak put those additional hours to good use.

>——<

The family lived in a first-floor apartment at Elektoralna 1. Some of the windows faced onto the courtyard. In those days that was a major advantage.

Her husband was an engineer. I think that before the war he was somehow connected to the film industry. But Mrs. Slepak was the one who had connections with the world of literature and art. She had been very much involved in the Russian-speaking and Yiddish-speaking intellectual elite of Vilna and Riga. But at the same time she was at home with the Polish-speaking Jewish intelligentsia of Warsaw. One of her major achievements had been her translation of Dubnow's *World History of the Jewish People* into Polish. Mrs. Cecilia was also close to the Niger-Charny dynasty, corresponded with Bella Chagall, and was in contact with Professor Segal of the Judaic Institute.

I got to know her at Tlomackie 13. Before the war I visited her at home for some reason. There I met her husband and their only daughter. She was a lovely girl with plump cheeks, not too tall, dressed in a school outfit, and with a thick braid tied in a black ribbon that rested on her shoulder. Her mother was not tall either. She wore her hair in an old-fashioned braided style knotted at the nape of her neck.

That's how they remain in my memory—mother and daughter. They looked so much alike: the same color eyes, same smile, same wide neck. And they shared the same fate, early victims of the deluge that carried them off to Treblinka.

>——<

Once I happened to meet Mrs. Slepak in the corridor of the ZTOS,[1] which had moved into the building at Tlomackie 5, the former home of the Judaic Institute. She took me into an alcove and discreetly invited me to drop by around 5 p.m. on a Sunday afternoon "for coffee." "A few other people will be there," she added.

Considering our situation, I was intrigued by the idea of inviting people to a "five o'clock." I immediately said yes. That Sunday, accompanied by Miriam Orleska, I appeared at Elektoralna 1. In a big room, with a piano that luckily had not yet been confiscated, we met a group of guests seated in upholstered chairs around a low table. Some we already knew, some we didn't: the historian Edmund Stein and the Folmans from the Judaic Institute; the Kirschbraun brothers, one a lawyer, one with a doctorate in philosophy, and a few other guests. The Kirschbraun brothers were known to be gifted amateur musicians, a pianist and a violinist. Thanks to them, the get-togethers at the Slepaks gave us a chance to hear beautifully played classical music.

One of the brothers, the lawyer, had lost his wife during the bombing. He didn't take part in the conversations and the guests treated him like someone in mourning.

In those days, just inviting ten or fifteen people to come to your house was a dangerous thing to do. I think it was expressly forbidden. All that had to happen was for a passing German patrol to hear some strains of music and enter the apartment. Everything could have ended very badly. Nevertheless, the Slepaks and their guests paid no attention to the danger or perhaps didn't understand what kind of risk they were taking. In retrospect those gatherings might be seen as an act of civil resistance; as one of the first attempts to fight back against the German determination to reduce the oppressed population—and especially the Jewish and Polish intelligentsia—to a state of fear and bovine passivity.

The Slepaks probably had stores of flour and sugar, which allowed them to bake large cakes to serve with the five o'clock coffee. Despite the permanent feeling of hunger, which probably bothered us in those early days more than it did later, what really attracted us to this wartime salon was our hostess: her friendly smile and the warm atmosphere she fostered. We could, if only for a short time, forget about the nightmarish present, converse with interesting people, and free ourselves from the viselike grip of a frightening reality. We exchanged rumors, talked about the latest news from the BBC, discussed and analyzed the political situation, and told jokes.

During those talks a topic that came up over and over again was how to escape the trap we were in. We talked about those who left the city "as men," in response to the appeal during the first week of September, and about those who left "as Jews," after the arrival of the Germans, to cross the Bug River and reach the Soviet zone of occupation. This odyssey lasted the whole of that winter. Many journalists and writers were killed on the road trying to flee, killed by bombs or shot by Germans. There were those who returned, having been unable to cross the demarcation line, as well as some who had made it to the other side but then returned in order to help loved ones escape or to look for ways to get out of Europe altogether.

The return of two arrested Jews—Yitshak (Itsik) Giterman and

Moshe Indelman—whose fate had caused much worry created something of a sensation. Mrs. Slepak was close to the Indelmans, and she had taken care of Mrs. Indelman after the arrest of her husband and his removal from Warsaw. She was among the few people who met and spoke with him after his return, and discreetly told the guests the story of a good German—Fritz was his name—who had helped Indelman in jail and had shown him sympathy. Indelman came back a sick man. He didn't go outside and was wary of receiving visitors. Then another sensation! He and his family were able to leave Warsaw, almost as if it were normal times, and go to the Land of Israel on the basis of an immigration certificate and with tickets purchased through the travel agency "Lloyd Triestina."

It turned out that the Italian travel agency, thanks to the alliance of Hitler and Mussolini, had reopened its business in Warsaw with an office on Marszalkowska Street. If Jews had the right papers they could use it. A privileged few could leave occupied Poland as clients of a well-known travel bureau that supplied passports, train tickets, and passage on a ship. Some of these lucky ones were among Slepak's guests.

For a time the question of whether to stay or go was the main topic of conversation. But soon a new dictum appeared: "Not everybody has the right to run away." This was a maxim supported both by the Judenrat and by the Aleynhilf, which was made up of more radical and populist elements. We also heard the terrible news that the Germans had arrested and shot several Jewish professionals, mostly lawyers, including Braverman, the director of the CENTOS.[2]

The gatherings at the Slepaks' stopped for a couple of weeks, but then they began again with the same guests and a few new ones.

Miriam Orleska and I were not regular visitors at Elektoralna 1. But one of my visits—or to be specific, one of my return trips—is fixed in my memory.

It must have been in February or March; or at any rate, after the occupation of Norway.[3] That news did not worry Cecilia's salon too much. In those bright late-winter afternoons the guests were more preoccupied with predicting what would happen in the spring: the chances for the "great, general offensive of the western powers against Nazi Germany."

That day I left for home in the company of Hersh-Tsvi Rakovski, a

Hebrew writer and activist. We were going in the same direction, and Mrs. Slepak put us together so that he could "see me home." It was just before curfew. The devastated street going from Bank Square to Chlodna Street was almost completely empty. The eerie hulks of shattered houses jutted out from both sides of the street. There were no street lamps, and in the pale light of the moon those dead houses looked like surreal stage sets. The moon itself, peeking out from between the ruins, looked like a theater prop.

Winter was fading away. In the daytime the piles of snow and lumps of ice covering the streets were beginning to melt. But at night the soft spots where the ice had melted froze over again, and you had to be very careful not to slip. As a "well-brought-up gentleman" Rakovski should have given me his arm and guided me along the dangerous walk. But such a thing never occurred to him. Tall, somewhat stooped, spectacles perched on his long, thin nose, he strode by himself down the middle of the street, paying no attention to the fact that I might break my arms and legs.

His behavior struck me as very funny. I somehow managed the walk in my snow boots. But when we got to the corner of Solna Street, where our paths diverged, I could no longer resist and asked him good naturedly if this was how he always escorted a lady. He took me absolutely seriously, made heartfelt apologies, and then told me what had happened to him.

A few weeks ago at the Slepaks', one of the departing guests had mistakenly put on Rakovski's rubber boots. So he had no choice. He wore the boots of the guest that took his, even though they were a bit small. Since then he visited the Slepaks each Sunday in the hope that he would find the person who had started this "crisis of the boots" and put it right.

"Do you know who it is?" I asked.

"How should I know?" he replied. "I try to get there after everybody has already arrived and I try on all the boots in the anteroom. But I haven't been able to find my pair. I don't even have that first pair of boots that I took instead. This is the fifth pair of boots that I'm wearing. These are too big."

On Solna it became lighter. I took a look at Rakovski's long and narrow feet. They seemed to be swimming in boots that were too big and too wide. Just like a heron who bends his beak low to protect his catch, Rakovski's long thin nose was fixed on his feet, anxious not to lose the boots.

I was already living with the Feldshuh family. Having made it home just before they locked the gates, I told them about Rakovski's fifth pair of boots. My cousins knew Rakovski and they had a good laugh when they heard about it.

The story became popular. People told it in different versions. Five pairs of boots became ten. People could still laugh then. They were eager for anything that would make them less depressed. We still wanted to believe in a happy ending. We thought that we'd get a chance to jovially retell the incidents and jokes of the occupation days. That we'd recall our troubles and have a good laugh. Even disasters and misfortunes produce their own clichés and platitudes. After the First World War people wrote memoirs. Even in our most pessimistic predictions, we could not have foreseen what would happen to us two years later.

Looking back after many years it was clear that the writing was on the wall. One could have predicted and understood what would happen. But we turned away from the truth. We didn't want to face it.

>———<

In the spring of 1940 the Slepaks had to leave Elektoralna 1 and the "five o'clocks" ended. I would run into Mrs. Cecilia in the offices of the Aleynhilf. Toward the end of 1941 she visited me in the soup kitchen as well as in my room at the Feldshuh's. She asked me questions about my work in the kitchen and about general matters. I guessed that she was collecting information for an essay for Dr. Emanuel Ringelblum's contest, "Two Years in the Ghetto."[4]

What happened to Tsvi Rakovski? To the Kirschbraun brothers? What happened to the other guests who came to Cecilia Slepak's Sunday evening salon?

After the war I couldn't track down any details about their fates. Except for Mrs. Cecilia's husband, the engineer Slepak-Juszynski, I never heard from any of them again.

Part 2: The Story of a Kitchen

6. THE KITCHEN AT LESZNO 40

In those days we walked around covered with ash and soot. The fires that engulfed the city had finally died down. The heels of our shoes were torn from slogging over the stones and bricks of ruined buildings. The smell of smoke and death was everywhere. It filled our nostrils. The echoes of roaring planes and exploding bombs were still ringing in our ears.

The city looked like a scene from an earthquake. The Polish state was dead, but its unburied corpse was splayed out in full view. We were like mourners standing in front of an open grave. These were the last days of September 1939. Warsaw had just capitulated, and the German army was about to march into the city.

It was during that time at the end of September—those black days when the first German proclamations appeared on city walls—when the poet Reyzl Zychlinski dropped by and said that Emanuel Ringelblum was looking for me. He asked her to tell me to see him in the offices of the Joint Distribution Committee.

After its building at Jasna 11 had been destroyed, the Joint moved to a new headquarters on Wielka Street. People were saying that Ringelblum showed up for work during the entire siege, even on days when the bombing was especially heavy. He even came in on that terrible Monday, September 25, when the bombing raged nonstop from eight in the morning until six in the evening. That day was the prelude to Warsaw's surrender.

I was feeling broken, helpless, depressed. I was totally penniless. When I came to Wielka, Ringelblum told me of a decision to employ as many members of the Jewish intelligentsia as possible. It was important to save its cadres. He also told me in no uncertain terms that not everyone should or could run away.

The Germans were expelling Jews from the western provinces. Thousands of them were already in the city, as well as many refugees. We could not simply abandon these people. Ringelblum sent me to Leszno 40, the old headquarters of the retail association. Since their building was undamaged, we could set up a soup kitchen there. Ringelblum introduced me to Tsalel, the association's secretary. I received some cash and then Tsalel and I stumbled our way through rubble, the remnants of barricades, and antitank ditches that had not yet been filled in. We rummaged through the apartments of shopkeepers and looked for cooking utensils, dishes, and food. In a warehouse of the Joint there were still some sacks of provisions that had not been burned or soaked. On October 1, the very day that Hitler came to Warsaw to review the victory parade on Saxon Square, I was making my way with Piotr Sulin, the Polish janitor of the retail association, through the rubble of a side street that we were forced to use so as not to interfere with the German military.[1] I was carrying a packet of blank forms to set up the paperwork as well as a box of dried prunes to start cooking. Piotr lugged a half-full sack of rice on his shoulders. The day before we had received several packages of dried saltwater fish.

>——<

That's how it began. On that first day the kitchen served fifty portions of a random meal that a woman who lived at Leszno 40 offered to put together from the various items we had brought. The first clients came from the literary world, mostly the wives of men who had left with the retreating army. These women were also preparing to cross the Bug and reach the Soviet zone. Among the first volunteers to work in the kitchen were two teachers from the Yiddish schools, Rivka Kogan and Sheyna Pat, who was the sister of Yankev Pat, as well as Miriam Orleska. Except for Orleska, everyone—those I mentioned and those I didn't, volunteers as well as clients—soon left for the Soviet zone.

A kitchen reserved exclusively for journalists and writers and their families was organized at Karmelicka 5, which expanded to two other kitchens: one for writers in a wing of Tlomackie 13, and one for journalists at Graniczna 13, right next to the building which had housed the writers union on the eve of the war and which was destroyed by a bomb in the very early days of the siege. The journalists' kitchen was located in the apartment of Y. M. Apelbaum. That kitchen, along with Apelbaum and his family, later moved to Leszno 14. The kitchen at Leszno 40 was registered as a regular public kitchen.

The first day we served fifty meals. The last meals were served at the end of July 1942, during the Great Deportation, just before it became a "shop kitchen" serving the workers of the W. C. Toebbens factory. That whole time I kept working in the same kitchen; I was one of those people who seemed to be able to hang on no matter what. For almost three years I found myself at the epicenter of Jewish troubles, in the front lines of the battle against hunger, as close as one could get to the suffering of the Jewish masses.

>——<

A public kitchen . . . it is not that simple to define what it is. A kitchen could be many things. This was a microcosm of the Jewish community, the critical foundation of welfare activity. Over time—and especially in the ghetto—it also became a base for clandestine and semi-clandestine political and cultural activities and, at the very end, even for the resistance movement.

The Aleynhilf took over all kinds of Jewish institutions, including party headquarters, offices, welfare organizations, schools, and unions, and it brought together and employed large numbers of communal activists along with the Jewish white-collar intelligentsia. All other forms of public, political, and cultural life were forbidden. But in time Jews resumed these activities under the protective cover of the one type of organization that was allowed to help the homeless and hungry masses: the public kitchen. Each kitchen had its own specific character, and together they reflected the wide-ranging political and intellectual diversity of Jewish life.

Jewish leaders, at some personal risk to themselves, shrewdly wheedled German permission not only to legalize the Aleynhilf but also to allow it almost complete independence of the Judenrat. It would operate as a parallel organization. Such an arrangement was unique in occupied Europe.[2] The Aleynhilf functioned on the basis of a clandestine arrangement between political parties, which allowed Jewish groups and organizations some autonomy and the chance to secure posts for their own people.

>—<

The network of kitchens was organized in a uniform manner and worked under a first-class administration. On paper Yehoshua Broyde directed the kitchen department of the Aleynhilf. But because of Broyde's lung disease, the real administrator was the energetic and capable Dr. M. Shpindler. Menakhem Linder, the young statistician and YIVO scholar, oversaw the records of the 100,000 adult clients as well as of the thousands of children who used the kitchens. Three indefatigable instructors, directed by the university-trained nutritionist Gina Berkenheim, went from kitchen to kitchen and taught us hygiene, proper cooking technique, and accounting. They were always experimenting, trying to figure out how to take the food that the Germans allotted—of the worst quality and often half rotten—and make it as tasty and nutritious as possible.

The kitchens worked under enormous pressure. Their employees were undernourished and had to worry about their own families. There were masses of refugees, as well as destitute local Jews, for whom that soup at the kitchen was their only meal of the day. Unfortunately, we quickly realized that the only people we really helped were those who had access to another meal somewhere else. As for the neediest, even the best soups did not keep them from swelling up from hunger and perishing. Entire families and displaced communities were dumped into the ghetto, passed through our kitchens, and expired in front of our eyes.

The kitchen department went through different phases and changed its location a couple of times. There were periods when the department had a large storehouse full of products. Then we would hand in our orders and go there every day to pick up food. There were also times when the department would give us money to buy food on our own. There were meetings and consultations. The director of each kitchen had to stay on top of things, know what was going on, and visit the office every day to find out what the leadership was thinking. They had to cajole, prod, and battle for the interests of "their" kitchen.

So the same people would run into each other every day in the corridors and waiting rooms of the Aleynhilf headquarters, especially when it was located in the former Judaic Institute at Tlomackie 5. The kitchen directors formed a cozy group, and they would linger a while to pass along information, shoot the breeze, tell the latest jokes, and discuss hopeful rumors about the imminent defeat of Hitler and Mussolini. They also heard war news gleaned from secret radios and transmitted it to the ghetto at large.

In time the prophecies about Hitler's defeat came true. But of the hundred or so directors and the thousand to fifteen hundred workers and employees of the kitchens, not even 2 percent lived to see it.

Now I see faces, and remember certain people, especially the women who were kitchen managers. Two of them ran neighboring kitchens: Pola Elster, who ran the kitchen of the Left Labor Zionists on Elektoralna Street, and the manager of the kitchen at Leszno 29, one of whose co-workers was a Soviet citizen. During the first year and a half of the war, that was a mark of privilege. We had close relations with those nearby kitchens, lending and borrowing food products from one another.

Genia Ber, a young woman with blonde curly hair, was another popular manager of a Labor Zionist kitchen. I remember the face and smallish figure of Mlinek, who ran the big Bundist kitchen on Muranow. I remember three managers of religious kitchens. One of them, a refugee from Lodz, with a blond beard and blue eyes, tried to persuade us just before the first wartime Passover in 1940 not to cook legumes.[3] He used psychological arguments. The inner turmoil that a religious Jew would suffer from violating the laws of Passover would harm his health and far outweigh the nutritional value of the protein that a few beans might provide in the course of a week. When the second wartime Passover came along, there were no longer any discussions about legumes. Nor was there any sign of the man with the blond beard.

I remember a refined gentleman who before the war had been the director of a free loan society in some larger provincial town. I also remember that dark day when I heard the news that the Germans seized this gentleman along with the entire staff of his kitchen, among whom were several former co-workers from Leszno 40. That evening a Jewish policeman told me how this director, a respected personality before the war, showed dignity and courage as he marched to the cattle cars, followed by his entire staff.

I also remember some teachers who ran kitchens for children. One of them, Genia Silkes, I knew from before the war. She supervised the general activities and educational programs in the children's kitchen at Nowolipki 35. Once I also visited the children's kitchen at Nowolipki 22, where Ms. Mostkov taught the children in Hebrew. And since I am mentioning kitchens that I visited, I shouldn't forget to include Gęsia 14, where the poet Yitshak Katzenelson organized a Hebrew dramatic circle.

We were especially impressed by the relationships that developed between activists from rival organizations. Before the war they never had much to do with each other. But now that the Aleynhilf had brought them together in a shared mission they worked in concert, often very harmoniously. It was here that Dr. Ringelblum developed a close friendship with the young religious activist Rabbi Shimon Huberband, who became one of his most diligent partners in the secret archive. Rabbi Zysha Frydman was a popular and intelligent speaker at our meetings. I also became friendly with Khaim Leyb Kozlowski, who had been a publicist and an active figure in the Aguda.[4]

I remember my visit to the biggest of all the public kitchens, which was located in the premises of the prewar Tomkhey Aniyim (Supporters of the Poor) Society on Pawia Street. It had a potato peeling machine as well as a facility to wash dishes. If I'm not mistaken this kitchen served the largest number of soups, four thousand a day. I met the manager of this kitchen after the war. Try as I might, I can't remember her name.

7. HUNGER

I remember a scene from my early years—something that happened during the Polish-Ukrainian war of 1919.[1] The Ukrainian army was retreating from Galicia, and our village was one of the last places they passed through. The young Ukrainians were a hungry, thirsty, and dejected band. And there was my mother, standing in front of the house holding a big loaf of bread. Those were perilous times of endless fighting, as different armies came and went. That loaf of bread was one of several prepared for some sudden emergency: the need to make a run for it, or as a bribe to buy off a dangerous assailant. But that's what we did during the First World War. Every soldier, every Cossack who came to the house, got some bread. This time my mother was behaving just like a mother. Maybe at that moment she was thinking about her own son. Was he asking for help from strangers? She didn't see those men as soldiers, or as potential robbers or killers. She saw them as exhausted, hungry sons. And somehow the bread seemed to expand as she held it. Her loaves of bread seemed to feed an entire army. I remember what my mother was thinking, and what one soldier said: "Mama, don't slice it, Mama give me what's left of the loaf." He bent down to touch her hands, almost praying. He didn't grab the bread from her hands. He implored her, like a son to a mother.

But my mother, in tears, implored him as well: "Look at the others who are waiting. I have to give them some too . . ."

That's what I thought about when I began work at Leszno 40: to give everyone their share! It was so hard for me to deal with those throngs of hungry people!

The directors of the Jewish "government" surrounded themselves with gatekeepers and hid in offices and corridors. But the manager of a public kitchen was also reckoned to be part of the "government" and became the easiest target for people who needed to unload their anger, pain, and despair at the injustices of the world, at this historical cataclysm that played itself out in an infinite number of individual variations. The kitchen director found herself on the receiving end of the deep resentment a declassed person felt after losing everything except that daily bowl of soup, that identification card, that ticket to the kitchen: the sum total of disaster broken down into tiny bits of small change.

Such a person naturally expected the director to accept everything he said. Look at what I once possessed: so many rooms, so many houses, so many sawmills, businesses, restaurants. Even though he now needed charity, he still believed that because he had been better off than others before the war he should get better treatment than those who had lived in poverty and want.

At the same time, there were some others—a few—who showed nobility of spirit, integrity, humility. It was their pain that gripped the heart.

So many tragic episodes took place at the door to the room containing the cauldron of soup. Each crisis in the food market affected our kitchen. So many scenes—the kind one might see in a rabbi's anteroom or in the office of a doctor or divorce lawyer—played out in room no. 12, our office. So many tears: the soft tears of women, the bloody tears of men, the tears of broken people in total despair. I tried to be consistent, to go by the book, and to follow the rules of the kitchen department. But real life always got in the way and turned those rules into a joke.

In those days I was a novice. In a way I remained a novice until the very end.

This is what I wrote in the autumn of 1941:

> Who knows whether those scenes we are seeing now in this closed city will not disappear along with all of us into oblivion? Just like the panic on a sinking ship, or in a burning house, from which there is no escape. Or like the horror of miners in a coal mine who are being buried alive.
>
> I see many things in our kitchen. It's here that you first see all the suffering of the ghetto. Even before the ghetto began the kitchen was the first and often the last

stop for people who ended up on the "trash heap." It's here that one can observe the whole process from beginning to end.

People who never saw this firsthand tend to think that if you see such suffering day in and day out, you get used to it. That you become numb, even callous.

I would not say that is true.

>——<

What is the relevance of all those descriptions of hunger and poverty that we used to read long ago? No one who did not spend a year in the Warsaw Ghetto has any idea what hunger really means. If you haven't seen somebody dropping to a filthy floor to lick what's left of a dropped bowl of grits, or slurping the vomit of a passing drunk from the sidewalk, or picking the lice off one's own body to eat them—even then you haven't seen the half of it. Melech Ravitch in one of his travelogues described a Chinese coolie who ate the vermin off his body. Nobody believed him.

Once I saw a sudden tumult in the anteroom of our kitchen. I did not know what was happening. Then I suddenly understood, and I yelled at our janitor for having left open a garbage bin full of half-rotten and moldy leavings of beetroot preserves, virtual poison on an empty stomach, as well as some sour strips of rhubarb peelings.

That day we were supposed to use those two "food products" to cook a borscht, sweetened with saccharin and served with an eighth of a loaf of bread that the bakeries supplied from the allocated flour ration. The Germans provided the beetroot preserves and the black bread, adulterated with clay and glue, to feed the Jewish refugees. If you put that flour in a sifter, not even half would remain. But we did not do that.

There's no nutritional value in those delicacies. But you can fill your empty stomach. How your stomach will digest that "meal" is something you can worry about later. Statistics showed that apart from the typhus epidemic there were many cases of dysentery as well as intestinal and gastric bleeding.

44

A bunch of children once moved into the corridor of our kitchen, found themselves a dark corner to hide themselves, and stayed there, strangely quiet. It turned out that there was a basket of cabbage leaves. Like a bunch of young rabbits, they pounced on the raw leaves and stuffed them as quickly as possible into their mouths. They were afraid that we would chase them out. Their teeth busily chewing away, they packed their little bellies with a little bit of wormy, filthy vitamins.

>——<

Once, in the fall, our cook arrived at daybreak and told me what she had seen on the way. Most of the time the people who came early described the naked corpses they saw, stripped bare of every bit of clothing by the human hyenas who sold rags in open-air markets. Now she described something even more shocking. She was passing a garbage bin on wheels and noticed a figure, covered in a white sheet, who was picking through the garbage with both hands and putting bits of food in his mouth. Maybe this was someone who had sold everything and spent his days lying naked on some plank. Unable to go out into the street and beg in the daytime, his only remaining garment was this filthy sheet. It was also possible that in the dark that figure only seemed to be dressed in white, as if wrapped in a shroud. Along with the cook, a Jewish policeman on night duty also saw the figure in white. No one else was around.

"You see this?" he asked the cook. "Can you believe this?"

"You see this?" answered the cook.

>——<

Here are more excerpts of my writings from 1941 and '42:

> So many of our clients have disappeared. I think about how many acquaintances I'll meet when my turn comes and I arrive in the world to come. I'll find myself in familiar company. "Oh, Miss Director is here too!" they'll greet me. And they'll surround me on all sides and demand all kinds of forbidden things: soup tickets without ID cards, lunches on tomorrow's ticket, lunches on yesterday's

ticket. They'll all be shouting at me at the same time and for so long that finally I'll have to call the dead kitchen attendant to help me escape from the throng. And as always, I'll feel a special surge of sorrow when someone simply leaves on his own, without making any fuss.

This was all because of their longing for a spoonful of food. Their faith in that bowl of soup was so strong that they kept it even in death—and so too their faith in the all-powerful Miss Director, who could supposedly feed the entire ghetto with that vat in her kitchen.

They thought that all you had to do was implore, beg with the right words, plead with bloody tears, and the miracle would happen: the vat would never empty.

"We are hungry people! We are all swollen from hunger! Don't refuse a person who is bloated!" That's what they're yelling at me, and the attendant in the world to come will not help me and will not rescue me from the siege. I'll remain there, helpless, not knowing what to do, in total despair. For a short time I'll think that I'm still alive and at my normal job.

People who had suffered through the Zbąszyn refugee camp; young survivors of the labor camps; decent-looking Jewish men and women along with some professional beggars; women from the provinces who looked a little like peasants, carrying jostling infants suckling at empty breasts. There were children who were expert scroungers, first-class specialists with their childlike heads and eyes, children meowing like kittens who were tossed over a fence into the mud.

And what about that clan of refugees who could have marched straight out of a Zalman Shneour novel? They were tough, these rural Jews, down to earth, and looked as if they were built of solid oak. One fine morning they swept into the kitchen with healthy complexions, smelling of the forest and the butcher's bench, of sacks of flour and bundles of straw, part of a fresh transport of refugees thrown out of some shtetl whose name I never would have come across in a thousand years. But when they

reach the world to come, up there, they no longer look so
ruddy and healthy. They too wound up on the scrap heap.

Over two and a half years clients would try their luck with me;
some succeeded. I remember Beila Strumpfeld, a German Jew with
Polish citizenship, who begged me only for *brosame*, the crumbs that
fell off the bread we processed on "bread days," when we added a 125-
gram slice to each bowl of "borsht." There was Abraham Brocks-meier,
the man from Dachau. Those two became privileged characters, the
first clients who enjoyed special status. I also remember the Zarchin
family along with the Lemonade troupe, magicians from the Sta-
niewski circus. Zarchin wore clown trousers, probably because nobody was willing to buy them. The day before he died, Zarchin, stoical
and subdued, came to say goodbye. He thanked me, handed over his
ticket to the kitchen, and was true to his word.

A few days later his wife showed up with a pot to get some soup.
She confirmed that he had just died. Looking back, I think that he
must have committed suicide. How else to explain the uncanny fact
that he chose to die on the "Day of the Clown," 1941?

I remember the Bronstein family, the Auerbach family from
Leipzig, the Waldman family from Posen, that boy from Krakow, and
a certain young man from Vienna. Over and over I explained to them
why I couldn't do this and shouldn't do that; why they couldn't use
the kitchen unless they filled out certain forms and applied for a ticket. This back-and-forth went on until somehow, even without proper
tickets, they managed to become regular clients. They came regularly
until we were temporarily forced to suspend our operations. When
they returned they were all swollen. Once they reached that point not
even ten free soups a day could have helped them.

I remember Nachtgeboren, the artisan with bags under his eyes.
And Shimon Hokhtsayt with the harelip. One fine morning he showed
up to tell me that he had reached a certain decision. He saw no point
in torturing himself any further. He had no way out. Therefore, he
informed me, he had decided to "entrust himself to my care."

Who else? There was the "brother and sister," Avrom and Gutche
Tsuker. And what about Paula-Tsele, from Lemberg? Mentally she
was not all there. She thought that I was her secretary. Every day she
came to my office with piles of letters to be dispatched to different

institutions in the ghetto as well as memoranda addressed to Hitler and Mussolini, Churchill and Roosevelt. Each memorandum was formulated in the appropriate language.

I remember "Oliver Twist"—Henyek Gliksztok, the blond "nobody's child" who was there when the kitchen opened. And yet another character from the kitchen's early days, Nokhem Ostri. I would tell him to wait by the wall and he would stand there, stroking his whitish goatee. As I walked past him, his whisper echoed like gurgling water: "*Tokhtershi*, just a little something to eat."

I see Lerer from Dobrzyn. He was flashy, with a certain swagger. When he came to the kitchen there was always a hearty "good morning." Just like a Pole, he would greet a lady by kissing her hand. He wore a short fur coat and high boots, like a Polish nobleman. Lerer delivered important items: bottles of sauce and ground pepper. But by the time he appeared in the world to come, with his red hair and effeminate voice, he was gaunt and covered in a layer of dust. That's how we saw him the last time—Lerer, the provincial member of the retailers association—as he made his final gesture of despair. He sprawled face down in front of Leszno 40, affecting the stance of a goner, a man in his final agonies. Yes, he was going to teach them a lesson, those bigwigs in the association who had not helped him. It turned out to be no idle threat. The next day he died.

What about the doctor who came from some small town near the Baltic? He was tall with broad shoulders and arrived wearing a stylish coat. Soon enough he had no decent clothes to wear. His suffering made him unbalanced, unable to work as a doctor. He looked like a ghost as he passively waited to die.

There was one day when we couldn't serve soup. "Hallo!" He yelled from the courtyard below. He waved his stick at us and shouted all kinds of threats and curses. Yes, there he was, that doctor, another client who had once been a respectable citizen of some small town.

>——◂

I recall the words from Markish's "The Heap," written right after the First World War.

They are here, they are all here

They stacked them up here, all of them

The Jews in Warsaw who died of hunger during this war against the Jewish people are not piled in some heap. They are lying naked, without shrouds, in the mass graves of the Gęsia cemetery.

>——<

Here's another excerpt from what I wrote then:

> *Zey pekhnen oyfn pisk far hunger*—they are swelling up and starving to death. I heard that expression often. In my native village of Lanowitz, that's what Jews used to say about a family that was dirt poor. In those days that phrase was just a phrase, a kind of metaphor, and no one bothered to think about its literal meaning. Those words must have originated when famine, especially among the peasants, was a more common occurrence. More recent generations didn't actually have to suffer that way. In those days Jewish poverty meant "a thin slice of bread, potatoes Sunday and potatoes Monday, tea and bread, bread and tea, may we all be spared from such a treat." That was how we used to describe what it meant to be hungry. But children in the Warsaw Ghetto would have regarded such expressions as descriptions of luxury. Potatoes every day? You get hot tea and bread? Maybe real tea, with real sugar?
>
> Once I met a Jewish refugee in the street, a weaver from Lodz. He was carrying a pound of turnips to eat with his wife on the Sabbath. "God favored me with a bargain." Those were his exact words. A bargain for sixty groshn. Today that Jew is no longer alive. He was the young grandfather of an odd girl who would get free soups. Her name was Topche.
>
> Anyway, now we know exactly what the phrase *pekhnen oyfn pisk* means. There are plenty of opportunities to see it up close in the Jewish quarter of Warsaw.
>
> The special color of the cheeks, the little swellings

on both sides of the nose, the bleakness in the eyes . . . I think that each director of a kitchen has become a kind of expert in this area.

Hunger is one of the four horsemen of the apocalypse. We need a new Goya to come and draw the worst sufferings of this new "Jewish War" that the Crazy Man is waging against the Jewish children of the sealed city.

I have often heard people expressing surprise at the stoicism of the hungry masses. The windows of the food shops on Karmelicka Street are full of products: big fat cakes with mysterious stuffings, loaves of bread and challah. There's no lack of delicacies or fruit, almost like before the war. The windows are full because there are few customers. In the stalls of the open-air markets and in front of the courtyard gates on Nowolipie and Smocza Streets there are strange and disgusting displays of new food products that attract the stares of thousands of hungry people. And yet no one smashes the shop windows and only rarely, maybe on the eve of some holiday, does a crowd attack and rob a street stall. I understand why this is so. It's not the fear of the Jewish policeman that keeps the hungry masses from committing acts of despair. Anger and despair are not the last step toward the bottom. Hungry people without jobs can feel that—until they swell up. Once they become swollen—after a long period of malnutrition—they undergo a psychological change. They become apathetic and develop a frightening fixation on their own bodies.[2]

"My body is scrawny," a woman lamented to me, with a note of surprise. She was splendid, with dark eyes and curly hair, the mother of quite gorgeous children. "Each day I get thinner, and my legs and thighs are swelling, growing bigger." I actually don't know why she was so surprised. She had already buried her husband. And with each passing day, the cap of her lovely son, who had the same eyelashes as his mother, fell lower and lower over his eyes.

It's very hard to save someone who has already begun

to swell. It's no longer a matter of stilling hunger but of providing fats, fruit, sugar. How will we find that for them and for those we want to keep from becoming bloated? In our own circle only the most naïve try to convince themselves that you can save a Jew with a bowl of soup.

>———<

These pessimistic observations of mine were cited by Emanuel Ringelblum in his writings on the Aryan side. That was what I was thinking in the ghetto.

Now, as I look back many years later, I think that I was too rash when I underplayed the impact and social significance of the public kitchens and children's kitchens, or the colossal effort that went into them. Neither the kitchen administration nor the Aleynhilf were to blame for the fact that the 100,000 soups served once a day could not solve the problem of massive hunger and widespread mortality. The monthly rations that the Germans allocated to the ghetto could not feed someone for more than a week. We should also remember that most of the unemployed and uprooted families lacked the money to buy food, even at the lower ration prices. So our social welfare institutions, no matter how much they tried, were unable to feed them adequately.

But we shouldn't forget that the kitchens made a real difference in feeding the ghetto, along with massive smuggling and economic ties with the Poles. Those clients whom the kitchens really helped were those who could get other meals, ample or meager, from some other source. In those wartime conditions no social welfare organization would have been able to feed tens or hundreds of thousands of needy refugees and destitute Warsaw Jews. But their efforts, along with smuggling and illegal trade, made a difference and are the reason that 75 percent of the ghetto population survived the first two and a half years of the occupation.

If, as German statistics show, 350,000 Jews were still alive in the Warsaw Ghetto,[3] it was a result of the amazing will to live, the ability to organize, and the intelligence that was exhibited not only in the public institutions but also in spontaneous efforts of civil resistance.

Entire bands of traders and smugglers sprang up in the ghetto and on the Polish side. They ignored all the edicts and warnings. They didn't care about the dangers and the shootings that took place on both sides of the ghetto wall. They supplied the ghetto with everything necessary to live. Of course, the Jewish and Polish smugglers were doing this to support themselves, to make money. The smuggled products cost a lot. But this did not diminish their significance in allowing a great part of the Jewish population to survive.

The German occupiers were not used to dealing with these kinds of Jews and gentiles. (They didn't see the likes of them in the Reich.) They wondered why the process of liquidating the Jews through economic pressure and administrative decrees was going so slowly. Before long they decided to move on to more effective methods.

Therefore, despite the tragic fate of the providers and consumers of smuggled food, and notwithstanding my reservations and pessimistic appraisals of welfare activity, it all reflected an impressive effort by public and private aid organizations. From a national and from a human point of view it was a positive achievement. Furthermore, smuggling and trade were examples of an incredible dynamism on the part of large sectors of the Jewish (and Polish) population, who did not allow themselves to be crushed and paralyzed in their struggle for survival.[4]

8. ADOLF AS IN HITLER. BUND AS IN *FELKERBUND*[1]

That's how he used to humorously introduce himself in the early days. I don't really remember how he ended up in Warsaw. He originally lived in Vienna. Perhaps he escaped from there, or was deported, or maybe he was one of those who came through Zbąszyń.

He wasn't much younger than thirty. Not too tall, he cut a nice figure, with an attractive head of hair: a real Viennese "Herrchen."[2] He was well groomed, always wore a polite smile, and cared about his appearance. He turned up at the kitchen after he spent the last złotys he received for selling his family heirloom, a solid gold watch, that he had managed to hold on to until he arrived in Poland. He applied for a ticket and became a client of our kitchen.

He would buy his ticket and eat his soup with other clients from Germany. As his very last złotys gave out he moved from the front hall to the seats near the kitchen and began to take his soup in an old food jar, which he hung over his arm with a piece of string. At the same time, he started trying—in a seemingly lighthearted kind of way—to attract my attention. He had probably convinced himself that if I really wanted to I could do something for him. After he finished his soup he would not leave but hang around reading an old German newspaper. When the kitchen got less busy he would start up a conversation.

His common sense told him that it was pointless to walk around and bemoan his fate. So he kept up the pretense of a normal conversation, the kind you would have in a café or on a train. One time he worked up his courage, knocked on my door, and inquired if he could ask me something. Since he had heard that I used to write in the press before the war, he would like to know my opinion about the situation in Germany. We should get some sense—"*nicht wahr?*"—about what was going on there.

He had read Ernst Haeckel's *Die Welträtsel* (*The World's Riddle*), which tried to give a rational explanation for how a simplistic paranoid like Hitler could rise to power in the country that had the world's best scholars and philosophers. How did he manage to mobilize their support to become the ruler over all of Europe?

"What? In the twentieth century for such a thing to take place?" Every other German-Jewish refugee was always bringing up the twentieth century.

Bund wound himself up. His voice got louder. Standing in the middle of the room, his speech took on a note of pathos. I got the sense that he had some hidden agenda.

"Herr Bund," I said. "Excuse me. Somebody is coming to see me soon. Can you tell me something about your personal situation?"

It was as if I had given him his cue. In that same intense tone he tried to convince me that saving him was worth the trouble. Knock on wood, he had something to live for. As soon as Hitler cleared out of Vienna, a fortune was going to fall into his lap. His parents of blessed memory fled Galicia in 1914 and remained in Vienna. His father, a watchmaker, worked his way up and built a prosperous jewelry business in the second district. After Hitler marched in his father got very sick and died. His blessed mother had died earlier. A Catholic partner, a "decent Christian," was running the jewelry store. Business was good. As soon as the Nazis collapsed, "which can happen any day now," he would have no trouble retrieving his fortune, or at least a large part of it. He also had a fiancée. She had stayed in Vienna after they deported him. There were no letters from her. But, he remarked drolly, that was something he could worry about later.

Bund said a courteous goodbye and asked me not to be angry with him. He only wanted me to consider that he had good reasons to try and survive.

>———<

The weeks went by. Bund moved into a refugee shelter. In our kitchen he got one soup daily with or without a ticket. He probably got another soup in the shelter. After a time I found out that some people had independently arranged for "impoverished members of the intelligentsia" to get a supplemental breakfast, which consisted of a cup of ersatz tea sweetened with yellow sugar and a 50-gram slice of bread. With the help of Dr. Vaysberg, the director of the refugee shelters, I got Bund's name added to this list. A few weeks later I was able to get Bund a package of uncooked food products. That was all I was able to do for him. When he began waiting for me again in the corridor, I gestured to him that there was nothing more I could do. After that he stopped following me. He had enough sense of shame and enough dignity not to put me in the position of having to avoid him.

Once someone told me that Bund was standing in front of the open-air market at Leszno 42 and was trading our soup kitchen tickets. How could that be, I wondered. He was entitled to one ticket a day. But I also knew that people thought up various schemes to trade our tickets. The 20 groszy price of a ticket, which bought a soup worth more than a złoty, tempted poor people to try and make some money. The price of the daily soups varied depending on what we were cooking that day. When people heard that the kitchen prepared soup with beans, they bought the next day's tickets and, without too much trouble, changed the date and sold the ticket for a higher price. Because of that there were days when there was not enough soup for those who came late. That caused us major problems. We caught on to the trick and stopped selling tickets for the following day. Other kitchens had the same problem and the kitchen directorate demanded that we show absolutely no tolerance for these abuses. They asked us to confiscate the kitchen passes of those involved in selling tickets.

I sent for Bund, and he showed up around three or four in the afternoon. I served him a bowl of soup that had been reserved for clients who got off work late. He thanked me courteously and declined.

"Do you feel insulted, Bund?" I asked him. I began to explain to him that his actions made no sense, that his dealings were pointless. Anything he earned from selling the tickets would not be able to buy anything more nutritious than the bowl of soup. I talked and talked until I realized that he was silent. Suddenly my speech just wilted away.

"Dear lady," he said in German, "take a look at me!"

I stared at him. He pinched the skin under his eye sockets with the thick fingers of both hands, leaving two deep dimples that did not fade quickly. In his eyes there was a glint of irony and devilish vindication. It was as if he was telling me: "OK, lady, take a look, this is what your 'help' amounts to." His fingers and the bags under his eyes sent a clear message: swollen! Such a person should no longer eat liquid food. Bund could now do without my friendly advice or my soups. With a shake of the head, he said: "You are right, you are right, I kiss your hand, dear lady."

For a time I did not run into Bund. Spring was coming and with it the first warm days.

One day, as I was walking on Leszno, I saw him from a distance. It seemed that he saw me too, but he didn't greet me, didn't move faster to meet me. He turned back into a crowd of people and moved toward a nearby wall, the large double building of Leszno 52–54. Bund was totally barefoot. His tiny, almost childlike feet were deathly white, as if they had risen from a clump of dough. They were covered in filth from the melting snow.

Seeing him sent a pang through my heart and I felt an impulse to run up to him. I racked my brain about what I could do for him now. But by the time I reached the gate of the double building he was gone. Perhaps he could no longer get his shoes onto his swollen feet. Perhaps he sold his pair of worn-out shoes, hoping that he could use the money to do a little buying and selling on the street. But as soon as he held those few złotys in his hand, he could not resist the temptation to buy a loaf of bread, to eat his fill, for once, with real food.

A new spring was beginning . . .

He ran away from me. Maybe he was ashamed for me to see him barefoot, filthy, unshaven. Or maybe he just didn't want to meet me and hear my cheap words again.

Adolf as in Hitler. Bund as in *Felkerbund*.

9. FAMILIES

In that terrible time there were families who held on to bonds of love and devotion that were beautiful and sad to see.

I remember the brothers Malavantshik-Perlmutter. I don't recall which shtetl they came from, only that they had been thrown out of their homes and were totally uprooted from their livelihoods and trades. As they trudged toward Warsaw they were robbed of their clothes, their money, perhaps even the jewelry that their wives still might have had. Ordered to keep pace with the police motorcycles at their heels, they were forced to abandon the packs they carried on their backs. They only managed to bring one treasure with them to Warsaw: their old, blind father. The father would not come to the kitchen. But the sons told me about him, perhaps asked me for an extra soup to take to him, and every time they did not forget to add, "Father, may he live to 120." That old blind Jewish father who was richer than King Lear.

>—<

I remember a woman in her thirties who came to our kitchen along with that group of husky rural Jews I already mentioned. They ate at our kitchen only once, when they first came to Warsaw. Then they were placed in some refugee center that arranged for them to get a kettle of soup. The woman was surrounded by four children, each one smaller than the next. She paid the most attention to the fifth, the youngest, who was not even a year old. The little tot perched on her arm and she held it close to her heart, speaking in a tone that was a mixture of joy and sadness: "Look at this little guy! Some little refugee, some little wanderer, expelled from home . . . look at this little guy!" She embraced the child with a squeal and a laugh, uncovered her breast, and stuck the nipple in his mouth. "He could care less about what's going on! He has his meal!" This devoted mother was sure that she wouldn't have to worry about him. Her breasts were full.

They didn't come to us again but sometime later I saw the woman on Leszno followed by her entire flock. Someone, it seems, had given her a baby carriage. In addition to the baby she put two other children in the carriage, their feet hanging down from the sides. Two others walked along as if providing an escort. She looked confident as she pushed the wagon across the street, holding a basket with something she wanted to sell as well as coins that people tossed in. Despite the crowds and the many beggars that thronged the street, the sight of this caravan evoked the pity of passersby. People cleared a path for her and looked out for her. Her thick curly hair, her arms with their rolled-up sleeves stood out among the crowd of sallow and scrawny beggars. A blaze of hope and a wave of optimism seemed to be present in her expression and in her energetic gait. She was sure that she was in the right and would prevail in the end.

I never saw her again, those Jews she came with, or her five children. I can only imagine what they looked like months later. Thank God I did not have to see it.

I remember the Kobriner family, three sisters, who managed to rescue a fine aluminum pot from what had once been a home and a life. In the early days one of the sisters would come to get soup for all three. Maybe the others were working somewhere. I didn't really know the family at first. About half a year later a woman approached me. She had a chit and was carrying the pot. "My sister is sick," she told me. That happened before they organized the ghetto. Our kitchen was serving about five hundred to six hundred soups a day. The woman who doled out the soup—Miss Halina—knew all the customers. She served them with a smile and a warm word. She knew about their lives and their troubles. She asked the "new" sister how the older one was doing. So it was: one sister took the other's place. A while later Halina informed me that the third sister was standing in the soup line. So now the second sister no longer had the strength to come. Only the pot remained as before, well cleaned and glistening brightly. That pot told volumes about a way of life, about a tidy home, about the dignified decline of yet one more Jewish family.

10. People and Pots

I am writing this chapter in January 1972. About thirty-one years have passed since I woke up early one morning, lit a lamp, and after lowering the blackout shades over the one window in the tiny room at Leszno 66 where I lived began to write about our kitchen. Now I'm no more than a pale shadow of that young woman who outlined and partially completed a "Study of a Public Kitchen." I had promised to write it for the secret ghetto archive as part of the "Two Years in the Ghetto" competition.[1]

That second anniversary of the ghetto happened to be November 15, 1942. But in the meantime the Great Deportation began, and on the sixth day of the roundups, on July 27, I handed over my outlines and finished texts. I got those same writings back in September 1946 when the first part of the Ringelblum archive was dug up. To be more precise, the originals remained in the Jewish Historical Institute in Warsaw. When I immigrated to Israel in 1950 I took along a written copy of that manuscript. It is only now that the time has come to publish it.

It was easy to edit and prepare those sections of the essay that had already been completed in the ghetto. But I cannot promise the reader the same degree of accuracy in those sections that existed only in rough outline (section headings, themes, the names of people) despite weeks of hard work going through those pages of faded onion paper.

Yet human memory is remarkably resilient. The human brain is the most perfect computer that God Himself devised. If one is ready to invest enough energy and determination then it is possible over the course of many years to retrieve from its hidden recesses all the microscopic traces of ideas and emotions that were once inscribed there. What one has seen, experienced, and suffered in the past reemerges to be seen and felt again. That's just what one would expect from the "computer" that processed, reorganized, and reformulated those psychic traces left from the ghetto.

What I have just said applies to the chapters that describe the inner workings of the soup kitchen and my co-workers. Day in and day out we witnessed and endured calamities and tragedies, and experienced the pain and toil of that time.

>——<

The very first person who became a permanent member of my staff at Leszno 40 was an older lady named Halina Gelblum. She was a real *Warszawianka*—Warsaw born and bred. She went to school in tsarist times, completed some kind of business course, and had some old-fashioned office experience. In the early days of the occupation, before she came to us, she was involved with selling hats. She knew which private apartments contained essential items that we needed. So she was able to provide us with a real "office," setting up my desk with a whole set of writing materials as well as an abacus with red and black buttons. As a native of Galicia I was not used to having such a contraption on my desk. I never used it once. But no matter how many times I took it away and placed it in some corner I would always find it back on the table the next morning.

The instructors of the kitchen department were happy to see such an "authority" in our kitchen; they had much more in common with her than with me. In addition to the director's office, located in a smallish room, we established a locked storeroom for food products, supervised at first by Halina. The department sent us a bulk scale and a table scale. Halina brought her brother Abram to the kitchen and told him what to do. He got hold of some old boards, which he used to build shelves along the office walls. In one corner Halina cobbled together a kind of closet, covered with an improvised curtain. There, hanging on coat hooks, were white aprons and work outfits for the cooks and other members of our steadily expanding staff. She went out and bought all the little things that we needed, such as washing towels and wire bands for coat hangers. She managed to obtain for herself and for me a pair of aprons with blue stripes and pockets. I came to like that work outfit so much that I would wear it for days on end. For almost three years the uniform that Halina gave me enveloped my entire life. My private identity, outside the kitchen, faded into the background. Halina also had her little private space inside the big kitchen hall, consisting of a smallish cabinet on the wall near the window whose drawers contained thread, needles, and thimbles. The job of a hostess, established in all the public kitchens, fitted her perfectly. When the kitchen served soup, she stood there in her striped apron with a white starched doily on her head. It suited her ash blonde, neatly combed hairdo.

Starting with absolutely nothing, she established a kitchen that was well organized, well staffed, and fitted out with all the necessary accessories. Her brother helped a lot. Abram was a little deaf and taciturn. He spoke Polish to her, softly and quietly, in a low-pitched hum. I don't really know which of them was older. But it was clear that Abram loved his sister and did whatever she desired. Now and then he would kiss her hand, just as if she were his mother.

I never found out what happened to Abram. I heard nothing about his fate. I probably did not ask. But in those days he was an important part of our little world. As in all tragedies there was no lack of minor characters, whose roles all ended in the same sad finale.

All of these recollections stored in my memory are coming back to me. From the ruins and debris of those years the one thing I held on to was a long blue silk scarf with a red and white stripe down its length. I wore it around my neck when I left the ghetto and I was still wearing it when, disguised as a Polish woman, I was driven out of the burning city during the Warsaw uprising of August 1944. If Jewish law allows it I would want that scarf to be buried with me in my coffin. Halina gave it to me on her first day in the kitchen. It was left over from the clothing she had bought and sold before she started working there.

Halina had a wide face. It was soft and bright with limpid, light-blue eyes. There was a sad undertone in her Warsaw accent. She brought a spirit of homey familiarity and intimacy into a world that had become mean and alien. She was unpretentious, without guile, unflappable, and blessed with real empathy for human suffering. It was largely because of her that I, along with my co-workers in the kitchen, found the inner strength to bear the unrelenting burden of a difficult job and a desperate struggle against a frightful reality: on the one hand no end of human tragedies and suffering, and on the other hand our inadequate ability to really help those unfortunate people.

And now . . . Gutsche. There was probably another cook in the kitchen before she arrived, but if so, I remember neither a name nor a face. Not only that: I can't remember the name of the last professional cook that they sent us just before the deportation. But Gutsche was a personality, an individual who stood out. I remember Gutsche very well.

Before the war she ran a small restaurant in Praga.[2] She earned a reputation for Jewish delicacies: gefilte fish, cholent, and piquant jellied dishes set in deep pans.

Gutsche was a talented cook who had verve and a sense of tradition. She loved to cook for people who would truly savor her dishes, and she herself loved to eat. One of our clients was a Jew who had been driven out of Praga. He used to tell us about her prowess. First of all, he said, before the war she was twice as broad as now. That was hard for us to believe because large folds of flabby skin hung down from her double chin, from her chest, and especially from her stomach. Before the war she must have weighed 90 or 100 kilos. She was short, but her round, smallish legs moved quickly and deftly around the big pots resting on the four burners of the large kitchen stove. She carefully tended the flames and saw to it that the chimneys were properly cleaned. She had her own tricks to bring the pots to a boil.

She used to come in very early. The burners were already heating the first pots of water. The food products had been peeled and prepared the day before.

A respected member of the retail merchants association, Nokhem N., a refugee from Nowy Dwor, lived with his family in one of the three small rooms in the corridor that connected the back part of the premises with the front. The room was on the first floor and the large kitchen space had its own anteroom, which you entered through a door going off the stairs of the annex.

Nokhem's main job was to get up very early and start the fire. After the kitchen expanded in 1941, we installed a large new soup kettle encased in ceramic tiles. Nokhem attended a special course organized by the kitchen directorate to learn how to heat the pots with a minimum of coal.[3]

As I have mentioned, I lived at Leszno 66, a distance of twelve buildings from the kitchen. Every now and then, when I would get to Leszno 40 before the others, I would enter the kitchen and eavesdrop on Gutsche as she spoke to the pots. She shouted at them or pleaded with them in a gentle tone of voice to boil faster. Her favorite was the newest pot, a vessel that held 100 liters. Covered with a handsome lid made of thick sheet metal, that pot was always scrubbed to a shine. When it came to softening the hard barley stock that was the basic ingredient of all our dishes, it outdid all the other pots. So that's where Gutsche would pour in the whole bucket of rinsed groats. After that she would distribute equal measures of the cut and rinsed vegetables into the other pots, add the boiled and swollen groats from the first one, and then cook the whole concoction.

A few hours later it was time to test the taste and readiness of the soup. That was quite a show, attracting spectators and imitators, both from among the kitchen staff and the clients. But when the first act of the show began, I was the lone spectator. Gutsche fussed with that favorite pot of hers, the newest one. She pinned her hopes on its powers and even gave it a name, "Maciusz." She stroked it, praised it, gave it a few knocks and said, "*Nu*, start cooking, come to a boil, you rascal!" Finally, when the sounds of simmering and boiling came from under the lid, her face became happy. Then she would wipe the sweat from her forehead, put a cup of ersatz coffee on the burner, and start singing. I remember the words of her song:

> *Once there lived a girl*
> *She had nothing*
> *She lived in a field*

After we acquired the tile-encased urn our work routine changed. From then on the other pots lost some of their importance. That urn was five times the size of "Maciusz." You couldn't see its surface because it was encased in ceramic tiles. In order to clean it a girl had to take off her shoes and crawl inside. That giant of a pot had the power to cook enough stock for two thousand soups. After heating the burner beneath it we would put out the flame, screw the top on tight, and let the hot coals do the rest. In two hours, all the groats, vegetables, beans, or potatoes were soft and ready, and the vegetables did not get overcooked. The groats produced a kind of paste that sealed the softer ingredients so they did not break apart. One of our janitors would take a pail attached to a long pole, climb up on a bench, and ladle the thick concoction into the other pots. We added hot water, oil, and chopped onions. Gutsche took a taste, smacked her lips, and the soup was ready.

We then used Gutsche's urn to bring the soup into the big hall. We would scour it clean, make it shiny, and fill more than half of it with hot soup. Two employees would carry it carefully into the hall, place it on a low table on the platform, and ladle the soup into dishes which the "waitresses" brought to the tables.

In any event, "Maciusz" was relegated to that platform with the fresh soup. The food was hotter, and probably tastier, than before. Gutsche certainly understood that, but she still disliked the new way of doing things. Soon after the encased urn appeared I happened to be alone with her early in the morning. She patted "Maciusz" on its side and stared at me morosely. "*Nebekh*, this pot has been dishonored," she said to me, and tears of sadness and pity glistened in her dark eyes. It was as if to say: "Before, he was the most important pot, and now look what's become of him . . ."

>—◂

Gutsche had her little tricks. When she wanted to see if the food was ready she did not use a spoon; instead she raised the lid, and when the soup simmered and the bits of carrots and parsley danced in the boiling water, she would snatch a bit of carrot with her fingers and rub it in her hands to see if it was ready. She never scalded herself but it got on our nerves, both because she risked her finger and because she put her paws in the food.

Cleanliness was not one of her priorities. We would argue with her about the white aprons that we would dress her in each morning. At first she didn't want to wear the apron at all. She tied some rag around her belly and didn't mind walking around covered in soot and stains. Only after she got used to the job did she agree to get rid of the rag and put on a clean and pressed apron. She did this only because we reminded her that an inspector from the kitchen directorate, or even the director himself, might make a surprise visit and she would embarrass the entire kitchen. In the end the white apron didn't help much because within half an hour it was stained and smeared.

But Gutsche knew how to pay attention to her head covering. She tied the kerchief in her own style so that it looked like a pointed bonnet, which set off her features nicely and gave her face and dark eyes a look of intelligence and dignity.

>——<

Gutsche knew all the secrets of cooking, how to coax flavor from a dish even without the necessary ingredients. She could prepare a two-liter pot of "chicken soup" from the smallish wing and neck of a hen. When she made that soup she used a bit of salt and a pinch of sugar, a little juice from a marinated onion, and she did not scrimp on vegetables. Her "unkosher" secret was to flavor a meat soup with a bit of butter the size of a pea. But although she knew that secret, she did not use it. She was careful to observe the dietary laws because she had a husband at home, a Talmud scholar. She called him "my *Kiddush makher*" whenever she spoke about him in the kitchen.[4]

We had a delicate problem. In a hungry ghetto that contained hundreds of thousands of starving people, we had a storehouse that contained food products and vats full of soup. We had to feed our eighteen employees, and everyone had a mother, father, brother, sister, or close friends at home. We couldn't expect the people who ladled out the food to go hungry themselves. But one of the hardest and most painful tasks of a director was to prevent the theft of the products that provided soup for hungry clients, many of whom ate nothing more than that one daily bowl.

Of course, our employees could eat as much soup as they wanted. They had to buy bread, which each of them stored in a special bag hung from a peg on the wall. But I knew that this did not solve the problem, and if I refused to cut them any slack the kitchen would not be able to function. I thought about it for a long time before I hit on a solution. When we weighed the products we also had to include the weight of the sacks and pots that held the food. Since we weighed large quantities, those "extras" might total two or three kilos a day in potatoes, barley stock, vegetables, flour, and a little oil.[5] Gutsche took advantage of this to bake and cook dishes that were filling and tasty. She made an ample meal for herself once a day and took the rest home for her family.

I told the entire truth to the instructors who came to the kitchen two or three times a week. They were very familiar with this problem. They accepted my "solution" and even recommended it to other kitchen directors.

I was not able to totally eliminate the temptation to do a little pilfering. Once I noticed that two girls who worked in the kitchen would cook a daily pot of potatoes together. None of us could afford the luxury of being able to eat half a pound of "dry" potatoes with onions every day. After we observed this for a couple of days, Halina and I discovered their secret. Each day a man holding a can would meet the girls at a side door and get a few helpings of soup.[6] We sent the man away, reprimanded the girls, and hushed up the whole matter. Did this kind of pilfering continue, but hidden better? I can't say for sure that it stopped.

At home Gutsche had to feed her elderly and respected husband. I think that he was a lonely widower who had been a steady customer in her restaurant for many years before the war. Though long retired, he had been a teacher in a Jewish religious school that also taught secular subjects. Now he sat at home all day and "studied holy books," as Gutsche put it, thereby giving him a certain mark of dignity. Gutsche herself had been a childless widow. Before the Praga Jews were forced into the ghetto she agreed to the match and stood under the wedding canopy. Both parties were satisfied. The elderly man knew that if he had to rely on his own resources he would go under very quickly. He never came even once to our kitchen.

Then something happened that causes me shame even now. After the affair with the girls, who complained that "they weren't the only ones," I took a peek once into Gutsche's basket. I searched and I found. Aside from the cooked food from our "employees table" and a jar of soup, I also found a little bag of beans and soup vegetables. Perhaps she intended to stop in a street market on the way home and buy a few kosher chicken scraps—a couple of feet, a gullet, a tiny wing—and cook a broth for her husband. I didn't take the bag with the vegetables away from her. I probably warned her not to do it again.

I don't remember what she said. But whatever I said or didn't say to her, I now feel a lot of remorse.

Why did I shame and sadden her? Why couldn't I understand that by means of this little trespass she wanted to gladden and strengthen her old, helpless husband, who was now her vulnerable child. How blind we were then, how stupid—as we stood on the brink of death.

11. INSTRUCTORS

There were three of them: three middle-aged women. I would like to dedicate a few words to their memory.

The leader of the instructors was Gina Birkenheim, a university-trained specialist in nutritional science. She had studied at an American university and worked for a time in the Land of Israel, where she supervised kitchens on the kibbutzim.

I don't remember the family name of the second instructor, Pani Eva. She was an elegant, sportily dressed lady. Before the war she was employed in the administration of a Warsaw state hospital.

The third was Mrs. Lola Berkenheim-Szereszewska, a former opera singer who, I think, had no prewar experience with the challenges of feeding large numbers of people.

The Department of Kitchen Instructors was established before the ghetto. Although it was constantly criticized, and sometimes even harassed by the directors, it played a major role in ensuring the proper functioning of the public kitchens. The operations of the kitchens, which at one time fed up to 100,000 people a day, were always expanding and improving. Thanks to these tireless and dedicated instructors, who worked without letup, most of the meals that the kitchens served reached a tolerable standard of cleanliness, orderliness, and above all nutritional value, despite all of the obstacles and difficulties.

One or two of the instructors would visit each kitchen at least a couple of times a week. Nothing escaped their attention. They helped organize the work, assigned tasks to the staff according to their abilities, and had them change jobs so they would be able to teach each other new skills. They showed us how to stand when we did different jobs, so we would not tire as quickly.

The key point was the constant struggle to ensure the nutritional value and taste of our product—that bowl of soup. They wrestled with the problem of how to extract the maximum number of calories from the substandard allocations that we got from the German authorities. And thanks to the dangerous large-scale smuggling, as well as trade with the Poles, we were also able to buy better food on the illegal "free" market.

>———<

In both the central administration and in the individual kitchens the instructors had to work with staff who lacked any prewar experience feeding large numbers of people. To get things done and to cope with the challenges of the job they needed a lot of tact and patience as well as an ability to persevere in the face of constant abuse. In all these respects Gina Birkenheim was exceptional. She was inspired with the spirit of her pioneering past, with the sense of a mission that had to be accomplished despite all difficulties. Her unassuming affect and her idealism also inspired her two co-workers.

I admit that I caused her difficulties more than once. But over time she won me over. She was the first person from the Jewish settlement in Israel that I got to know well.

>———<

Planning a meal for thousands of people was no simple matter. A major problem was how to soften the very hard barley or oat pellets so that they would infuse the rest of the ingredients and provide optimal nutrition. Our starting point was to calculate one portion and then estimate how much to put in the vat to ensure proper caloric content. The instructors introduced a point system. Each soup had to have ten to fifteen points, one point being ten grams of beans, grits, or flour or fifty grams of greens or potatoes. Mrs. Birkenheim also believed that satisfying the "craving for taste" made people healthier and helped them feel satisfied with their meal. She worked with the cooks so that they could make the food as tasty as possible. She advised us not to spare any money to buy pepper and spices.

>———<

Here is the little I know about the fate of the three instructors.

All three were taken away in August 1942. They were deported to-gether with the officials of the kitchen administration who would all report to work, probably because they saw the office as a safer place to be. They relied on the green identity cards of the Aleynhilf, which even the Jewish police had stopped honoring by the second half of August. The first rumors about Treblinka had already reached the ghetto. But Gina Birkenheim reassured everybody. She declared that it was simply unbelievable that they would just murder people for no reason. Resettlement meant resettlement. That's what she said even on her way to the Umschlagplatz.[1]

When Mrs. Berkenheim-Szereszewska arrived at the Umschlag-platz, she bribed her way out with a diamond brooch, something she used to wear when she sang opera. After the *aktion* ended, she slipped out to the Aryan side of Warsaw with her daughter. That daughter was killed during the Polish uprising in 1944. I met Mrs. Berken-heim-Szereszewska after the war in a Jewish institution, where I heard her describe the march to the Umschlagplatz.

After the war I learned something about Gina Birkenheim from Ringelblum's notes written on the Aryan side. He wrote that there were people who tried to free her. But she refused, not wanting to be freed without her coworkers from the kitchen directorate.[2]

12. THE KITCHEN STAFF

Once about 400,000 Jews had been imprisoned by the Germans behind the walls of the Warsaw Ghetto, their economic situation worsened dramatically. Jewish organizations pushed back, doing everything that was possible, and even impossible, to save lives. The volume of relief work doubled and tripled, with organizations that distributed food playing an especially important role in the desperate struggle against hunger. They redoubled their efforts to deal with hunger, homelessness, and epidemics while trying harder than ever not to collapse in the face of administrative and economic persecution. German action or inaction all had the same aim: to destroy the Jewish population by increasing the death rate.

Our kitchen also doubled and even tripled the number of daily meals handed out. The staff grew. Today I often only remember their first names and faces. Once again, I can see their images, the people who were swept away. I'll describe them according to their jobs.

Mrs. Nelken was a middle-class woman from the Posen region and the wife of a landowner. She did not know a word of Yiddish. Until I met her I did not imagine that this type of Jewish landowner or well-to-do leaseholder existed outside of Galicia.

Before I met Mrs. Nelken I had become friends with a family that had a similar background: the Beldigers from the Rypin district. I got to know the patriarch of the family, Abraham Beldiger—nicknamed "The Count"—two weeks after the Germans entered Warsaw. He would come to visit a Polish tenant in the six-room apartment at Przejazd 1 where I lived. That tenant also owned an estate in the Rypin region. During the short time that he lived in that apartment, where many people from the same milieu would come to see him, I got a chance to observe the reaction of Polish society to the September catastrophe.

The landlady of the apartment, Mrs. Kaczańska, did not return from her summer vacation. So Janka the maid, along with her boyfriend, took over the job of renting out rooms. Janka soon became a turncoat, a newly minted "Volksdeutsche." (That's a long story I won't get into now.) It was clear that I could no longer stay there, so I moved to the apartment of my cousin Dr. Reuven Feldshuh at Leszno 66. But I still kept in touch with The Count. He was about 60 years old and was living with a friend from his younger days, a fellow townsman from Cholewa, at Leszno 52. This was just a few gates down from the kitchen at Leszno 40. I soon got to know Beldiger's children, three sons named Jurek, Dawid, and Jakub, and the youngest, a daughter named Ista (Esther). Their mother had died before the war.

Thanks to their Polish friend Kalasiński, the Beldigers, now refugees, were able to get funds from the property they left in Rypin. Now and then Kalasiński would bring food for the Beldigers and some other Jewish families. Later on, in a transaction based on trust, he bought a portion of the Beldiger's land for a sizable sum, which sustained the family in Warsaw. Jurek, the oldest son, also engaged in trade.[1]

Three people from that family joined the staff of our kitchen. The father and daughter helped serve meals as volunteers. Jakub had a regular position in the storeroom, where he was always punctual and meticulous. He was a somewhat reticent but wonderful young man, a Jewish version of a *panicz*.[2]

In the early days of the kitchen I took on a couple of young girls to help out, and over time additional girls joined the staff. In the mornings and after meals they peeled potatoes, cleaned up, scraped vegetables, swept the floor, and washed dishes. At lunch time they put on white aprons, triangular white kerchiefs, and served bowls of soup to the clients sitting at the tables.

There were Dora, Stella, and Dina—the daughter of a deceased Jewish actor whose name I have forgotten. There was a fourth member of that group, Khava (Ewcia). She was young, pretty, and limped a bit. In addition to these four young girls there was Genye, who was a bit older than them, funny and smart. She helped with the cooking and could replace the head cook in a pinch. Then there was Henye, the youngest of them all. She had flaxen hair and looked like a little shiksa. Henye would take on the toughest jobs. She could scrub the floor and hoist large sacks on her shoulders. Henye, who also came from Rypin, was quite a character. She liked to "pilfer." When I would send her to the main warehouse with one of our caretakers, she would always come back with something extra for the kitchen and didn't mind bragging about it. Henye was a born master at bamboozling the manager of the warehouse as the food was weighed; when his back was turned, she would add potatoes or something else.

The Beldigers knew Henye from back home in Rypin, where they had their farm. Mr. Beldiger would commandeer her to carry heavy loads. For her it was fun. Now and then two sisters and their mother would visit Henye in the kitchen. A couple of times I caught her giving them a pot of cooked food as well as raw vegetables. But I didn't want to fire her because she was an efficient and fast worker, as well as a likable and happy soul. Along with her usual jokes and pranks, Henye was capable of pulling some real surprises—like the time when she came to the kitchen very early in the morning and cleaned the whole main hall with the six long tables. Or the time when she graced my office with a vase containing a blossoming sprig she had broken off from some tree.

Henye was only 16 years old. I can see her now. I miss her. I thought about her one night when she was no longer among the living, when I was on the Aryan side writing my lament for those Jewish girls who evoked that Slavic earth where we Jews lived and worked for hundreds of years: fields of wheat rustling in the wind, thick rye bread, coarse flax shirts draped around the body of the Jewish people. She could have easily saved herself by going to a village and passing as a peasant girl. But they grabbed her at the very start.

At the beginning of 1942 I found myself caught up in a plan devised by advisers from the central office to transform our place into a model convalescent kitchen.[3] Since we had attractive rooms and a reputation for personal honesty, the directors chose our kitchen for major renovations and improvements. There were also some changes in the staff. They transferred the cook Gutche, Mrs. Nelken, and Henye to a reorganized kitchen on Nowolipie. All three were angry with me for having agreed to let them go. Now I realize they were right.

We got a new cook and a new supervisor. I don't remember if we got a replacement for Henye. The Great Deportation was still half a year away. I never saw those three again. After the Great Deportation began none of them came to us to seek protection or to find out what was going on with us. I found out something about Henye from a Jewish policeman who would visit our kitchen. Twice he managed to extract her from a column marching to the Umschlagplatz. The third time she marched there with the entire staff of her new kitchen, including the supervisor and the director, who had formerly run a free loan society. That day she made no effort to escape. She was ramrod straight and dignified, maybe even proud to be marching together with the entire group. Then again, she was still little more than a child. This happened just a couple of weeks before the mass selection, when the staff of our own kitchen marched to the assembly place in a group. They never returned.[4]

>—<

I have described the women who worked in the kitchen. But I should add one more name, Masha Liberman. Her father served on the board of the retail merchants association. She was the cashier who sold tickets for the portions of soup.

The male staff initially consisted of one, and then two, custodians. The first janitor, Pinkhes (Pinnie) Shraga, came to work in our kitchen just before the establishment of the ghetto, when the Polish janitor of the retail merchants association, Piotr Sulin, had to leave Leszno 40. Pinnie belonged to some political movement, but I don't remember which one. Nor do I remember what he did before the war. He was a healthy man in his early 40s and did not shirk hard work. But it was interesting to see, as we compared him to the former Polish janitor, that he never carried heavy loads. Instead he managed to finagle a small cart that he would use to pick up products. He was divorced, or maybe a widower, and raised a son, Davidek, by himself. Davidek would spend entire days in the kitchen and accompany his father on all of his errands.

Pinnie's job became more critical as the kitchen grew and after the installation of the large ceramic-encased pot. The job of carrying large pails of soup from kettle to kettle, suspended from a long rod, demanded physical strength and agility. One had to be careful not to get burned by the boiling soup.

I see Pinnie standing before me now; he is of average height, with steel-gray hair parted on the left side, a head of hair that would never grow bald. He spoke in a thick, low voice with a slight raspiness on the higher notes. I remember his voice, his face, the blue work frock spread over his slightly hunched back. He carried out all my orders, but we never established any friendliness or empathy between us. He did not like my attempts to single out certain eaters for special attention and help. He regarded that as unfair to everybody else and would ironically refer to them as "privileged characters." Maybe one can agree that from a purely abstract and theoretical point of view he was right. But I think the real reason for his disapproval of the privileges (if that's what you can call them) that I extended to certain people was not so much a protest against the injustice being committed against "everyone else" as it was a feeling of jealousy and unease that arose when he saw a hungry and depressed person get better—albeit for only a short time. Unfortunately, an incident would soon demonstrate how his neuroses would cause me major problems, and in very painful circumstances.

>———<

One day we learned of the sudden death of one of our eaters. He had been a champion sportsman from Karlsbad. After the Germans occupied the Sudetenland he was sent to Dachau and from there—since he was a Polish citizen—to Zbąszyn.

"You failed to keep the German alive," Ringelblum reprimanded me when I ran to him with the news that Abraham Brocksmeier, "the man from Dachau," had died. In the whole time that we knew each other, this was the only time that Ringelblum admonished me. Ringelblum had wanted me to write down detailed testimony from Brocksmeier about his experiences in a Nazi concentration camp. Of course, neither Pinnie nor the other workers at the kitchen had any idea that this was the reason why Brocksmeier got special attention from me. Most of them felt like I did—they liked Brocksmeier and wanted to help him survive. After he began to swell up, we used our own staff allotments to give him some solid food (*konstantes*, as he called it), rather than the usual all-liquid diet. It was only after Brocksmeier died that we realized how much this special attention enraged Pinnie.

Because of Ringelblum's intervention, Shakhne Zagan gave me a voucher for 50 złotys, which he had scrounged from some account, and a letter to the directors of the Gęsia cemetery instructing them to bury Brocksmeier in a separate grave.

When I got back to the kitchen, still unaware of Pinnie's special animus toward Brocksmeier, I gave him Zagan's letter and money and sent him to the cemetery to tell the staff to put a special tag on Brocksmeier's body. This would prevent the gravediggers from simply dumping him into a mass grave with no shroud and no name. The next day I planned to go to his funeral, accompanied by some members of the kitchen staff and some neighbors from the tiny corner where he lived.

At that time we still had no inkling of the mass graves that would contain hundreds of thousands—or millions—of Jews from all over Europe. I just wanted to make sure that the friends and family of that Czech-Jewish athlete would have a grave to visit. He died from hunger in the very center of Polish Jewry. It would be an outrage and a terrible shame if they would someday learn that he vanished into some mass grave without a trace, buried alongside the poorest and loneliest Jews of the Warsaw Ghetto.

When we got to the cemetery, we discovered that the body was not there and was nowhere to be found. It turned out that Pinnie did not go to the cemetery with the letter and the money, and didn't even think that he had to inform anyone about what he did. He handed over the 50 złotys to Halina. I could not forgive him for what he did, and for a long time I could not speak to him.[5]

13. THE BLUE OVERALLS

Our second caretaker, Joseph (Yosele) Erlich, was especially well liked by the whole staff and by all the eaters and visitors who came to the kitchen.

I don't remember whether he had parents, but he had close relatives in some shtetl in the Warthegau.[1] I knew this because sometime in the winter of 1941–42 he came to the kitchen with a postcard. It had been addressed to his grandparents, with whom he lived. I gave that postcard to the secret archive. There were hints in the Polish text that some of us understood all too well.[2]

BESAKONE GEDOJLE ANACHNU they wrote in big Polish letters.[3] They urged us to go to the great "doctor" and pray for medicine that would save them. That meant we should go to the cemetery, to the grave of a great Hasidic rebbe, and pray for them. The postcard began with the words "We've paid and we're waiting." Those of us who had been reading the secret press knew that the Jews in the Warthegau had to give the Judenrat a payment for their transportation to Kulmhof (Chelmno).[4] Chelmno was the last stop, where the Jews had to disrobe in the cellar of a manor house. Then the Germans forced them into a large truck, where they were told that they would undergo disinfection. But as soon as the truck began to move, a special pipe connected to the engine filled the hermetically sealed compartment with exhaust fumes that suffocated them.[5]

We already knew that in the German-occupied territories of the Soviet Union there were similar trucks without windows and that there they were called *dushegubki* (people killers). We also knew that in other occupied areas—Volhynia, Galicia, and Ukraine—there were mass shootings of Jews at the edge of large pits. We were terribly shaken but not entirely certain that this was really happening. And we began to ask: When will it be our turn?

Around the beginning of 1942 some wise guy, one of the kibitzers who would hang out in the kitchen, started to "entertain" us by asking: "So, what have you decided? Will you travel first class or second class?"

Those who didn't understand the "joke" and asked where they were going were told that traveling to the next world courtesy of bullets was "first class": death in fresh air, in the middle of a fragrant pine forest. Those in the know answered that since they were "democrats" they preferred third class: a dash from your apartment to the cellar. They recalled the advice of a "good German": *Der bester ausweis ist der keller ausweis* (the best safety pass is the cellar pass).[6] Someone on the administrative staff of the kitchen opened a registry for those who expressed a wish to be born a second time.

In early spring of 1942 the Germans changed the ghetto boundaries to exclude the Judaic Institute building on Tlomackie, which had been the headquarters of the Aleynhilf. We had to transfer the main offices of the soup kitchens to a cramped locale at Przejazd 9. For a time the kibitzers stopped hanging around. After the night of April 17–18, which was the beginning of many nocturnal Gestapo murder sprees in the ghetto, it appeared that the jokers decided to hang it up once and for all.

>—<

The caretaker Yosele Erlich was the grandson of a rabbi, but he grew up in Hashomer Hatzair.[7] He had a light brown head of hair and a young, bright, slightly childlike face with a healthy color, a sign of his earlier days in the fresh air of the provinces.

Our kitchen had a large supply of work clothes: white robes for the women, gray and blue smocks for the men. One day I came back from the central offices with a nicely sewn pair of light blue men's overalls. Halina and I immediately decided that they were perfect for Erlich. When he tried them on they fit perfectly, and the blue color matched his eyes and highlighted his boyish charm. The girls began to joke among themselves, saying that we should install a mirror so he could straighten his hair and check out how the overalls looked. Joking, of course, was reserved for early morning, before the daily crush of hungry eaters arrived. The big cauldron was already boiling, and we'd take a short break to eat. We poured the staff some thin soup, along with a slice of bread topped with grated onions and washed down with fresh porridge.

Like a young rooster showing off his colorful plume, Yosele strutted in front of the girls in his blue overalls. Khavetche, the girl with the slight limp, fancied him the most. Her girlfriends laughed and joked with him; she couldn't say a word. She sensed that something was going on between him and Dina. Looking at her you could almost hear the quiet tune she hummed and the hidden tears she wept. Erlich was also very shy. But when he wore those overalls, he became a bit bolder. Now and then he would blurt out some lame joke. Genye, the older girl, would egg him on and make fun of him. Once she pretended that she was about to give him a kiss. The group took this all in fun and laughed. The boy blushed a deep red. But he laughed along with everybody else. As time passed, he became more mature and self-confident.

Those girls of ours, and their young friend, did not go hungry. It was so wonderful to watch them as they ignored the hell around us and enjoyed their youth. They had no inkling that this would be their last spring.

>—<

Terrible events edged closer. Two weeks before the Great Deportation the "shop panic" began, as Jews frantically looked for security and safety in the German industrial enterprises in the ghetto. News of what happened during the deportations in Lublin and other places convinced people that only those who were young, healthy, and able to work had a chance. Only they might remain. People became obsessed with getting work clothes. In the days before the Great Deportation genuine and bogus workers, as well as physicians, druggists, nurses, and people who worked in laboratories, all began to walk around in work smocks, white medical coats, or nurses' uniforms, convinced that those garments served as a kind of body armor and gave them more hope of survival than a mere shop ID card.

Then came that terrible day of July 22, when the Great Deportation really began.

One stage followed another. Each day the angels of death from the German Sonderkommando[8] would descend on the ghetto, accompanied by their Ukrainian, Latvian, and Lithuanian collaborators. Each day a cohort of Jewish police stood ready to help them comb through buildings and streets, checking the documents of each Jew. During the blockades Jews stayed off the streets. Only during lulls in the manhunts, or after a particular block had been searched, did they dare appear, and then only with some document in their pockets. But in the very first days of the deportation a white smock or nurse's uniform could actually help save someone caught in a random search.

It just so happened that a week before the beginning of the Great Deportation the kitchen sent a load of work clothes to the laundry, including Erlich's blue overalls. Usually after a week or ten days we would get the laundry back, clean, ironed, and starched. But because of the shop panic and the general state of confusion in the ghetto, the shipment of laundry did not arrive. Days went by, the deportation was in full force, and there was no sign of the clothing. The laundry was located on Dzielna Street. Each day Erlich ran there to get the laundry, and each day he returned depressed. Clean or dirty, there was simply no way now that we could get the laundry back. Erlich became convinced that his fate depended entirely on that pair of blue overalls, which made him look young and healthy and which symbolized his luck and his future. When he told me once again about another failed mission to get the clothing, I noticed how nervous tension caused a tiny red speck in his eye to swell up like a little pea or a cataract. Maybe he noticed it as well. That's all he needed: to appear before a German with a visible physical defect!

Our kitchen still had some white robes and smocks. Some staff were no longer coming to work. Jakub Beldiger's work smock, neatly pressed and now ownerless, was hanging in our supply room; in the kitchen there was the new apron of the tall stout supervisor who came to work with us at Leszno 40 after we became a model convalescent kitchen. I told Erlich that he should wear one of those. But they were too big for him. And besides, I could see that he was reluctant to wear the clothing of those who had already been taken away.

The Great Deportation continued. More and more categories of employees, along with their families, lost their right to remain in Warsaw. A husband's work documents could no longer protect his elderly parents. Nor could they protect his wife if her children were under 10 and she had no work documents of her own. Even the documents issued to the most important categories of workers, who were employed in factories, shops, and sites outside the ghetto deemed essential to the war effort, could no longer shield family members from deportation.

In the middle of all this, Erlich's grandmother—a short, likable *yidene* in a *sheytl*— turned up in the soup kitchen.[9] Yosele brought her to my office, even though at that time my own situation was very tenuous. Her clear and aged countenance radiated a religious faith and trust in the Almighty that I admired. While she sat at my table, she reached into her pocket and pulled out a little carrot and a small knife. Then she peeled off little juicy slices and gently guided them into her tiny, toothless mouth.

She wouldn't go to ground in a cellar or find some other place to hide. She felt safe because she was sure that God in Heaven would show His mercy and grace. He would not abandon people like her in their old age. She also put her trust in God's messenger, Moritz Kon, who gave her husband, a rabbi, and herself two ID cards showing that they were employed in his firm. That good deed, she was sure, would redound to the credit of Moritz Kon in this world and the next.

In the end the blessings of the religious Jews did not help Moritz Kon. The day after his grandmother's visit, Erlich dashed into our kitchen looking even more agitated and depressed than before. He had just heard that Kon and Zelig Heller had been shot in the courtyard of Jewish police headquarters on Ogrodowa Street.

A few days later around dawn, Pinnie ran into the kitchen in a total panic. His ten-year-old son Davidek had been missing since the previous day. That little rascal had already snuck away twice from a column marching to the Umschlagplatz. This was a little boy who could crawl through the tiniest cracks or scale a tall building without a ladder. Now Pinnie's last hope was that maybe Davidek had found a hideout in the kitchen. But when he failed to find him there, he grabbed his head with both hands, sat quietly for a minute, and then dashed out. He didn't say a word to me or to anybody else. And that was the last time we saw him. I think that he ran to the Umschlagplatz to find his boy, or to follow him on his journey.

>—<

The kitchen now prepared meals for the Jewish workers in the Toebbens shop. The new boss discharged Halina, and my own position became very precarious. Sometime during the third week of the Great Deportation I saw Halina run into the kitchen from the front entrance. (The side entrance was blocked by a long row of people waiting for soup, real and bogus tailors who were Toebbens employees, people who were very different from our previous clientele.)

"I've just come from the Umschlagplatz," Halina stammered. She was deathly pale, disheveled, disoriented. She put her arms around me and began to softly wail. I brought her into a side room, near where the ticket window was before the start of the Great Deportation. I caught the eye of one of the girls and told her to bring some valerian drops.

Ten minutes later Halina, who was seated on a bench and leaning on a wall, dozed off. Suddenly the new boss of the kitchen, Shtivl, came in and motioned for me to follow him.

When we were in the corridor Shtivl grumbled, "What's she doing here?" His expression was dour, his voice angry. "She doesn't work here anymore. She must leave immediately!"

"Have you no shame?" I answered him. "She worked here almost three years. She just escaped from the Umschlagplatz."

"I know, I know," he mumbled, his mouth lopsided and distorted. "But if we take in everybody like her, the Germans will deport us all tomorrow."

He disappeared into the office and locked the door behind him. Nothing surprised me anymore. Just the day before he and I had a terrible quarrel. His wife and his daughter Tunie (who had been named after the same woman as Esther Beldiger) overheard us, and their faces burned with embarrassment. They had spent the entire day in deadly fear, in a small room in the kitchen. They both knew that not long before I had been the director. Until a month ago they received me with the greatest courtesy when I visited the Beldiger family. The Beldigers were relatives of theirs who shared their apartment. By now not only Jakub Beldiger and Ista, but also the younger son Dawid and his wife, had been deported. At the height of the shouting, Jurek, the oldest Beldiger son, came into the room. He tried to comfort me. "Does it really make sense for you to cry like this? What are you letting yourself get insulted for? For what? Don't you know what's going on in the ghetto? It's all one big catastrophe! Nobody can rely on any documents. That idiot will keep doing the most shameful things until his own turn comes."

Jurek spoke like a true sage. He also perished, even though the Pole Kalasiński was prepared to rescue him. But the elderly patriarch Abraham was sick and totally shattered. There was no way to take him anywhere, and Jurek would not abandon him. They would die together. Of that entire family, my close wartime friends, not one survived.

They took away Shtivl's wife and daughter a week later. He sent a Jewish policeman to the Umschlagplatz who called out their names. They were ready to let the daughter go, but Tunie would not leave without her mother. Shtivl sent another policeman to call out their names, and he returned to Leszno 40 with two women who had pretended to be Shtivl's wife and daughter. One of them had been the sister of our friend Stella, and after the first phase of the Great Deportation she worked in the kitchen as a potato peeler. Shtivl saw her every day in the kitchen, but he didn't say a word. He suffered a total emotional collapse. I have no idea how and when he disappeared. I think he died during the second *aktion*.[10] Neither he nor Stella's sister, nor Stella herself, who had managed to escape from the "cauldron" selection by herself—not one of them survived.

>——<

Just a few days after the incident with Halina, the people who took over our kitchen fired me. In the early hours of September 6, 1942, the day when the entire ghetto population was ordered to appear by 10 a.m. in a cordoned-off block of streets, I still had no idea what my relatives at Leszno 66 were planning to do. We had a tiny cellar where we could hide. The German order issued that day also suspended all existing restrictions on moving around the ghetto. Around 5 a.m. I went to Leszno 40. I wanted to say goodbye to the people I had worked with and find out what was going on with them.

Those who had evaded deportation were still in the kitchen when I arrived. They had spent the night there and had gathered their family members along with little bundles containing their few possessions. Dora was there with her mother, who had washed dishes and peeled potatoes. The Germans had announced that everyone going to the selection had to bring enough food for forty-eight hours. The Toebbens supply chief had sent over two days' worth of food the previous night. They put everything into the warehouse, and what they couldn't fit there they put in my old office. There were hundreds of loaves of bread, a barrel of marmalade, big jars of fats. Some German entrepreneur had begun to sell a kind of butter-margarine, and that too was to be given to the Toebbens employees.

The Jews who worked for Toebbens, along with everyone nearby, soon heard about the cornucopia in the kitchen. The allocation of food awakened hope. If they're giving people food, isn't that a sign that they need their work? So what does the selection really mean? Maybe they'll choose the strong and the healthy for work, those who look good. Many people stuffed their pockets and bundles with bits of sugar, drops to strengthen the heart, cologne to rub on their temples. Women and men took little tins of makeup, lipstick, pomade, and small mirrors.

A long line of people at Leszno 40 filled the courtyard and extended as far as the steps of the building's right wing. People were holding pots, soup bowls, saucepans, mess kits. When I saw that there was no way I could get through the mass of people I turned around, went up to the front entrance, and used the doorbell of the retail merchants headquarters to send a signal. Sure enough, in the office were Graf, the office manager, and Masha Liberman, our former cashier. They glanced through the peephole, removed all the screws and bars from the front door, and, worried that others would dash in behind me, quickly let me in. I went through the office, past an anteroom, and came to a corridor with small rooms that were part of the kitchen.

I saw a scene that you see only once in a lifetime. Some of the crowd downstairs entered the building and climbed the stairs. When they saw the piles of food at the end of the corridor—loaves of bread, sacks of flour, big jars of marmalade and margarine—they went completely berserk. There were three or four kitchen employees in the storage room. One of them was holding a pencil and a notebook. They were supposed to count the people, weigh the food, distribute the rations, and register it all in a proper way. But they found themselves helpless to control the situation.

Some tough characters pushed their way toward the food and

caused absolute mayhem. They jimmied open the barrels of ersatz honey, margarine, and beet marmalade. The louts shoved aside the kitchen workers, who were standing, ladles in hand, ready to dole out rations. They stuck their paws into the barrels and filled entire pails, slopping margarine on top of marmalade and then, their arms full of bread and their hands totally soiled, shoved their way back through the crowd downstairs. Then a new group came to the storeroom and did the exact same thing.

I heard a voice call out from the corridor: "People! Where's your shame? They'll photograph you behaving like a bunch of wild animals!"

"People, have mercy, let me out, I'm being crushed!" a woman cried.

"Me too, me too," some other voice bleated softly. Someone yelled out and made a scene.

"Don't be afraid of them. Take what you want! They'll be sure to fill their own knapsacks and will leave nothing for us. Push them away!"

I made my way to the tail end of the crowd where people were leaving and took a quick look around the storeroom. I saw the walls, the doors, and the faces of people all smeared in marmalade, like a coating of tar. Cooking oil was leaking from some pot on a high shelf. The faces of those doling out food seemed insane. They stood there with mouths wide open. They were saying something, but I couldn't make out their words. One of them must have been the new caretaker, a Jew from Sierpc, Shtivl's protégé who had replaced Pinnie.

The second employee standing there was Joseph Erlich. His young, clear face was unshaven, and there was a wild look in his eyes. He held a smallish shovel, which he used to stir the soup in the cauldron. He was also screaming, and I saw him wave the shovel over the heads of the crowd, yelling in an otherworldly voice: "What a ruckus! Get out! Out! Don't take anything! This is a zoo!"

The crowd stopped pushing forward for a moment.

"Aren't you all ashamed? Ashamed?" he yelled. "Show some shame for your own sakes. Have some mercy on yourselves."

The crowd made another move. Some retreated with their loaves of bread and pails of marmalade down to the exit. Others, now a bit calmer, waited their turn.

I was crushed between those coming in and those going out. I no longer wanted to go into the storeroom to see people. One of the people handing out bread recognized me, pointed me out, and passed me a loaf of bread over the waiting people's heads. I put it under my arm.

>——<

That was the last time I saw Erlich. He stood guard, trying to defend his post in the kitchen. He didn't notice me at all.

A few hours or a few days later—when we were all packed into the "cauldron" and the Toebbens workers faced the selection—I wondered if he tried to get one last look at me as they sent him and those pretty girls, his coworkers, to the Umschlagplatz, to the cattle cars, to Treblinka.

What happened to him then? Was he among those who were killed jumping from the train? Was he among those selected to work in the camp, to suffer for a few days or weeks? Or did he—this 19-year-old—simply run with all the others, young and old, along the "Himmelstrasse" to the "baths"?[11]

He was not wearing that handsome outfit of his, those blue overalls. Maybe he thought that if he had only been wearing them, he might have been able to survive.

14. They'll Take You Too

How can you figure out why one person survived and another person died when you knew both and assumed that the one who died had better connections and better chances?

As for myself, you could say that during the occupation I had more luck than brains. Or maybe it was my mother's love that protected me like a talisman, when random strokes of sheer luck repeatedly threw me a narrow footbridge over the abyss. It was a bridge that I stepped over as if I were blindfolded, unable to see a step in front of me. Without that blindfold, I would never have dared to take the steps that saved me.

You can talk about coincidences. Well, right up until I left the ghetto for good I never had to change my apartment; not when the ghetto began, nor during the Great Deportation. Both times it turned out that living on the even side of Leszno helped me continue living, and I mean that literally. Both Leszno 66, where I lived with my relatives, and the kitchen at Leszno 40 where I worked happened to be in an area that I did not have to leave during the Great Deportation. That area became an integral part of the work and residential enclave controlled by the W. C. Toebbens firm. Since I was employed in the kitchen, I did not have to change either my place of work or where I lived.

Even before the Great Deportation the Toebbens firm had established a headquarters in the school building at Leszno 74. Now it took control of the entire street between Karmelicka and Żelazna.

What a name! Walther C. Toebbens, one of the biggest vultures, who made millions from Jewish suffering and who deceived many Jews by offering false hope of survival in return for their work tools and raw materials. If that wasn't enough, they also had to pay him off with foreign currency and jewelry for the privilege of becoming one of his slaves—until they faced a selection and death, or until the agent (the very one they paid for their job) sent them away to die and sold their place in the shop to someone else.

———

One more vignette from those days:

In the very first days of the Great Deportation our kitchen, which was well equipped and well organized, had the chance to be taken over by a shop. The only problem was that I didn't have the right personal connections, I didn't know how to pull off such a "deal." It was only after the odd numbers of Leszno were removed from the ghetto that the machers—wheelers-and-dealers and tough guys—who had ignored my previous efforts to get official German recognition for our kitchen suddenly realized that it could give them cover and protection. They brutally began to throw out the people who had worked with me during the three years of the occupation and who had helped me build the kitchen.

The takeover of our kitchen was carried out with the participation of Toebbens' supply director, an assimilated Jew from the Posen region. I had some knock-down, drag-out fights with the kitchen director he appointed as I waged my losing battle to protect the jobs of the eighteen employees I had brought into the kitchen during the three years when I was the director. As for myself, each day he thought up some new way to downgrade my status. Both of them did as they pleased with the kitchen and the staff, without any trace of shame. As for those of us who actually did the work, it was as if we didn't exist.

In addition to the new boss of the kitchen, the supply director foisted on us a mother and her daughter, who was the wife of a Jewish policeman. Without her husband's knowledge she became the director's lover.

In those stifling days, those days of our great disaster, such scenes flashed by at lightning speed. The first two victims of the new order in our kitchen were two employees of the storeroom: Jakub Beldiger, our supply person, and Ista Beldiger, his sister. They were deported during the first big blockade of Leszno Street. Neither the kitchen manager who owned the apartment they lived in nor the almighty new direc-

tor—a supposed friend of the family who came from the same town—
lifted one finger to try to rescue them from the Umschlagplatz.

What is left to say? After all, this director looked on while his own
wife and two children—along with her parents—were sent "east." And
he knew better than anybody where they were going. His wife had
been angry with him because of the affair. When he finally showed
up at the Umschlagplatz, they were about to be shoved into the cattle
cars. She refused to say goodbye. But he didn't let this depress him
too much. He returned to Leszno and resumed his fantasy of power
and love as he romped with the policeman's wife.

As for myself, the director treated me to a lecture about the difference between the old kitchen that I had run—based on the principle of serving the public—and the present setup, based on "military
discipline," that had to be enforced in these new circumstances.

Another week went by, and he gave me no assignments. Instead,
he politely told me that I was "on leave." Each day he sent me a jar of
soup and some bread.

Maybe he had some inside knowledge of the mass selection that
was about to affect the Jews who remained in the Warsaw Ghetto.
He had already managed to calculate the number of "life tickets" the
kitchen would receive and had decided who would get them. None
would go to the employees. So he let me go on in order to avoid an
embarrassing scene when the Germans showed up.[1]

>——<

I survived those days of the "cauldron" hiding out with ten other people in a tiny, concealed coal cellar in the building at Leszno 66, where
my cousin Dr. Feldshuh lived. Then another miracle happened. This
bunker was not discovered by the patrols that combed through the
empty buildings after their inhabitants were marched off to the selection. This was because a fire had broken out in a nearby apartment,
and the firemen, after they put out the fire, were so preoccupied with
loading loot onto their truck from the unlocked apartments that they
didn't think of looking under the rug, and under the table and chairs,
that masked the entrance to our hideout.

We sat through it all and didn't make the slightest sound. The
firefighters finally left, and the leaders of the manhunt took no fur-

ther interest in the burned-out apartments of our wing of Leszno 66.

>—<

When the *aktion* ended and I returned to the kitchen at Leszno 40, I found an entirely new staff, headed by that mother and daughter. They now wore on their heads odd, starched white bonnets with the initials of the firm Walther C. Toebbens nicely sewn in with silk garland thread. Attached to the bonnets and hanging down over each shoulder were two long white ribbons that also contained those magic initials, additional talismans of safety to go along with the life numbers that they carried in the breast pockets of their white aprons.

One day a Jewish tailor and his assistant came to the kitchen with a handcart to pick up soup for his shop. He glanced at those people with their uniforms. What did those initials stand for? *"Wezmą Cie Też!"* ("They'll take you too!") he exclaimed behind their backs, with a look full of hatred and contempt.[2]

The director's mistress and her mother—who had harassed me at every step and tried to turn the staff against me—now left me alone. For a couple of weeks I hung around in limbo. I peeled potatoes and cut vegetables. Every few days I would stay longer to cook a meal for the potato peelers on the night shift. When the surviving communal activists learned that I was still alive they asked to see me in the new ghetto and began arranging for me to move there.[3]

Of all the people I came to know in the kitchen at Leszno 40, before and after the Great Deportation, the only person who survived apart from me was one woman whom I worked with peeling potatoes. For a while after the ghetto uprising she hid out in the charred ruins and then survived on the Aryan side. I met her once after the liberation, but I don't remember her name.

The supply director of the kitchen—the Jew from Posen—was sentenced to death before the uprising by the Jewish Fighting Organization and was executed.[4]

That other woman who survived told me that between November 1942 and April 1943, and probably during the uprising itself, that coal cellar at Leszno 66 served as a hideout for one of the combat groups. Her brother had been one of the boys in that group.

I never saw Leszno 40 again.

Part 3: The *Zamlers*[1]

15. THE DEATH OF A RIGHTEOUS MAN

I have a childhood memory of an icon that hung on the wall of a peasant hut. Painted on the icon, in descending rows, were three different worlds. The top row showed the sky, the bottom row, hell. Between the sky and hell was this world. There were two beds. In each one lay a dying person. In the left bed there was a wicked man, his body decayed, his face distorted in an expression of wild fear. Two devils glowered over him, branding irons and flaming pitchforks. In the other bed lay a gaunt righteous man. He rested peacefully, his body straight, his hands clasped on his chest. At his side there was a white angel, serene, his wings fully spread. The angel stood ready to usher his soul through the beckoning gates of paradise. "The Death of a Righteous Man": those words were inscribed over the bed.

>——<

Now a quote from something I wrote, from the second notebook of the journal I kept when I was hiding on the Aryan side.

> Shmuel Lehman was one of those lucky enough to die in his own bed. He died of cancer in the fall of 1941 and had the privilege of an almost normal funeral in the Gęsia cemetery.
>
> Only in his very last years did he get to enjoy the respect and recognition that eluded him his entire life. Thanks to Emanuel Ringelblum, Yitshak Giterman, and Shiye Broyde, all of them higher-ups in the Aleynhilf, he

did not suffer from hunger and want in the ghetto. When he got sick toward the end of 1940, they sent a secretary to help him. The secretary helped him decipher his old handwritten notes, cataloged and sorted his materials, and typed his writings, which included material he had gathered since the outbreak of the war.

After the First World War Lehman had published a study, edited by Noah Prylucki, of Jewish wartime folklore. And now, as soon as the present war began, Lehman set out to write down the new words, the puns and expressions, that showed how Jews reacted to Hitler's triumphs and to the persecutions, humiliations, and assaults that beset them after the Germans marched into Poland.

The occupation also raised a new issue that interested Lehman: how Poles reacted to what was happening to the Jews. In those last months before he became sick, Lehman began to supplement and update the materials on Polish-Jewish relations that he had been gathering for many years.[2]

Lehman's wife had always shown a lot of understanding for the constant travels demanded by his research, which produced very little income. And when he got sick she stood by him as a loyal partner, helping him endure with dignity the physical pain and mental agonies of an incurable disease.

She survived her husband by only one year. They took her away near the start of the Great Deportation, in the first week of August 1942. Lehman's only son managed to hang on a little longer. Once I saw him marching with a group of workers along Leszno street. That was the last time I saw him.

I believe and I hope that Lehman's work, that enormous treasure, has been successfully hidden. Maybe it's in a safe place.[3]

>—<

According to Zalmen Reyzen's *Leksikon* of Yiddish literature, Shmuel Lehman was born in Warsaw in 1886 and began to *zaml* in tsarist days.

Until the outbreak of the First World War Lehman collected folklore material mainly in the Jewish communities of central Poland. When Galicia became part of the Polish Republic he began to cross the former Austrian-Russian border and was flabbergasted by the differences in folk culture and social custom that had arisen between the Jews of Russian Poland and Austrian Galicia during the 150 years that they had been separated. There were different religious customs and different forms of apostasy. The learned Jews were different and so were the untutored common people. Hasidim and rebbes seemed to be everywhere. But there were also large numbers of young people with university degrees and doctorates.

I got to know Lehman in Lemberg in the late 1920s, when he was collecting material on Galicia. Melech Ravitch urged him to meet me, and he came to see me in the editorial offices of the *Nayer morgn*.[4] Before I knew what was happening he turned me into a source for the folklore of Podolian Jews. Later on, when I moved to Warsaw, he continued to bring me questionnaires to fill out and dragged out of me enormous amounts of information about everyday life and language, proverbs and jokes, even how Podolian Jews ate and baked. Podolian Jews had more contact with the Jews of Russian Podolia, Ukraine, Bukovina, and Bessarabia than they did with the Jews of central and western Galicia.

What Lehman loved most were my stories about how shtetl and village Jews mocked each other, about the pranks and practical jokes they enjoyed at each other's expense, and about how shtetl quarrels played out in the villages. "Passover yeast" was how Lehman and I referred to these stories.[5]

As a student and disciple of Noah Prylucki, Lehman was especially interested in the macaronic Ukrainian-Jewish songs that Jews in our region would sing at festive occasions and holiday meals. Prylucki believed that a "prehistoric" Ukrainian Yiddish had developed in the lands that would later become the southwest territories of the Russian Empire, and that its influence could still be seen in the many Ukrainian words that Jews used in their everyday speech.

The kinds of songs that interested Lehman also existed in certain parts of central Poland, but the Galician-Ukrainian versions were funnier and more emotional.

There's a song, half in Yiddish, half in Ukrainian, where a Jew reprimands the patriarchs and the angels in heaven. Why are they just hanging about in the Garden of Eden and doing nothing to speed the coming of the Messiah? Why can't they convince God to redeem the Jewish people from exile and return them to the Land of Israel, rebuild the Temple, and renew its daily service? When one sings these verses one after the other it quickly becomes clear why the redemption does not come: every single one of the patriarchs and angels is burdened with a defect:

> *O our beloved little Isaac, O our dear father,*
> *You are blind, yes father you are*
> *O our beloved little Jacob, O our dear father*
> *You are lame, yes father you are*

Even Moses is flawed.

> *O our beloved little Moses, Moses our dear father,*
> *You stutter, dear father, yes you do*
> *Why don't you go up,*
> *Why don't you plead for us,*
> *Before God,*
> *Before God?*

And so on and so on, one "cripple" after another is asked to plead before God:

> *So you may redeem us*
> *So you may forgive us*
> *And rebuild the Temple*
> *So the priests can offer their sacrifices*
> *And the Levites sing their song*
> *In our land*
> *In our own land*

I also recalled the ditties that Berl and Shmulik, the sons of the village butcher, sang in my grandfather's prayer house in Lanowitz at the end of the Simchas Torah holiday. They regaled all the Jews of the village: men, women, and children.

There's one particular Ukrainian Jewish folk ballad that Lehman somehow got me to dredge up from the deepest recesses of my childhood memories. Maybe this lurid ballad, violent and tragicomic, was connected to an incident that really happened. It was about a romance between Khantsye, the daughter of a Jewish shopkeeper, and Vasyl, the son of a gentile widower. Khantsye orders the young gentile to come to her house on the Holy Sabbath, "when mother and father will be in the synagogue." They load the Jewish "gold and silver" on a wagon, along with heavy quilts, and ride away. They come to "the shore of the deep river." And then the young gentile groom tells his Jewish bride:

> *Khantsye, you did not want to eat kugel,*
> *So now, Khantsye, you must drown yourself in the river.*

In 1941, just before the German hordes arrived in our region, peasants from the village of Niezhvisk, not far from Horodenko, tied together about ten Jewish families with barbed wire, pushed them onto a raft along the deep waters of the Dniester, and cast them into the torrent. These criminals were never tried or punished, not then, and not after the Soviets returned.

However, this particular Jewish Ukrainian ballad from Habsburg days does not have a pro-Ukrainian "happy ending." In the last verse the emperor's gendarmes arrive and Khantsye's Vasyl is hanged on a tall gallows.

> *You wanted to sleep on a Jewish feather bed,*
> *And now Vasyltchko, you must pay with your head*

Lehman liked this song so much that he could sing almost all of it by heart. When I came to Warsaw once he wouldn't let up until I agreed to sing the ballad before a group of writers and kibitzers at the Jewish writers union, and everybody picked up the refrain in no time.

I felt at home with this group because the guardian angel of all the literary Galicians, Melech Ravitch, was the head of the writers union. If I'm not mistaken, Dov Ber Malkin was also part of the group that hummed along.

>———<

A few years later—when I was already living with Itsik Manger in Warsaw—Lehman encouraged me to transplant another Ukrainian song.

> *A fowler is sailing down the big river*
> *A fowler is sailing down the big river*
> *And I don't know why I'm so sad.*

It had the same refrain repeated over and over again, each time with more pathos and more yearning. This was a cerebral song whose words and melody resembled the Jewish song *"Di alte kashe"* ("The Old Question").

Manger liked this song a lot and mentioned it in one of his later writings. As people picked it up they added different Jewish "wrinkles." Somehow this song became associated with a popular hit written by Victor Henkin, based on Ukrainian motifs and melodies but with added Jewish words.[6] Henkin described a peasant who was a philosopher and a ne'er do well. Each time he complained about his bad luck he ended with the words:

> *I drink by myself, I do everything by myself,*
> *I go to bed all by myself, I fall asleep all by myself*

In Yiddish, the word that means "alone" in Ukrainian (*sam*) means "poison." Moyshe Nadir once opened a number in New York with the same pun: "I am so sad. So I go to Maurice Shwartz. All alone!" Or—"Poison!"

Embittered Yiddish writers in Warsaw—those connected with the writers union or the journal *Literarishe bleter*—often repeated this ironic pun that connected loneliness and poison.[7] They did it as they vented their anger at editors who, they were convinced, could help them if they only wanted to. It didn't really matter whether their rage at the editors was justified. Neuroses. Complexes. These were the hallmarks of the Warsaw Yiddish literary milieu.

At least then it was still there, those people and organizations that we mocked and criticized. Today we can only mourn them and honor their memory.

>——<

After I moved to Warsaw I would often run into Lehman in the writers union. He was very popular with the writers. In the late afternoons a small crowd would gather around him to hear the stories he loved to tell about various characters of the Jewish underworld.

Lehman's understanding derived from a basic psychological premise. What mattered to him most were not the moral defects of Jewish criminals or the harm they caused others. Instead, he preferred to regard them as individuals who had lost their way, tragic examples of souls cast adrift. He also believed them to be more sincere and honest than many "normal" and "decent" people, who were just pious hypocrites lucky enough to be spared the blows that life had inflicted on the criminals.

It's possible that Lehman was influenced by Maxim Gorky's stories and by the great interest shown then in the psychological and sociological aspects of crime.

Yiddish literature and the Yiddish theater were fascinated with themes and characters from the underworld. Sholem Asch's *Motke the Thief* was a big hit, as were several of Froym Kaganovsky's stories about the Warsaw Jewish underworld. In the 1930s Lehman himself became an important source for those seeking to portray the "cheerful thief with a heart of gold," like the characters sketched by Broderzon and Gebirtig and staged by the cabaret theaters Azazel and Ararat.

Shmuel Lehman knew as much about the lives and doings of the heroes of the Warsaw Jewish underworld as any chief of police. He knew their conflicts, their jokes, their stories, and their songs. The only part of his folklore collection that ever appeared in book form was his *Ganovim lider* (*Songs of Thieves*).

Lehman's studies highlighted the specific Jewish background of their customs and habits. He described the principles and rules by which they created their own "jurisprudence." They lived as an organized caste with their own synagogue, court, and religious functionaries to preside over funerals and prayers. They even had their own free-loan society. The Warsaw Jewish underworld! It was truly a world unto itself.

Shmuel Lehman was proud of "his" crooks, of their juicy Yiddish, of their resourcefulness, their rhymes and their songs.

Even today I remember one of his hits—the lament of a Jewish prostitute:

> *I went to Buenos Aires*
> *To have a better life*
> *And I met a shegetz*
> *A petty little thief*

> *I went to Buenos Aires*
> *And then to Brazil*
> *So my boyfriend, the shegetz*
> *Could drive in flashy cars*

And the refrain:

> *O woe is me,*
> *The whole night*
> *I toss and turn*

One of the jokers who used to come to the writers union once decided that he would tease Lehman a bit about his fascination with this subject and interjected a barb that was not so subtle: "Why is that — — crying so much? Give her a sleeping pill and she'll conk right out."

Everybody laughed, including Lehman, but you could see that he was also a little insulted.

>——<

I mentioned Manger in this chapter, and I want to say something about his relationship with Shmuel Lehman. Manger, himself a passionate devotee of Jewish folklore and folk songs, regarded Lehman as a fellow sufferer, a genuine member of the circle of the maligned and insulted: that is, another devoted defender of Yiddish culture.

And there was nothing Manger liked better than insulting people who had wronged a fellow member of the club. That was Manger in his natural element.

I remember one banquet in Lehman's honor at Gertner's restaurant at Leszno 2. The evening was Manger's idea. The purpose was to console and encourage Lehman, while highlighting that he was a persecuted victim of the indifferent and callous powers-that-be in the Yiddish cultural establishment.

Part of this feeling was connected with Lehman's sense of resentment toward the YIVO, feelings understandable from a psychological perspective but probably unjustified. The founders of the YIVO made it clear to Lehman that they respected and admired him as a pioneer in gathering Jewish ethnography and folklore. They certainly involved him in the work of various commissions they set up. But still, the YIVO had intruded on Lehman's domain. It was not easy to soothe his ruffled feathers and make him feel that he was being included.

As the YIVO mobilized an ever-expanding network of *zamlers* and correspondents throughout the large and small Jewish communities of Poland and the entire Diaspora, and as it crafted guidelines to direct and train them, Lehman, perhaps unwillingly, began to feel that he was being pushed from his perch.

He asked, "Why do you need wisdom when stupidity works just fine?" Who, besides him, could really do this work? In his heart he probably understood that broadening the collection of Jewish folklore and bringing it up to date was a good thing. But people are who they are, and one was well advised not to broach this subject with him. For Lehman to use any of the YIVO's questionnaires was absolutely out of the question. In his heart he felt angry and insulted.

The banquet must have happened in 1935, just before the world conference of the YIVO was to take place. At that conference Lehman was scheduled to give a talk. After all, his friend and guide, Noah Prylucki, sat on the YIVO board.

But now, at the banquet at Gertner's, Lehman arrived in a bad mood, like a member of the family bearing a grudge. The group pushed together some tables, produced some bottles of liquor, a few dishes of chopped herring, a pile of bread on a plate—and the banquet was ready to start.

The painter Yankl Adler, who had recently fled Nazi Germany, loved such events.[8] He and Manger were at the head of the table, with Lehman between them. Seated around the table were other admirers and friends, including Mateusz Mieses. Mieses was a scholar and historian of the Yiddish language and the genealogy of Jewish family names in Poland. More and more of Manger and Lehman's buddies kept arriving, and they had to drag in one extra table after another. Everybody made a toast and had a bite to eat. Then Manger got up to speak. In the beginning he stumbled a little—as often happened with him—but then he hit his stride. In words at once intense and inspired he spoke about Lehman as the "uncrowned prince of Jewish folk-wisdom"; about the mission that he had for so long carried on his own shoulders; the treasure that his materials represented, a treasure that would inspire Jewish writers and artists for generations to come.

"Nobody can hold a candle to him," Manger declared. "Certainly, none of those university educated characters. He is in fact the great sage of our forsaken Yiddish culture."

Having now climbed to the Olympian heights of poetic lyricism, Manger suddenly realized that it was time to come back to earth. He bent down, all aglow with liquor and friendly feelings, grasped Lehman's head in both hands, and planted a big kiss on his forehead.

Everybody applauded, everybody drank some more, a few more people spoke. The mood became ever more lighthearted and playful. Lehman began to cheer up. He ate and drank and a smile began to form around his lips.

Then they asked him to say something. He got up, began to murmur some thanks for the big bash arranged in his honor, and then trailed off. Perhaps he simply had too much to say. A vodka tear glistened in his eye. Then he suddenly ended his speech and sat down.

For about a minute an awkward silence filled the room. I don't remember who the clever character was who jumped in to rescue the banquet. He banged on the table three times with the palm of his hand and told Lehman: "A song!"

Lehman let out a breath, swayed back and forth on his chair, and began to pound the table to the beat of a new number from his repertory:

Harshl was the sharpest guy on the block
Then Yoyne Buzik came along and nabbed his broad

So what now, Harshl, what's up?

Whattaya gonna do
With those fat paws of yours?
They're gone now,
Along with your dough
No more shakedowns
On Swietojerska Street

Lehman's sad expression vanished. A joyous, impish light lit up his face. He stuck out his finger and pointed to his chest. It seemed like he wouldn't mind if people compared him to Harshl, the de-throned has-been of the underworld.

An ecstasy gripped the room. It was as if a taut violin string had suddenly snapped. The whole group began to sing along and clap, a look of spellbound concentration on their faces. A few minutes later some other patrons of the restaurant peeked into the banquet room and joined in the clapping and singing.

Around 10 p.m. each evening Gertner's restaurant would turn into a dance hall. The musicians had already arrived. In the blink of an eye, the band began to accompany the primitive melody resounding from the literary table, a melody that could well have been lifted some years before from an old Warsaw hit tune.

Long after Lehman and his fellow banqueteers had gone home the dancing crowd and Polish girls jumped around to the tune of "Harshl the Tough Guy."

When Lehman showed up at Tlomackie 13 the next day, everybody greeted him with that song. For a long time, everywhere you went you could hear young and old warbling:

Harshl vi gaysti
Harshl vi shtaysti
Harshl vi hosti dayne grobe hent

I think after that evening the YIVO thing stopped bothering Lehman. Maybe he realized that the network of folklore *zamlers*, far from being in competition, actually represented the triumph of the cause to which he had given the best years of his life.

And a triumph it certainly was. That effort to collect Jewish folk-lore, based on the help of volunteer *zamlers*, sparked a major upsurge of cultural activity and remained a major achievement of those who fought to promote Yiddish culture—a new dawn on the very eve of destruction.

Lehman's methodology developed in the course of the pioneering work that he carried through with so much devotion. The method he applied to get people to retrieve the passive knowledge lodged somewhere deep in their memories was especially effective. How did he do it? Instead of starting off with a question, he often got his informant's attention by telling them words people in a certain region used to describe a skinflint, a hag, or a wastrel. These expressions caught on precisely because they were funny and creative. As Lehman's informants heard them, they began to recall similar terms from their pasts, terms that had been long buried in their subconscious minds, stored in that marvelous computer, the human brain. Lehman never lived to see the computer. But he constantly explored the unique wonder of human memory.

It was Lehmans's mnemotechnical methods to stimulate repressed memory that I recalled and applied when I formulated directives for how staff members at Yad Vashem should take down testimony from Holocaust survivors.

Lehman called his informants his "victims." When he was working he liked to enjoy himself, regale his companions, and hear some good stories in turn. He believed that humor played a key role in encouraging effective communication, and this helped him a great deal in his work. Of course, humor is only one part of a person's emotional makeup. In our conversations with survivor-witnesses of the Holocaust we also understand the impact of traumatic memories. Sometimes, all of a sudden, there's a moment when a spark of shared feeling or interest brings two people together. And that's when the memories of events suffered long ago spring to the surface. Happy memories and sad ones both.

Lehman discovered the secret of how to do this thanks to inspired intuition and the lessons of long experience.

>——<

After Lehman managed to wheedle out of me all kinds of yarns and expressions about "hicks," "blockheads," and "dumbbells," he shifted gears and probed for expressions to make fun of "better class" people or religious Jews. Could I tell him stories about "learned simpletons" or "scholarly ne'er do wells"? What did I remember about the ordinary conversation of common people?

When Lehman first asked me these questions I was flustered. "How they mocked people? Is that what you're after?"

"Strife and peace, each has its place," he answered. And I suddenly understood what he meant. A Jew might admire his leaders and mentors. Yet a tiny bit of jealousy gnaws at his heart and he dreams of just a little bit of payback. In the lofty matters of the spirit he knows that he can't compare himself to the rabbi or rebbe. But that's all the more reason why he needs to show his own talents and his common sense in the here and now.

"Rabbis, scholars," I tried to object, "that all has to do with men." But he continued to tell his story of a rabbi who lost his yarmulke in the town bath and almost drowned when he tried to retrieve it. And I suddenly remembered a whole collection of similar stories.

In Galicia we used to have a one-syllable epithet that we always added to the word *melamed*.[9] We couldn't say it in front of a Polish Jew, who would have considered it very vulgar. Also, the synonym for a "pathetic woman" was a "melamed's wife." That memory led me to tell Lehman about the term we used for somebody who had a stupid expression on his face. This originated in the shtetl Suchastov near Tarnopol. Jews used to call it Sechlestov. They added the "l" to make it easier to pronounce. After all, why contort your tongue just to call a no-account shtetl by its proper name?

And so, whenever somebody did something really stupid or embarrassing, we used to say: "He looks just like the rabbi of Sechlestov when the bottom fell out of his bathtub."

Younger people will certainly not understand what I'm talking about. After all, such short and wide wooden tubs held together with iron hoops don't exist nowadays. And just as it often happened with milk buckets, basins, and deep bowls, those tubs would dry out, separate from their iron hoops, and scatter all the nails. Then they'd have to be refastened. Often the bath attendant might not be able to find a loose screw. Then we'd say "he's missing a screw" or something like that.

The gentiles also used that expression to describe a certain kind of person. Go figure whether they got that from the Jews or vice versa.

Anyway, to come back to Sechlestov for a minute. As a matter of course the rabbi was assumed to be impractical and absent-minded. But to the great merriment of shtetl society it went without saying that the rebbetzin was no better. She had to be a do-nothing, a forgetful nobody who couldn't even remember to fill her pails with water. So wherever there was a room that was particularly filthy, with everything piled up topsy-turvy, we would say the "housekeeper kept house the way the rebbetzin made her bed."

>——<

After the war began and the Germans occupied Warsaw, I did not run into Lehman for a long time. We started seeing each other again after I met him once in the offices of the Aleynhilf. Lehman, like other friends and acquaintances from Tlomackie 13, would come now and then to see me at the soup kitchen at Leszno 40. I learned that he was keeping himself busy. Ringelblum got him a job in one of the refugee centers. And he began to record the remarkable phenomena that he observed as a collector of folklore.

After the first mass exodus from Warsaw, caused by the bizarre command of Colonel Umiastowski the night of September 6–7, a second wave of refugees headed east, hoping to cross the Soviet-German demarcation line that ran along the Bug River. This second mass flight consisted entirely of Jews, and it continued until the end of that first wartime winter. During the first week of the war the street vendors in the Jewish section hawked "gas masks," a ridiculous contraption of cardboard and gauze that looked like some toy. Now they pushed home-produced rucksacks for the trip "over there."

These two mass departures gave rise to one of the first wartime jokes. People who met after a long absence asked whether so-and-so had gone east "as a Jew" or "as a man."[10]

Crossing the German-Soviet border was far from easy. It did not take long for many left-wing young men and women to receive their first nasty shock from the Soviets. Most of the Soviet border guards showed no more sympathy for young Jews than the former Polish police or even the German border guards. Many of those who left returned to Warsaw with hands and feet frozen after waiting in vain for permission to cross to the Soviet side.[11]

Many weeks or months later, refugees who had been on the Soviet side and returned told stories about what they had gone through. Refugee jokes became quite a fad. Young and old sang the song "Bialystok" in Yiddish and Polish, set to a popular Jewish tango melody. Later the beggars in the ghetto added it to their repertory of street songs.

Lehman diligently transcribed all these jokes, songs, and beggar tunes. But he was more interested in a different kind of folklore that emerged in those days: how people coped with inescapable danger. Trapped in an atmosphere of trauma and confusion, they sought to assuage their terror and despair with fantasy.

Dreams of redemption and salvation flourished in that defeated, shattered, humiliated city, where rubble still lay in the streets. It didn't take much effort to notice bizarre psychological phenomena. Even people blessed with a logical mind and a gift for critical analysis would read newspaper communiques and deduce just the opposite of what had been printed. They would listen with the utmost attention to the most stupid and primitive drivel and then pass along the nonsense with their own embellishments.

>——<

One example of this mood was the clairvoyants.

The story would begin in a queue and the chance meeting of two people as they waited for bread, water, or soup in a public kitchen. Character number one would be a specific person, with a name and address. Or perhaps he might be a friend of the person who told the story. The second person was usually more mysterious. He might be a refugee from Zbąszyn, or some important person who could not risk the danger of revealing who he really was.

Yes, a genuine prophet should be incognito . . .

The first person is terribly agitated because she has no news about a son or husband who had been mobilized and disappeared. To make a long story short, the second person takes the hand of the unfortunate father or mother, inspects the fate lines on their palm, and intones in a low voice that they should not worry. In three days, news will arrive from far away.

And guess what? A few days later there's news from the Red Cross. The missing loved one is a prisoner of war. And soon the son or the husband comes home. But this story is just a come-on to prove the powers of the person who told it.

Once the "clairvoyant" had proven his bona fides, his authority expanded to explain political events. One example: a neutral nation offered to mediate peace talks with Hitler. Or America proposed an international commission to visit Poland and negotiate the removal of occupying forces. One story people really latched on to predicted a great spring offensive by the western Allies. It would be launched with help from America. (There was yet another version that had America joining the war in January 1940!)

If all these pipe dreams were not enough, "well-informed" circles suddenly buzzed with a report that dwarfed all previous fantasies. Hitler was dead, assassinated in the famous Munich beer hall. His henchmen were just using every possible trick to hide the truth until they figured out how to stay in power.

This good news was based on an alleged unsuccessful attempt on the Führer, which had been staged for internal political reasons in November 1939.[12] Neither Hitler nor his closest associates suffered any injury. But the political experts in Warsaw didn't pay the slightest attention. For weeks the "secret" spread through the city that the plot had succeeded. What was the proof? There were no pictures of Hitler in the newspaper and no speeches on the radio. If some naïve fool remarked that he saw Hitler's picture and heard him on the radio while doing forced labor in some German apartment, he was quickly put right. He had been taken in. What he heard on the radio was an old recording of Hitler's voice. What he saw was simply a collage of previously published photos.

Lehman recorded such examples of wishful thinking and added his own comments. Lehman was an autodidact. He could read the academic literature in only two or three languages. But what he lacked in erudition he made up for with a colossal degree of intuition, observation, curiosity, daring, passion, and above all the experience that he had gained through hard work.

He independently attained a deep understanding of the psychological mechanisms that emerged as individuals reworked and refashioned, in accordance with their needs and desires, their understanding of the environment and events surrounding them. This was especially true in a time when people were essentially powerless.

Those dreams and fantasies multiplied like algae on the surface of a swamp. They had a certain grotesque charm. Lehman ran around like a man possessed. He resembled some medical professor who observed, classified, investigated, and tracked the course of a progressive disease. That's how he was. He wanted to get it all down and understand what it meant.

He wrote down the jokes, derisive songs, songs of comfort, fabricated news reports, stories, legends, and prophecies.

The Jewish masses, Lehman believed, used them all as psychological defense mechanisms to fight off despair and depression.

There was one basic reason Jews told anecdotes, why they passed along mysterious information based on "well-informed sources," why they related imaginary political or military news. The stories made them feel better. They instilled hope, allayed fears, and gave Jews the strength to persevere and not break down under the atrocities and persecutions of violent German thugs who had total freedom to torture and humiliate them, to steal their property and kill them. It was from Lehman that I learned to recognize the different varieties of psychological self-defense that enabled such a large number Jews to maintain their emotional equilibrium in the face of so much fear, anxiety, worry, and torment. This struggle waged for deliverance could not have been emulated by gentiles, who had not suffered the centuries of persecution that the Jews had endured. Had the gentiles been in the Jews' place, they would have gone to pieces.

"Why haven't the Jews gone mad?" an SS man shouted during one of the *aktions* in the Warsaw Ghetto. Menakhem Linder, our demographer, did a statistical study in the first year of the war showing that the suicide rate had fallen markedly in comparison with the prewar period. This happened because in an extraordinary time Jews mobilized inner reserves of strength and psychological resistance that in normal periods remain repressed.

>——<

Months passed. At the end of the winter of 1940 we heard the terrible news that the Germans had established a closed ghetto in Lodz. A new wave of refugees from Lodz arrived in Warsaw. For a lot of money they could get out of Lodz and the surrounding area, which had been annexed to the Reich. Using what they had managed to salvage from their former savings, they settled into rented rooms. But half a year later they too found themselves inside the closed-in "Jewish residential area."

Shmuel Lehman wrote down more stories in his notebooks: hostile jokes and anecdotes about "Lodz fat cats," "hustlers who land the best jobs," "apartment grabbers," and any other possible evil that you can imagine.[13]

>—<

Finally, during that first year of the occupation, spring arrived, that long-awaited spring we hoped would bring about a radical change in the military situation. But we all know what happened that May and June. And once again the Warsaw Jewish "military specialists" hunkered down and exclaimed: no and no! They weren't changing their minds. No, they wouldn't read the falsified, out-of-date German military communiques. They refused to listen to the howling of the German loudspeakers in the public squares of the city. Their struggle with the German victory and the French defeat lasted longer than the fight put up by the French army itself.

One year later, on the first anniversary of the French capitulation, when Germany attacked the Soviet Union, nobody seemed to have learned the lesson of the year before. The Warsaw Jews could hardly contain themselves and anxiously expected news that finally "the wheel would turn."

Everybody suddenly became historians. They analyzed the reasons for Napoleon's defeat in 1812—the enormous distances, the frosts, the snowdrifts. And, wait a moment, what about the million Germans who had voted for the Communists in the last Weimar elections? Surely they would do something? Once again, they mocked and ridiculed the German communiques that described the retreat and disarray of the Soviet army. The few air raid sirens sounded to us like the trumpet of the Messiah. When the bubble burst and we came back to reality, it was under much worse circumstances than the year before. The outbreak of the Soviet-German war removed the last barriers to the "Final Solution of the Jewish Problem."

By that time Shmuel Lehman was no longer around.

>———<

Just before the spring of 1941 Lehman disappeared somewhere. Several weeks later I learned that he was sick—terribly, incurably ill. I had been intending to pay him a visit. Before I could, Lehman's wife appeared at Leszno 40 and said that he wanted to see me.

They lived two minutes away from our kitchen, on Orla, near the corner of the odd side of Leszno. A few days later, in the afternoon, I went straight from work to see them.

Lehman was lying in bed, almost sitting actually, propped up high on heavy old-fashioned pillows. Besides his wife, his sister-in-law was also there in that tidy, comfortable room. A young man, a YIVO graduate student I believe, was sitting by a table at the window arranging Lehman's collections.

That must have been in March. There was snow on the ground, and it got very cold that evening. But the room was warm. Lehman was very happy to see me, and he told me that he invited me because he had a surprise. As soon as I sat down, he offered to give me a "Galician treat."

I didn't know what he meant. As soon as I saw him I felt terrible. It seemed that his face, thin and emaciated to begin with, had shrunk to half its size. But I soon found myself laughing nonetheless. The "treat" that he had prepared for me turned out to be my own "dumplings," as it were. The young man approached and presented me with a stack of index cards. Each one contained my name and a different Galician saying about dumplings that I had told to Lehman. Each saying, each word, was like a different part of the recipe for a dish that Podolian Jews regarded as both ordinary and special, usually prepared to mark the new month. In winter they would cook meat dumplings mixed with chicken cracklings and stuffed with potatoes, buckwheat, or sauerkraut. Most of the time, though, people ate dairy dumplings filled with potatoes and thin porridge, fried in butter and onions. In summertime Jews prepared them with sour cherries, sweet cherries, and blackberries. Jews ate them in the middle of Hanukkah, or on weekdays to honor a guest, or simply to mark some family occasion.

"He cried and cooked his dumplings." That's what they used to say about a Jew who was always complaining about life yet always seemed to have enough to spend on his own pleasure.

"He's putting all the cheese into one dumpling." That's what they used to say about somebody who didn't know how to allocate his resources properly, such as a parent who gave one child a bigger dowry than the other.

"He's swelling up like a dumpling in the pot." That expression would be used to describe someone who exhibited his joy in an exaggerated or stupid fashion.

"When a poor man cooks dumplings the smell always brings a guest." There are different ways to interpret this. One is that a poor man never has any luck.

I think there were many more dumpling sayings on those index cards, but I can't remember them now. Lehman's idea to invite me over and show me how valuable I had been as an informant was an example of his sincere and modest sense of humor. It was also the gesture of a friend who knew that I would be happy to see the results of his labors.

I was deeply moved by this turn of fate. For the first (and maybe the only) time in his life, he got to feel like a respectable scholar who finally got the chance to work through and interpret all the material he had collected. It was too bad this only happened in such bleak times and after his personal situation had become so hopeless.

I guessed that Lehman must have taken some kind of pill before I arrived to ward off pain. He began to talk about what he hoped to publish, thematic guidelines for the different volumes, and how they would be edited. Of course, that would all have to wait until after the war.

He never let on that he might never live to see those books in print. But I was convinced that he knew exactly how sick he was and how it would end. Suddenly I felt that I shouldn't overstay my visit. Without much ado I said goodbye, promised to drop in again soon, and left.

I never saw him again.

>——<

A few weeks later—a short time before Lehman died—a birthday celebration was held in his honor in the large hall of the former Judaic Institute at Tlomackie 5. According to the *Leksikon* of Yiddish literature, this would have marked his fifty-fifth birthday and the thirtieth year of his work as a folklorist. But what mattered was not the pretext for the celebration, which was organized by the Yiddish Culture Organization (IKOR).[14] They wanted to lift his spirits and show him respect. Perhaps it would give him some comfort in the last days of his life.

A big crowd came. The organizing committee and the speakers sat on the rostrum. But the honoree was not there. As was customary on such occasions the committee sent Lehman good wishes and hopes for a speedy recovery, just as if it had been normal times.

In the second volume of Emanuel Ringelblum's published works[15] there is a section entitled "Shmuel Lehman: The Man and the Institution." Ringelblum describes that evening and lists the speakers and their themes.

A striking omission was that Ringelblum forgot to mention the main speaker of the evening, his own teacher and mentor, Dr. Ignacy Schiper, who treated us all to a fine academic discussion of folklore and ethnography.

I was there that evening. I heard the talks. And my mind went back to that remarkable prewar birthday celebration in Gertner's restaurant. But now Lehman was not there. His wife sat in the first row and did her best to hide the silent weeping that we could see on her face.

>—◄

I described how it all ended at the very beginning of this chapter. Lehman died on October 23, 1941, and enjoyed the privilege of a dignified funeral. Emanuel Ringelblum gave a moving and heartfelt eulogy. He was buried in the literary section of the cemetery, near the grave of I. M. Vaysenberg.

There was one thing that puzzled me and caused me bitter disappointment. I wrote in 1943 that Lehman's materials were safe and secure. I was referring then to the underground caches of the Ringelblum archive, where Lehman had been an important collaborator and organizer. But Lehman's materials were missing both from the ten tin boxes dug up in September 1946 and the two milk cans discovered in 1950. I assumed that they must have been in containers buried under Nowolipki 68, which had not been discovered.

But in 1961 the second volume of Ringelblum's notes, made while he was hiding on the Aryan side, were published in Warsaw. At the end of the essay on Lehman he wrote, "We were not able to rescue Lehman's materials. They were destroyed."

This will remain an eternal, insoluble riddle. How could this have happened?

It simply defied belief that Lehman, an organizer of the secret archive, who had devoted the last reserves of his strength to work with a trained expert to properly organize his scholarly legacy, should have neglected to tell his wife and son to hand over his materials to Dr. Ringelblum.

And it's hard to imagine that Ringelblum, who took such interest in Lehman's work and who supported it financially, would have forgotten about it.

Hersh Wasser, the former secretary of the archive, confirmed my hunch. More than once Ringelblum asked the widow and son to give him Lehman's collections. But they did not do this. He couldn't tell them about the secret archive that concealed and protected documents. So he failed to get Lehman's materials. And this wasn't the only time when Jewish cultural treasures were lost because of such blunders by heirs.

That's why I tried so hard in this chapter to describe, on the basis of my personal experience, the enormous dedication behind Lehman's determination to learn and describe ethnographic and folkloristic information about an individual, a region, and his own era.

In 1926 Zalmen Reyzen wrote that "Lehman visited and described fifty towns in Poland."[16] He interviewed and investigated hundreds of individuals. What wealth of information did he learn from them? And afterward, how many more places did he study with his expert and refined methodology?

We feel a deep pain and bereavement as we realize this loss to Jewish culture and scholarship.[17]

16. A Remembrance for Menakhem Kipnis

Half a year into the German occupation, after countless individual odysseys and return journeys, about 150 Jewish writers and journalists, along with their families, found themselves in Warsaw. Among them were individuals who even before the war had been some of the most helpless, destitute, and vulnerable members of the writers union.

Menakhem Kipnis, A. Gavze, and Y. Rayzfeder, leaders of the union before the war, played a key role in organizing relief and welfare for these writers.

The very first kitchen for writers was the one that I organized at Ringelblum's initiative on October 1, 1939, in the former headquarters of the retail merchants association at Leszno 40. This had also been the location of the Hazamir society.[1]

But this place, which was shared with other groups, was not well suited to serve meals and meet these writers' special needs. After a few days they moved to a small locale at Karmelicka 5. This arrangement was also short-lived, and the literary kitchen then shifted to the private apartment of Y. M. Apelbaum, a former staff member of *The Moment*, at Graniczna 13. This was near the former premises of the writers union, which had been shattered and burned during the bombardment. Sometime later the kitchen relocated to Leszno 14 and served journalists. That kitchen, after a few more changes, survived until the Great Deportation.

Meanwhile the actual literary kitchen, which served writers, finally found a stable home in the well-known address Tlomackie 13. The address was the same as the former headquarters of the writers union, but the kitchen itself was not in that renowned front-facing section. Instead it took over a couple of rooms in the right wing of the building, which had belonged to a former trading firm.

Kipnis's dedication to the kitchen, his determination to turn it into an effective provider of relief, and his personal reputation all persuaded the directors of the Joint Distribution Committee to give him ample support. These JDC leaders, notwithstanding their isolation from the wider Jewish world and the draconian restrictions imposed by the German authorities, were able to raise large sums of money by promising repayment after the war.[2] This money from the JDC made it possible for the literary kitchen to distribute packages of uncooked foodstuffs and in some cases even to give writers small amounts of cash.

Nobody could blame Kipnis for the fact that this effort couldn't even meet the minimal needs of those writers who had no job, no other means of support, and were unable to find some way of staying afloat.

There's something I want to say about what some Warsaw publicists wrote after the war. The book *Di umgekumene shrayber fun di getos un lagern un zeyere verk* (*The Lost Jewish Writers in the Ghettos and Camps and their Works*) blames the JDC and the "writers and journalists of the bourgeois press" for the death of several writers who died of hunger before the Great Deportation. This is a reckless, even malicious, accusation that certain postwar historians and publicists bandied about. These accusations were based not on fact but on tendentious ideological prejudices dating back to prewar days.[3]

In Issachar Fater's book *Yidishe muzik in poyln tsvishn beyde velt milkhomes* (*Jewish Music in Poland between the Two World Wars*) I read how Kipnis supported young Jewish musicians, helped them get settled in Warsaw, and encouraged their talent. This same determination to help colleagues became even stronger in the Warsaw Ghetto, when he made incredible efforts to support the most destitute and unfortunate Jewish writers.

People said that Kipnis died of a heart attack. Fater wrote that he was 65 when he died. In Israel today people would consider that too young an age to die. Before the war people in our circles thought that Kipnis was an old man. We used to joke in the writers union that so-and-so was pretty old because he remembered the days when Kipnis—who in later years sported a head of dyed, thick black hair—had gray hair.

>——<

I was present at Kipnis's funeral. I don't remember the exact address where it took place, but it was some courtyard on the even side
of Leszno. Pallbearers carried out the casket. That was the first and
only time I saw the notorious "editor" Abraham Gancwajch, head of
the gang of Jewish criminals and informers known as the "Thirteen."
He came with a photographer in tow. He quickly moved over to join
a group of Jewish writers, and the photographer snapped a picture.
Clearly, he very much wanted to be seen with respected figures of the
Jewish community. Perhaps he wanted to prepare an alibi that might
come in handy later. This bizarre wartime opportunist did not live to
face a court of justice.[4]

I accompanied the funeral procession until the Gęsia cemetery.
Kipnis had once been a cantor, or a singer in a synagogue choir, and
then became a regular contributor to the Yiddish press. Readers
loved the feuilletons he wrote for *Haynt*. For years he wrote reviews
about new talents, mostly vocalists, in the world of secular and religious Jewish music. Since he was also an amateur camera bug he
made sure to take their pictures. Before the war, he and his wife, Zimra Zeligfeld, would also sing folk songs together in cities and towns
all over Poland.

Kipnis deserves a lot of credit for his contribution to Jewish folk
music. He didn't only sing. He collected songs, classified them, and
published many popular Jewish folk songs with musical notes and
annotations.

Kipnis died in the early fall of 1941, when it was still allowed to organize funerals and follow the casket to the cemetery. All the surviving cantors and prayer leaders from the many Warsaw synagogues,
large and small, now officially closed, came together and organized a
spontaneous choir. David Eisenstadt, the director of the choir of the
Great Synagogue on Tlomackie, dressed in ordinary shabby clothes,
planted himself in front of the choir and led them in a searing rendi-
tion of "El Maleh Rahamim."[5]

This was an original and fitting tribute by colleagues and cantors
who would themselves soon die without funerals and without songs
of remembrance.

Unfortunately, when Kipnis died, his treasure, that archive of unpublished essays and notes on Jewish folk music that he planned to publish in future volumes, also disappeared. It had not been secured. He possessed a marvelous collection of Yiddish poems set to music, which many different composers and poets had sent to him. Unfortunately, his wife Zimra Zeligfeld didn't want to give up the collection and they were lost, together with Zeligfeld herself, during the Great Deportation in August 1942.[6]

Kipnis was a living encyclopedia of Jewish music, and so much of that knowledge, etched in his memory, went to the grave with him.

FATHER AND DAUGHTER

All those who prayed in big city synagogues in tsarist Russia or in Warsaw between the wars remember David Eisenstadt as *the* choir director. That was his profession. For devotees and cognoscenti of liturgical music he was the maestro, the fiery master of the vocal art. That's how he was remembered by professionals. But for those who were active in Warsaw proletarian circles, he was known as an educator and a devoted organizer of youth choirs.

The wider public had little idea, however, that David Eisenstadt was first and foremost a composer with a God-given talent. He used texts from Yiddish poetry for his vocal compositions. He was very interested in Yiddish lyric literature, which was how I got to know him. About a year before the war started—Manger had already left Poland—he came up to see me at Przejazd 1. He was looking for a volume of Manger's poems. We got to talking, and although he had not brought any instrument he soon started singing his extraordinarily beautiful oratorio set to the words of Maria Konopnicka's poem "When the King Went Off to War." I don't know if any Polish composers had thought about this poem, which was a perfect text to set to music. No poet in his wildest dreams could have asked for a better composer to immortalize his work than Eisenstadt.

The rich melodies, the phrasing, the subtleties of tone: that's what we remembered. We were intoxicated by the interplay of words and sound and were carried away in a flood of emotions; we encouraged Eisenstadt to continue what he had started. That night he sang me some more of his compositions. Though I was no musical expert, I can say that David Eisenstadt's song compositions were among the most meaningful and authentic works ever created in that genre. If only the world might have heard of him: a new Schubert or Schumann setting the words of poets—Yiddish poets—to music. Unlike Heine, these were not poems written in the language of the German salons but in the mother tongue of the Jewish masses.

>——<

"Do not ruin my circles!" That's what the mathematician Archimedes supposedly cried to the Roman soldier who disturbed him in his garden as he was drawing circles and triangles in the sand. But the soldier was thirsting for blood and murder. With one blow of the sword the head of that mathematical genius tumbled to the ground, the rivulets of blood creating new lines in the sand. A three-dimensional shape came to rest alongside the two-dimensional figures in the earth. According to legend the Roman general who conquered Syracuse had wanted to spare Archimedes and ordered the soldier be decapitated.

There's also a story that right after Genghis Khan conquered Beijing he wanted to save an elderly Chinese scholar and, in a gesture of great respect, asked the wise man to visit him in his tent.

Very different stories will be told about Odilo Glubocnik, the Higher SS and Police Leader of the Lublin District who supervised the mass murder of Jews in central Poland, and about Karl Brandt, sub-executioner of the Warsaw Jews.

>——<

Before the war Eisenstadt was so busy with his day-to-day conducting and public activities that he did not have time to arrange and prepare his compositions for publication. He did not believe that the amateur and proletarian choirs he directed were accomplished enough to give his works a public performance. I remember that in 1941, when artistic performances in the Warsaw Ghetto were all the rage, people failed to convince him to give a concert of his choral pieces. He demanded the maximum from himself and others. He had a dream that someday after the war, be it in Poland or elsewhere, he would put together a proper choir that would sing all his work at once.

During the first winter after the establishment of the ghetto, sometime in January or February 1941, Eisenstadt asked me to his apartment near the Tlomackie synagogue and played on the piano the music he had composed to accompany Mani Leyb's ballad "A Winter Story." The ballad was about an elderly Jew who wandered from town to town collecting charity. One night, caught in a terrible blizzard between two shtetls, he froze to death. Eisenstadt got the idea to do this a year earlier, during the first winter of the war, when he heard stories of Jews trying to escape to the Soviet zone who froze to death in the no-man's-land between the German and Soviet border guards.

Eisenstadt took that motif of the lonely person wandering in the wilderness, unable to find a way home. He used music to express the essence of that confrontation between the human soul and the elemental forces of nature. The dreamlike aesthetic revealed in Mani Leyb's ballad came alive in his music.

An amazing faithfulness to the poetic text, a slow and deliberate development of the various registers of narration, the dramatic presentation of the death motif, the themes of wandering, fear, gradual surrender, the lapse into eternal rest . . . Did Eisenstadt have any idea at the time that death in the snow was a blessing compared to the mass murder that would come a year and a half later, which would engulf him as well?

There was also the motif of mercy. As the peasants discover the body of the frozen Jew in the snow, people still blessed with the gift of life remove their caps and pay homage to the majesty of death. From a nearby village come the strains of church bells sounding the Angelus, signaling sunset and evening prayer. It was a symphony of twilight, a harmonious combination of Slavic and Jewish themes, a word concert of floating snowflakes wafting over a low-lying landscape. The cosmos was shaken by the death of one human being who was lonely, old, and poor.

This is how humanist culture honors the death of a person. Because respect for the dead also means respect for the living. Culture also means mercy. It means sensitivity to the pain of each living thing and to the fate of everyone. How important it became to uphold these fundamental humanistic principles in a world of mass murder and contempt for the dead, a world marked by the rejection and wholesale violation of human rights.

I can still hear the sound of those Slavic church bells, those same sounds that an entire generation of Jewish poets once heard—before the peasants suddenly turned around and began to rob and murder Jews on the open roads as they tried to run from their killers.

I can still see David Eisenstadt as he threw back his head and opened his lips in an expression of musical ecstasy. I can still hear how he hummed along in his deep voice as he marked the notes that he played on the piano.

Do I remember anything else? One phrase sticks in my mind. It's part of a refrain that Eisenstadt played in many variations throughout his composition:

The frost draws little flowers, the frost draws tiny garlands
Little flowers, tiny garlands,
On the windows

>——<

When I was in his apartment Eisenstadt presented yet another of his creations: his one and only daughter, the 17-year-old Marysia.

She was the apple of his eye, his pride and joy, his greatest treasure. In the community of artists he stood out as the proud father. Thanks to his teaching, his daughter inherited a musical talent that she developed in a spectacular way.

Musical talent. A beautiful voice. And such a father! Her musical training began in the cradle. Was it any surprise that she turned out the way she did?

Marysia Eisenstadt made her debut after the war began. In no time at all she became very popular. Her father came to see me again to talk about her concerts. He asked me for the text of the lullaby in Manger's *Khumesh lider:*[1] Mother Sarah sings little Isaac to sleep.

I explained to him that this was a lullaby for a boy. I proposed that he use one written for a girl—a lullaby that Manger had written at my request and that he included in "Velvl Zbarzher Writes Letters to the Beautiful Malkele." The idea of lullabies for both a boy and a girl pleased Eisenstadt, and he began to compose a new number for his daughter. In the end, nothing came of it.

Each time we met he talked about his plan to create a repertory of folk songs and lyric poetry that Marysia could perform. I somehow got hold of Bassin's anthology[2] and looked up suitable folk songs, which I then transcribed.

Eisenstadt's real plan was to turn his daughter into an opera singer. She had already begun to perform well-known arias from the classical repertory. She put so much effort and expression into her singing that when she stood onstage that oval face of hers—full featured but still somewhat childlike—broke out in little reddish-blue spots.

Now a few words about their end.

They did not have to wait long. A short time after the Germans removed the Tlomackie synagogue, the adjoining Judaic Institute, and the attached apartments from the ghetto area, Eisenstadt, his wife, and his daughter moved to a new apartment on Ogrodowa Street. Three months later the Great Deportation began. In the first half of August, in either the second or third week of the deportation, the Germans liquidated the so-called "small ghetto." With few exceptions they sent all the Jews who had not yet managed to flee, and who were still living in the odd-numbered buildings on the south side of Leszno, to the Umschlagplatz.

Marysia Eisenstadt might well have remained in the ghetto. It's quite possible that somebody gave her a work certificate that afforded her some temporary protection. Perhaps it was still early enough for young people to get a reprieve simply because they were young and able-bodied. That day the Germans were simply doing what was obvious and self-explanatory: they were sending off the elderly, all those who were "dispensable." And that meant her father! Marysia could never accept this. Did she scream? Cry? Go down on her hands and knees and beg for her parents' lives? Did she try to shield her parents with her own body, shouting that she had to stay with them? I don't know exactly what happened, but there's one thing I heard for sure: because she resisted, the Germans shot her on the spot. Thus ghetto Jews, already wounded and traumatized, had the chance to mourn her and grieve. She was so special, and they could still embrace her with love and light.

The rest of the story followed the familiar pattern. They sent her "elderly" father and mother to Treblinka. Should we be angry that nobody on that terrible day had the presence of mind to rescue Eisenstadt's musical notes and compositions? That might have given us just a little bit of comfort. The loss of those works was a terrible blow for Jewish music.

Part 4: The Record of Our Struggle and Destruction

17. THE MISSION AND FATE OF EMANUEL RINGELBLUM

Before the war the Jewish public already knew him as a historian and the author of important studies of the history of the Jews of Poland, as a leading associate of the YIVO, and as a political activist in the Labor Zionist movement.

Emanuel Ringelblum was born in 1900 in Buczacz, a town in Galician Podolia, and finished high school in the West Galician town of Sanz.[1] He earned his doctorate in 1927 from Warsaw University and worked for several years as a history teacher in the Polish Jewish gymnasia of Warsaw. In 1938 he was appointed to a major position in the central administration of the Joint Distribution Committee in Poland.

While many leaders of the Joint and other international organizations fled Poland in the face of the German invasion, Ringelblum became one of the most capable and energetic new leaders, organizing aid for the ever-growing mass of refugees, people in need, and those the Germans had expelled from western Poland. Those public figures who stayed in Warsaw did not stand idly by when the great disaster began. With extraordinary shrewdness and political finesse they were able to create an umbrella organization in Warsaw that coordinated and supervised relief activities and was largely independent of the Judenrat. After the Germans marched into Warsaw this organization, the Aleynhilf, inherited the mantle of the Jewish section of the former Polish Coordinating Committee that had been established by the Polish authorities and the Warsaw city government.[2]

The authorities were willing to legalize the "Association for Jewish Self Help" in large part because the Joint Distribution Committee, as an American organization, enjoyed a special status. That's how it became possible to establish an impressive network of soup kitchens, hospitals, first aid stations, vocational training courses, refugee shelters, and children's care centers in Warsaw as well as in several cities in the provinces. In addition to the relief work that was their official remit, these organizations gave the Jewish community effective cover to carry on many other cultural, communal, and even political activities.

In these new conditions, and working in two different spheres, Ringelblum emerged as one of the most diligent, resourceful, courageous, and inspired public figures. As the head of the public sector of the Aleynhilf, which included house committees and district committees,[3] he directed an effort to alleviate the terrible suffering of Jews who, for the time being at least, "only" had to suffer the near-fatal effects of German administrative decrees. Despite the terrible burden of that unrelenting responsibility, the 40-year-old Ringelblum also found time and strength to take an active role in the underground Yiddish Culture Organization (IKOR) as well as in many other areas before and after the establishment of the Warsaw Ghetto. Ringelblum himself began one of the most important and most clandestine cultural initiatives in the ghetto.

>—<

Times marked by extraordinary events, major psychological shocks, and social disruptions intensified certain kinds of behavior. Some people showed themselves to be cowards and petty egoists. Some succumbed to hysteria and, in some cases, descended into treachery, lasciviousness, or criminality. Then there were others who grew in moral stature and attained the highest level of initiative and devotion to the common good.

Shaken to his core by the disaster that engulfed Polish Jewry after the German invasion, Emanuel Ringelblum was transformed from a teacher, a modest scholar, and a Left Labor Zionist cultural activist into a wide-ranging public figure. His incredible energy and commitment, his powers of imagination, his intellect, his ability to love—and to hate—all helped create that great collective project now known the world over as the Ringelblum archive.

>——<

According to notes he wrote when he was in hiding for seven months on the Aryan side, Ringelblum began to keep a diary from the very first day of the war. The historian sensed that "real history" was beginning. Each evening he wrote down and recorded what he had seen that day; he used initials and abbreviations and probably intended to make more detailed notes when conditions improved. These notations, camouflaged with many condensed allusions and fictitious salutations, were the beginning of that great project of documentation that later included dozens of collaborators. For more than three years he continued to write his own notes, and therefore, despite the many people who worked with him, the most important member of the Ringelblum archive was Ringelblum himself.

Following the methodological path charted by the YIVO, Ringelblum anchored his project on a firm organizational base. According to Hersh Wasser, the secretary of the archive who survived the war, a circle of people collecting documents about the occupation existed in Warsaw as early as the winter of 1939–40. There was also an informal group that was soon transformed into an executive committee.

Besides Ringelblum it included two secretaries, Hersh Wasser and Eliyahu Gutkowski, as well as the writer Israel Lichtenstein, who worked in the children's soup kitchen located in the prewar building of the Borochov school at Nowolipki 68. He was entrusted with the safe-keeping of the collected materials. Another important associate in that early period was the folklorist Shmuel Lehman.

A larger committee was then established to provide moral and financial support. It included figures such as Yitshak Giterman, engineer Aleksander Landau, Yehoshua Rabinowicz, and above all, the most devoted and loyal supporter of the archive, Menakhem Kon. Later on the noted YIVO activist and patron of Yiddish culture Shmuel Winter also became one of the most important pillars of the archive. There were yet others who collected placards (often ripping them down from walls), announcements, and communiques; who recorded eyewitness accounts, wrote reports, and noted incidents; who conducted research, studied, investigated, and described what was happening during the occupation.

"Oyneg Shabes"[4] became the code name of this organization. Why this name?

After the ghetto was established, at the beginning of the second year of the occupation, a group of friends who were in the top circles of the Aleynhilf began to get together Friday evenings in a private apartment. They would have something to eat, spend some time together, and began to call these evenings "oyneg Shabes." Now and then Ringelblum would drop in. And he decided to use that name for his secret documentation project.

Maybe the semi-secrecy of these get-togethers inspired Ringelblum and his circle to attach the same sobriquet to the very dangerous top-secret documentation activity. Protected by this double layer of secrecy, the documentation effort, whose goals became steadily more comprehensive and ambitious, was safe from prying eyes. This was a big stroke of luck. For more than three years the enemy never heard of it and never discovered the hidden documents.

They collected everything that was connected to daily events and to the activities of both Jews and non-Jews: posters of German decrees, reports of the Jewish police, the protocols of meetings of the Judenrat, the statements of delegates from the provinces, the stories told by spokesmen of Jewish communities forcibly resettled in the Warsaw Ghetto.[5]

The archive also collected samples of things that were sold in the ghetto: tickets to ride the horse-drawn ghetto trolley; labels in Yiddish; white armbands with a blue Star of David, which all Jews in the General Government[6] had to wear; the yellow Stars of David with the inscription JUDE that all Jews in the western Polish provinces annexed to the Reich had to display on the front and back of their clothing. The Germans made sure that the Star of David was always visible, wherever you went.

The archive gathered the lyrics of songs that beggars sang in the streets; it compiled statistics; collected copies of the illegal press, private correspondence, and reports from young Jews who had run away from labor camps. It took down the eyewitness accounts of the first escapees from the death camps.

The archive collected all firsthand accounts and testimonies in real time, as events were unfolding. Today this is something researchers value very much.

In 1941 the archive organized a secret contest entitled "Two Years in the Ghetto." Ringelblum called on teachers, writers, scholars, and other professionals to choose topics and problems based on their interests. They would study them, write them up, and thereby describe what life in the ghetto was really like.

Thanks to this project the archive received important monographs and studies of refugees, hunger, epidemics, smuggling, the plight of Jewish children, the role of women in relief activities, and more.

In 1941 the archive distributed a questionnaire asking respondents to describe the overall impact of the ghetto experience. This elicited many interesting reactions from well-known Jewish personalities, including Hillel Zeitlin, Dr. Milejkowski, Aharon Einhorn, Shaul Stupnicki, and others, none of whom survived.[7] Menakhem Linder, a passionate young activist, carried out an ambitious statistical investigation of nutrition in the ghetto. Since he worked in the statistical bureau of the Aleynhilf, he used its resources for his research, although his study was not presented as an official report.

Works of fiction and poetry, chronicles, and essays flowed into the archive, as did reportage that described street scenes and vignettes of everyday life. There were sketches and songs connected with ghetto themes, plays, and early chapters of stories. Ringelblum sparked a veritable literary movement within certain circles of the Warsaw Ghetto. There were no newspapers, no publishers, no contact with a wider reading public, even though there was indeed an underground press, as well as certain literary-artistic events organized under the pretext of raising money for relief activities. But in a time of dreariness, bloodshed, and hunger, the writer suddenly realized that his talents were needed; that somebody was eager to read what he wrote; that he had the chance to analyze and describe the tragic events that tormented his soul. He saw that he could reach out to a future that he might never live to see.

A number of talented authors wrote in the Warsaw Ghetto, including Yisroel Shtern, Yekhiel Lerer, Yosef Kirman, Yitshak Katzenelson, and Shlomo Gilbert. There was ongoing contact with Yankev Prager and Kalman Lis in Otwock. At the end of 1941 the novelist Yoshue Perle returned from Lemberg.[8] There were several lesser-known writers who had been active on the local scene. Ringelblum took the initiative and reached out to most of them. Some responded and some did not.

Yehuda Feld, M. Skalov, and Yitshak Bernstein were among the most diligent collaborators of the archive. There was also Cecilia Slepak, who had translated Dubnow into Polish. The most productive collaborator of all was Peretz Opoczynski, who gave the archive a trove of notebooks, chronicles, and reportage of daily life, which today read like the fifth page of a prewar Warsaw newspaper—except that the content is a little different.[9,10]

Some individuals began to keep diaries. Ringelblum also discovered a new collaborator, extremely valuable and loyal, who came from Orthodox religious circles: Rabbi Shimon Huberband.[11]

I have mentioned many individuals from literary and journalistic circles. But there were just as many people from other milieux who, thanks to Ringelblum's determination to cast as wide a net as possible, provided many valuable contributions that helped illustrate that particular period.

The work of the archive made steady progress. Without any fanfare, simply and modestly, Ringelblum remained the dynamo that moved the project forward. He imbued many of us with a spark of the same passion that impelled him to carry on this vital and historic mission. During the day he directed the house committees—whose constant problems made it a tough job—and served as one of the many leaders of the Aleynhilf. In the evening he wrote and read what fellow members of the archive sent in. Then, when he met them, he would discuss their writings, offer some words of encouragement, and spur them on to greater efforts.

In the spring of 1942, after the Germans murdered more than fifty printers, financial supporters, contributors to, and organizers of the underground press, signaling the beginning of the nightly killings that preceded the Great Deportation, Ringelblum spread a rumor among the participants of the Oyneg Shabes that he was disbanding the archive.[12]

In fact, Ringelblum resumed the work of the archive, but this time with a smaller core of the most dedicated and trustworthy associates.

>——<

I am not trying to write a thumbnail sketch of the Oyneg Shabes archive or a biography of Emanuel Ringelblum. Interested readers should consult the rich bibliography on the subject that has appeared over the years in Yiddish, Hebrew, and a number of foreign languages. A first step should be the two-volume edition of Ringelblum's wartime writings that were published in Poland with an introduction by historian Artur Eisenbach, Ringelblum's brother-in-law.[13]

To mark the twentieth anniversary of Ringelblum's death, the three leading institutions in Israel devoted to preserving the memory of the Holocaust—Yad Vashem, Beit Katzenelson, and Moreshet—in 1964 proclaimed a "Ringelblum Year."[14]

Ringelblum's close friend historian Rafael Mahler headed a committee that issued a special proclamation and organized meetings, lectures, and various other events in Israel and in Jewish cultural centers elsewhere. It also called for the naming of streets after Ringelblum in Tel Aviv, Jerusalem, Beersheva, and other cities. A history symposium took place at Yad Vashem dedicated to his memory. Hersh Wasser, the surviving secretary of the archive, gave a detailed report about the activities of the Oyneg Shabes, while the researcher and collector of Holocaust documents, Dr. Joseph Kermish, discussed the significance of the archive's materials for the historiography of that period. The proceedings of the symposium were published, adding yet another source of information about Emanuel Ringelblum and his work.

As someone who chronicled and witnessed that period thanks to Ringelblum's initiative, I would like to convey my own recollections of him and of the events that led to my work in the archive.

18. Personal Encounters

To write memoirs—that's easy enough to say. To transmit yet one more account of those times and events, to record yet another measure of the turmoil, of the alternating moods of hope and despair, of the fight for survival, of those struggles to help people hold out and to rescue them from hunger and hopelessness . . . Then we were thirty years younger, and everything was simultaneously easier and harder. The intensity of those experiences reached a fever pitch.

My first meeting with Ringelblum, at the end of September 1939, right after Warsaw capitulated, determined my fate during the German occupation.

We were not well acquainted. We had some friends in common who worked for the JDC: Mendel Blumenthal and Nokhum Bomze. Now and then we'd run into each other at the premiere of a Yiddish play, or at some event at Tlomackie 13. So I was totally surprised when I learned, on the first day of the cease-fire, that Ringelblum was looking for me.

I have already described my meeting with him after the capitulation of Warsaw and how he recruited me for the task of organizing and directing the soup kitchen at Leszno 40. That's how it began, that heavy responsibility he entrusted me with, which kept me in its grip right until the Great Deportation. That was the chief reason why I stayed in Warsaw and did not join the stream of people fleeing to Lemberg, where my family wanted me to join them. At the same time, I found myself in an ideal place to observe all the scenes and events that were taking place and that Ringelblum later asked me to describe.

One and a half years later he summoned me again and recruited me to join his other major project. And once again I did not disappoint him. I faithfully shouldered that responsibility and have been doing it ever since.

Max Frisch, the Swiss Jewish playwright, tried to explain in his autobiography the various directions one's future might take. When a person reaches a certain crossroads in life, those "what ifs" become especially palpable. Should I regret that I did not leave Warsaw and go to Lemberg? If I had been there, I might have escaped with my family to the Soviet Union before the Germans arrived. Or maybe, even if I had stayed, I might have been able to rescue one of my loved ones. Or perhaps I would have perished together with them. Of course it's useless to keep asking how things might have turned out differently, but at the same time you can't pretend that the question doesn't matter. There is one thing I know for sure as I look back through the prism of what happened then. If it was indeed fated that of the many people who collaborated in the most important project of Ringelblum's life only two would survive—Hersh Wasser and myself—then we can say that we fulfilled the obligation that Ringelblum laid on each of us: to search for, dig up, and reveal to the world what he collected.[1]

In the fall of 1942, after the first phase of the Great Deportation was finished, Ringelblum reached out to me again. He and Shmuel Winter asked me to write up the extensive testimony I had taken down from an escapee from Treblinka and prepare an explanatory brochure. Because of the outbreak of the second *aktion*, the brochure was written but never published. It was a preliminary version of my later book on Treblinka. I wrote then, "One must not only describe Treblinka. One has to define it." That is what I did.[2]

Ringelblum also gave me his blessing when I was about to leave the ghetto for the Aryan side. He gave me something else as well: access to the telephone located in the German carpentry firm Hallmann on Nowolipki Street, where he was registered. That telephone enabled him to stay in steady contact with Dr. Adolf Berman, who had already been on the Aryan side for half a year. When he received a telephone message from me after my departure from the ghetto, he arranged my first meeting with Berman. Had it not been for that meeting, and the help and advice I received from Adolf and Basia Berman, I would have been forced to return to the ghetto and would have perished a few weeks later in the flames of the uprising.

I see him now as if he were still alive, his tall figure standing before me. I can hear his voice, his distinct accent with that slight lisp.

The different phases of those years, months, and days, of all the conversations we had, pass before me once again.

>—<

The first offices of the central administration of the soup kitchens were located at Leszno 13, the same place where the infamous "Thirteen" later established their headquarters. Before the war it housed the Association of Jewish Insurance Agents. I would go there almost every day and see Ringelblum's colleague Meir Korzen, who worked for the JDC before the war. Shortly thereafter he crossed the Bug to the Soviet zone.

I remember yet another detail from that first wartime autumn. After the bombardments of September not one whole pane of window glass was left in the city. Winter was coming. Once when I was talking with Ringelblum the subject of covering the open windows came up. "Come see me," he said. "We've already covered our windows with boards, and we have an extra one. Maybe you'll be able to use it." His apartment was at Leszno 18. When I knocked on the door late in the morning a blond boy who looked to be nine or ten years old opened it. He was the only person there and received me as if he was an adult. He had been told to give me the board. Very polite and quite friendly, he helped me carry the big board down to the street. "He's a lot like his father," I thought as I looked at him. That was Uri, Emanuel Ringelblum's only son. A few years later he and his father would both share the common fate of other Jews.

>—<

In the late spring or early summer of 1941 I visited Ringelblum's apartment on Leszno again. It had been about half a year since the ghetto was established. The whole routine of that massive, sealed ghetto was already in place: the hunger, the trading in the streets, typhus, the refugee centers, mass death. No sooner did one terrible interlude pass than another began. We were at the threshold of yet a new phase, one even more horrible than the previous one. Once again a messenger sent by Ringelblum came to see me. I was buried in work at the soup kitchen. But I took a break and went to visit him. That's when I learned about a group that collected documents and compiled accounts of what was happening. The group had been active for some time. Ringelblum invited me to join it. He told me about a contest for writers. With the straightforward, guileless candor of a person who is conscientious about everything he does, he explained the principles and ground rules of the work ahead. His attention to detail even led him to formulate rules that protected the copyrights of those who wrote essays about life in the ghetto. There would be an honorarium, he told me, a stipend to make the task a bit easier. Authors would retain the right to eventually publish what they wrote. As I was leaving, he warned me with a gesture and a smile not to talk too much. Everything had to stay very secret.

I needed to pick a topic. I kept it simple and chose to write about my kitchen: about the people, families, and entire communities who passed through there, so many of whom had already died of typhus and poverty. I also thought that it made sense to write about my co-workers, and even about the purveyors of food products, much of which we received in the adjacent market at Leszno 42 or at the back exit on Nowolipie. I wanted to write about Leyzer, a wonderful Jew, an ordinary man of the people who loved to come into the kitchen to pick up the money we owed him, and then stretch out on a long bench in the office and take a nap until the busy lunch hour was over. He refused to count the money he got for the products he delivered. "One shouldn't count money," he said. "If you count too much, you lose the blessing that comes with it." One day, after he left, we found a wad of paper money that must have fallen out of his pocket. Still, he was no slouch, and he knew what was what. He liked the work that we did, and he gave us a discount on what he sold us. He told us various stories about the market and smuggling. Then one day he came with a bag of carrots and refused to lower the price. He had to pay off his "partners," he explained. It turned out that they were the extortionists of the "Thirteen" who demanded that he pay them a share of all his proceeds.

And what about the double and triple eaters? Or that gang of hangers-on who frequented the kitchen? I suddenly felt an intense desire to describe my experiences and all those impressions that had accumulated during a stretch of time when I imagined I would never write again.

During the first winter of the occupation, memories of September were constantly in my mind. The smoke. The flames. The shriek of the Stukas that dived lower and lower, right above our heads. The loud whine of falling bombs. Relief when they hit another building and missed you. I remembered a soldier, his bloody face lacerated by the flying glass of a shattered window pane. His voice was so submissive, so meek, when he begged us for help, "just a little bit of help." Then there was a dead couple, each with a rucksack, lying facedown on the street. I remember the dead horse with his head resting on the pavement. Under each eye there was a teardrop, no longer warm, that looked just like a bean. It was as if that horse had wept for the city and for the country that collapsed. There were scenes from the day when Warsaw surrendered: how people climbed out of the cellars after about twenty-four hours of round-the-clock aerial and artillery bombardment.

September 1939 was the first mass tragedy that I witnessed and experienced. I began to write but then stopped. I couldn't write just for myself.

Ringelblum suggested that I read the works he collected from writers who remained in Warsaw, and then write a critical study of Jewish literary activity during the occupation. I found out that much of the material was already in Ringelblum's possession and a lot of it had already been typed.[3]

>——<

It's easy to get excited about an assignment. Finishing it is harder. Weeks passed, maybe even a couple of months, before I completed my first ghetto reportage on August 4, 1941. Ringelblum, of course, didn't expect that I would send him material just because we had a talk. He sent a "deputy" to see me, Eliyahu Gutkowski, one of the secretaries of the secret archive. Gutkowski, a former high school teacher and a refugee from Lodz, was a warmhearted Jew and a devoted friend. He soon began to take meals in our kitchen, so I would see him every day. And he goaded me nonstop. There would be small advances on my promised honorarium, empty notebooks that he would hand me, constant reminders. So whether I wanted to or not, whether I was able to or not, I began to give him material. He would then give me feedback from Ringelblum and his colleagues.

I wrote at night. Actually, it's more accurate to say that I wrote in the predawn hours. I couldn't write in the evenings, not after I returned from the kitchen exhausted from twelve hours of work and various painful experiences. Even now, in normal times, my best time for writing is when everybody else is still asleep and I feel more or less rested. As if any of us who lived through those days might ever again experience normal times.

When I would run into Ringelblum I would tell him, half jokingly, half seriously, that he turned me into a writer again.

And we did meet, for various reasons. When I tried to help one of our eaters, or a member of my staff, I sought out Ringelblum. When I had a conflict with the central administration of the soup kitchens—when they would try to place somebody on my staff or take someone away for reassignment without my consent—once again it was Ringelblum that I turned to.

Since in those days of hunger I had the power to give somebody an extra bowl of soup, Ringelblum often sent people to me with chits. We agreed that each day I would serve ten bowls of soup to people who were not formally entitled to them. Their password was that Wasser had sent them. (At that time, I did not know Hersh Wasser.) This was part of the compensation that people who worked for the archive received.

Time passed. War broke out between Germany and the Soviet Union, then between Germany and the United States.

In the fall of 1941 contacts were reestablished with territories that had been occupied by the Soviets. Just like two years before, Jewish refugees once again moved through the city, except this time in an opposite direction. A few Jewish writers returned from Lemberg, including Yoshue Perle and Kave-Vanvild. I saw them once in Ringelblum's office. I understood that he was trying to get them to write.[4]

Winter, 1941–42. We heard the first ominous reports of mass shootings in the eastern areas recently occupied by the Germans. News came from Lodz: "They're moving people out." Lodzers in the Warsaw Ghetto, frantic with worry, asked, "Where to?" They still didn't know about the gas vans. Rumors began to swirl about "Chelmno-Kolo," but people still had no idea what that meant. Then the terrible spring of 1942 arrived: the news of the first *aktion* in the General Government; the deportations from Lublin; the stories told by refugees who had fled this new horror. The first mass killing on the night of April 17–18, when the Germans targeted fifty-two activists connected with the underground press. The noose around Warsaw tightened.

>—<

Semi-clandestine meetings of the Yiddish Culture Organization (IKOR) had been taking place for some time. That terrible Friday evening a discussion forum was scheduled to meet in our kitchen at Leszno 40. After we served lunch we prepared the premises for the meeting. We moved the tables and placed benches in front of the podium. Ringelblum was supposed to share some thoughts on the concept of kiddush Hashem.[5]

I saw Ringelblum that Friday night and the next day as well. He was the first to arrive. We barely had time to exchange a few words when Mordecai Mazo appeared. He appeared pale and confused and whispered something to Ringelblum. Ringelblum turned deathly white.

"The meeting is off," they told me, and immediately left.

My hunch was that the same agents who compiled the lists of people to be killed (perhaps they were the Gestapo agents Kon and Heller) also warned some of them. It seems that they also tipped off Ringelblum and Mazo.

That night, between Friday and Saturday, those who either got no warning or didn't believe them were taken from their apartments. The Germans shot them in front of their buildings and left their bodies on the pavement. That night one group of killers came to our place looking for Menakhem Linder.

Groups of three or four Gestapo men carried a list of addresses. In each group there was one who carried a machine pistol. By the next day the Jews had come up with a nickname: the executioner. When they didn't find a person on their list, they murdered the people they happened to run into in the building or apartment. At Leszno 40 they woke up the Jewish janitor and followed him to the first floor of the right wing of the building, where the entrance to our kitchen was located. Nokhem Neufeld, together with his wife Khane and 9-year-old son Elik, lived on the premises of the kitchen, just past the big cooking area in the first of the small rooms off the corridor. They were refugees from Nowy Dwor. Since he had been a member of the board of the retail merchants association before the war he was allotted a living space within the kitchen area as a kitchen employee. His job was to heat the large kettle.

Nokhem was a very clever man. He wasn't very tall and had very semitic features. He immediately understood what was happening and responded quickly to their questions. Maybe it's for that reason that he escaped with his life. Inside the kitchen they demanded that he open the large, enclosed cauldron so they could see if Linder was hiding there. When they entered the large hall, all tidied up for Friday night with the tables along the walls and rows of chairs facing the podium, one German shouted: "A meeting?!" Nokhem quietly explained that the people who took soup home in pots sat on the benches and waited for the soup, which was distributed from the podium. When they asked him about Linder, he told them that he hadn't seen him but that the office where he worked was on Tlomackie Street, which was not far away. Of course, he was playing dumb. No one lived in the offices of the Aleynhilf on Tlomackie.

The German was satisfied with these answers and told Neufeld that he could go back to bed. He and the others left the building, taking the janitor to show them the way out and to lock the gate.

>———<

As soon as it became light out and it was permitted to go outside, Neufeld came to tell me about the late-night search of the kitchen, which, by some miracle, did not end as badly as elsewhere. He woke me up with a careful knock on the door and then, just as carefully and quietly, with frequent interjections of "don't be frightened," gave me all the details. They seared my soul like tiny droplets of poison, made even more painful by his description of how they finally discovered Linder. They also shot the baker Bleiman, along with his wife. Just now, on his way to see me, Neufeld had seen their bodies lying in front of the bakery where they lived at Leszno 56. He added that there were other bodies on the street; dozens of corpses were lying everywhere in the ghetto in puddles of dried blood. The Jewish police had no idea what to do with them.

Nokhem Neufeld continued his report. He was terribly shaken by the fact that "nothing had happened" to him and his family. I was the first person he spoke to about it.

He quickly realized that I was no longer listening to him. I had fainted.

He woke up the Feldshuh family. They rubbed me with wet towels and forced me to take valerian drops. To this day I can't forget the bitter smell of those dark green drops; or Nokhem Neufeld's long, pale nose that protruded from a face that looked like death itself; or my own fear reflected in the frightened expressions of my cousins.

"It's like Lublin—it's starting." That was the first reaction to what happened that night. I saw before me a harbinger of the violence that would engulf Warsaw on a much greater scale three months later.

Sometimes we suffer a terrible blow. We think that the end has come, but it hasn't. It's just a harbinger. The real danger is still far away. The blow is a warning that reaches us when we still haven't reacted to the danger by mobilizing our biological reflexes of self-preservation.

I recovered a little bit, but I stayed in bed. I felt crushed and depressed. I could not and did not want to get up.

Three months later, when the real blow fell on us with full force, and when disaster engulfed the entire ghetto and put us all in immediate danger, I did not break down.

>——<

Some hours later I joined the others in saying a final farewell to Linder. The Judenrat had already hung up "reassuring" placards in the streets. A large group of young people and workers in the social welfare organizations gathered in the courtyard of Leszno 52, where Linder had lived.

I saw Emanuel Ringelblum, Itsik Giterman, and Shakhne Zagan standing close together. I still remember the impact that encounter had on me. Of course those three were just as worried and shaken as the rest of us. Yet their dignified and determined expressions radiated a great deal of strength and calm.

I joined them and felt an inner surge of strength. I realized that I could maintain my dignity and composure in the face of danger and death.

Of those four who followed the coffin of the murdered Menakhem Linder the short distance to Zelazna Street, on the edge of the ghetto, I was the only one who survived.

We know how Itsik Giterman and Emanuel Ringelblum died. They maintained their moral stature until the end. I am certain that we can say the same for Shakhne Zagan when they sent him, his family, and a transport of other Jews on that last road to Treblinka.

>——<

Time moved forward. Despite the reassuring announcement of the Judenrat, that first large-scale nighttime murder was followed by other, smaller killings that took place both in the day and night. The excuse for that first large killing was the need to liquidate the illegal press. And there were always explanations for the later murders, which the Jews probably took more seriously than the Germans. Once they heard the "reason," the Jews "calmed down" a little.

I heard the news that our kitchen would be reorganized. This would also happen to a few other kitchens: Orla 6, where exhibits and chamber concerts used to take place; Orla 13; and the Bundist kitchen on Muranowska, run by Mlynek, a Bundist activist. It turned out that the nighttime visit and search for Linder was no coincidence.

Several times the girls who worked in the kitchen drew my attention to a character who hung around the corridor when they distributed bowls of soup for people to take home. He would wait in line but did not move forward. In his hand he held something wrapped in paper, supposedly a bowl or a jar, but never took any soup. Then I realized that he was the hired scoundrel. I felt terrible but did everything I could to make light of what was happening. Maybe, I thought, he was waiting to see someone. I did not allow any of our janitors to approach him. The character sensed that we had noticed him, and he disappeared for a few days. Then he returned, sat down in the dining hall, bought a ticket—without showing a chit—and took a bowl of soup. The girls were no longer interested in him. But I knew that he was there. I am still proud of myself for never sharing this knowledge with anyone else. I didn't want to start a panic or deprive our staff of the fragile feeling of stability that they had. A few times I spent the night with friends in the small ghetto.[6] But soon I stopped doing that; I was too tired and lazy to rush to get off the street before curfew, to sleep in strange beds.

In May one of the nocturnal killing sprees cleaned out the agents of the "Thirteen." The liquidation of that gang of agents and informants clearly frightened our "minder." We no longer saw him in the soup kitchen. And perhaps—you can never know—he was in the gang they shot that night?

>——<

The situation in the ghetto grew steadily worse. The tension grew from day to day. The terror—or the prelude to the terror—continued until the beginning of the Great Deportation on July 22.

Despite everything, Ringelblum and his group kept working.

To all appearances the archive no longer existed; Ringelblum planted a rumor that he had wound it up. But in fact the Oyneg Shabes quickly got back to work, this time with fewer people and even more secrecy. After another visit from Gutkowski, at home rather than at the kitchen, I went to Leszno to see Ringelblum again. He put a finger over his mouth in a gesture not to say anything to anyone. But he wanted me to remain in the Oyneg Shabes, which was now much smaller. I got back to work.

Night after night I wrote about what I saw and heard during that dreadful time just before the Great Deportation. It was the prelude to disaster, weeks of fear, daily violence, and ominous rumors. On the other side of the wall the Poles spoke about "the forty days of the ghetto."[7] It was the eve of destruction.

On those hot and humid summer evenings just before curfew, when I left Leszno 40 to go back to Leszno 66, I would often see Dr. Ringelblum hurrying down that big street through the crowds of beggars and street peddlers. Sometimes he walked at a brisk pace with his party comrade and close friend Dr. Adolf Berman, who lived on Ogrodowa Street, not far from Zelazna and close to the headquarters of the Jewish police. Perhaps Ringelblum intended to spend the night with the Bermans, thinking that a surprise nighttime search was less likely next door to the police station. Once, I was able to get him to stop. I asked him—as discreetly as I could—about something I had picked up in the underground press about our fate.

He remained optimistic about the military situation, even though the Germans seemed to be winning everywhere. When Germany had invaded the Soviet Union Ringelblum, along with many other Jews, had clung to another source of hope: the million Germans who had once voted Communist. Now, surely, they would "show what they were made of!" That hope burst like a soap bubble. Yet he remained optimistic.

On the other hand, he harbored no illusions about our own personal fates. He did not want to fool himself, or anybody else, with groundless optimism.

>—◄

One phase followed another. Now we know how it all ended, that last chapter of Warsaw Jewry. We also know Ringelblum's fate. We are no longer gripped by tension and curiosity and can linger on the final chapters of that long story.

I will mention two further meetings I had with Dr. Ringelblum. The first occurred between the first outbreak of resistance, in January 1943, and the uprising in April 1943. The second, the last one, took place on the Aryan side.

During the Great Deportation my only contact with Ringelblum was through Gutkowski. At the end of that first week I handed him a packet of materials to hide. They included a first draft of my essay on the soup kitchen at Leszno 40, which I wrote for the Oyneg Shabes writing competition. I also attached a final testament. It was a goodbye letter, a scream of protest. I wrote it on the fifth day of the deportation. I wrote that testament in Yiddish, although my reportage and notations were in Polish. Why did I write in Polish? The best explanation is that I was using the empty pages of a thick bound notebook, the second volume of a diary I had been keeping since I was a girl.[8]

I gave Gutkowski the last pages I had ripped out of the notebook, where I described what happened during that final week before the deportation began. At the same time I asked him to take both volumes of my diary, which included the period from 1917 until 1927. I threw in some more writings I had with me that dated from before the war. The entire previous night I sat with a small pair of scissors and cut out a large collection of my newspaper articles from the Polish and Yiddish press. I assembled various materials published before the war, some manuscripts, some published and unpublished stories, as well as chapters from the story I was writing about the village Jews of Lanowitz.

Gutkowski had no hesitation about taking both the prewar materials and what I had written during the occupation. He arrived after the daily blockade had ended, in the late afternoon, when one could move more freely in the street. Gutkowski took what I gave him to the archive.

I was still not finished with the prewar writings. After the night of April 18 and the search of our kitchen, when I felt threatened by the nocturnal visits of the Gestapo, I removed from my apartment the most important part of Itsik Manger's prewar literary archive as well as my own writings. I handed them over to Ruth Karlinska, who lived at Przejazd 1 on the fourth floor of the courtyard wing. Right after Gutkowski's visit at 5 a.m. I went there to take back the materials I had promised to give to the archive.

The writings were kept in a very large leather briefcase that had been bought in Romania. They included not only copies and early versions of poems and ballads Manger published later but also a libretto he had begun but not completed of *Megile lider* (*Songs of the Megillah*) along with a drawing of Ahashverosh's court and various characters that were not part of the *Songs*.

There were also my handwritten version of the *Kishef-makherin* (*The Sorceress*); our collaborative translation of Buchner's *Wozzeck*, staged by the Yung-teater with Kurt Katsch in the lead role; and a translation of Bruno Frank's drama *The Twelve Thousand*, which I had prepared for the Yung-teater after Manger left Poland in 1938.[9] I hope these manuscripts still exist.[10] There was also a joint "anthology" of poems that we copied into a notebook belonging to both of us; Polish and Ukrainian songs that Manger, with my help, was going to translate for the second volume of *Felker zingen* (*Folk Songs from around the World*); and a batch of letters dating from the time we lived together, which Manger sent to me during his trips to Romania.

I took the briefcase to Leszno 66 with no difficulty. But during the

Great Deportation Gutkowski did not get a chance to see me again.

That was also the last I saw of Ruth Karlinska and Hela Herman. When I went there to get my briefcase, Ruth, her son Ury, and Hela had already been taken away during one of the blockades. Hela's mother, the sister of Professor Schorr, was too old to travel. They shot her on the spot.

I hid that Romanian briefcase in the coal cellar where I, together with ten other tenants of the building, successfully hid out during that mass selection between September 6 and 12. After that I handed it over to a policeman who lived in our apartment, Ber Warm. He took it to the woodworking shop on Gęsia run by a friend of the Oyneg Shabes, Aleksander Landau. The shop was called the O.B.W., short for *Ostdeutsche Bautischlerei Werkstaette* (East German Furniture Workshops). During the Great Deportation Hersh Wasser and Eliyahu Gutkowski were registered as workers there.

Four years later, after the discovery of the first cache of the Oyneg Shabes on September 18, 1946, I was able to find all the materials I handed over during and just after the Great Deportation. I describe these papers in such detail because they are still being kept in the archives of the Jewish Historical Institute in Warsaw. As I said before, I had more luck saving manuscripts than saving people.

The papers in the black briefcase remained in Warsaw. For various reasons neither Manger nor I came forward to claim them right after the war.

A few years ago, during the last year of Manger's life, a literary committee and I made a joint request to the Jewish Historical Institute to send the materials to Israel—or if that was not possible, to send microfilms or photocopies. But those who were then in charge of the institute, either because they lacked permission or lacked courage, sent us nothing.

After the Great Deportation each of us wound up somewhere else. Ringelblum and Israel Lichtenstein lived and worked on Nowolipki Street, which was occupied by the Hallmann woodworking firm. This allowed them to guard the entrance to the building at Nowolipki 68, where the first cache of the Oyneg Shabes was buried on August 3, 1942. After that they stored materials as they arrived. While he was there Ringelblum stayed in touch with what remained of the Jewish administration of the ghetto. Once or twice a week, on the official pretext of obtaining supplies, and escorted by a German soldier, Ringelblum would visit the provisioning department run by Shmuel Winter. This enabled him to maintain contact with Shiye Perle, Yosef Kirman, and myself, who were all working at Franciszkanska 30.

Wasser and Gutkowski, who worked in the Hallmann woodworking firm, lived on Mila Street and therefore had access to the central ghetto. This new ghetto, along with the shops, now consisted of work camps under the control of the SS. It was forbidden to be on the street during working hours or to go from one zone to another without a special pass. Each day the Germans killed and wounded people whom they caught in the open. Nonetheless, for the 35,000 Jews who were officially registered, as well as for the "illegals," life went on, in all its intensity.

People looked for—and often discovered—new ways to stay alive and to prepare to resist. By this point Ringelblum was not just gathering documents for future historians. The Oyneg Shabes was working together with the fighting organization. It began to publish a mimeographed bulletin that recorded each step and each act of the growing resistance movement.[11]

>——<

Between the first and the second *aktions,* from September 1942 to January 1943, I did not see Ringelblum. Now and then Winter would tell me something about him. Shortly before I left the ghetto, after the second *aktion,* I went to Franciszkanska to say goodbye to Winter and unexpectedly saw Ringelblum in the waiting room. He told me that the archive was secure, that the documents were "protected from fire and water"—something he had told me a few times before. He didn't tell me where the documents were hidden, and I did not ask him. I found out only much later, after the ghetto uprising and after all the buildings left in the former ghetto went up in flames. He did tell me, though, that the order to finally seal and conceal the hiding place for the duration of the war could be given at any moment. He had already sent out the "call number" (legenda) of the archive to the Aryan side.

Historians use the term "legenda" to refer to the reference number of a document, as well as the date and place of its origin. But when

I heard Ringelblum say that word I understood it in the way that lay people would. It was a "legend." For a moment I felt transported to some point in the future, when everything that we did and saw would become, for the Jews who survived, a legend.

That was at the beginning of March 1943. It never occurred to me that Ringelblum—who had a better chance than any of us to survive—would himself become a legendary figure, one part of a terrible and catastrophic saga.

19. TESTAMENTS

> I knew that we wouldn't make it. It's impossible to survive these horrible killings. So with all the energy and enthusiasm I had, I threw myself into collecting as much material as I could for the archive. They told me that I would be the guardian of the treasure. I hid all the materials—I hid them well! May the day come when someone will find them! And then we'll be the redeemers of all the other Jews in the world. I believe in the survival of our nation. They will not destroy the Jewish people.

This is what Israel Lichtenstein, the guardian of the secret ghetto archive, wrote in his final testament, which he buried along with all the other documents on August 3, 1942, the thirteenth day of the Great Deportation in the Warsaw Ghetto.

His two young assistants also left notebooks with letters of farewell. They had been students in the Borochov school at Nowolipki 68, where Lichtenstein had been a teacher before the war. It was no coincidence that it was here that they buried the archive. During the occupation this was also the location of a kitchen, one of the kitchens for children run by the CENTOS.[1] These two former students were part of the kitchen staff.

> We made a decision to describe what we saw. Yesterday we stayed up late into the night because we were not sure that we would live to see today. Right now, even as I am writing, I can hear the terrible sound of shooting coming from outside. If there's any one thing I am proud of, it's that during the very worst of the terror I helped bury the treasure. I hid these documents so that you might know

about the suffering and the killing that marked the Nazi tyranny.

Those words were written by the 18-year-old Nakhum Grzywacz. David Graber, all of 19, with the keen insight of someone facing death, wrote:

> We have to hurry. We don't know what the next moment will bring. Yesterday we worked until late at night. I want future generations to know what we lived through, our sufferings and our pain. They should know that during such days of disaster, there were those who had the courage to carry through this kind of task. Just look at our devotion and energy as we dug holes for the containers. We received each new batch of documents with such enthusiasm. We have fulfilled our responsibility. The dangers did not frighten us. We all realized that we were working for history, and that this was more important than individual lives. Where did we bury this treasure? They can cut pieces from our bodies, and we will never divulge the secret. I would love to see the moment when they dig up the treasure and cry out the truth to the world. But we ourselves will not live to see it . . .

This 19-year-old added at the end: "And now we can die at peace with ourselves. We fulfilled our mission."

A week earlier, on the night of July 26–27, 1942, as I was preparing to hand over to the archive a package of writings by Manger and myself, as well as newspaper clippings, I also added something like a final testament. The original remains in the Jewish Historical Institute in Warsaw. Fate decreed that it would be Hersh Wasser and myself—after more than a year of struggles—who would live to see those ten tin boxes dug up from under the ruins of Nowolipki 68, who would be able to touch the writings of those terrible days, both documents that we wrote ourselves and those written by others. I want to cite another final testament that was dug up from the hiding place in September 1946: the farewell letter of Israel Lichtenstein's wife, the artist Gela Sekstajn.

I knew them both before the war. I would see him from time to time when I lived at Idusia Meyzl-Blumental's at Ciepla 19. Teachers from the Yiddish schools would often visit there. I got to know Gela years later in the writers union, where she would spend time in a group that included the Hebrew poet Ber Pomerantz. Now and then, when I had a moment, I would join their table. We would kibitz, gossip, laugh. I think that the writers union had already moved from Tlomackie to Graniczna. I remember well how a romance blossomed at that table between Pomerantz and a soloist from Shneour's choir. She became his wife and the muse of his last poems, in which he was already writing about a son. I read those poems when I was in Israel. I learned about his life and his tragic end in the memorial book of Yanov, a town not far from Pinsk.

Gela Sekstajn was a woman in her thirties with a broad Slavic face, slanting eyes, and largish, protruding lips. That's exactly how she appeared in her self-portrait; a smiling countenance that radiated feminine charm and attraction. A visitor from abroad fell madly in love with her at first sight in 1938; he was ready to do anything. He wanted to get her out of Poland before the war began. But in the end Gela resisted temptation, and the visitor had to settle for a platonic friendship, which also included Gela's husband.

Gela Sekstajn's very fine portrait of Pomerantz was retrieved from one of the ten tin boxes of the first cache of the Ringelblum archive. This artistic memento of their friendship was found in the same box that contained those final testaments. I want to quote from the last, and most heartbreaking, message that Gela Sekstajn wrote:

> When I find myself on the boundary between life and death, now that I am convinced that I am more likely to perish than survive, I want to bid farewell to my friends and to my work. For ten years I drew, sorted my paintings, tore some up and started again. I was preparing to exhibit my works, with the title *A Portrait of the Jewish Child*. Now I am trying to rescue paintings to the extent that present circumstances and available space allow. So, I am forced to abandon to their fate dozens of oil paintings, portraits of Yiddish writers, sketches, and other works, which will not fit into the box.

I am not asking for praise. I only want my name to be remembered. I want my daughter's name to be remembered, that talented little girl Margalit. She's twenty months old and shows a talent for drawing. She is a Jewish little girl, speaks a nice Yiddish, and is well developed both physically and mentally.

Israel Lichtenstein, in the farewell letter he left in the box, also wrote about the not-quite-two-year-old Margalit as if she were already a big girl. There being no chance and no hope that she would grow to see adulthood, her parents convinced themselves that she was already a grown person, endowed with talent and with the promise of a future that would never be.

In that last letter Gela then turned her attention to the children she drew in her paintings.

I leave my drawings to the future Jewish museum that will revive the Jewish artistic creativity that existed before the war and before the horrible tragedy of Polish Jewry.

She then appended last goodbyes to relatives and friends who lived in distant countries far from the scene of German mass murder. She omitted her relatives and her husband's relatives, who still lived in German-occupied Poland. Clearly, she did not think that any of them would survive. She sent regards to her husband's sister and brother-in-law in Argentina, as well as his brother and sister-in-law in the Land of Israel. She asked to be remembered to the Jewish communal activist Bentsion Hariton, who was the first person in New York to recognize the talent of I. J. Singer.[2] She also sent her goodbyes to the Jewish artists and painters from Warsaw who had fled to the Soviet Union. "Now I am at peace," she ended her final letter.

I will die but I have fulfilled my mission. I am trying to hide away some memento so that my work will be remembered. Farewell, my comrades and friends! Farewell, Jewish people! Never allow such a disaster to happen again!

>—<

Gela's testament was dated August 1, 1942. But that year, during which more Jews were murdered in Poland and Europe than any other, did not turn out to be her last. The same was true for the remaining members of the Oyneg Shabes on Nowolipki. They lived to hear news of the first major German defeats: El Alamein, which ended the danger that Jews in the Land of Israel would fall under German occupation; and the destruction in February 1943 of the almost 500,000-strong German army in the pocket around Stalingrad.[3] They survived to see the first outbreak of Jewish armed resistance during the second deportation *aktion* of January 1943 and, three months later, the ghetto uprising. They had gotten a nine-month reprieve from the death sentence that they expected at the beginning of August 1942. They had the opportunity to collect, sort, and bury the second cache of the Ringelblum archive, this time in two hermetically sealed milk cans.

During those last, most terrifying days of the Great Deportation, when the Germans forced the remaining Jews into a sealed square bounded by Gęsia, Smocza, Niska, and Zamenhof Streets and sent more than 100,000 to Treblinka, that building at Nowolipki 68 proved that it could shelter people as well as documents. The Lichtenstein family, other staff members of the children's kitchen, activists including Emanuel Ringelblum and Hersh Wasser (along with their wives), and Eliezer Lipe Bloch, the former director of the Keren Kayemet in Poland, all hid in a concealed classroom of the former Borochov school.

In the interlude between the first and second deportations, as well as the one between the second and third, that part of Nowolipki Street numbered in the 50s and 60s housed the workers attached to the German woodworking firm Hallmann. It was here that the Oyneg Shabes began a new, extremely important stage of its activities.

The recovered milk cans of the second cache of the archive contained the proclamations and handwritten warnings that hung on the walls of the shrunken ghetto and of the shops. They warned the remaining Jews of the ghetto not to believe German promises, to stay in the ghetto and resist blandishments to move with their shops to the provinces.[4] These documents also described the preparations to fight back against that inevitable and final blow that the Germans planned to unleash on the remaining Jews. During this time Jews were building bunkers, buying and smuggling weapons, assembling grenades and bombs. The secret archive was a powerful part of this movement.

>—◄

Can you imagine how young people who are awaiting death experience and feel each extra, unexpected day? There they are, embracing a few more precious hours of love and bittersweet joys. That's how Gela Sekstajn, in her maternal pride, must have felt as she watched her child play, grow, become smarter and more beautiful with each passing day. Was it even possible that the thought wouldn't have crossed her mind: "How can I save my child, how can I get her out of here?"

Days and months passed. The reprieve was about to expire. The rush of good news from the big world outside the ghetto slowed to a trickle. And maybe a thought began to take hold in the minds of Israel and Gela Lichtenstein that they had done their mission and were no longer needed. Maybe now there might be some way to save themselves and little Margalit? Certain members of the Oyneg Shabes had already gone over to the Aryan side, where the chances to survive and see the end of the war were infinitely greater.

>—◄

Another spring arrived and another Passover. Emanuel Ringelblum, who for some time had been on the Aryan side with his wife and son, decided to return to the ghetto to join a Passover Seder. So did Hersh Wasser. Perhaps Israel Lichtenstein got some kind of message from them because that Sunday, the day before Passover eve, he and the teacher Nathan Smolar left his building to go to Brauer's shop on Nalewki, where Ringelblum was staying as someone's guest.

They spoke late into the night. That Sunday was the last day before the third and final *aktion*—the outbreak of the ghetto uprising.[5] Ringelblum wrote that during this last meeting they discussed how to help Nathan Smolar, who was in an exceptionally difficult situation. He had already survived two big *aktions* and was still not officially registered in any shop. I suspect that another purpose of Ringelblum's visit was to find ways of getting certain people over to the Aryan side, including the Lichtenstein family.

It was too late. That night people in the central ghetto had already learned that special detachments had arrived in Warsaw and the ghetto was surrounded. The Jewish Fighting Organization (ZOB) went on high alert. They knew that a new *aktion* was about to begin, that long-awaited final ordeal.

The last news about Lichtenstein was provided by Ringelblum. Late that night Lichtenstein and Smolar left in order to get back to Hallmann's shop on Nowolipki, to that tried-and-true hideout that had already protected their families and friends so many times.

And that's the last we know about what happened to them. Ringelblum thought they were both killed on their way back. No one ever learned any further details about the subsequent fate of Lichtenstein, his wife and child, and the other members of the Oyneg Shabes on Nowolipki Street. For such a long time they had prepared themselves to face death. But when it cut them down they were alone, separated from their loved ones, denied that final comfort of at least dying together.

20. ONE LAST CONVERSATION

For a long time we knew nothing about what happened to Ringelblum during the fighting, the conflagrations, the mass executions,
and the transports of workers from the shops to labor camps in the
Lublin region. It was only in July that a postcard was sent to a Polish
address in Warsaw carrying the news that Rydzewski (Ringelblum's
Polish pseudonym) was in Trawniki.[1] It was important to get him out
of there and bring him to Warsaw. People were sent with messages,
at great cost but with no success. I finally suggested that they should
send the Polish railroad worker Tadeusz Pajewski, who extricated
me from the labor site at the Pelcowizna train station in March[2] and
who did the same for Jonas Turkow in April, during the uprising. In
time Tadeusz would become a vital courier and go-between for the
Council to Aid Jews.[3] He was accompanied by a young, courageous
Jewish woman who went by the name of Emilka (her real name was
Rosa Kossower). The two of them were able to bring Ringelblum to
Warsaw. That's when I met him again.

Yes, those days . . . It was the summer of 1943, just after the fall
of Mussolini. Like most people in Warsaw I was full of excitement,
totally obsessed with the significance of what had just happened. I
fantasized and spoke nonstop about what would come next. And after having suffered for so long, who could blame us for getting carried
away with this tiny bit of good news?

In the meantime, like everybody else, I took care of business. Although I received a monthly stipend from our organization, which
barely covered my personal expenses, I had to earn a lot more to meet
the needs of the large group of people in hiding that I was helping.[4]
So I also traded, which was the way much of the unemployed Polish
intelligentsia (which supposedly included me) earned a living during
the occupation. I sold socks. All my "Aryan" friends (the real Aryans

and those just pretending to be) bought them only from me.

I had some socks to deliver at Radzyminska 2 to a Miss Stacha, a sister-in-law of that same railroad worker Tadeusz Pajewski who had gone to get Ringelblum out of the camp.

Several Jews from Emilka Kossower's circle knew Stacha's address. I had also stayed with her for several nights after I was forced to leave my first "normal" apartment. As I entered the apartment with the socks and met Stacha, I noticed that something was bothering her and that she wanted to get rid of me as soon as possible.

Stacha had already gotten me halfway out the door. As I was about to leave, I suddenly heard a ring from a front room that I recognized as a code. Stacha glanced at me and decided to open the door: Dr. Berman was there! Then I learned the reason for this unexpected meeting. Ringelblum was here! Yes, right here, in the other room! If I was willing to wait, I could see him.

And that's exactly what happened. When Berman left a short time later, he gestured to Stacha that she could let me in to see Ringelblum.

He was very happy to see that I was alive and looking like a genuine Aryan woman. During the next half hour, we talked about many different subjects. He told me that compared to the camp, Stacha's two modest rooms seemed like a paradise of cleanliness, comfort, and space. He mentioned the names of the different activists that he left behind in Trawniki and described the underground organization that functioned there. It had acquired some weapons and become so well entrenched that it helped compile the lists of transportees to be sent to Sobibor, supposedly to dig peat but in reality to die there. That was a good way of getting rid of the informers and scoundrels among the prisoners.

Then Ringelblum began to ask me about what was happening in Warsaw. Since I was so obsessed with the news about Mussolini, I started to bombard him with what we had heard on our illegal radios, hardly bothering to conceal my own excitement.

"Now it's happened," I said. "This is what we've been waiting for so long. So many times during this war we got our hopes up, only to see them dashed. But now fascism has suffered a decisive blow at its very center. There's no longer any doubt. Its fate is sealed; the final collapse is just a matter of time." I even cited a prewar article, "Without Mussolini, no Hitler."[5]

I went on to say that Hitler's collapse would not surprise us as much as Mussolini's because now all our doubts were gone. Now we knew that his end would come.

"Oy!" Ringelblum answered me. "When that time comes, we Jews will once again suffer personal heartbreak. Even more than now. Because then we will be able to say that we, personally, actually survived. That's how human nature is."

He was right, as we learned. But he never lived to see that moment.

21. The Martyr's Crown

Dr. Ringelblum left Radzyminska. I only learned where he went eight months later and under very tragic circumstances. Now and then I would ask the Bermans how he was doing. I once used one of our contacts to ask him something about a documentation project. But I guess he never got my letter, because I received no answer from him.

March 1, 1944. Dr. Ringelblum and Dr. Berman completed a comprehensive report about the cultural life of the Warsaw Ghetto and about the fate of its many writers, artists, and cultural activists. Thanks to the Polish underground that letter, addressed to the YIVO in New York, to several Yiddish writers, and to the historian Rafael Mahler, reached its final destination. And there was a postscript, added on May 20, that reported what happened to Ringelblum and his family six days after the completion of the letter.

Both this letter, as well as the message sent on behalf of the underground Jewish National Committee and signed by Adolf Berman, Yitshak Zuckerman, and David Guzik on November 15, 1943, mentioned my name as well. Thanks to that message, transmitted through the channels of the Polish underground and addressed to Dr. Ignacy Schwarzbart, a Jewish delegate on the National Council of the Polish Government in Exile in London, and to certain other details picked up by the Yiddish press, my relatives and close friends who were living abroad learned that I had managed to leave the ghetto and was living on the Aryan side.

>——<

It happened on March 7, 1944, a bitterly cold day. The terrible news became the talk of the city. The Germans dragged out thirty-six hidden Jews from a well-made bunker underneath a hothouse at Grójecka 81, which belonged to a Polish gardener. The Germans took them all to the Pawiak prison and shot them three days later.

Among those thirty-six Jews was Emanuel Ringelblum, his wife, Judyta, and their 12-year-old son Uri.

Those of us who had been his friends and co-workers on the Aryan side were crushed by the calamity. After surviving so many close calls, he perished. And less than a year before the liberation.

To this very day, his death gives us no peace.

>——<

Some months before the Germans discovered the bunker, Adolf Berman ran into blackmailers on the street. There's reason to think that the scoundrels who recognized him were Jews from Radom. They knew exactly what he was doing and demanded a very high ransom. They also went with him to his flat, where his wife Basia also resided with Aryan documents, posing as Berman's sister. After this incident they were both forced to get new names and documents, give their physical appearances a makeover, change the way they dressed, and move from the center of town to a new neighborhood. For a while they also had to avoid showing themselves on the street. They went to Żoliborz and for weeks and months they curtailed their clandestine activities.

When that happened, it became even more urgent to increase Dr. Ringelblum's involvement in the ongoing political and relief work of the underground. He was asked to leave his hideout and participate in clandestine political activities on the Aryan side. Ringelblum was tall and blond, an ideal representative of the Nordic race. He could have moved about the city much more easily than Berman.

But there were two reasons why he did not leave the bunker where he was hidden with his wife and son. First, he was very absorbed in his historical writings. He had written accounts of the Aleynhilf in Warsaw and, most important, essays about the Oyneg Shabes archive and about murdered Jewish writers, actors, lawyers, public activists, and scholars. In addition, while sitting in that bunker, Ringelblum wrote a work about Polish-Jewish relations during the Second World War.

There was another reason he kept putting off the decision to leave the hideout: it was hard to leave his family. His wife Yehudis (Juzia) did not have the "right look."[1] When he left the bunker to visit the ghetto on the eve of the uprising, she suffered agonizing bouts of fear, and it took her months to regain a semblance of her former self. So she could not decide to let him go, although it was a firm rule that Jews who lived as Aryans should not have their entire families with them.

It was also a careless mistake to put a person of Ringelblum's importance in a hideout where, besides him and his family, there were more than thirty others. By and large they were not the kind of people he would normally have associated with. There were too many of them, and they were neither discreet nor prudent. Just sending in enough food for such a large number attracted unwanted attention from the neighbors. The Polish landlord had suddenly become very rich, and conflicts broke out with his relatives. Complicating matters was his wife's suspicion that he had a lover on the side. As the days wore on the situation became steadily worse.

For many months there was a place in Izabelin to which Ringelblum could move. Finally, another ghetto activist moved in there, and he survived the war along with his family.[2] But Ringelblum—who was so courageous and so full of energy—kept putting off the decision to leave the bunker. The last letter that the courier Wanda Elster passed on from him to the Jewish underground committee was full of despair and foreboding. But as for clearing out of that place without delay, that was a decision he had to make for himself—he and his wife.

Then it happened. It was a bitterly cold day in late winter. During those three days between March 7 and March 10, 1944, a ghastly, freezing wind lashed the city.

Among the Jews dragged out of greengrocer Mieczyslaw Wolski's bunker was a tiny infant who had been born in the hideout just days before. This little soul was the thirty-seventh Jew, along with the landlord Wolski, that they took to the Pawiak prison. That same day they arrested the Polish midwife who delivered the baby.

>——<

In the Pawiak prison there were workshops where a number of Jewish artisans worked, some of whom managed to escape during the Warsaw uprising of August 1944. Jozef Lehman, who hid out for a while in the ruins of the ghetto, and Treblinka survivor Aron Czechowicz, who worked at Pawiak, later related that when the Jews in the workshops found out that the Germans had brought Ringelblum to the prison, they tried to figure out how to get him into the shops disguised as an artisan. Lehman said that as he was walking through the courtyard with a load on his back he heard whispering through the bars: "Ringelblum is here. Ringelblum is here." The news spread from mouth to mouth.

There is a story, which is hard to believe, that the Jewish shopworkers' plan actually worked. Ringelblum's wife and son were shot along with all the other Jews from the bunker, but Ringelblum himself supposedly survived for some weeks among the Jews in the workshops and was shot during an unsuccessful escape attempt.

The journalist Yehiel Hirszhaut, who left Poland after the war for France and later the United States, tells a very different story in his book *Dark Nights in Pawiak*.

Hirszhaut, who was disguised as a Pole, arrived at Pawiak in late 1943, after being swept up during one of the periodic street roundups in Warsaw. Having made up many different stories about himself, he secured the help of a Polish official who worked in the prison administration, and he got access to the Jewish workshops. Hirszhaut, as a fellow Galitsianer, had known Ringelblum before the war. When they brought Ringelblum to Pawiak, Hirszhaut decided to sound him out about a possible rescue. While a bribed prison guard looked the other way, Hirszhaut managed to enter Ringelblum's cell.

According to Hirszhaut, by that time Ringelblum was totally resigned to his fate, and he showed little interest in plans to rescue him. He understood that even if they managed to get him out there was no hope for his son or his wife, who was together with the other women from the bunker in a separate cell. With his wonderful, handsome, and talented son sitting before him, Ringelblum asked Hirszhaut: "And what will happen to him?"[3] There was no doubt that Ringelblum would never have abandoned his wife and child in order to save his own life.

Hirszhaut's plan probably had little chance in any case. The execution of all those caught in the bunker took place only three days after they were brought to Pawiak. Those working-class Jews who labored in the workshops were ready to risk their lives to save Ringelblum. But there was little they could do.

Of course, people outside Pawiak also tried to rescue Ringelblum.

In those days a good bribe went a long way. But this incident was too well-known. Everybody was already talking about the thirty-six Jews caught in the bunker. His friends could only arrange for Ringelblum to send a secret letter from the prison, in which he asked for poison. And they couldn't even do that.

The Germans discovered the bunker on Grójecka on March 7. If the information we received was correct, Emanuel Ringelblum, along with his family and the other Jews, were shot in the ruins of the ghetto on March 10, 1944.

>—◄

Thus they murdered, in his very prime, Dr. Emanuel Ringelblum, the organizer of the secret ghetto archive, the Jewish historian, the activist who worked tirelessly for his people.

He could not escape the gears of the colossal murder machine. Like millions of other Jews, he became a victim.

Ringelblum was a person who combined pragmatism, modesty, and diligence with an inner core of human decency and deep devotion to his people. All this explains the project he started, which produced such a great national treasure. His life, and what he accomplished, should serve as an example for generations of Jews to come, a model of Jewish humanism, cultural vitality, and youthful creativity.

Perhaps such an elegy, set in such a terrible time, would not be complete unless it mentioned the personal, individual tragedy of his death and evoked the pathos of martyrdom. So let that too be part of his memory. For us survivors, we still feel the pain of an eternal, incurable wound.

The work that Dr. Ringelblum began during the occupation is being carried out today by individuals and institutions in Israel, Poland, and other countries. But what the murderers tore away from us that cold, late-winter day left such a void within our already meager ranks that even today we can't replace what we lost.

>—◄

Afterward, events followed one after the other. Warsaw's fate was sealed, and with it the fate of the 20,000 Jews who were hiding on the

Aryan side. The destruction of the whole city followed the destruction of the ghetto. It is as difficult to change the fate of a city as it is to alter the destiny of an individual. Yes, there were mistakes. But how can we be sure that if those mistakes hadn't been made, matters would have turned out differently?

We buried documents. And then we dug them up. Many papers were destroyed during the Warsaw uprising. The archive that contained Ringelbum's writings on the Aryan side mostly survived.

Sometimes documents are more durable than people.

Part 5: Before the Great Deportation

22. Old Man Zaks

Any habitué of the Jewish writers union in prewar Warsaw knew the regulars who were always there.

To give you just one example: There was this Jew whom everybody called "Old Man Zaks." He resembled a typical Russian *intelligent* who never missed a chance to show off his knowledge of Russian literature. He worked for years as a proofreader for *The Moment*. Nobody knew very much about his private life. Maybe he had none. He had washed up in Warsaw, a remnant of that vanished world of prerevolutionary tsarist Russia.

You could see Zaks at Tlomackie 13 any time of day, except when he was working at *The Moment*. He was a regular fixture at the restaurant and buffet. In the afternoons he was usually drinking tea at Mrs. Ravitch's table. Only a few Russian-speaking guests and habitués of the union belonged to this circle, which was led by Madame Garielov, the "impresario." After they left, Zaks would move on to the next part of his daily routine—curl up somewhere and take a nap.

His favorite spot for that afternoon siesta was the piano that stood in the left corner of the stage. Zaks would move the piano stool off to one side. Then he would bring a bench, sit down, make himself comfortable, and plop his arms down over the piano keys. In no time, there he was, quietly snoring. The cat lay right next to him, sprawled on the stage carpet as she took her own afternoon nap.

Downstairs in the hall there were no tables near the piano, which stood at a distance from the windows. But in front of the stage was some space the poet Joseph Rubinstein named "Saxon Square."[1]

Anyone who dropped by the writers union around five in the afternoon would witness a scene of peaceful serenity: on one side of the hall there would be a table with a couple of chess players, totally wrapped up in a game that never seemed to end. On the other side, the cat and Old Man Zaks, sleeping away by the piano. The papers carried bad news, the communiques of the wire services became steadily more alarming, and a few writers in those last years before the war migrated to new continents. But who among us saw those portents of danger as something that could reach us so directly and quickly? How could anyone who looked at this innocent idyll in the writers union have suspected that somewhere else the forces of darkness were getting ready to lay waste to Poland and its capital with fire, iron, and bombs?

Who could have guessed that one flick of a match would spark a conflagration of satanic hatred that would destroy forever all those moments of peace and serenity here at Tlomackie and in every other Jewish sanctuary throughout Poland?

23. Hershele

His muse was no bigger than he was. And he was no bigger than his muse. Hershele Danilewicz, a folk poet. Hershele for short.

Throughout its entire existence the writers union had to take care of this 50-year-old, who spoke in a thin reedy voice, as if he were an actual child. His problems never seemed to end, even when the union married him off, gave him a dowry, and set him up in a little store in the town of Henrykow—which from that moment on came to be called Hershelov.

Each evening he would go back to Hershelov on the narrow-track train with a basket of merchandise and a little pail of kerosene. By day he held court at Tlomackie 13. Aside from a little shop, which he left in the charge of his wife and mother-in-law, Hershele earned his living from copying manuscripts. Hershele's beautiful and elegant handwriting could easily compete with any typewriter. And there were members who appreciated a nice script. Hershele, sitting for hours near the window of the big hall, worked diligently. He belonged to that category of folk calligraphers who in our day would compete to set a record for putting the text of an entire book on a postcard or for creating a portrait of an author using the letters of their text. If one looked with a magnifying glass, it was all there. There would not be one letter missing.

Hershele was also, if you will, a "miniaturist," a calligrapher, a scribe. But the holy texts that he toiled over with such patience were short stanzas of poems, his own "collected works." They were written in finely crafted tiny letters and all fit into one "volume": a miniature address book that Hershele always carried in his pocket and which was surely one of the greatest bibliographic rarities in the world.

Not everyone had the honor of getting Hershele to show him this "volume," or the opportunity to read a poem written in those characteristic, Hershelese rhymes.

—

In his younger years Hershele spent some time in Switzerland in a milieu of students and political emigres, where he rubbed shoulders with some big-shot political activists. Some of his poems from those days were included in an international anthology of proletarian poetry. This was something he never bragged about very much. But then again, occasionally, at the right moment, his face would take on a solemn and dignified expression (obviously well rehearsed), and he let drop a word about that anthology. And then, as if the idea suddenly occurred to him, he would produce the collection and hand around his poems translated into French.

It was also in Switzerland that Hershele came up with his ontological proof of the existence of God. The proof consisted only of questions.

"Were you in Switzerland? Did you see the mountains? And the boulders? So who put them there? Me, perhaps? Maybe you? So there, it's clear that there's a God in this world!"

There could well have been some impish humor in his playful allusions to those days in Switzerland and to those French translations. But there was one thing in his life that filled his soul with genuine pride. The person who bestowed on Hershele his seal of approval and brought him into the family of Yiddish writers was none other than I. L. Peretz himself!

When Hershele was a young man, Peretz's favor and grace rested on his shoulders. Hershele carried around the issue of *Yontev bletlekh*,[1] edited by Peretz, where his first poem appeared. In that same journal, where Peretz mentioned several rising literary talents, he did not forget to include Hershele. (By the way, as a young man, Hershele was once given the honor of transcribing Peretz's works.)

When Hershele wanted to show someone respect and let him know that he admired and liked him, he would pull out that *bletl* and let that person read both pieces: his own poem and the article where Peretz mentioned him. That was his real proof of status, his lifelong source of solace and pride. There is a Latin saying about a sage: "All he is, he carries with him." So did Hershele carry around in his breast pocket, close to his heart, that old yellowing issue of *Yontev bletlekh* along with his volume of poems.

How did that issue survive all those years in the pocket of a worn-out jacket? That secret might have something to do with Hershele's special relationship with the printed word gained through years of copying.

Hershele addressed everybody with the familiar *du,* and many writers also addressed him with *du.*[2] They enjoyed spending time and being friendly with him. One funny pair was Hershele and Zusman Segalowicz. Segalowicz was tall, rather formal, and the paragon of elegance in the Yiddish literary milieu. They called him the "king of ties." He loved to have his picture taken with Hershele. When Itsik Manger, just as tall but quite thin, was in a good mood, he would hoist Hershele into the air and carry him through the hall of the writers union. Hershele would flutter his tiny legs and squeal with delight.

When Hershele turned fifty, Tlomackie arranged a birthday party with all the trimmings. I was not in Warsaw at the time, but I heard about that celebration many years later.

When the banquet was over, it was already too late to catch the little train to Hershelov. So one of the writers took Hershele home to his place and they bedded down together.

"You're just lucky that you're not my wife," Hershele said to him when they turned off the lights. That's how happy Hershele was that evening ...

A popular saying about socks also came from Hershele. One of the writers (maybe Segalowicz) asked him what he wanted as a present: flowers or socks. (This was either for the birthday party or for his wedding.) Hershele supposedly replied that he wanted socks.

"Flowers fade," he said. "Socks are forever."

>———<

How have I gotten so far ahead of myself? I set out to give the survivors of that once-vibrant Yiddish literary circle in Warsaw—survivors now scattered throughout the world—some description, some idea of how Hershele perished.

By the standards of those terrible days his fate could have been worse. Hershele passed away before the Great Deportation. He died his own death, in his own bed, surrounded by friends.

When they expelled the Jews from Henrykow, Hershele, along with his wife, his two children, and his mother-in-law, wound up in one of the infamous refugee centers on Nalewki. Thanks to his literary connections he and his family lived in a separate room.

How would he support himself? Before the war the writers union was a vibrant, public organization. When it took on the responsibility of supporting Hershele it gave him subsidies meant to supplement his basic income, which came from the little shop in Henrykow, where the family had put down roots. Once they were taken from their home and robbed of their modest economic support, the family now had to depend entirely on the writers union, which in fact no longer existed.

Yes, there was a kitchen that served free bowls of soup to the writers and their families. It also handed out dry products and now and then some small cash grants.[3] But that was the extent of the aid. There were spiteful gossips, people from our circle who remained in Warsaw, who snidely complained that those who received this help were better off now than before the war. They joked that the needy members of the writers union anxiously asked whether the war would end soon. They hoped not. They were now living well . . .

It was true that the kitchen administration, which included Menakhem Kipnis, Aaron Gavze, and Y. Rayzfeder, cared about the handful of writers who stayed in Warsaw as if they were members of their own families. They did all they could to help them survive. The "Jewish powers that be," the leaders of the Aleynhilf, also tried as much as possible to meet the needs of the Jewish writers. But they lacked the necessary resources, and whatever help they gave fell short.

That's how Hershele went under, along with his wife, his children, and his mother-in-law.

He was not a schnorrer. He didn't accost anybody and make a scene. He quite simply and without any fuss did what others did not so simply and with much more fuss: he suffered hunger pangs, lost weight, and looked twenty years younger. In fact, he came to resemble a little boy.

The last time I saw Hershele it must have been in the winter of

1941, a few months after the closing of the ghetto.

Y. M. Apelbaum, who had worked for *The Moment*, ran the kitchen for the journalists. Until the establishment of the ghetto that kitchen had been at Graniczna 13. Then it moved into the annex of the building at Leszno 14. The premises were larger, and there was a stage. The locale became a kitchen for the intelligentsia and served meals that were a little more nutritious.

Apelbaum also introduced literary *shaleshudes* gatherings. On Saturday afternoons, when religious Jews gathered in the synagogue for the third meal of the Sabbath, the small stage turned into a venue for a mixed repertoire of lectures, small concerts, recitations, and more. Two traditional candlesticks stood on a table covered with a white tablecloth as a reminder of the Sabbath. Cardboard decorations depicting Hasidim covered the lower wall.

The kitchen had its regulars, and its staff included writers. Among them was the poet Pesi (Peysekh) Vayland. The programs were staged for invited guests, while writers and artists could come as they wished. Apart from the cultural fare each guest received a glass of coffee and a piece of fresh soft cake, baked from a combination of white flour and potatoes. In those times this was no small enticement. Some of these programs were on a very high level, especially when Yisroel Shtern spoke about poetry. It was at that time that he became especially creative, as a poet and as a public figure, more than he ever was before the war.[4]

>——◄

That particular Saturday afternoon the speaker was not Yisroel Shtern but, if I am not mistaken, Yitshak Bernstein. His lecture—may he forgive me for this—was a little confusing. The audience was bored, and everyone was relieved when Apelbaum's young daughter and another girl, wearing white aprons, began to serve the ersatz black coffee with real brown sugar along with an ample piece of fresh cake.

Hershele was a regular at these Saturday afternoon gatherings. This time he was sitting (or maybe he was standing) at the same table as a Jew from Lodz who happened to be one of the well-known Kon brothers, industrialists who were prototypes for the main characters in I. J. Singer's *The Brothers Ashkenazi*. If memory serves me right it was Elisha Kon. His finely trimmed beard, protruding cheekbones, and wide eyes made him look like an old-time Russian merchant or landowner, a type we know well from films and plays. It was amazingly funny to see the look of confusion and disappointment on his face after he had drunk a bit of coffee, looked at the speaker, and then reached down for another bite of the cake he had started to eat. He touched the plate with his fingers and—the plate was empty.

This was Hershele's doing. He took advantage of a moment when Kon was distracted to swoop down and gobble up the whole piece of cake in one gulp. The scene was worthy of a Charlie Chaplin film. Elisha Kon withdrew his hand, brought his fingers together, closed the mouth that had been all set to eat that cake, and said nothing.

The Lodz industrialists had a tradition of supporting scholars and authors, as well as various types of unworldly intellectuals. Perhaps Elisha felt bad that he couldn't give his fellow Lodzer Hershele the help he needed. Or maybe he was only imagining that he couldn't help him, that he had to husband the fortune he brought with him from Lodz for whatever would come later.

I was sitting at a nearby table with Ruth Karlinska. We exchanged glances, nudged each other under the table, and quickly turned our heads away in order not to break out laughing.

The way we reacted to this tragicomic scene was so silly. We later told this story to a friend, just another funny anecdote about the Hershele that we all knew so well.

I decided to invite Hershele to come every day to our kitchen to eat a bowl of soup and take home a container for his family. But before I had a chance to do it, I heard that Hershele had died.

This happened at the beginning of the second winter of the war. I was not able to go to Hershele's funeral. I heard that he was buried in the "literary alley" of the Gęsia cemetery.

He thus had a privilege that eluded most of the other Jewish writers who stayed in Warsaw: his own grave and his own funeral. A friend gave the eulogy and his son said Kaddish. There was no chance to erect a tombstone.

24. ONE MORE HERSHELE

There's another Hershele that I want to recall—Hershele Shtern, the brother of Yisroel Shtern, though the brothers didn't resemble each other in the least. You could call him "Hershele the parodist."

This second Hershele was very musical. Whenever he heard a beautiful song he could quickly remember the tune and sing it. I remember how he taught me two songs. One began with the words:

The sun had already set on the other side of the river

Another started like this:

My sister digs a well
And the water gleams like a shining bell

As far as I remember those were the words of Mani Leyb. I don't recall who composed the melodies. But even now they echo in my ears. The joy with which he sang those songs! The pleasure he took in those lyrics and in that tune!

He possessed an inner quality of "muse-ic." He also exemplified a certain pattern in Jewish culture: If someone in the family became a writer, then his brothers followed in his footsteps and sometimes even established a dynasty.

Hershele Shtern's "muse-icness" revealed itself mainly in humor. He could deftly imitate the Jewish singers, male and female, who used to perform on the stage of the writers union. I remember one performance he gave before a small audience of intimates. His parodies had us rolling on the floor.

I also remember the plan, avidly supported by Hershele, to put on a puppet show in the writers union. He would recite the texts and croon the tunes. But for some reason the show was never staged.

His best numbers and skits were send-ups of his own brother. This family, which I believe all came from Ostrolenka, was unique and original.

Hershele was also in Warsaw when the Germans marched in. I remember, as if in a dream, hearing the news that this frail, thin little Jew, Hershele Shtern, died of tuberculosis in the spring of 1941.

25. Our Gandhi

If you really wanted to understand Tlomackie 13 it wasn't enough to know just the top tier of the writers union. You had to pay attention to the second tier, those other writers and hangers-on who were not as famous or prestigious.

One of the most popular "Tlomackie paupers" in Warsaw was Borukh Trzebucki. Before the war people called him "Gandhi" because of his bald head and his frequent bouts of hunger. I remember an evening that Tlomackie arranged as a benefit for Trzebucki. The posters billed the event as a "A Literary Evening for Our Gandhi."

Trzebucki-Gandhi was the subject of endless banter. Endowed with genuine, if not quite first-rate, talent, Trzebucki once contracted an illness (perhaps sleeping sickness?), and from then on remained a semi-invalid who depended on the help of Jewish writers and journalists. May God forgive me if I describe what this help amounted to! Trzebucki wandered like an emaciated phantom around Tlomackie 13, around the city, and even further afield. Trzebucki always had the look of a sleepwalker, so frail that he could collapse at any moment.

Now and then he would actually have a fainting spell, usually at night. When that happened someone would awaken the chairman of the writers union to send for a doctor.

Trzebucki also suffered from a speech defect. You could barely understand what he said. So his stammering and puny figure made him the butt of good-humored teasing and mimicry by the writers. Nokhum Bomze, to cite one example, gave a masterful imitation of his barely decipherable mutterings. When Y. Y. Trunk was the chairman of the PEN Club, Trzebucki would follow after him and nag: "Eh wan' the Pen Club to publish ma' little book too." Just like a little boy begging his mother for an apple.

Those were the days when the PEN Club would finance the publication of "PEN books," and Trzebucki acted like a child who wanted what the other children were getting.

"Draw a book cover fuh me, draw it." That's what he constantly demanded from the artist Mendel Reif, whose book covers and graphic designs won him a lot of recognition from literary circles in the second half of the 1930s.

Such a book was far from ready for publication. It probably didn't even have a title. But no matter. If Reif was preparing jacket designs for other writers, then Trzebucki had to have one too.

Yet in the middle of it all Trzebucki had a wife and children and a normal family life, just as if he had been a famous literary star. His wife and children even boasted that their husband and father also belonged to the world of letters.

>——<

After the war broke out Borukh Trzebucki and his family found themselves in a difficult situation. At the very beginning of the occupation, in October 1939, when the soup kitchen opened at Leszno 40 and word got out that I was the director, Trzebucki showed up among the other clients. Of course, he never had the 20 groszy to buy a ticket for a bowl of soup. Since I didn't want to set a bad example for the staff, each day I had to figure out some clandestine stratagem to pour him a jar of soup without a ticket.

His container had once been a pickle jar. During the siege of Warsaw some of the big food enterprises burned down, and the city was inundated with jars that had been salvaged from the wreckage. The process of adapting to a new life under occupation began with one of those pickle jars. People would bore two holes at the ends, insert a string through both holes, and just like it was a pail, loop the string around their arms and go to the Vistula to fetch water, or to the soup kitchen to get soup. Just like everywhere else, there were long rows of people lined up in front of our big soup cauldron. Trzebucki stood in line, his pail draped around his arms, and waited patiently. When he went past me he would lightly tap my apron and signal that he wanted to get his soup ahead of the line. He didn't do this because he was impatient but because, facing the catastrophe that engulfed us all, he yearned for a little attention, for a little recognition from a fellow writer, for some tiny bit of moral support from somebody who had more power than he did.

But Trzebucki was not somebody who just took. He also gave. He radiated a feeling of warmth. He never left without a final *"zay gezunt."*[1] When he didn't see me near the soup line he would wait in the corridor outside my office until I came out and then murmur his thanks. Sometimes he would also mumble barely understandable requests or grievances, which I could easily satisfy with a clasp of the hand, a smile, some words of encouragement, or by simply ladling some extra vegetables into his bowl. Appeased, he would thank me once more and leave.

As time went on Trzebucki's mumbling and stammering became harder and harder to understand. Then one day he did not show up to stand in line. His wife came for the soup instead and carried a note. Since I imagined that he was in a very bad way, I was surprised by the note's clear script and polished style.

A short time later, Trzebucki's wife, a respectable person who looked serious and trustworthy, became a widow. A major and far from unimportant part of her husband's legacy was the privilege of getting free soup at our kitchen. Actually, Trzebucki left not one but two legacies. His family inherited his place in the soup line while I inherited the entire family. That happened quite often. When one of our charges died, we inherited the rest of the family. The survivors would come to me for sympathy, for advice, and for a chance to talk about their misfortune.

Trzebucki's wife came to see me along with her young daughter. During that first period of the occupation, even as she depended on the pathetic bowls of soup and the meager slices of bread that we handed out, this child nonetheless blossomed into a stunningly beautiful young girl. She was charming in a typically Jewish way, graceful and modest. Each time I looked at her, at that old-fashioned braid that fell back on her shoulder, at those lowered, bashful, dark eyes that reminded me so much of a Jewish bride, I would think about Thomas Mann's depiction of Rachel, narrated by Jacob, who loved her so much—about her face, about those twisted eyes of her father's that became beautiful.

That girl looked so much like her disabled, unattractive father— and yet what a beauty she turned into! Perhaps she also inherited the quiet grace that rested in her father's soul. It gave her an inner light that radiated from her young face and from her entire delicate figure.

You had to see with your own eyes how mother and daughter moaned, the tears they shed, whenever somebody mentioned her father. More than one Jewish writer would have longed to have left behind a loved one to mourn him and to mention his name.

The trouble was that Trzebucki was soon fated to lose even his modest share in the world to come. His wife and daughter disappeared from the soup line in the very first days of the Great Deportation in the summer of 1942. I didn't even notice exactly when that happened.

>——<

I once read one of Trzebucki's novellas in a journal. It was about an unemployed textile worker. Finally, he got a job. But he became so excited by his change of luck that he became confused when his new employer asked him to pass a simple test. He jumbled the threads, failed to finish the task, and lost his position. He thought that he would finally work again and dreamt about his new life, when his money worries would finally be over: "A little bit of soup, some noodles, a taste of compote ..."

Even before the war Trzebucki was well acquainted with hunger. He had a deep affinity for the little man with his humble desires. He was also that kind of little man, with a quiet, unassuming soul. But the time came when his little wish for just a bit of modest comfort became an impossible mirage. Just as "our Gandhi" lived quietly, so did he leave this world, in silence.

26. The Holy, the Worldly, and the Polished Boots

In the soup kitchen at Leszno 40, every now and then, without informing or getting permission from the central kitchen administration, I would decide to support a needy friend. The Hebrew writer M. D. Widrewicz, the eternal "budding talent," was one of the first.

Before the war his beautiful countenance and dignified bearing graced many group photographs taken in the summer resorts and vacation camps run by Jewish organizations. In October or November 1939 he paid the soup kitchen the honor of a personal visit. After that he began to send his unassuming and likable son, who did not feel at all insulted when his father once explained to me, in his presence, why the boy was so "average."

Yes, that Hebrew writer Widrewicz was also a part of our literary milieu. I don't remember any specific details about how he died. I only recall that I saw him once in 1940 or the beginning of 1941, just before he passed away. Instead of being swollen he was emaciated. His face was covered with dark blotches, but he still took care of his appearance. He was clean-shaven and neat. His collar was clean. That's how I used to see him before the war when he would come to Tlomackie on a Friday evening just before going to a nearby synagogue to pray. I still remember his deep voice, his clear diction, and his correct literary Lithuanian Yiddish.

> The holy, the worldly, and the polished boots. Blessed be the day when he died. It came at the right time, early enough to allow old Widrewicz to hang on to some shred of his dignity and refined persona.

Those are the words I wrote in the winter of 1943–44, during one of my nocturnal writing sessions at Smolna 24. After the war, when a short sketch appeared in the Lodz journal *Nasze Słowo* as part of the series *Z ludem pospołu*,[1] an engaging young woman got in touch with me. She was Widrewicz's daughter who had survived the war. She came to thank me for the information I had provided about her father. She brought me a gift: a photograph of him taken in the Polish resort Ciechocinek. There was an inscription on the left side of the photograph:

> At home a good for nothing
> But in Ciechocinek a prince
> And I know what they say
> A prince who has a nice hat,
> And not a penny in his pocket.

I was glad to hear that at least someone from his family survived.

27. THE SELF-TAUGHT SCHOLAR

He was just another client in the soup kitchen at Leszno 40—a normal person with a ticket. Before the war he was known in Warsaw literary circles as a translator, a transcriber, and as somebody who prepared books for publication. He also wrote popular articles about science and translated from French into Yiddish.

In my reportage from that time, which was found in the first cache of the Ringelblum archive in 1946, I wrote this about him:

> We just heard in the kitchen that Yitshak Weintraub died. He was a reserved and intriguing person who wrote interesting articles about Yiddish dialects. He titled one of the books he planned to write *How Ordinary Jews Spoke Yiddish.* He helped Shiye Perle prepare his books for publication, and he was planning to analyze Perle's literary style in that work he was hoping to write.
>
> He was deaf and for that reason spoke very quietly. A couple of times I heard him, again in that softly pitched voice, confess his true plight: "My dear friend, I am dying!" he lamented, with the heartbreaking frenzy and constant cough so common among those swollen from malnutrition. He said that after Hershele "went into the box" he would be next in line. I tried to comfort him as much as I could, but my heart told me that he was right. I had become an expert at diagnosing the first signs of that swelling that 99 percent of the time ended in death. His fate was already sealed.
>
> I tried to get the central kitchen administration to allocate a package of dry provisions and some money for Weintraub. The last time I saw him was a couple of weeks

ago, on the front steps of our kitchen. I had gone to the head office to get some authorization slips, and I saw him making a great effort to climb to the first floor, one step at a time, to get a bowl of soup. He paused at each step and rested his hands on his swollen knees.

"My dear friend. I am dying."

All I could do was get him a ticket for a free bowl of soup and, when there was a "bread day," to provide him with an eighth of a loaf of bread. But the bread could no longer help him, and the soup even did him more harm than good. He needed special injections as well as fats, sugar, fruits, green vegetables—a special diet to control his swelling. Weintraub lost his strength even before he stopped coming to the kitchen. I asked Kirman a few times to go see him, and to give him the 50 złotys that were left from my failed attempt to arrange a funeral for Brocksmeier.[1] But 10 złotys, even 100 złotys, could not save somebody whose swelling had gone that far. What's needed are thousands. They found those thousands to save the poet Yisroel Shtern. But when it came to saving the less-well-known Yitshak Weintraub, those thousands were not there.

That's what I wrote then. When I read these words now I get very depressed. We felt so happy when we saved Yisroel Shtern from dying of hunger. May God only spare us that kind of joy! We put so much effort into saving him from starving to death, only so he could suffer a much more painful death in the Treblinka gas chambers.[2]

>——<

Weintraub's literary legacy consisted of unknown studies of Yiddish dialects and unpublished translations from French literature. These works were compiled with great care and were written on the Yiddish typewriter that was also a part of his legacy. Despite his terrible poverty he could not, it seemed, bring himself to sell it. I remember how angry Yosef Kirman became with him when he refused to sacrifice the typewriter to help save his own life. The typewriter ended up with

1 The Great Synagogue of Warsaw on Tłomackie Street, destroyed by the Germans in May 1943, was the largest in the world when it was completed in 1878. During the war the adjacent building at Tłomackie 5, which had housed the Institute for Judaic Studies, became home to the Jewish Social Welfare Association, or Aleynhilf. Today the same building houses Warsaw's Jewish Historical Institute.

2 Girls in a tailoring workshop in an orphanage directed by educator Janusz Korczak on Krochmalna Street. Photographed in April 1940, after the occupation of Warsaw but before the creation of the ghetto.

3 A watchmaker's workshop near the entrance gate to the ghetto at Nalewki Street. Many Jews hoped that employment in ghetto workshops would save them from deportation.

4 A children's soup kitchen at 16 Świętojerska Street. The sign in the background reads, "Have you washed your hands before eating?"

5 Emanuel Ringelblum, a historian and social activist who created the secret Oyneg Shabes archive, was determined that the Jews of Warsaw would write their own history, even from beyond the grave.

6 Shmuel Winter, a grain merchant and patron of Yiddish culture before the war, was a sympathetic member of the Judenrat who worked with Emanuel Ringelblum and helped save Rokhl Auerbach's life in the fall of 1942.

7 In the ghetto, Basya Temkin-Berman dedicated herself to creating libraries for children. After escaping to the Aryan side in September 1942 she became a leader of the Council to Aid Jews, or Żegota. Like Auerbach, she survived by assuming a false Polish identity.

8 Before the war Jan Żabiński had been the director of the Warsaw zoo. During the German occupation he and his wife Antonina used the zoo grounds to save hundreds of Jews in hiding, including Auerbach. Żabiński was also a leader of the Polish underground and fought in the Warsaw Uprising of 1944.

9 Menakhem Linder was a young statistician who worked for the Aleynhilf. He was also the lead organizer of the Yiddish Culture Organization, or IKOR. He was murdered along with other cultural figures and members of the underground ghetto press on the night of April 17–18, 1942.

10 Before the war Mordecai Mazo had been the director of the acclaimed Vilna Troupe. In the ghetto he served as chief lecturer for the IKOR. According to Emanuel Ringelblum, he died during the Warsaw Ghetto Uprising.

11 Miriam Orleska was a friend of Auerbach's and an actress in the Vilna Troupe who had played the lead role in S. An-sky's The Dybbuk. In the ghetto she worked for the Aleynhilf in addition to acting. She was murdered at Treblinka in September 1942.

12 In addition to being a leader of the Association for Jewish Writers and Journalists, Menakhem Kipnis was a singer, photographer, music critic, and pioneering ethnographer of Jewish folk music. According to Auerbach, he died of a heart attack in the fall of 1941.

13 Shmuel Lehman, center, was a pioneer of Jewish ethnographic research, which he continued to conduct in the ghetto. Despite the efforts of Emanuel Ringelblum and others, much of his work was lost.

14 Both a modernist poet and a traditionally observant Jew, Yisroel Shtern was something of an oddity in the Yiddish literary world. According to Auerbach he composed some of his most powerful work shortly before his death in 1942.

15 Abraham Ostrzega was a sculptor renowned for his gravestones and other monuments, including the famed Ohel Peretz in the Warsaw Jewish cemetery. In 1942 his studio at Mylna 9 became the site of a short-lived grindstone workshop for Jewish artists.

16 Before the war, David Eisenstadt had been the choir director of the Great Synagogue of Warsaw on Tłomackie Street. He was also an accomplished composer whose works were lost in the destruction of the Warsaw Ghetto.

17 Eisenstadt's daughter, Marysia, was a popular singer known as the "nightingale of the ghetto." She was shot to death in the Umschlagplatz in August 1942.

18 An opera singer performs on the streets of the Warsaw Ghetto. Despite the crushing conditions of ghetto life artistic productions flourished, partly as a way to raise money for social welfare causes.

19 This self-portrait by artist Gela Sekstajn was included with other of her works in the Ringelblum archive. The exact circumstances of Sekstajn's death are unknown.

14. Courtesy of the Congress for Jewish Culture, New York 15. & 17. Ghetto Fighters' House Museum, Israel / Photo Archive 16. From JewishGen, Inc. 18. United States Holocaust Memorial Museum, courtesy of Leopold Page Photographic Collection
19. From the collections of the Emanuel Ringelblum Jewish Historical Institute

20 *Guitar Player,* a prewar oil painting by Roman Kramsztyk, who had lived in Paris before the war. Kramsztyk died of a gunshot wound in August 1942, on the same day that many of his colleagues were deported to Treblinka.

21 *Still Life with Vegetables,* by Feliks Frydman. As Auerbach relates, Frydman was in the hospital with tuberculosis during the summer of 1942 and was spared deportation to Treblinka by a nurse who gave him a fatal dose of morphine.

22 *In the Countryside,* by Roman Rozental. According to Auerbach it was Rozental who succeeded in organizing the artists' grindstone workshop at Mylna 9, falsely believing it would save its workers from deportation.

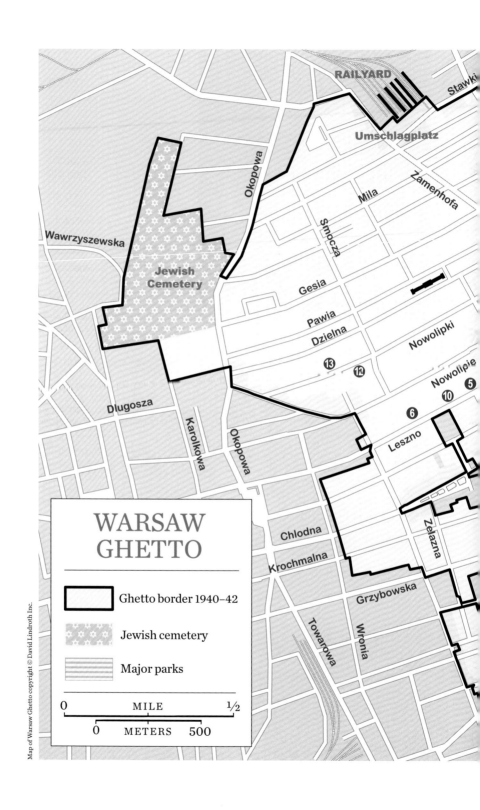

RAILYARD

Stawki

Umschlagplatz

Okopowa

Zamenhofa

Mila

Smocza

Jewish
Cemetery

Gesia

Pawia

Dzielna

Nowolipki

⑬

⑫

Nowolipie

⑩ ❺

❻

Leszno

Wawrzyszewska

Dlugosza

Karolkowa

Okopowa

Chlodna

Krochmalna

Zelazna

Grzybowska

Towarowa

Wronia

WARSAW
GHETTO

Ghetto border 1940–42

Jewish cemetery

Major parks

| 0 | MILE | ½ |

| 0 | METERS | 500 |

Map of Warsaw Ghetto copyright © David Lindroth Inc.

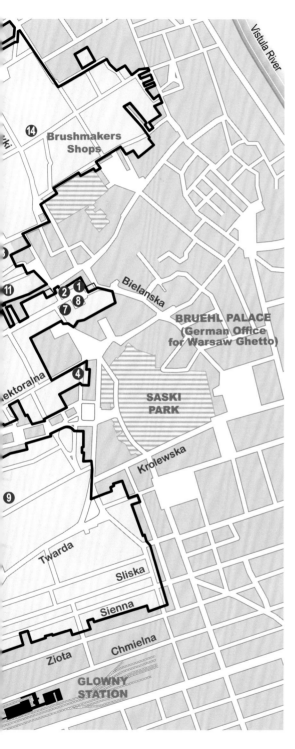

❶ Tlomackie 13
Longtime home of the Association of Jewish Writers and Journalists

❷ Przejazd 1
Auerbach's apartment at the outbreak of the war

❸ Nowolipki 7
Print shop of Nasz Przegląd, the Polish-Jewish newspaper where Auerbach was working at the outbreak of the war

❹ Elektoralna 1
Cecilia Slepak's apartment and salon in the fall and winter of 1939–40

❺ Leszno 40
The soup kitchen that Auerbach directed from 1939–1942

❻ Leszno 66
Home of the Feldshuh family, Auerbach's cousins with whom she lived from 1940–42

❼ Leszno 13
Central administration offices for ghetto soup kitchens

❽ Tlomackie 5
Headquarters of the Jewish Social Welfare Association, or Aleynhilf, and former home of the Judaic Institute

❾ Grzybowska 26
Offices of the Judenrat

❿ Leszno 56
Apartment, and briefly library, of Leyb Shur and Borukh Makhlis

⓫ Mylna 9
Prewar studio of sculptor Abraham Ostrzega and artists' grindstone workshop during the Great Deportation

⓬ Nowolipki 59
Hallmann woodworking shop and a refuge for Oyneg Shabes members during the Great Deportation

⓭ Nowolipki 68
Children's soup kitchen, Borochov school, and site where the first cache of the Ringelblum archive was discovered

⓮ Franciszkanska 30
Artificial honey factory where Auerbach worked after the Great Deportation

23 The first cache of the Ringelblum archive was excavated from the ruins of the ghetto on September 18, 1946. The second cache was discovered accidentally by construction workers in December 1950.

24 The Ringelblum archive was preserved in tin boxes and milk cans. The third cache of the archive has never been found.

23–24. Yad Vashem Photo Archive, Jerusalem

his landlords. They insisted that Weintraub owed them rent money. They also wanted to hold on to the manuscripts. We were forced to pressure them and even give them some money.

Before the war that typewriter was Weintraub's livelihood. He was not only Shiye Perle's typist but also Froym Kaganovsky's. Both Perle and the other writers who entrusted Weintraub with their manuscripts heeded most of his stylistic and syntactical suggestions and took his comments seriously. So I understood quite well why it was so hard for Weintraub to give up his typewriter.

People were often saying that somebody had to protect Weintraub's manuscripts. I reminded Kirman about that a few times, but nothing came of it. We did not know then that many such unpublished manuscripts would disappear forever along with their authors.

And little did we suspect that colleagues more famous than Weintraub in the pantheon of Yiddish literature would come to envy him his quiet death. He died of hunger, but in his own bed.

Part 6: The IKOR Group

28. THE ORGANIZER

Certain states of mind might make little sense to anyone who did not live through the German occupation and endure years in a closed ghetto. One has to drill down and try to grasp the abnormal psychological realities we faced as we lived under the jackboot, suffered living conditions that only became worse, and confronted draconian anti-Jewish edicts and ever-escalating dangers. How did we do this and still manage to work and to maintain a semblance of health, despite the meager rations? In a place where everyone was engulfed in disaster, how did we preserve that last little bit of psychological equilibrium?

When I say "we" I am referring to those of us who were physically weakened but not yet totally crushed, the people who were somehow hanging on to life and thereby taxing the patience of the German "administrators."

Locked behind the walls of a huge prison, we were surrounded by yet another wall, a circle within a circle. This was the wall of hatred and monstrous lies that were meant to convince the Aryan population that we deserved our fate: total annihilation.

As Heine once wrote, albeit in very different circumstances:

> Yet I bore it, and am bearing—
> Only do not ask me how . . .

>———<

How can one explain the extraordinary intensity of cultural and civic life in the ghetto? The explanation is simple: every positive initiative served to protect life, to provide strength and the will to live. To that end the fight against despair was just as important as the battle against hunger. In fact, both struggles were closely intertwined. Anyway, my purpose here is more to describe these activities than to explain them.

I would like to mention the topic of cultural performances. People who never lived in the ghetto might well ask: Who needed them? Who had the patience to take part in them or to attend them when we all faced such misery, troubles, and dangers?

But there's no denying it. They happened! Even at the very end, even in the face of death.

That's How It Was. Jonas Turkow chose this title for his memoir of the Warsaw Ghetto, which for the most part gave a good and accurate description of theatrical and musical activities, as well as of other public performances. Turkow had been an actor and a theater director before and during the war. In the ghetto he directed the cultural performance department of the Aleynhilf.

I don't intend to repeat what Turkow said so many years ago, nor do I pretend to have his expertise. But I also touched on this subject in the winter of 1943–44, in the notes about the ghetto that I secretly wrote on the Aryan side. I relate these observations based on personal experience and the contacts I made in my own social circle.

>—<

Fate decreed that after all the wandering and false starts, after all the fleeing and returning, a very large number of actors, singers, and musicians ended up in the Warsaw Ghetto. In addition to the artists who had always performed for Jewish audiences there were a great many artists of Jewish descent who had performed for the Polish-speaking public and found themselves forced into the ghetto. All of these performers had to earn money to survive. This is one factor to keep in mind.

Another factor was the formidable network of people and organizations trying to raise supplementary funds for the official relief institutions and to allay the terrible misery of the masses of refugees and destitute Jews in Warsaw. This network included the Aleynhilf, various patrons and sponsors, private ad-hoc groups, house committees, and district committees. The number of potential contributors was not very great. One way to reach them was to return to a tried-and-true idea used so often in the past: raise money through artistic productions. This explains the bizarre fact that there were so many performances and that they indeed flourished in the ghetto.

Reb Mendele, the "grandfather of Yiddish literature," once hit upon a solution to the problem of Jewish poverty: divide the shtetl of Kabtsansk (Beggarville) into two parts.[1] During the first half of the week the householders in the first section would collect alms for Jews in the other half, and in the second part of the week the roles would be reversed.

This pretty much describes how we hoped to raise money. But as more and more performances took place, we realized something else. It turned out that people bought tickets because they wanted to relax, to forget for a while the terrible reality that surrounded us, to fight back against the mental assault that was slowly eating us alive, whether we knew it or not.

Thus, during that period of not quite two years between November 1940 and July 1942, artistic activities of all kinds flourished on a colossal scale. New talents appeared in music, theater, and recitation. One could even say that audiences received them with more enthusiasm than in normal times.

In addition, that traditional Jewish passion for reading, self-education, and the study of Jewish literature and culture became stronger than ever. This was especially true for those who had been distant from Jewish life before the war and who had been deeply assimilated.

One must, however, make a distinction between two aspects of this upsurge in cultural life. Performances staged as popular entertainment might pay for themselves. More nuanced programs that were on a higher cultural level had to be organized in a different way.

The group that encouraged, and to a large degree organized, all of this activity was the IKOR—the Yiddish Culture Organization—which came into being after the establishment of the ghetto. The IKOR was a semi-clandestine unofficial branch of the Aleynhilf, which was recognized by the German occupation authorities. It emerged from the same circles that constituted the Aleynhilf, which gave it financial support and a social base. But the IKOR also pursued its own agenda and relied on its own circle of activists.

The heart and soul of the IKOR, its devoted promoter, was Mena-khem Linder.

>——<

I knew Linder before the war. We both came from the same region, and although I was older and left Galicia before he did, I heard things that made me want to get to know him better. I noticed that we shared a common intellectual trajectory and had similar views on issues of Jewish culture, language, and Zionism. The first article that I ever published, in the Lemberg journal *Nayer morgn*, was entitled "The Zionist-Yiddishist Misunderstanding." And I heard that he too, while he was a student at the University of Lemberg, had begun to distance himself from the Zionist student milieu because of its insistence on "Hebrew or Polish," a convenient fig leaf for de facto assimilationism and denial of the importance of Yiddish in maintaining the survival of the nation.

Menakhem Linder grew up in the Hashomer Hatzair youth movement. He had a brother in the Land of Israel who was an engineer and a sister who was one of the founders of Kibbutz Mishmar HaEmek. To this day his widowed sister-in-law, whom I contacted for biographical details, calls him "Munie." She also came from Sniatyn and enjoyed a long, productive career in Israel as a teacher. There is no doubt that Munie would have migrated to Palestine along with his siblings except that he became enthralled with Yiddishism and began to go in a different direction.

I learned more details about Linder's life from the warmhearted eulogy that Ringelblum wrote about him on the Aryan side and that was included in the second volume of Ringelblum's published wartime works.[2] In 1936 Linder took part in a competition sponsored by the central bureau of the Joint Distribution Committee for the best essay about a Jewish community in Poland. He was awarded first prize for his historical-demographic study of our own familiar East Galician town Sniatyn. After he finished his studies in economics and his examinations for a master's degree at Lemberg University, Linder went to Vilna, where the leaders of the YIVO welcomed him with open arms.[3] They regarded him as a rising star in modern Yiddish scholarship, encouraged his work, published his articles in the YIVO journals, and took him in as one of their own. Incredibly dynamic, talented, and hardworking, Linder felt totally at home in Vilna. This was certainly the happiest time of his life. Just as he fell in love with the city, he also fell in love with a Vilna girl. He even began to speak Yiddish with a Vilna accent. A year or two before the war Linder became secretary of the YIVO's Warsaw branch, moved to the capital, and took on new responsibilities. He became co-editor of the journal *Yidishe ekonomik*[4] as well as the secretary of the Commission to Study the History of Polish Jewry.[5]

Noah Prylucki was the director of the Warsaw branch of the YIVO. Jakob Lestschinsky, who soon made Linder the sole editor of *Yidishe ekonomik*, served on the board.

I was also connected to the Warsaw branch of the YIVO and was often asked to come to meetings, which mostly took place in Prylucki's apartment.[6]

The apartment was an attractive salon with an expensive Persian rug and a life-sized portrait of Prylucki's wife, the writer Paulina Prylucki. It was there, in the presence of those two important Jewish scholars, that I got to know Linder. Neither Linder nor I could have guessed how different the circumstances would be when we renewed our acquaintance a few years later.

>——<

When the occupation began, Linder showed himself to be one of the most talented and dedicated leaders of the new, expanded relief organization that worked under the auspices of the Joint and that, over time, gave cover to an array of political, cultural, and civic activities, both legal and illegal, carried on by the Jewish community.

Linder organized an evidence department inside the Aleynhilf that compiled a card file of important information on the work of the soup kitchens and other organizations. It also provided a base for an ambitious, semi-clandestine statistical project. Under the cover of the Aleynhilf, Linder gathered important data about the ghetto population including health, nutrition, and employment. Above all it collected information about mortality caused by German policies that aimed to impoverish, starve, and systematically destroy the Jewish masses, albeit, for the time being, through "administrative" measures.

The semi-clandestine IKOR organized lecture series on Jewish culture and history. These lectures, as well as artistic performances— small-scale get-togethers that sometimes featured a buffet, games, and even dancing—usually took place in the large, overcrowded War- saw tenement buildings, with their sprawling inner courtyards and annexes. When curfew began the outer gates were locked. All of these buildings contained some large space—an apartment, office, or busi- ness—where dozens of people could gather, bring plates of food, and buy tickets. Thanks to Linder, many of those evenings, in addition to raising money for the poor, became opportunities to teach Jews more about their literature and culture.

>—<

After the *Einsatzstab Reichsleiter Rosenberg*, the German body tasked with looting books and cultural objects, plundered the collec- tion of the Judaica library at Tlomackie 5 in the first months of the occupation, the IKOR used its main auditorium to organize a kind of popular university. Its lectures attracted growing audiences, mainly members of former worker and youth organizations. Every Saturday and Sunday, and often on weekdays, there were recitals, academic evenings, and concerts. Certain programs attracted so many specta- tors that the IKOR had to stage many repeat performances.

The IKOR also commemorated important milestones in Yiddish literary history, which gave it the chance to reach and educate young people cut off from normal schooling. It paid special attention to the assimilated intelligentsia in the ghetto who knew nothing about modern Yiddish literature before the war. Now, for the first time, they wanted to learn.

One could say that nowhere else in the entire world was the hun- dredth anniversary of the birth of Mendele Moykher Sforim cele- brated with such reverence as in the Warsaw Ghetto—albeit a couple of years late. Perhaps no other Yiddish literary milestone aroused such excitement, ever.

There were also yahrzeit programs dedicated to the works of I. L. Peretz and Sholem Aleichem, which included lectures and recitals; a presentation about Avrom Reyzen; and talks, readings, and surveys all focused on contemporary Yiddish poetry and prose. The speakers and lecturers who had been members of prewar political parties would liven up their talks with political allusions that would elicit waves of stormy applause from the audience of young people. It often happened that one sat there totally incredulous. You could easily imagine that you were at a political rally. People seemed to forget that they were in a ghetto, trapped between the jaws of a ferocious beast.

Linder was intoxicated by the incredible success of all this cultural activity in Yiddish. He proposed that the Aleynhilf conduct all of its internal business in Yiddish, including internal correspondence and administrative forms. He certainly implemented this in his own department. I remember an incident when Linder composed a blank complaint form to be used by the soup kitchens to combat the problem of "double eaters." He did not get very far. The clerks who worked in these departments—at least the typists—rarely had mastered Yiddish or its orthography. Some couldn't even read the Yiddish alphabet. Getting the Judenrat offices to use Yiddish was more of a pipe dream, though Ringelblum recalled that Linder tried to do this and won the support of Judenrat members Shmuel Winter and Yosef Yashunsky.

Linder loved to fantasize. That's what Ringelblum wrote about him. He dreamed of an autonomous, Yiddish-speaking Jewish life in the Diaspora. He believed that the curse of the ghetto had a silver lining: after the war the entire Jewish intelligentsia would adopt the living language and culture of its people; that a new era of Jewish creativity would emerge, its path blazed by Jewish suffering and pain; that very soon, at any moment, the dreams and ideals embedded in the struggle for Yiddish culture would emerge triumphant.

>—<

In the winter of 1941–42 a discussion group began under the auspices of the IKOR that included a diverse group of participants. The discussions took place in various soup kitchens. I remember that one evening the well-known lawyer Gustaw Wielikowski dazzled his audience with a lecture in a polished, modern Yiddish.

Zionists and assimilationists, Hebraists and Yiddishists, even Polish speakers who had been totally alienated from Jewish culture showed up. They listened with rapt interest, took part in the discussions, and offered their own observations about Jewish philosophy and history, which had been a closed book for so many of them before the war. Ringelblum lectured on "The Issue of Kiddush Hashem in the Past and Today."[7] The first evening devoted to this topic turned out to be the last. The discussions ended and the real kiddush Hashem began.

>——<

Its first victim was Menakhem Linder.[8] Along with several other activists, Linder received a warning that something was brewing. (Perhaps he was tipped off by the same informants who drew up a list of organizers and participants in the Jewish underground press.) For a few nights Linder did not sleep in his own apartment at Leszno 52. But on that Friday night he was at home. The Gestapo agents politely "requested" that he take a toothbrush and a towel and follow them. They reassured his wife and then drove him to the small square at the junction of Mylna, Nowolipie, and Karmelicka Streets, where they shot him in front of the locked gates of the Evangelical hospital. People who lived in nearby buildings looked on through gaps in their curtains. They saw that he suffered for a long time before he finally died.

For a long while it had seemed that the Germans were totally uninterested in the political and cultural life of the Warsaw Ghetto. Over time the number of underground newspapers and proclamations put out by different groups greatly increased. The aim of that first massacre was to suppress them. Alongside people connected with the underground press, some printers and bakers were among the fifty-two victims whom the Germans shot that night.

Everyone understood why bakers were on the list. During the war and the ghetto period bakeries were the most important productive enterprises. Bakers became the financial elite of the ghetto and a major source of support for the underground press. Before the war Bleyman's bakery was well known for its delicious bread and Passover matzos. That night Bleyman and his wife were among the fifty-two who were murdered.

Menakhem Linder, who was a beloved mentor of young people, had fed the underground press a great deal of information. In his case, the Gestapo knew exactly what it was doing.

The Mousetrap at Mylna 9

The Germans winnowed and decimated the Jews without letup.

The days when the Germans honored the green-colored identification cards were long gone. When the Great Deportation began, the Aleynhilf had liberally distributed these cards to real and fictitious employees. The less numerous gray cards, sent from Krakow and adorned with a swastika-and-eagle stamp, were already null and void. Along with the bulky identification cards that the Judenrat issued in large numbers, these documents protected for a short while the professional intelligentsia as well as lesser-known writers, artists, and former political and community activists.

As the weeks went by, any document issued by a Jewish institution became increasingly problematic. In the best case it was only the Jewish police who respected them. The cards issued by German-owned firms offered more protection, but as time went on those documents also declined in value. Jews bought them with their last bits of cash and property, with their remaining gold coins and foreign money. They offered all they had left. But when those pieces of paper became worthless, their owners paid with their lives.

"Combing." That's the word the Germans liked to use.

In the early days any German work document protected not only the worker but also his close family. In some cases, "family" included parents and younger siblings. But with each passing week and day there were fewer protected categories. The comb's teeth became tighter and sharper. And so the Jews finally realized that the German firms had become an efficient trap to lure them to their deaths.

>——<

It began with the small fry, the fly-by-night shops put up by German vultures who flew in from everywhere to alight on the field of slaughter and stuff themselves with wealth wrested from the dead and dying.

Scam. Trick. Fake. "AKL."[1] That's how the doleful ghetto jokesters parsed the initials of Aszmian Karol Leszczynski, a textile and weaving firm. During the third week of the Great Deportation it was liquidated, and all of its "protected Jews" were sent to the Umschlagplatz and then to Treblinka.

A week later the Jews employed in the large network of shops established by another one-day wonder—Karl-Heinz Müller—met the same fate.

These German entrepreneurs did not suffer too many pangs of regret. It was only yesterday that they had welcomed with warm smiles the Jews who organized the shops for them. They magnanimously allowed them to bring in the machines, tools, and raw materials that the Jews had somehow managed to protect from many rounds of German looting. When the shops closed, these German entrepreneurs were nowhere to be seen. They simply vanished, discreetly, without too much fuss. Of course, they did not forget to pocket the Jewish wealth and transfer the machines and materials somewhere else, where they could start the same criminal game all over again. Could anybody be surprised that they didn't tip off their Jewish associates about the looming liquidation?

This is what happened to the twenty or so Jewish artists and sculptors of the Warsaw Ghetto who moved with their families to the Karl-Heinz Müller firm in order to sharpen and polish German bayonets with grindstones.

>——<

The shop was located at Mylna 9 in the former studio of the sculptor Abraham Ostrzega.

There were many other shops on that street, all engaged in light industrial production for the German war effort. They employed hundreds of Jews, including many with an art or theater background, who saw those shops as their life ticket. Next door to the artists' shop was a shop with theater people who worked at such "vital military tasks" as the production of shaving kits to trim soldiers' beards and garters to hold up their socks. The noted actor Jonas Turkow became especially adept at organizing this work. His postwar memoirs depict the anguish and monstrous subplots of the ongoing horror show that was being simultaneously staged in the adjoining shops of the Karl-Heinz empire. His memoirs contain a lot of important information including many names and descriptions that I do not need to repeat here.

What I remember most vividly and know best is what happened in the artists' shop. As far as I know for sure, the artists who worked in the shop at Mylna 9 included Abraham Ostrzega, Władysław Wajntraub, Izrael Tykocinski, Józef Sliwniak, Hersz Rabinowicz, Hersz Cyna, Simcha Trachter, Roman Rozental, Max Eliovich, and others. They were about twenty in all, and they were all assigned to various buildings on Mylna Street together with their wives and children.

The big piles of marble and granite located in Ostrzega's workspace provided the raw material. These precious blocks had been meant to become gravestones, paying homage to lives lived in dignity and comfort. Now Jewish artists hoped that marble and granite would help them survive.

The shop at Mylna 9 was the last chapter in the history of the Jewish Sculptors Union in Warsaw.

>———<

Before the Great Deportation began, the artists had organized a garden café, which they called the "Artists' Garden." It was located on the site of Ostrzega's former workshop at Mylna 9 and was open throughout the summer of 1941 and in the early days of the summer of 1942. It was a relatively large space, surrounded by a fence. While there weren't many trees, one could look at the planted potatoes, beets, carrots, tomatoes, onions, and parsley. In one corner of the garden, not far from the shop where the orchestra set up its bandstand, there were a few flowers.

This garden became an important source of income for Jewish sculptors. They earned money by renting out fresh air. Who were the customers? Just like all other Jews they had to put up with the stifling and overcrowded ghetto. But unlike the others, they had a little money.

>———<

In the garden a first-class orchestra gave afternoon concerts and a stand-up actor entertained the guests, some of whom had their own reserved tables. People played cards and met friends. The artists even found a large piece of colored linen with a floral pattern, which they used to make two large garden umbrellas. The actress Klara Segalowicz would often sit under one of them and play bridge with her friends. She was decked out just as if she were in a prewar spa with an elegant, wide straw hat perched on hair that had turned gray since the start of the war. She radiated a mood of clever humor and optimism. One could go to her table and hear the latest secrets, news gathered from illegal radios—not to mention fresh jokes about Hitler.

This was when the Germans were running their "V for Victory" campaign. Big signs festooned the façades of the train stations: "Germany is winning on all fronts." Polish boys, in acts of what was called "small sabotage," would change the letters on such signs to read "Germany has collapsed on all fronts."[2]

These details of how Polish kids sabotaged the placards made their way into the ghetto through the same channels as the daily shipments of smuggled food. To the merriment of the entire table, Segalowicz did the Poles one better with her own witty puns on the German slogans.

The bitter truth, however, was that Germany was powerful everywhere and even more so in the lands it occupied. But the Jews in the Warsaw Ghetto were trying to put up a good front. They hadn't yet thrown in the towel.

In the early afternoons there were women on chairs who shut their eyes, faced the sun, and tanned themselves. There were strollers with sleeping infants parked between the carrots and parsley while older children ran around the scraggly pair of trees and played tag. Girls with colorful kerchiefs on their heads and boys holding balls enjoyed a privilege denied to most children in the ghetto: they could look at real plants. Your heart broke when you watched those kids hop like little sparrows around the narrow lanes of the garden. In the ghettos we had already heard the vague, dark rumors about what was happening to children under the age of ten in Lodz and Pabianice. There was already news of roundups and special transports.

Now and then special benefit performances would take place in the garden. During such open-air concerts the artists would walk around the garden radiating the pride and authority of true proprietors. You could see how happy the older children were then, as they imagined what their future would be like after the nightmare was over. The concerts seemed to give the artists a feeling of holiday cheer, which made them even more friendly and warmhearted than usual. Jews who had been part of the literary community and who couldn't afford tickets got discounts. Some even got in for free, just like the families of the artists themselves.

>——<

Even though the Karl-Heinz Müller firm specialized in producing furniture and other wood products, it agreed to sponsor the rather unconventional grindstone project of those gullible Jewish sculptors. The artists naively believed that all those blocks of granite and marble and all those bags of stone polish would somehow protect them from death. And Karl-Heinz Müller? What did he care? In this case, as in everything else, it was no skin off his back.

This is not to say that it was easy to organize that special shop for the sculptors. They had to defy the dangers of the street blockades and roundups and sound out hundreds of contacts in the hope of finding someone with "pull." They banged on the doors of the labor department, of the Jewish police, of machers connected to the Judenrat. And what do you know! They pulled it off without having to fork over bribes or hand over big wads of cash. They were able to establish a refuge in the storm: their own shop!

The project demanded an amazing degree of initiative and ingenuity. Nowhere else on earth did Jews show so much resourcefulness as they did that summer in the Warsaw Ghetto. The chief initiator of the grindstone shop was the artist Władysław Wajntraub, while the artist Roman Rozental did most of the running around. The story of that shop on Mylna, its rise and fatal fall, was all a result of their initiative and energy. It turned out to be a fatal mistake to concentrate so many talented individuals in one place. I think that Rozental had a brother living on the Aryan side, a doctor who was married to a Polish woman. Other artists had colleagues and friends on the other side of the wall. Many of them might have found a place to hide and even to survive. If only they hadn't been so eager to organize that shop! Those shops created their own mania and psychosis.

>——<

I would often run into Roman Rozental in the ghetto. Like other artists whom I knew, he would drop in now and then when he happened to pass by the kitchen at Leszno 40. Surrounded by the hubbub of so many hungry people, we would exchange a few words. Before he left I'd hand him a bowl of hot grits from the big pot. In those days that was an offer nobody would refuse.

Sometime in the winter of 1942, after Rozental got sick, he was able to take daily meals in our kitchen, which had been reorganized in January 1942 as a kitchen for convalescents. Many other colleagues from the literary and artistic community also ate there; some were genuine convalescents, others not. Yes, I plead guilty: this was yet another rule of the soup kitchen administration that I broke.

Then Rozental appeared in our kitchen again. It was during the Great Deportation. Having learned that we were still preparing meals, he showed up every day with a pot to take soup home to his wife and mother-in-law. In the meantime, the Walther Toebbens firm had taken over Leszno 40. Our public kitchen became a kitchen for the Toebbens shop. The new boss did me a big favor by letting me stay there at all. I no longer had any say in running the place. But I could still wangle some food or a bowl of soup for a friend. So every day, when the blockades were over and I could go out, I would run into Rozental with his pot. That's how I learned what was happening with their grindstone shop.

Rozental was tall, and his drooping shoulders conveyed an expression of sadness. He was never known for his high spirits. But he was bursting with creative energy, which had found an outlet before the war in painting stage sets for literary reviews and in composing melodies for the witty cabaret numbers put on by the Azazel and the Ararat.

The Rozental that I saw on the day in 1942 when he signed the papers giving Karl-Heinz Müller ownership over the shop was like a man transformed. Nobody had ever seen him so excited. He was covered in sweat, as agitated as a racing hound straining to burst from the starting gate. His entire expression radiated joy and hope. He had a new surge of vitality and a determination to stay alive. He was full of enthusiasm and pathos as he boasted how he and his colleagues from the artists' garden had managed to overcome many obstacles and secure a legal workplace not only for themselves but also for their wives and children.

He was so kindhearted and generous that he was even willing to do his friends a favor. Rozental asked me if I was interested in going to work there. He offered to accept any of his friends from the literary community free of charge. In fact, he registered Y. Y. Propus, Brokha Einhorn, and the director Max Wiskind.

The shop began to operate. Rozental would now come to Leszno 40 dressed in a studio smock. Like everyone else he appeared in the street only in work clothes.

He told me that they would soon open a shop kitchen at Mylna 9 that would receive regular food allotments from the provisioning bureau. All the artists in the shop had already received work certificates from the labor department. Any day now they would get their papers stamped by the Sicherheitsdienst (SD), and then they would be able to freely walk the streets.

By that time ordinary Jews were no longer as naïve as the artists.

It happened in the last week of August 1942. Rozental came for his soup as usual and promised to come the next day with a present for the kitchen: a grindstone to sharpen knives. We never got that grindstone. The same day—Turkow wrote that it was August 25—there were empty wagons on the train that stood at the Umschlagplatz. The liquidation of the Karl-Heinz Müller shops was already decided.

When they came for the artists, they all lined up in the street. Not one of them tried to hide or run away. No one grabbed the knapsacks they had prepared just in case, nor did anyone think to take along any extra clothing. Dressed in their smocks and aprons, they marched out. They were not worried. After all, they had that work card from Karl-Heinz Müller.

What I know about the last hours of the artists at the Umschlagplatz comes from the testimony of an eyewitness, a Jewish policeman who survived the war. A painter himself, his beat had included the shop at Mylna 9. This time he tried to warn them about the blockade but came too late.

As the policeman, "P.," recalled (his memoirs are in the Jewish Historical Institute in Warsaw), the artists waited on the corner of Karmelicka and Nowolipie streets.[3]

They did not seem particularly frightened. Each of them

held his work card in his hand. That very morning at 8 a.m. the workers in Müller's shops received those SD stamps. But at 6 p.m. that evening the order came to liquidate those shops. The artists were in a group of a couple thousand workers who were escorted by Ukrainians and a few Germans. I rode after them on a bicycle hoping that I might be able to save a few people. But this time the Germans did not lead them through the main entrance of the Umschlagplatz but herded them through a side gate that led directly to the cattle cars. I moved with them as they approached the train. Until the very last minute they all believed that the Germans would order a selection and let them go. It was only when they lined them up in groups of five facing the tracks that they realized how they had been deceived. Wajntraub, who thought up the idea of the shop, kept repeating: "Colleagues! Forgive me! It's my fault!"

After they entered the cattle cars bareheaded and dressed in their soiled work clothes, they screwed up their eyes and took a long look around, as if they wanted to take in one last image of Warsaw. Maybe I'm mistaken, but to me they looked completely different from everybody else there.

"Save our wives. They're still in the garden." Those were their last words. They each gave me a farewell smile as they stared at my face, hoping in some way to learn something about their fate.

>——<

That same day the policeman P. witnessed the death of the artist Roman Kramsztyk. Kramsztyk was not connected to the artists' shop on Mylna 9. But as fate would have it, he died the same day as the other artists.

As P. remembers it:

Like most doors in ghetto apartments, the locks had been knocked out. I found nobody in Kramsztyk's room or in the entire apartment. The building seemed totally abandoned. I called out many times before I came upon a living soul. A man's head peered out from a basement window. He asked me to wait. It was the janitor. "You want to see Kramsztyk? Then come with me." He took me along a meandering route into a long, narrow tunnel, which led to the cellar. I had to slide on my stomach through a hole in the wall until I entered a large subterranean room with a few dozen people. Then I noticed Kramsztyk. He was lying on a cot in the corner.

His face was terribly pale, almost white. When he saw me he tried to summon up one of his beautiful, legendary smiles. "I asked someone to bring you to see me," he said. "They killed me today. Yes, I'm not dead yet, but I will be soon."

I discovered that in the morning Kramsztyk had left the hideout to retrieve some watercolors from his apartment. But at about 10 a.m. he was trapped in the daily roundup. There was nowhere to hide, and a random bullet pierced his lungs. Covered with blood, he collapsed unconscious, and the Germans left him for dead in the courtyard. A few hours later, when the screams and shootings died down, people left the hiding places near the courtyard and dragged him into the cellar. A doctor who was there gave him several injections, but offered no hope. Kramsztyk had a high fever. Now and then he regained full consciousness, but then lapsed back into delirium. I did not have the courage to leave. It was as if his burning stare chained me to the spot. He held my hand in a convulsive grip.

"Tell the artists to keep drawing. Tell them goodbye for me!"

I had to give him a solemn oath that I would implore our artists to draw scenes of the ghetto when the war was over.

"Tell them to stop drawing portraits, études, and still-lifes. The world must find out about these crimes. Tell them that Kramsztyk begged them to draw ghetto themes. They should make sure to hide their work so that the world will understand the Germans' bestiality."

He was slipping away. Blood began to spurt from his mouth. He was suffering terribly but kept on whispering to me. He then pressed some Sangwin crayons into my hand.

"Give them this. These are good crayons, originals from Le Franc."

But nobody was left to take the crayons or to hear Kramsztyk's dying wish. Kramsztyk would never know this. His friend did not want to take away his one remaining bit of comfort.

>——<

The artists' wives had spent the blockade in a hideout, and for the time being they survived. They emerged from the hideout to a scene of total emptiness. Nobody had the time yet to loot the workshop. The tools were still there.

The artists had been so sure that the work certificates would save them that they took nothing along. Or maybe they already had some idea of what Treblinka meant. The first escapees from there had already arrived in the ghetto. The policeman P. said that in the garden shop they were already talking about it. Maybe the artists sensed where they were going and knew that there was no need to take anything along.

Their wives did not understand this. Rozental's devoted and loving wife, the rather homely pianist Stefania Feltenstein, could not stop fretting that her husband had forgotten to take along a jacket, pajamas, or a sweater. The wives still believed that they were "somewhere," and Mrs. Rozental was convinced until the very end that Roman would return to her from that "somewhere."

A few days later she started showing up at Leszno 40 with that soup pot. One day, as she was waiting along with the Toebbens workers for soup, I passed by. She embraced me, rested her head on my shoulder, and broke out in short sobs. As I caressed her hair I noticed for the first time what lovely and youngish azure-blue eyes she had. Suddenly bereft of the fatherly love and masculine devotion with which Rozental had surrounded her for so many years, she acted like a child. Now and then I would have to hug her close, console her, and whisper words of comfort. She waited for those caresses as if she were an orphan.

After the end of the first phase of the Great Deportation I saw Stefania Feltenstein a couple of times in the company of the wife and daughter of the sculptor Ostrzega. They were all wearing several layers of clothing, just like the women who smuggled merchandise to sell on the Aryan side. With their heads covered in warm kerchiefs and their stocky figures wrapped in men's thick leather belts, they hung around the remaining Jewish institutions and warehouses looking like shepherds and lost sheep whom nobody cared about any longer, wanderers ready to set out on a journey if only they knew where to go.

Yes, they looked like wanderers without a today and even without a yesterday. They were like neutered creatures whose age was difficult to tell. Totally lost, fearful, helpless, they looked for support and dreamed that someone might be able to set them up on the Aryan side. Ostrzega's 13-year-old daughter was talented, and her mother was ready to do anything to save her, even give her away to strangers. But all her attempts to save her child failed.

Their end came later, and it could not have been worse. They sat out the January *aktion* in a hideout of the Aleynhilf at Zamenhof 56. They died in May in the flames of the final liquidation.

>—<

Roman Rozental was a landscape artist with a very subtle sense of color. He was also musically talented. He would compose melodies for Moyshe Kulbak's poems and for other poets. Many of them entered the repertoire of the Yiddish *kleynkunst* theater, in which Rozental played an important role as a cofounder of the Lodz-based Ararat, and as a set and stage designer in its early years. In the spring of 1942 we celebrated the twentieth anniversary of Rozental's artistic career in the public kitchen at Orla 6, which was also a semi-clandestine literary club. There was a musical recital in which his wife played. I remember that we had to exclude Liszt from the repertory because the Germans had just banned Jews from playing the works of German, Italian, and Hungarian composers.

One of Rozental's paintings hung in my room in Reuven Feldshuh's apartment, a picture of a sun-drenched landscape in southern France. On the opposite wall were two watercolors by my Galician friend Mendel Reif. A tin etching by Józef Sliwniak hung in the corridor. These were just a sample of the artistic riches created by Poland's Jewish artists that Feldshuh collected over the years.

The annihilation of the artists was followed by the destruction of their works. Feldshuh's art collection and his rich library went up in the flames of the ghetto uprising. The paintings in private homes, in Jewish institutions, or the ones that artists kept in their own collections met the same fate.

➤—◄

During the war the artists were able, to some degree, to live from their work. The Judenrat and the Aleynhilf made it possible for cultural activists to help artists and writers. For example, the CENTOS proclaimed a competition for the best poster to mark "The Month of the Child." It also sponsored an exhibition in the Aleynhilf headquarters in the Judaic studies institute and awarded prizes for the best works. A talented young female artist created placards for the IKOR, the organization to promote Yiddish culture, which disguised its activities as benefit events for various social welfare institutions. I don't remember her name, but I can still see her young, attractive face. I recall that her first name was Rachel. She was a previously unknown talent, discovered and sponsored by a man named Wallach, who was a cousin of Maxim Litvinov and a higher-up in the Aleynhilf. Adam Czerniaków, the president of the Judenrat, engaged artists to paint works for his office at Grzybowska 26 as well as for his private apartment, the so-called "White House" at Chlodna 20. The artists Trakhter, Fridman, and Puterman painted a large canvas, or perhaps a fresco, entitled "Job." Other institutions, such as the merchants union, which was also active in the ghetto, tried to support the artists by ordering signs, advertisements, and labels. Artists as well as writers received food packages from the Aleynhilf warehouses.

That's how they lived and struggled to get by—as much as it was possible.

➤—◄

Once before the beginning of the Great Deportation I was present when some of the artists were discussing what they should draw. Somebody asserted that they should be painting people who were swollen from hunger, child smugglers, and street peddlers. They should not miss the opportunity to study and depict scenes never witnessed by the artists of any other people. They had the obligation to leave meaningful artistic documents of that extraordinary and horrible time that would convey these new, unplumbed depths of human suffering. I also recall that one of them—I think it was Hersz Rabinowicz—got up and said that he did not agree. Especially now, he argued, artists should draw sunny images full of light, paintings that would allow both the artist and the viewer to escape, if only for a short while, from the terrible reality that surrounded them. Only later, after the horror was safely in the past, should artists take up the theme of ghetto suffering.

Nonetheless, Rabinowicz and the other artists amassed bulging files full of sketches and drawings of ghetto life. Unfortunately, most of them were lost in the liquidation of the ghetto.

There were frequent debates about the mission and purpose of art. One had to look no further than a random street to find abundant models for drawings of hell, scenes that all but implored artists to make a quick sketch and then fix the image on canvas. Expressionistic license, not to mention artistic embellishments or interpretations, were totally unnecessary. If anything the artist might have had to minimize and soften what he saw on the ghetto streets. The feverish, sick reality of the ghetto provided a ready-made palette and seared the senses with a unique urgency.

The artists used to say that this was not just another theme. No, it could be an enormous source of inspiration. But you had to be both a genius and a madman to capture and express what we were seeing and feeling.

"Leave me alone," one artist retorted. "When I look at the desperation all around me, my eyes refuse to see and my hands refuse to move. But I'll settle for this: may the time come when German artists get the opportunity to sketch and draw such scenes from hell in their own country."

The young director Max Wiskind, a pupil of Leon Schiller's, also went with the artists on that transport to Treblinka. I had gotten to know him before the war in connection with the translation of Bruno Frank's play *Twelve Thousand*, which he was going to stage in the Yung-teater. We both agreed that film was the best way to convey what we were seeing in the ghetto; we should be collecting material for a grand and tragic movie of the drowning, singing, trading ghetto.

We were especially interested in the ghetto's "brilliant lunatic," Rubinstein.[4] We had already tagged him as the main character in our version of a Jewish "Till Eulenspiegel."[5] At that point we had no idea that we were seeing only a pale preview of what would happen later. And when that happened, Wiskind perished, along with all the artists.

>—<

Of all the Jewish artists one survived for a while as a sole remnant of the entire group. During the Great Deportation Feliks Frydman was in Otwock and did not join the others in the grindstone workshop. I don't remember exactly how he was able to survive the roundup on the Otwock line, although I heard the story once. His wife was a young woman with a pale complexion. She fought without letup to stay alive. It was thanks to her that he made it through the Great Deportation. In the autumn of 1942 Frydman was sick with an inflammation of the lungs and his tuberculosis reappeared. After his wife was somehow able to find a place for herself in Schultz's shop on Nowolipie street, she sent Frydman into the new, post-deportation rump ghetto, where conditions were a little easier and freer and where one could live among friends.

It was in that ghetto, sometime between September 1942 and the second *aktion* in January 1943, that I ran into Frydman in the waiting room of the provisioning department at Franciszkanska 30, which was run by our beloved protector and guardian angel, the councilman Shmuel Winter.

Frydman was wan and shriveled, thin as a rail, weak and gaunt. He seemed as meek as a sick child. His bony, protruding nose made him look like a buzzard. I thought about Adolf Dygasiński's tragic story of a buzzard in autumn, who had broken one of his wings and, unable to join his brothers flying south, was fated to remain alone in the freezing swamps.

The hopeful flight to warmer climes that Frydman's colleagues began ended in Treblinka. Frydman missed them terribly. It did not take long before he caught up with them.

Because of his bad lungs, Frydman was admitted to the hospital at Gęsia 6 at the end of December 1942. He was still there when the second *aktion* began on January 18, 1943. But something happened to him that gives us some consolation. A truly merciful nurse, a Jewish caregiver who had worked to get him admitted to the hospital, performed a wonderful act of kindness. On that black Tuesday, the second day of the *aktion*, the Germans came in the morning and announced that within one hour the entire hospital—patients and staff—had to leave for the Umschlagplatz. And this nurse, in the middle of all the confusion and chaos, had the wits to think about Frydman. She gave him a dose of morphine. Of course it was much more than normal.

She was able to do this before Frydman had any idea what was happening. In his eternal sleep he did not have to make that march to the Umschlagplatz with the others, walking in 20 degrees of frost with slippers on their bare feet and some blanket slung over their hospital pajamas. He was spared the journey to Treblinka in a sealed cattle car. He did not enter the gas chamber.

All of us who knew Frydman owe that heroic nurse a great debt of thanks. And since it's probable that she also perished, we bow our heads over her nonexistent grave.

29. THE LECTURERS

While Menakhem Linder organized cultural activities in the Warsaw Ghetto, it was Mordecai Mazo who provided these programs with content. He was the chief lecturer, the one who organized and supervised the IKOR's presentations and activities.

Before the war, when he had been director of the Vilna Troupe, Mazo often addressed theater audiences in the name of the ensemble. Blessed with self-assurance and a strong work ethic, Mazo could finish any task he faced. Now, well over sixty, Mazo showed himself to be a first-class speaker and lecturer.

His insights and wisdom enchanted his listeners in every sense of the word. He enlivened his talks with humor, fables, and traditional Jewish commentary. He made his points in a pleasant tone of voice as he transitioned from one topic to another. And of course it was impossible to overlook the attractive masculine timbre of his voice or his fine, precise diction. He had read much and worked hard, and each of his well-organized talks featured a unique theme. From having once been a theater entrepreneur and, more often than not, a hard-nosed businessman, he turned into a superb teacher. In this he resembled Chaim Zhitlowsky, who had combined the traditional and the modern, the atmosphere of the old *bes medresh*[1] with the wider world.

Mazo, who was so much a part of the theater world; Mazo, the actor in Yiddish dramas, died during the very last act. I saw him in the rump ghetto in the winter months of 1942–43. He was languishing in some kind of "office" having to do with Judenrat relief activities. After the January *aktion* ended, I heard that he was still alive, along with his last wife, the actress Esther Goldenberg. They moved into one of the shops, but that's all I was able to learn. Ringelblum wrote, and this was published in the second volume of his works, that they both perished during the Warsaw Ghetto Uprising.

>——<

A fragment of my last conversation with Mazo remains etched in my memory. I met him by chance on the premises of the new Judenrat, between the January and April *aktions*. I had already learned the circumstances that surrounded the death of Miriam Orleska.[2]

"They sent her to Treblinka on September 13," I told him.

"Yes," he replied. "They sent Chana Braz as well."

Strange. Miriam Orleska, one of the actresses of the Vilna Troupe—and he talked as if she meant nothing to him.

That saddened and angered me. I did not realize then that such a reaction could be a sign of deep anguish, of a need to blot something out.

And—go know—it was actually Esther Goldenberg, Miriam Orleska's former friend, the woman who stole her husband away, who asked for more details about "Polye" and her close family.[3]

>——<

In addition to Mazo, Binyomin Wirowski, a Bund activist from Lodz, became quite popular in the Warsaw Ghetto. I can still see him: restive and fidgety, the Jewish face with a long nose, the small frame. He was the one who always wove unmistakable political allusions into his lectures and garnered enthusiastic applause. Ringelblum mentioned him as one of the leaders of the IKOR.

I was also an IKOR lecturer, although Jonas Turkow erred when he wrote that I served on the board. Even though I was swamped with work running the kitchen at Leszno 40, I could not refuse Linder's stubborn pleas that I prepare something for his "people's university." I prepared and gave two lectures. The first was entitled "Work and the Folk Song," modeled on Karl Bucher's "Arbeit und Rhythmus." The second was "Jewish Life in the Mirror of Jewish Literature," based on my own reflections.

Perhaps I was lucky that I lacked time to do more for the IKOR. Look at what happened to Sonia Nowogrodzka, the Bundist teacher and school activist who had diligently tried to get material from Yiddish writers for the Bund's underground press. Her name was on the fateful list. The emissaries of the angel of death did not find her at home that night. But from then on, and right up to the Great Deportation, she did not spend the night in her own place.

>—<

Fortunately for herself, and to the relief of her friends, Rosa Simchowicz, a psychologist and pedagogue, also survived that April night. She played a major role in the Yiddish literature courses that she helped organize and in which she lectured. Rosa Simchowicz, a shining light in the Warsaw Ghetto, was one of the finest people I have ever met.

I got to know her before the war because of Riva and Vita Levin, two well-known sisters from Vilna. Whenever they came to Warsaw for a visit they would stay with a relative on Marszalkowska Street, where Rosa was also a lodger.

Rosa had a solid reputation as a long-established scholar. She participated in international conferences on pedagogy as the representative of the Central Yiddish School Organization in Poland. I was absolutely enchanted by her personal charm, her wisdom, her far-ranging intellect, her modesty, her professional expertise. Rosa's thin, delicate hands would often tremble when she tried to lift a door latch or serve a cup of tea. I thought this might have been an aftershock of some personal trauma she suffered long ago, and each time I noticed it I would feel a rush of compassion and worry. My heart would go out to her. Then I would realize how much I cared about her. Even today I can't be nonchalant when I see somebody's hands tremble.

>—<

I remember two tearful encounters we had during the occupation.

The first took place before the ghetto was established. I was on Bielańska, on my way back from the office of the Medem Sanatorium on Fredro Street. I had been trying to arrange a multiweek stay for the young daughter of a war widow from the provinces who ate at a kitchen. I hoped that a visit to the sanatorium might reverse the symptoms of serious malnutrition that the child had begun to exhibit. This little girl was the third child I had taken under my wing and tried to save from starvation through a stay at the Medem Sanatorium.

While I was in the office I learned that the second child I had sent there, Yeshaye G., a boy of thirteen or fourteen, had persuaded two other boys his age to rob the sanatorium's clothing storehouse. The administration discovered the theft and expelled the thief but did not tell me what happened. The little fellow returned to our kitchen with rosy, puffy cheeks and said nothing. As I sat in that office and heard about this incident, I ended my intercession for the little girl. On my way back from Fredro Street, I cried nonstop.

Just then Rosa was leaving the main offices of the Aleynhilf on Tlomackie Street. She could barely make out what I told her, but she took me by the arm and walked with me as far as Leszno. In a quiet voice, she comforted me. The boy was also a victim of the situation created by the war. He was going through the difficult time of puberty, and he might still turn out to be a decent person. She counseled me to treat him with empathy.

I did not take her advice. I could no longer bring myself to speak to Yeshaye. He understood and tried to apologize by sending me a strange, pathetic letter. When that did not change anything, he disappeared for good. I later learned that he went somewhere in the provinces. It's not hard to imagine what eventually happened to him. Suppose I had tried to help him further. Suppose he had turned into a well-behaved young boy. In the end he would have perished anyway.

About a year later Rosa and I met again, but our roles were reversed. At the same place, in front of the entrance to Tlomackie 5, I saw her leaving the building. This time it was she who was crying.

"Rosa, my dear, what happened?" I said as I ran toward her.

"England," she stammered. "They're bombing London with heavy explosives. They don't want to surrender. The people take cover in the stations of the underground. All the men are learning how to repel parachutists. The attacks have been going on for months . . ."

Rosa had lived and studied in London for a while. She had probably just gotten news about the blitz from the staff that hung around the Aleynhilf offices, and it pained her heart: the last redoubt in Europe, the last hope! Thinking about how the British held on and refused to quit plunged her into emotional turmoil.

I saw and spoke with her one more time after that. I would mention her in the weekly reportage that I wrote for the clandestine archive and cited the highly original observations she made about aid for children. In early winter 1941 I sought her help to find a place for four little orphans—three brothers and a sister—who loitered around the corridor of the soup kitchen the entire day and slept at night in an attic, where they were sure to freeze to death when winter got worse. As Rosa listened to me, what drew her attention was that the children absolutely refused to stay in an enclosed children's shelter. They had already run away twice: the first time on their way to the shelter and the second time as they were being registered in the reception area. Once, the emissary we sent to take them from the kitchen to the shelter came back with a "receipt" for the children, signed and sealed, but no sooner had he returned than the children were all back in the corridor of our kitchen.

As Rosa listened to what I had to say, she observed that one had to take their fear of being confined in a closed building seriously.

At that time we still hadn't heard about the roundups of children in Lodz. The mass murder of Jewish children had not yet begun, during which the orphanages became easy targets for a one-way journey to Treblinka, Chelmno, or the shooting pits in White Russia and Podolia. But this great pedagogue, with her profound intuition and a heart so full of empathy, already had some sense of what might happen.

"Those children's instincts, their fear, is something we should take seriously." That was her verdict.

>——<

"She was an angel who lived on this earth." That's what Emanuel Ringelblum wrote about Rosa Simchowicz in his essay about the destruction of the Jewish intelligentsia in Warsaw. She tried so hard to ensure that children in the ghetto would have not only bread but also a little happiness. She organized children's programs and translated texts from Russian and Polish children's literature. She enlisted Klima Fuswerk, the director of a Polish children's theater, to make sure that these programs were successful.

Rosa experienced the blessing of an early death, which spared her the frightful trauma of the Great Deportation and the horrors of

Treblinka. This favor was a just reward for the love that she bestowed in such great measure on children and their mothers.

>—<

"Restricted Area. Danger of Disease" the placards warned. During that first year of the occupation the Germans displayed those signs on every street that led into the Jewish neighborhood. "JEWS. LICE. TYPHUS." This was the shrill message trumpeted in Polish and German by the posters that festooned walls and signboards after the establishment of the ghetto, which did so much itself to spawn and spread the typhus epidemic.

Lice . . . the Germans were terribly frightened of those tiny creatures, who had become their most reliable allies in their crusade against other nations. Yes, they feared lice and they spread this fear to other peoples as well. At the same time, they did all they could to make sure that their deadly germs infected as many people as possible.

On the Aryan side one could protect oneself against these typhus-bearing lice. But in the overcrowded Warsaw Ghetto it was just not possible, especially if you were working with the impoverished crowds and with the refugees, who were always waiting in long lines.

Nevertheless, certain community activists and officials in ghetto institutions looked for ways to protect themselves from direct physical contact with the tightly packed crowds of needy supplicants. Railings were erected in the offices, which kept those seeking help at a distance.

They also wanted to build a barrier for Rosa's reception room in the CENTOS so that the lice-infected mothers with their lice-covered children would not be able to get too close to her.

Rosa would have none of it. She could not bring herself to keep those poor, unhappy mothers and their starving, sick children at a distance. That, she believed, would be insulting and demeaning.

She received no vaccination against typhus and became sick. Already exhausted and weakened from two years of war and occupation, she could not survive the high fever.

Close friends or relatives who lived on Grzybowska Street took her into their apartment. The doctors did all they could to make her stronger and save her. It was in vain. On a late autumn day in 1941 a large group of people gathered to accompany her on her last journey. As we stood and waited for the coffin we couldn't understand the reason for the delay. Then a wagon harnessed to a single horse suddenly appeared, but it did not stop. Instead, the horse went off at a fast trot toward Solna, and then ran even faster along Karmelicka in the direction of the Gęsia cemetery.

At that time it was still possible to follow the dead to the cemetery. A few people managed to hail some rickshaws and hurried off in pursuit of the cart. Others were left behind. Insulted and aggrieved, people went home. They never learned the reason for this outrage.

Of course, what did all this really mean in the end? You look back now and think about what happened to all those people who wanted to pay their last respects to Rosa and were unable to do so.

A few months later Shmuel Winter asked me to find out whether we could erect a gravestone for Rosa. This too never happened.

After the war I did not go to the Gęsia cemetery, just as I did not visit the desecrated cemetery in Lemberg, where nothing at all remained of the graves and tombstones of my father and brother.

The tombstones of our nearest and dearest are carved into our hearts for as long as we live.

30. THE LIBRARIANS

There were two of them: Leyb Shur and "Pani Basia," or Basia Berman, who worked for the secret Jewish aid organization on the Aryan side.[1]

Leyb Shur founded Tomor, the Vilna publishing house. He was the *lamed vovnik* of the Jewish book trade, one of thirty-six hidden righteous men who live in each generation and in whose merit the world survives.

Basia was a professional librarian and had been on the staff of the Warsaw public library on Koszykowa Street. Before the war Basia had developed an interest in Yiddish books and, in conjunction with the TSEKABE, had published an article titled "Jewish Libraries in Warsaw: A Statistical Survey."[2]

In the ghetto she and Shur set themselves a special task. Other Jewish communal activists were agonizing over how to feed, clothe, and house the ever-greater masses of impoverished Jews. Basia Berman and Leyb Shur tried to figure out how to provide these Jews with cultural nourishment. They were the first to realize how books could be a powerful weapon in the battle against despair.

One would think that when people were starving and displaced, books were the last thing they needed. But this would be a false assumption. Never had the passion for reading been as intense as during the years of the occupation. This was true of both Jews and non-Jews. This was partly because people needed some relief from omnipresent danger and a depressing reality. But they also sought mental stimulation and yearned to nourish an individual identity that had become battered and compromised.

What was true for adults was even truer for children, and especially for Jewish children in the ghetto.

The Germans had robbed these children of an entire world: of rivers, trees, freedom of movement. Perhaps the magical power of the written word could give some of it back.

>——<

Both Basia Berman and Leyb Shur began their work in 1940.

The Germans issued an order in the early days of the occupation forbidding Jews to use public libraries. By the spring of 1940 all the communal and most of the private lending libraries in the Jewish section were closed. Jewish Warsaw, which before the war had boasted more than 50 libraries with over 250,000 volumes, now had no access to books. But the Jews of Warsaw found illegal and clandestine ways to sabotage German measures to deny Jews books and force them into a cultural desert.

Leyb Shur began to collect the partly scattered and dispersed holdings of the Grosser Library.[3] Somebody, I do not remember who, authorized him to do this. He also began to receive gifts from private individuals. Blessed with a Litvak's indefatigable stubbornness and with the devotion and fanaticism of a true idealist, Shur threw himself into this task. In the first months of the ghetto, and perhaps even before then, Shur stuffed his briefcase with books and delivered them to his "clients," providing many people with reading material.

In secret, and perhaps with just a hint of self-conscious embarrassment, he nourished another dream: to publish, under the Tomor imprint, at least one small book in the ghetto, an edition of a few typed pages.

In the spring of 1941 the Judenrat got permission to issue permits to establish some lending libraries, but only for books in Yiddish and Polish. Leyb Shur tried to get a concession to take over the rich collection of books in the Lebn library on Dzielna Street, which the Polish authorities had closed before the war on the grounds that it was a cover for communist activity. It just so happened that it was this library, with its large number of books, that survived the bombs and conflagrations of September 1939.

Shur had become weak and emaciated. The puffy bags under his eyes signaled the first signs of hunger edema. Still, he sought no financial help for himself, neither from the Judenrat nor the Aleynhilf. If a friend gave him a food package from a Joint warehouse, he would take it. If I invited him to visit the soup kitchen for some soup, he would come and eat. But he never spoke about his own problems. All this time, his thoughts focused on his one great dream—to organize a large Jewish library. What? Now? In these terrible conditions? Yes, that was precisely the point.

It so happened that the dream became reality.

Shur brought all the books to a three-room apartment at Leszno 56 he shared with Borukh Makhlis, his colleague who had been a typesetter for *The Moment*. In Makhlis, Shur found a devoted friend and a collaborator in thought and deed. Shur used the term "metrika" to refer to a catalog card, and he cataloged books according to his own original system. Hour by hour, day by day, lovingly and devotedly, Makhlis and Shur cataloged dozens and dozens of volumes, pasted on the proper labels, and turned heaps of damaged books into a well-organized cultural resource containing wisdom and knowledge from the entire world. Every inch of the walls, from floor to ceiling in the three rooms they shared at Leszno 56, were covered with bookshelves. They had to hustle, beg, petition, and cadge subsidies even as they hunted down each board and screw that went into those bookshelves.

When many books had already been cataloged and arranged on the shelves, certain privileged insiders, including myself, showed up to borrow or exchange books. One day I was going home from the soup kitchen at Leszno 40 a little earlier than usual. Along the way I peeked into Leszno 56 to congratulate Shur on his achievement. We needed to keep each other's spirits up in those days and weeks of rumors, new edicts, bad news, and the nightly killings of "proscribed" individuals.

That was how they did it: terror and murder on the one hand, concessions and the issuance of new identification papers on the other, all to lull us into a sense of false security before the final, fatal blow. The lending libraries that the Germans finally allowed had not yet opened when the Great Deportation began.

>—<

Not all the boxes of books had yet been unpacked; Shur and Makhlis had not yet finished sorting and cataloging them all. They still had not finalized plans for the low-key, clandestine dedication ceremony that, defying all obstacles, they planned to hold, if only symbolically.

Shur was a first-class typesetter and machine mechanic, so despite his age and gray hair he had a good chance of finding work in some shop. But he made no effort to do so. Despite the general fear and panic, despite their worries about their own safety and that of their families, Shur's friends and colleagues tried to set him up in one of those places. Shur ignored their entreaties.

It was the fifth of August, the fifteenth day of the Great Deportation. That day everyone on Leszno Street who was not employed by the Toebbens Firm had to leave their apartments because the firm had requisitioned all the buildings on Leszno, from Karmelicka to Zelazna, to serve as workshops and living quarters for its workers.

Very early on that Wednesday morning, when it was still dark, Shur's friend and flatmate Makhlis jumped out of bed. He went into the kitchen, put on the kettle for tea, and called to Shur, who did not answer. He went into his room to wake him up and saw him standing near one of the highest bookshelves, his head jerked upward. Makhlis came closer, and when Shur remained silent, he realized what happened: Shur had hanged himself.

Terribly upset, Makhlis ran a few houses up the street to me, at Leszno 68. He banged his head against the doorpost. He wept and shrieked. He knew about my friendship with Shur, about his daily visits to the kitchen. I admit that I did not do what I should have done. I didn't go back to help him arrange the funeral or to find somebody to take away the books. Meanwhile the daily blockades were about to begin. A roundup on Leszno could begin at any second. What could we do for a friend who was dead when we couldn't do anything for him when he was alive?

That's how we were in those days. The most terrifying events were our daily routine. Our senses were dulled and jaded. We were steeped in a kind of psychological narcosis, our blood barely moving through our veins. As the knife cut into our bodies and ripped away our vital core, we reacted with a faint tremor, if at all.

Some people were surprised that Shur had killed himself. They envied him for having the inner strength to do what he did. They understood that he had suffered a breakdown, largely because of his library, which was impossible to relocate. Nonetheless, people saw in his suicide an act of courage and pride.

Such an old man! Such a gentle soul! But he did it! People envied him because he no longer had to carry on the ugly, futile struggle.

Did anyone accompany him to his final resting place? Was anybody there when they buried him? What happened to his friend Borukh Makhlis? I never saw him again, and I never heard anything more about either of them.

The newly arrived slave laborers of the Toebbens firm, who took over Makhlis and Shur's old apartment, did not bother themselves too much about the library whose fate had probably pushed Shur to kill himself. They wasted no time dealing with the books, which they threw from the windows into the dumpsters. Of course, there were too many books even for all the garbage cans in the three courtyards of Leszno 56. Books lay on the pavement, soaked in rain, covered in dirt, piled up in out-of-the-way corners.

For a long time afterward, during the rest of August and early September, when all the remaining Jews in the ghetto had to assemble for the mass selection, two members of our kitchen staff at Leszno 40, Joseph Erlich and his friend, would come back each day from the flour mill at Leszno 56 with stacks of books in their handcart. They found those books lying in the courtyard. Pretty soon Yiddish books were piled all over our kitchen at Leszno 40.

When the Toebbens workers stood in line for soup and coffee, they would often pick up a book, give the cover a tender pat, turn over some pages, perhaps even read a page or two, and put it back with a heartfelt sigh. They did not get even a second's worth of diversion to read those abandoned books, now held by totally forsaken people.

>——<

But the final days of the ghetto had not yet come. So I would like to write about Basia Berman, what she accomplished in those days, and what she lost.

It was the winter and summer of 1940. Basia was working in the department of the Aleynhilf that distributed clothing. While her colleagues distributed clothes and underwear for refugees, Basia collected books for their children. To make her initiative sound more legitimate, she called it a project to distribute both books and toys. Children who were Warsaw natives and had acquired their own books before the war exchanged them with kids from other families. More formal book exchanges were organized in buildings that housed better-off tenants. Certain house committees established children's corners. But the children who lived in the refugee centers were the ones who were the most deprived, not to mention the orphaned and homeless children who ended up in the children's homes.

So Basia Berman, along with Leyb Shur, began to carry books from the displaced libraries for the displaced children.

November 1940, just before the establishment of the ghetto. A branch of the Warsaw Public Library, where Basia had worked, was located at Leszno 67. That Polish library now had to vacate the premises. Basia enlisted the support of the CENTOS in her attempt to get control of the building. She succeeded under the legal auspices of the Commission for Children's Theater, which functioned very effectively under the direction of Klima Fuswerk—later known on the Aryan side as "Bogusia."

This kind of work had to be clandestine. The two rooms were festooned with collages of children's drawings. Dolls, little animals, and various toys lined the shelves. Books with colorful illustrations were spread on the tables. We were trying to make the place seem light-hearted and playful, less serious. This gave us the cover we needed to assemble a large collection of literature for young people in Yiddish and Polish. They procured the books the same way Shur did. One of the most important suppliers was Shur himself. He always culled books from his collections that were best suited for children. He was always saying, "We have to help Basia. We have to help her!" He enthusiastically encouraged her work and drummed up support for the children's library.

Rosa Simchowicz was another of Basia's true friends and partners. After she died in the fall of 1941 the children's library was named after her.

>——<

The library at Leszno 67 flourished. In a short time more than seven hundred children registered to use it. Many of the children were not used to reading Yiddish or did not know the Yiddish alphabet. Basia had her own way of winning these children over. She would give the children two books: one in Yiddish and one in Polish. For more than one child, that first Yiddish book was a real revelation. It spoke to their inner sense of self. Several children acquired a sincere love for Yiddish books.

Every now and then the library organized public readings. The children themselves did the recitals. The library also arranged lectures about Yiddish literature for teachers from an assimilated background. True lovers of Yiddish culture would meet at these modest events. They felt so comfortable here, in this cozy nook dedicated to Jewish children and to Yiddish books. It was here that I last saw Rosa Simchowicz before she died. It was in this place that I had my last meeting with Menakhem Linder before his murder. I can still hear his voice, how he hummed the melody "Don and Dunya" that day at Leszno 67, at a concert given by a woman singer in the children's library.[4]

Basia found and trained her most important assistants and helpers from among the children themselves. Her "girl friday" was Shulamis Brotshteyn, the seventeen-year-old daughter of a well-known cultural activist and YIVO supporter from Wloclawek. Other key assistants included three younger girls, Tobche Keitel, Royzele Szwartsberg, and Pola Blazer. One was thirteen, the other two were fifteen.

When Basia would mention their names after the war her face would light up with a sad and somewhat cryptic smile. Even after their murder, she could not say their names without that smile, that's how sweet and charming they were.

>——<

One of the most urgent priorities of the children's library was to provide books for the poorest and most distressed children. The library reached out to the full-time and part-time childcare centers that had been organized during the war, the children's hospitals, and even to children from families who had suffered from typhus and were isolated for many weeks in quarantine.

Many of the pathologies of ghetto life were reflected in the activities of a lending library.

Mostly because of health concerns, it was necessary to set aside separate stocks of books to lend out to children in the refugee shelters and childcare centers. Basia also had a special supply of books for children who suffered from scabies.

Despite the best efforts of their teachers and caregivers, many of the children in the refugee shelters and childcare centers lived in frightful conditions. Most of them had no warm clothing to wear in winter. They had no shoes. They lived in unheated rooms. But those kids loved to read! To obtain books they would dispatch special "representatives," fitted out in whatever warm clothes they and their friends could rustle up.

On certain days children from the refugee shelters would visit the library. Their appearance, as well as a peculiar unpleasant odor, left no doubt as to where they came from. Most had shaved heads, the result of the periodic "parówki" that plagued the shelters like a scourge.[5] Many had those swellings under their eyes that were the first sign of hunger edema. They would show up, totally focused and serious, in order to "arrange" a book. They stretched out their shriveled little hands to touch the only relief available to them.

In some of the refugee centers where children were not able to read because of the freezing cold in the unheated rooms, the library would organize a collective reading aloud. Basia used to speak about the teacher Przepiurko in the half-day children's center at Wolność 16. The teacher would read aloud and the children would curl up closer to each other under the blankets. With wistful expressions on their faces, they would listen to a story about a far-off journey, about an adventure that took place under distant skies, in the warm climes of Africa or Asia . . .

Among the children that Basia worked with, one stood out from the rest. This kid, named Meir'l, simply devoured books. Once Meir'l returned a book with lice crawling along the inside pages. But the library staff did not get angry. It was not his fault that lice crept over his book just as they crept over his emaciated body. But it became clear that disinfecting the books was a problem for the library.

>——<

The lending of books did not cease even during the Great Deportation.

Basia told me after the war that during the first days of the Great Deportation, there were children who came to the library at Leszno

67 during lending hours, determined to exercise their right to borrow a book. And so the library served the children one more time—the last time. There was one little girl called Simche. She was a tough little character and was not afraid to be on the street during the roundups. "My daddy works in the Toebbens shop," she boasted and showed her ID. We know just how worthless those IDs turned out to be.

The books that were lent out in those days were never returned. How many must have been stuffed into those little packages, packed in advance, for the children to take along on their journey "to the east." How many of those books must have ended on the junkheaps of Treblinka, alongside the prayer books and books of Psalms that the adults took with them?

I can still see that little boy during one of the roundups on Leszno. His father had been in jail for many weeks. His mother had decided to go to the Umschlagplatz voluntarily, hoping to see her relatives in Brisk.[6] She gathered provisions for the journey from her neighbors in the courtyard of Leszno 66. All around one could hear the noise and tumult of the nearby roundups. But that little boy, 12 years old or thereabouts, just sat in a corner of the courtyard; he was totally entranced by a book he was reading. He was so focused on those imaginary worlds that he paid no heed to what was going on all around him. It was a tattered book with a red cover.[7]

His mother was not the only one who voluntarily went to the Umschlagplatz at that time. The streets swarmed with people who had decided to obey the decree to leave their homes. Only when they arrived at Treblinka did they realize how horribly they had been deceived.

PANI BASIA

I got to know her during the first month of the German occupation, when she and her husband came to visit me. She was a young woman with girlish charm and very defined facial features, wearing a blue sweater with a high golf collar along with a string of genuine coral beads.

I have written more than once, on the Aryan side and after the war, about Basia's activities. Once in Israel she jokingly referred to me as her biographer. She was younger than me, and after we survived that time of mass killing I could never have imagined that I would be writing my memories of Basia Berman after her death. I have discussed elsewhere Basia's activities in the ghetto. Now I want to write about what she did on the Aryan side.

With the Great Deportation in July 1942, which ended her work in the children's library at Leszno 67, a new chapter in Basia's life began. She was one of the people who did not break down when she stood face-to-face with the murder machine. Instead, she was one of the first to seek out and discover new ways to rescue people and keep them alive outside the ghetto; to rescue not just herself but also other Jews, and to ensure not just the physical survival of as many Jews as possible but also the continuation of Jewish political activity. When the Bermans made that risky move to leave the ghetto, it was largely because of Basia's grit and her conviction that not everybody was doomed and not everything was fated to go under.

That stubborn faith in a better future determined how Basia looked at the world during the worst moments of the occupation. It continued even later, in the late 1940s and early 1950s, during the mass migration to Israel from Poland and Russia and during the unending war scares. This dogged optimism did not desert her even during her terminal illness, during the last days of her life.

>—<

The Bermans left the ghetto on September 5, 1942, just a day before the horrible and fateful mass selection, through which every Jew left in the ghetto had to pass. It took a lot of courage to take such a step at a time of constant shooting and ongoing murders of Jews on both sides of the ghetto wall, not to mention the dangers that Jews leaving the ghetto had to endure from gangs of blackmailers and thieves who were always ready to strip them of their last possessions and then hand them over to the killers-in-uniform.

They too were exposed to these dangers. But Basia, who was raised in a hardscrabble Polish-Jewish neighborhood in Praga, knew how to talk to these "wise guys" in their own lingo. So after they handed over their last few złotys to some *szmalcowniks*, Basia managed to convince them to escort her and her husband to the tram, thus shielding them from the next gang.[1] Eventually they managed to shake them off and get to a part of town where a prewar friend, who had worked with her in the public library, found them a place to sleep in a distant library branch. The next day another Polish lady led them to yet another Polish friend, who helped them start their new life.

As soon as the Bermans began to feel more secure they started mobilizing their friends from the Polish intelligentsia to begin the dangerous and difficult job of helping Jews find ways to survive on the Aryan side. After the beginning of the third *aktion* and the ghetto uprising in the spring of 1943, the number of Jews who escaped to the Aryan side greatly increased. The tiny group of helpers turned into a widespread organization dedicated to finding apartments, forging documents, building hideouts, and providing money for Jews in hiding or living in the city under Polish identities.

The work of the Council to Help Jews began, which became known by its conspiratorial name, Żegota. Basia became one of the most dynamic leaders of that organization, working on the front lines to lead and implement some of the most dangerous and critically important tasks. As time went on she assembled an entire staff of Jews and Poles who worked closely with her and who served as contact people. Among those who worked with Żegota were such leading Polish personalities as Maria Grzegarzewska, director of the Institute of Special Pedagogy; the famous actress Irena Solska; the Professors Ossowski, who were married; Polish activists Irena Sawicka, Sofia Podkowinska, and many other well- and lesser-known members of the Polish intellectual elite.

These were the organizers and leaders, and many of them had more than a drop of Jewish blood. You can regard this as a characteristic example of reawakened solidarity with their brethren. Then again, they were exposed to greater danger if their true origins became known. It's also a well-known fact that large numbers of right-wing Catholic activists, who before the war had called for the exclusion of Jews from Polish economic and political life, participated in this rescue work.[2] While they supported Jewish emigration from Poland they certainly opposed mass murder and annihilation. Now they saw it as their basic human obligation to help the persecuted and the condemned. It stood to reason that most Polish members of the council had a PPS or a Communist background.[3]

Adolf Berman attended the clandestine meetings, where he saw the organizers and delegates from different political groups. Basia usually worked with those who carried out the day-to-day activities of Żegota, although one should not assume a strict distinction between the organizers and the people who worked in the trenches. Sometimes the same person belonged to both categories.

No less active than the Poles was an entire staff of Jewish helpers and couriers who looked Polish and could "pass." They were at Basia's beck and call, and she worked closely with them. I will just mention some of them, those whom I knew personally and whom I would meet in Pani Janina Buchholc's office: Bogusia (Blima Fuswerk), Wanda (Bela Elster), Jozia (Jozef Zisman-Ziemian), Stasia (Helena Merenholc), the "Ukrainian Lady" (Genia Silkes), and Pani Zawirska.

I would also like to mention some of the Poles: Panna Jadwiga, Pani Sylwia (Rzeszczycka), Pan Władysław. There are other men and women whose faces I remember but whose names I have forgotten, including a certain "Aniela," a name I knew well since I used it myself for two years.

It would be interesting to describe the complicated "Aryan rules" for Jews passing as Poles, how they worked in practice, and how they saved lives. But only Basia would have been able to relate the entire range of courage, ingenuity, dedication, and cleverness it took to run the rescue networks that helped thousands of people. A large proportion of the Jews who survived on the Aryan side of Warsaw owe their lives to her work.

After the war I repeatedly asked Basia to write a book about Jewish rescue activity on the Aryan side. She discusses this in fragmentary fashion in the diary she wrote in the latter days of the occupation. But she never was able to write a more comprehensive monograph.[4]

>——<

It was an entirely different Basia that I met one afternoon in late March 1943 in a tiny café on the corner of Nowy Świat and Ordynacka: Basia, the poverty-stricken countess. The woman waiting for me at a table, sipping a cup of "abysinka," looked like an old-fashioned Catholic lady in mourning for a family member. A long black veil fastened to her hat covered her face. But behind this charade there was a sad reality.

The conversation we had there does not lend itself to casual description. We were both on edge and tense as we remembered the last time we spoke: eight months earlier, before the Great Deportation. But we had to put on a good front in order not to attract attention from the people behind the counter or sitting at adjoining tables. Basia had already gotten used to playing the role of a declassed member of the intelligentsia who was meeting a fellow declassed countess to discuss how to dust off and sell a used coat or knit new kinds of scarves or sweaters to trade. Without batting an eyelash or changing her manner she whispered in my ear the bitter news that they had just arrested Jurek (Arie Wilner), the delegate of the Jewish Fighting Organization (ZOB) on the Aryan side. Her heart bled as she thought about that heroic young man.

In March Żegota was already able to help Jews with money, rooms, and, most important, false documents. I met Basia on a regular basis— sometimes more often, sometimes less. The rescue work on the Aryan side was constantly expanding. Everything grew: the challenges and the resources, the obligations and the difficulties, the anxieties and the dangers. That whole time Basia herself grew. As her tasks multiplied her stature reached new heights.

Let nobody think that Basia was some meek soul, some good-natured, mild-mannered, sweet-tempered lady. Maybe that's the Basia who picked out books in the ghetto for little children to read, the Basia who told them nice stories about billy goats. But now a new Basia appeared. You could see it in the way she walked. This new Basia was a dynamo. She was assertive, aggressive, sometimes even despotic. She had become a fighter, a leader of the first rank.

Only God and she herself know what she suffered in private: the failures she endured, the personal transformations she experienced. She worked as a charwoman in some professor's house, a dishwasher in a restaurant, a student in a bookbinding course, an apprentice librarian. You had to have an alibi, a cover.

Then Warsaw suffered an onslaught of terror as the Germans and the Polish underground traded blows. In October 1943 and later there were assassinations of Germans and reprisals against the Polish population: terror and counterterror. As time went on the tension kept getting worse and worse.

In those days Basia would sometimes get very nervous. She would become distraught and experience setbacks and very hard times. But after a few minutes she would pull herself together. There was no question of neglecting her duties, even for a day.

So she resumed "taking care of business," trudging through the city with those double-bottomed carry bags. Concealed under a top layer of apples, onions, rolls, potatoes, or pickles were false ID cards, baptismal certificates, and wedding records. She carried large sums of Polish złotys and even American dollars smuggled in by foreign Jewish organizations with the help of Polish couriers. There were also letters, historical materials, memoirs, and testimonies written by Jews in hiding at the request of a committee that was trying to continue the work of the secret ghetto archive.

Every day Basia would meet members of Żegota in cafés, pastry shops, cheap eateries, and restaurants, where she instructed Polish and Jewish activists on the details of where and whom to meet. Even during the most dangerous days, when the Germans carried out street roundups, blockades, and public executions, days when Poles were afraid to go out, Basia never sat at home. Her activities had become so wide-ranging, the lives of so many people depended on what she did and whom she met, that she could not miss even one day of work. She stuck to that rule even after a certain scoundrel, who happened to be Jewish, one day "escorted" Basia and her husband home, forcing the Bermans to immediately change their apartment, their names, and disguise their appearance.[5]

I often wondered why Basia was never arrested. Despite her blue eyes, she looked unmistakably Jewish. Once as I was traveling on the tram I froze when I heard a Polish passenger in a casual voice tell his neighbor: "Take a look at that Jewish woman!" I carefully snuck a peek through the window and sure enough, it was Basia.

She was in that hat with the black veil. To make herself look poor she carried a leather bag held together by a cord.

After her run-in with the blackmailer she stopped wearing the veil and turned herself into an elegant lady, carefully groomed with the kind of little hat called a "budka." The brim overshadowed her face and to some degree obscured and blurred the Jewish nose.

I remember how, on especially dangerous days, I would take great care not to run into her in Pani Janina Buchholc's office on Miodowa. At those times she would order me to lie low, while she herself, who looked much more Jewish . . .

I wrote somewhere that what protected her as she got on with her work and her meetings were the prayers of all the people whose lives depended on her. But what really saved her was her own inner strength. The sheer importance of her mission animated her and cast a spell that inspired her at every step along the way, a kind of protective aura that shielded her from danger.

><

For others she would deliver medicines and real good luck charms. For herself she only had one lucky charm: a blue porcelain elephant.

Her whole life she loved the color blue. Blue dresses, blue coats, blue furniture coverings. When she left the ghetto she took along that thin, almost transparent elephant. It was her fetish and personal mascot. All of us on the Aryan side became superstitious; we needed something to hold on to. In the end you could just as well die because you were too smart as you could because you were too stupid.

So Basia the socialist, our rational Basia, never let go of that little blue elephant. Even as she was fleeing the conflagrations of Warsaw in 1944 she took it along in her knapsack. It was with her on the day of their liberation, when the Bermans were in some small village near Warsaw. And then, on that very day, the elephant slipped out of Basia's hands and shattered.

><

When the war ended Basia returned to her work as a librarian. She had the good sense and tact to drop her "Pani Basia" persona from the time of the occupation. There was nothing in her gait, demeanor, or attitude toward others that in any way hinted at the role of a professional hero, a living icon cast in bronze and surrounded by the halo of her past deeds. She was too intelligent to do that. On the third anniversary of the ghetto uprising she received a medal for valor from the Polish government. But she never wore it, not even once.

As soon as the war ended she started to retrieve those few Yiddish and Hebrew books, as well as books on Jewish topics, that survived the Holocaust. Using books that turned up in basements of Polish libraries, in German warehouses, in hideouts, as well as collections sent over from the United States, and with a great deal of professional expertise, she assembled a very large and important central Jewish library in Poland, which later became part of the Jewish Historical Institute. She also arranged the shipment of many crates of religious books and duplicates to the National Library in Jerusalem. For the fifth anniversary of the ghetto uprising, Basia arranged an exhibit of rescued books. The public library, where Basia had worked before the war and which had since resumed its activities, gave her many rare Jewish books. When she left Poland and migrated to Israel she brought with her a treasure trove of Jewish books and printed materials.

She arrived in Israel full of enthusiasm, bursting with plans and dreams. The fire that burned so intensely during the occupation—that dynamic energy, dedication, and Jewish faith—was rekindled in her soul and waited to be redeemed.

She was raised in a religious home, grew up in the crowded streets of Jewish Praga, was educated in the ranks of the Jewish labor movement, and was a lifelong member of the Labor Zionist organization. In her very being, in the way she spoke and thought, Basia was bound up heart and soul with her people, the Jewish masses. She had Jewish warmth and an inner Jewish spark. Her aliya was the natural destination of her life's journey.

In Israel she hoped to find that longed-for realization of her hopes, to work as a librarian in a Jewish state. Her dream was to establish a museum of Yiddish and Hebrew books. She sought out contacts, looked for ways to make it happen. But nothing materialized. Something bad began to happen to Basia. After the war she rebuilt her home, gave birth to a son, and organized a large library. But she somehow failed to match the success that she realized when she stood face to face with danger. She sensed that her strength had started to fail her. Even before she left Poland, her health began to decline.

Basia believed that her luck changed on the day that the blue porcelain elephant broke. She started looking for a new little elephant just like the one she had. Her friends also looked, in Warsaw and in Lodz. But nobody could find one in any Polish city. When I happened to be in Czechoslovakia in 1947 I went through all the antique stores and found many figures of elephants, some quite gorgeous. But I failed to find exactly that one, not there, not in Paris, nor anywhere else.

Basia glued together the pieces of the blue elephant and placed it alongside other little elephants carved out of genuine ivory that friends had given her as gifts. But it wasn't the same thing.

Basia's arrival in Israel was the natural culmination of a life's journey. It simply did not seem right that Basia failed to find her place there. And then her health collapsed. Death stretched out its talons to claim yet another survivor. Maybe this was not by happenstance. The delayed effects of trauma, horror, and the endless need to expend physical and mental energy now made themselves felt. How much joy can someone who lost so much find in that "victory"? Eventually there is a reckoning.

Basia died as she lived. She fought until the very end; despite every hardship, her strong will kept her spirit up until the last.

Although her health was failing and she was half paralyzed, she did not want to blame her illness and its rapid spread on the difficult climate. Her only complaint was that she could not find employment. She finally managed to find a part-time post in some school library, and despite her terrible health she tried as hard as she could not to miss any of the work that she loved.

Once again, just like in the ghetto, she became a children's librarian, watching over those little sabra readers. She served them enthusiastically and gave this new generation of Jewish children the books written by her favorite authors. Her own son, soon to be orphaned, became part of that generation.

Basia was depressed in her last days. She knew that she was dying.

She was sad to know that she was leaving her new country, the new home where she lacked the strength to go on living.

The blue elephant made of porcelain shattered forever.

31. THE SUPPLIER

His name was known to me before the war. He was one of a group of key YIVO activists who dealt with financial and organizational matters. Everybody who cared about Yiddish book publishing knew where he lived in Wloclawek. Shmuel Winter was a major patron of Yiddish books and Yiddish theater. Actually, he was a lot more than a patron. He was a guardian angel. If Jewish cultural autonomy ever really existed its foundation was those few people, including Winter, who were devoted to Yiddish with heart and soul.

When I think of Winter, I'm reminded of another "Jewish merchant": one of our Galitsianers, Abraham Zaynfeld, who was a righteous man and a saint. Like Winter he too joined his people on that final journey of martyrdom.

Winter certainly had his likes and dislikes in Polish Jewish politics. But when it came to secular Yiddish culture he was like a faithful husband who never strayed. He took on the burden and responsibility of supporting it and caring for its every need. Because he left no survivors and belonged to no political movement ready to burnish his memory, he has been overlooked and forgotten. Here I want to relate what I remember and know about the last period of his life: the Warsaw Ghetto, Yiddish culture in the underground, and the struggle for individual and national dignity during the great catastrophe.

And finally, his help and financial contribution to the armed uprising.

>——<

You really had to watch Winter in those days and feel the trust he inspired in others—his tall, wide-shouldered frame, his drooping posture, his protruding head, his elongated face, the thick eyeglasses over his large, dark eyes. Yes, he was a Jewish merchant, but the kind of Jewish merchant whose eyes were aglow from staying up late into the night studying a page of Gemara after a long day of business.

That's how I remember Winter when we first met in November 1939, after the Germans marched in. He, his wife, and his three children arrived in Warsaw along with a large number of refugees. I got to know him in the headquarters of the Aleynhilf at Tlomackie 5. This building became a kind of safe harbor for the more radical elements of the Jewish intelligentsia in Warsaw. You might say it was the total opposite, the obverse, of that big building on Grzybowska, the headquarters of the Judenrat.[1] But this nucleus of Jewish communal activists based in the Aleynhilf had to have a trusted delegate and representative in that other place. Winter was the liaison between the two buildings.

Before the war Winter was a grain merchant and exporter. He was a member of the state chamber of commerce. Because of his commercial expertise he filled one of the most important posts in the internal hierarchy of the ghetto—administrator of the supply section of the provisioning department, which was headed by Abraham Gepner, previously a major iron merchant in Warsaw. How important it was that a man of integrity and honesty should run the bureau responsible for feeding the overcrowded ghetto.

Nonetheless Winter, with Gepner's full knowledge and approval, cut some corners. He diverted some of the allocated rations and products to help a core of ghetto activists and intellectuals, the "cadres." This policy was laid down at the beginning of the occupation.

There were those who looked out for the political leadership or for party activists, regardless of ideology. But Winter cared about those who were near the bottom of the ladder, people lacking the political connections and sharp elbows so important in the fight for survival. He looked out for writers and artists, for scholars, for young people and children, as well as for their teachers.

Apart from the tiny and low-quality food rations allocated by the occupation authorities, there were other sources of food for the ghetto. David Guzik helped raise money for this purpose. Guzik was in contact with very wealthy Jews who had large sums of money stashed away in German-occupied Poland and abroad. They agreed to lend him hefty sums with the understanding that they would be repaid after the war. That money paid for food products obtained through smuggling and illegal trade. This was the source of the special food allotments as well as of the monthly cash allowances for those who had no work and no source of income.

The same source later supported cultural activities for the Jewish masses who faced not only physical annihilation but also cultural deprivation. Winter in particular took a special interest in the secret ghetto archive organized by Emanuel Ringelblum.

>——<

I recall only one personal meeting with Winter in the period before the Great Deportation. It was a few months after the death of Rosa Simchowicz. Winter sent a messenger to ask me to come to see him after work. He asked me to find out if there was a tombstone on Rosa's grave. Entry to the Gęsia cemetery had already been cut off. I promised to see her friends on Grzybowska Street and to meet with Dr. Lajpuner, a physician long known in Yiddish literary circles and a personal friend or relative of Rosa's. During our conversation Winter mentioned an essay about a soup kitchen in the ghetto. That tipped me off that he was connected to the secret activities of Dr. Ringelblum. I realized that his obsession with secrecy did not keep Ringelblum from boasting a bit about certain essays he had collected. Hela Rajcher, who became my good friend on the Aryan side under the name Aniela Makarewicz, also knew about that essay.

I remember it now as if it were a dream. I reached Dr. Lajpuner after asking various people for the address. We agreed to ask some big shots to help put a tombstone on Rosa's grave. But I never got to tell Winter about that meeting. It was now April 1942, a few days before that tragic Friday evening when the nocturnal Gestapo raids began, which I already described in connection with Menakhem Linder. The tension increased from day to day, and nobody spoke anymore about erecting tombstones on graves. The time was approaching when the biblical warning came true: the living would envy the dead.

>——<

My second meeting with Winter took place between the first and the second *aktions*, a period from September 1942 to January 1943. It turned out that after the Great Deportation Winter was the first to find out that I was still alive, and he sent me a message asking me to come to Franciszkańska 30 in the central ghetto. One day in October I marched with a group of workers from Leszno through the "wild" area along Karmelicka through Nowolipki and reached the gate of the new ghetto on the corner of Gęsia and Zamenhof.[2]

In my essay "Weeping Over Abandoned Things," I wrote:

> It was like a journey through the landscape of a sad dream. That early morning slog of orphaned people along empty streets, the swirling flakes of the first snow falling alongside the feathers from torn Jewish bedding ... rows and rows of empty buildings, dingy shutters askew on broken hinges; the ghostly spectacle of open windows with swaying curtains that resembled mourning sashes— tattered, yellowed with rain, dust-covered, blown about by the wind, forsaken.

What I saw that day is forever etched in my memory.

The provisioning bureau was at Franciszkańska 30, where it had relocated during the Great Deportation. I found Winter in his office, which was in the front part of the building. He was so distraught following the deportation of his wife and son that he seemed drunk. Usually he was a quiet person. Now he clenched his fists and banged on the table. He seethed with anger and a thirst for revenge.

"I would like to kill a German woman," he stammered. "One who was just like my wife, as good a housekeeper and mother as she was ..."

After the war I learned that he had already taken his first steps toward exacting revenge. He was on the finance committee of the Jewish Fighting Organization (ZOB), and his mission was to raise money to buy weapons. His tragedy had ignited a white-hot inner flame.

After he pulled himself together he passed on regards from Ringelblum, who, I learned, dropped by each week to get food allocations for the Jews in Hallmann's shop. Winter told me that they had decided to move me from the Toebbens area and place me in the factory that made artificial honey and candy, which was in the same courtyard as the provisioning bureau. The director of that factory had been the prewar Danzig correspondent for the *Folkstsaytung*.[3]

His name was Grinberg, the same Grinberg whose tragicomic experience struck a personal chord. During the "wild *aktion*" on Yom Kippur, carried out by a Schupo unit[4] that was being trained in the art of organizing roundups, the Jews who were caught sat for some time in the Umschlagplatz.[5] Some of them were ransomed out. A rumor spread through the central ghetto that I was among those who were seized. When Grinberg heard the rumor he went right to Winter, put a 500-złoty note on the table, and proposed raising a sum of money for a Jewish policeman to buy me out of there. Now Grinberg was going to be my boss.

I learned that once I arrived my job would be to write down testimonies from Treblinka. There were already a number of Treblinka escapees in the ghetto, and there was a plan to publish a secret brochure about the fate that awaited each Jew they deported from Warsaw.

>—◄

Winter took me up to his apartment in the second entryway. He had moved there during the Great Deportation, along with his second son and daughter. Now they were not two but four. The son and daughter brought along a little boy and girl who had been orphaned during the roundups, and he registered these four with the provisioning bureau. I remember how impressed I was with that neat, heated apartment and with the home cooking that Winter's daughter-in-law served. The braid that rested on her shoulder made her look like a high school student. I was so moved by the expressions of tenderness on their emaciated faces. They shone with the glow of a first love that was already fated to end in death.

It began to get late. At 4 p.m. I had to join the workers' detail to return to Leszno. I said goodbye and moved through hacked-out breaches in the fences from courtyard to courtyard until I got to the housing bureau of the new Judenrat, where I could apply for a new apartment.

Two weeks later, at the beginning of December, I was living in a room at Nalewki 37, in a block assigned to the workers of the artificial honey and candy factory. My situation had greatly improved because I was now surrounded by friends and was less constrained. The work was easy. I could eat as much brown sugar and artificial honey as I wanted, there was enough bread, and soon I began to feel stronger.

I also got a generous allocation of carbide[6] and packages of large candles, so I could work late into the night. My neighbor in a nearby apartment on Nalewki was a young man called Abraham Krzepicki. He came from Danzig and two months earlier, on September 13, had escaped from Treblinka. Each night I sat with him and wrote down his terrible description of the eighteen days he spent in the death camp. Twice a week I called in sick and got time off in order to move the work along.[7]

Yosef Kirman was already working at the factory. Yoshue Perle was in the accounting section, while Y. Y. Propus, who before the war had been on the editorial staff of *The Moment*, also hung around the factory. We were all among the few members of the literary milieu who had survived the Great Deportation. The sorrow for those who had been deported, the fear for our loved ones who were outside Warsaw, the terrible news that we were hearing from other cities, the new disasters and dangers that threatened the now-shrunken ghetto—worries cascaded down on us from every direction. And still this place gave us the chance to catch our breath and gather a little strength for the trials that lay ahead. Like a father or a brother, Winter watched over us.

>——<

Then the inevitable happened. The second *aktion* began on January 18, 1943. It lasted "only" four days, but it showed that the mood of the Jews left in the ghetto had undergone a radical change. Nobody believed the German lies anymore; nobody reported for deportation voluntarily. The only people they caught were those they dragged out of bunkers. There were six or seven thousand victims who were either deported or shot in the streets. Those days saw the first Jewish armed resistance and the first Germans struck by Jewish bullets. When we left our hiding places we heard the news about Stalingrad. Our spirits lifted—tragically so—and the general state of confusion deepened. The Germans redoubled their efforts to mislead both the Jews and the Poles.

After that January *aktion* no trace remained of an orderly, routine life. No one lived in the present moment. The end was fast approaching, and everyone hastened their preparations. The Aryan side or a hideout: those were the two options for surviving to see a liberation that now, after the news of Stalingrad, seemed more palpable, more within reach, than ever before.

Which of those two options did Winter choose for himself and for his children?

I was finally ready to act on my plan to leave the ghetto for the Aryan side. In early March I went to Franciszkańska 30 to say good-bye to Winter. We began to talk about his two children and their partners who lived with him. Their shared lives had just begun and were so full of promise. What would happen to them? I could not imagine how I would cope "over there," living in the open as a Polish woman with a false identity. The thought of how I would get there seemed like an expedition to a far-off planet. I would have to reach Święto-jerska Street, where someone would hustle me out of the ghetto, and make my way to the corner of Marszalkowska and Pius, where a room was prepared for me to live—or so I hoped. How would I be able to help anybody else once I was over there? Nevertheless, I offered Winter my help in trying to arrange a way for him to escape as well.

Just before I entered Winter's room I ran into Dr. Ringelblum. We spoke and he gave me a telephone number in his shop he would use to enable me to contact Dr. Berman.[8]

I had heard talk about some committee run by Menakhem Kon that gave money to communal activists in the ghetto to escape to the Aryan side and survive there. I had no contact with that committee, and my own plan to leave depended on personal connections. But when I saw Winter I asked him why he didn't leave or at least help his children and their partners get out. Now another side of his character revealed itself to me. He seemed a little insulted at the insinuation that he might abandon his department and his co-workers. He was probably also thinking about the unofficial post he had in the combat organization.

"What? I just pick up and leave? Most people can't escape. So I just save my own hide? And what about those who don't have any money?"

"But I heard there's a fund..."

When I mentioned that fund, Winter suddenly exploded with anger. He turned red with rage.

"Who will take it upon himself to decide who deserves to go and who doesn't? When it's a question of who lives and who dies?"

Later I heard about Winter's impractical idea to organize a committee on the Aryan side. It was to be a top-secret organization that would draw up a list of the concealed bunkers in the ghetto and extend help until the end of the war.

Now I understood that he would not leave the ghetto. At most he would go bury himself alive in a deep underground ghetto fortress. When the killers made their final assault he would be counted among those who stayed in the fortress until the bitter end. He did not want to be like certain figures who thought they were more important than anybody else and thus deserved to survive. He had raised money for so many causes and for so many people, but he refused to spend any money on himself.

But what about the young people, his children? Would he sacrifice them as well?

I realized this was something he had not yet fully reckoned with. And just as I was saying goodbye, sadly aware that I would never see him again, he casually let slip the name of a Pole: Czesław Klarner. Maybe Winter was suddenly thinking of his wife, swept away in the deportations, who had left two children in his care.

At first I had trouble spelling Klarner's name because of Winter's Yiddish accent. "You don't remember that name? Find him. I think he's still in the country. Tell him, yes, tell him that Winter is asking him to save his children."[9]

After the war I made inquiries and learned that Winter, a major grain exporter, got to know Klarner through the state chamber of commerce. He wanted Klarner to do him this personal favor and he would then repay him after the war. Winter was not prepared to benefit from any official favors. In the five weeks between my leaving the ghetto and the outbreak of the uprising, I was not able to locate Klarner.

Winter also gave me a telephone number. We agreed that when I found a place for the two young couples I would contact "Zygmunt"— Zygmunt Frydrych of the Bund. The two of us would then arrange and settle the transaction. I made several calls to some locksmith's shop, which seemed to be Zygmunt's safe house. But each time I was told that he had not yet returned. They did not tell me where he was.

Days went by. Around April 15 I registered as a resident in a building on Próżna with another woman who was as "Polish" as I was. She used the name Stanisława Królikowska. (Her real name was Helena Merenholc.) We rented the room with the help of a Polish agent, and on Saturday, April 17, I telephoned "Mr. Zimowski"—Winter.[10]

He sounded flustered by the sound of my voice and worried by my call.

"What happened? Have you heard anything?" he asked.

"No, nothing. I want Zygmunt to meet me and go over the deal, as we agreed . . ."

I had to quickly end the phone call in the café on Stolowa Street. Too many people were hanging around who were "Polish" like me.

>——◄

I never spoke with Winter or Frydrych again. In 1948 I heard some details about Winter from Marek Edelman, the Bundist commander of the brushmakers sector on Świętojerska-Wolowa during the uprising. On the third day of the uprising the fighters retreated through attics to nearby Franciszkańska Street. Two weeks later, manning an observation point on the roof, he witnessed the tragic end of Winter and of the other Jews who had been in one of the underground bunkers.

Edelman was lying concealed on the roof of the annex of Franciszkańska 30. He saw the Germans hurl a tear-gas grenade into the solid and well-concealed bunker of the provisioning bureau and then drag out the people who were hiding there. The bunker had been built under the cellars of the annex opposite. If I am not mistaken, those must have been the cellars of the artificial honey factory to the left of the main entryway, where Kirman, Winter's young daughter-in-law, and I had worked a few months ago. Among the group of coughing and sneezing Jews who crawled out on all fours to be lined up and searched by the Germans Edelman saw Winter, with his tall, slightly stooped frame, and Abraham Gepner, small in stature but known as a great figure of Warsaw Jewry. Gepner was dressed in white overalls buttoned in the back or perhaps in an English woolen jacket. Gepner and Winter walked in front, followed by the others.

"Were there young people there? Did you notice Winter's son and daughter, his son-in-law and daughter-in-law?" I asked Edelman.

"I did not recognize them specifically, but there were more than four young people there."

I knew where they were all sent. Probably not to the Umschlagplatz but to the little square next to the Judenrat building at Zamenhof 19, where the ghetto monument stands today. There they were shot. They had the privilege of being buried in the Gęsia cemetery. This happened in early May.[11]

>—<

After the liberation and return to the ruins of the ghetto, Hersh Wasser, the former secretary of the Ringelblum archive, found in a courtyard of Swiętojerska 34 a bundle of badly damaged pages from Winter's diary.[12] There had been a bunker of the Jewish Fighting Organization that had been constructed under that building. According to Yitshak Zuckerman, numerous documents, including Winter's diary, were buried in a hole under the floor the night before the outbreak of the uprising. After the fighting ended and the fires died down, scavengers rampaged through the rubble looking for gold and money. They almost certainly rummaged through the bunker at Swiętojerska 34 and, finding only papers, in all likelihood dumped them.[13]

The papers had been lying around for more than a year. They had been scorched by flames and embers, soaked by rain. But a few pages survived, just like us. Just a few here and a few there, ownerless, to convey a description and reminder of those terrible days.

Part 7: Memorial Lights

32. THE FATHER

Yosef Kirman did not have to die. He had worked for
many years in Rigavar, a factory in Praga that made galoshes. Before I left for the Aryan side at the beginning
of 1943, I urged him to find the Poles he knew from there
and ask for their help. He did not react at all to my suggestion. He was murdered with the remaining Warsaw
Jews during the great massacre of the work camps in the
Lublin area in November 1943.

These are a few sentences from the report I gave in August 1945,
at the first postwar conference of the World Jewish Congress in London. The documents from the Ringelblum archive that were discovered also mention my contacts with Kirman during the occupation.
But our acquaintance began many years before the war started.

>—<

When a few of us, Galitsianers who had previously worked for the
journal *Tsushtayer,* found ourselves together in Warsaw in the early
1930s, the great excitement of the postwar *Sturm und Drang* in Yiddish literature had long since died down.[1] One by one the brilliant
firebirds of that scintillating literary gang, the *Khalyastre,* all took
wing and left Warsaw for the United States, the Soviet Union, or the
Land of Israel.[2] Gradually, and without much fanfare, new names began to appear on the scene. One such newcomer was Yosef Kirman,

who had been a young disciple of Perets Markish. Kirman continued to write blank verse in long unrhymed stanzas. But his well-crafted images and the themes that he wove into his poetry underscored a total lack of pretense and embellishment, a simplicity that marked an up-and-coming generation of young Yiddish poets. His tragic tone bore no hint of intellectual posturing but reflected feelings that he came by honestly, through his own experience.

The stiff way in which he moved, and his deep baritone voice, reminded us Galitsianers of Ber Horowitz. As we listened to his poems and to his terse, finely honed speech, we felt that we were in the presence of a new down-to-earth Jewishness, rooted in a unique, genuine Yiddish and permeated with a feel for authentic folk culture.

Kirman was born and raised in Warsaw, and the theme of urban poverty in his work had an autobiographical ring. That taciturn Jew, who came home with only one loaf of black bread, could have been his father, who died young. The pale, emaciated woman who cut ever thinner slices off the loaf for her children could have been his mother, who also died before her time.

He never stopped mourning his tiny little sister who crawled all over the floor and looked for the fallen crumbs of bread that she would put in her mouth. And there was another sister that he memorialized in his poem "The Death of My Sister."

Bread. Poverty. Death. *Broyt. Noyt. Toyt.* Even in his early poetry, in some stubbornly predictable pattern, these words, not always rhymed but often paired, kept turning up. In his cycle of poems entitled *Hunger*, inspired by the German occupation of the First World War, one can plainly see foreboding, a sense of inevitability and predestination. Because of their style and images, these poems could well have been written during the Second World War.

After a lot of effort, I managed to find an edition of Kirman's printed volume of poetry, *Iber shtok un shteyn* (*Running a Gauntlet*), published by Boris Kletzkin in 1930. I read it now and can't believe what I'm seeing. I'm sure that I read these poems shortly after they were published, but I can swear that Kirman read them to me in the Warsaw Ghetto in 1941 or 1942:

> Their faces frozen in cold fear
> These young giants, now in harness

Pull wagon loads alongside horses,
See them now, sprawled on the ground, their hands
    shriveled, yellow,
Their legs, thick and swollen, so bent they touch their
    eyes
And birds with scrawny claws flit over piles of knobby
    bones dragged here from God knows where
As they greedily peck at the moist earth . . .

Whom would he be describing if not those Jews from the provinces, Jews sturdy as oaks, who were dumped into the Warsaw Ghetto? In just a few short months, swollen from hunger, they were barely alive, their lives slowly ebbing away on the pavement next to a few coins tossed by Jews who, a few months hence, might well be lying in the same place.

Or perhaps this poem is about those who already died, piled in heaps of naked corpses in the death shed of the Gęsia cemetery, waiting to be shoved into a mass grave?

Whose bones is he talking about? Perhaps the bodies mowed down at some execution site?

Little birds, scrawny little birds—ten years later that's what he would call the hungry children on the ghetto streets.

>——◄

Even the most inexperienced memoirists of the Holocaust realize that they must begin with a chapter about life before the war, so the reader might better understand what happened next and feel the contrast between before and after.

We have not yet reached the days when the great disaster befell us. Let's linger just a little more in the brighter ambiance of the prewar years. (Bright? Well, everything is relative.)

I remember a story I heard just after I arrived in Warsaw. Kirman was the main character.

It happened in that legendary time when Markish and his disciples cut a swath through Jewish Warsaw each evening and late into the night with their public poetry readings at Tlomackie. In those days there were already novelists and journalists who were regular contributors to the Yiddish press and who earned good money from writing in Yiddish. A number of Yiddish writers had reached the point where they could afford to spend weekends and holidays in the nicest hotels and guesthouses on the Otwock line.[3] Some of these writers would send their wives and children to stay there the whole summer. Now it turned out that one such writer, the prominent Alter Kacyzne—who supported his family not through writing but through his artistically accomplished photography studio—was even able to buy his own dacha on the "line." This dacha became the butt of jokes (as well as an object of concealed envy) in the literary world, where it came to be called "the villa in Świder."

Our angry young men in those years were less aggressive than their post–World War II counterparts who wrote in other languages. So it happened that one day Perets Markish, perhaps in jest, issued the clarion call to "storm the villa in Świder"—and his disciples took him completely at his word.

No sooner said than done. The next Sunday morning a group of Markish's groupies left the station in Świder and marched to Kacyzne's dacha. Leading the column was, or so they told me, Yosef Kirman, a thick club in his hand, a bunch of stones in the pocket of his unbuttoned jacket.

It was said that one of the stones smashed one of the dacha's windows and roused the family from their blessed, late-morning sleep. Markish, it seems, was not there. But his friend Alter Kacyzne appeared on the veranda wearing his "petty bourgeois" house robe. He began wiping his spectacles, just as he would do before beginning a lecture at Tlomackie, then invited the whole crew into his palace for a glass of summertime vegetarian "*shmate* borscht." The young marchers were all flummoxed and hastily, surreptitiously, removed the stones from their pockets.

>——<

Zalmen Reyzen's *Leksikon* indicates that Kirman was born in 1896. When we got to know him in the early 1930s he was already a young man who made a decent living. Like Kacyzne, he did not rely on writing for his livelihood but on something that had nothing to do with literature. Perhaps, as time went on, Kirman made this a principled decision, preferring to make walking sticks for the elderly or galoshes for the autumn muck rather than write articles for the daily press and put up with the bosses who ruled the newsrooms.

He had a wide frame and, in the fashion of the time, copious locks of dark hair hanging down over his ample but not very high forehead. His large, smiling mouth perched over a wide, flabby neck that showed the tell-tale signs of goiter. Kirman's dark eyes sparkled with the light of Jewish irony and shrewdness.

Those who die young will always remain young . . .

That's how I remember Kirman. Today I am not certain if my memory is based on how he really looked or on some sketch of him hanging on the walls of the Jewish writers union on Tlomackie. Or perhaps I am remembering a portrait that appeared in the *Literarishe bleter* when it published one of his poems.

I don't know when Kirman got married. But I do remember when he began to appear at Tlomackie with a pretty and delicate girl—his wife. She had brown hair and brown eyes, a beige-brown outfit, and low shoes made of light brown suede. That's how I remember her: shy, taciturn, with a winning smile. When you addressed her, golden sparks glistened in her eyes.

That summer before the war I once ran into Kirman on Bielańska. He told me that his five-year-old was jealous of his little brother and how those two little devils romped around on a weekend morning when they would crawl into their parents' bed. One morning they jumped so hard on the bed and on their parents' bellies that all four of them fell to the floor, along with the mattress. They laughed so hard that it took a while to untangle themselves.

That's the last happy memory I have of Kirman.

>——<

In a ghetto reportage dated June 30, 1942, which I recovered in the first cache of the Ringelblum archive, I wrote:

> Y. (Yosef) is absolutely beside himself with worry about his children. He sent his two children and his young wife to her native shtetl to protect them from hunger and typhus. He misses them terribly, and he wanders through

the ghetto sad, preoccupied, always thinking about children—whom he treats with special tenderness. The love he had for his own children has turned into a love for all children, for those hungry, pleading, singing, haggling waifs whose wailing voices fill every cranny of the ghetto. Kirman walks along the crowded Leszno Street and gives the little beggars the last coins from his purse. These kids can already recognize him at a distance. They run after him and cut in front of him, blocking his way. Every word from his mouth is now about children . . .

We met often in those days. Kirman, like many writers, would drop in to see me from time to time in the soup kitchen at Leszno 40. Usually he would show up after we had finished serving all the meals. But a couple of times he would drop in at the busiest time and ask me to go with him to see the "boss," the director of the Aleynhilf.

"Come," he would order me. "You they would dare not refuse."

I don't know if he was involved in mutual aid activities before the war. But in the ghetto he zealously set out to provide help for impoverished and helpless fellow writers. In another chapter I describe how both of us helped rescue Yisroel Shtern from hunger dystrophy. But Kirman took on the task of watching over needy writers who were less famous. He brought doctors to treat them, procured medicines, brought them packages, and helped arrange their funerals.

All the while Kirman, like all the rest of us, had his own problems to worry about. He lived in a constant state of anxiety and mental disequilibrium. The nightly murders on the street, the prophecy making the rounds on the Aryan side about the "forty days of the ghetto" . . . in those days, during the summer of 1942, we had a premonition that a disaster was approaching that would dwarf the horror we had already experienced.[4] People spun fantasies and sought comfort in any lie. Writers—unless they were already crushed by what they saw around them—had certain outlets to cope with their fear. They could compose a poem, describe a scene, or merely note something that happened.

During his sleepless nights Kirman wrote. The written word tormented and disturbed him but it also soothed and comforted. So when he and I would be hurrying together through the thick crowds on Leszno, he would suddenly drag me into a doorway or a courtyard entrance and read one of his poems. Those poems were always about our common plight.

Kirman's poems became shorter and more folksy. In a sudden rush of inspiration he wrote song-poems that sounded like echoes of men crying without tears or the traditional liturgy of reverence and awe. He read those poems with that unmistakable intonation of a Jewish mourning dirge. It made the deep bass voice issuing from his chest sound more foreboding and more intimate.

By that time, the dying children in the ghetto had mostly succumbed to starvation. But one could sense, in the tone and cadence of the dirges that issued from this poet's soul, the frightening harbinger of more child-death approaching from all directions. This approaching death would be on an enormous scale, it would be horrible, and it would sweep away all the children from the streets of the ghetto.

It also destroyed him. The father.

>——<

In the last weeks before the Great Deportation the terror in the ghetto became so intense that I saw no writers during the whole month of July and the first weeks of August. The roundups began on July 22, and each day the panic grew worse. During the deportation one building after another was blockaded and searched, and everybody was totally focused on saving themselves. But in the second half of August there was a pause in the deportations because the murderers of the Rollkommando switched their attention to the Otwock line and began to liquidate the Jews in this area full of dachas and guest houses.[5]

Nobody believed the planted rumors that the roundups had ended. Most people in the ghetto had lost loved ones, neighbors, and good friends. Everybody knew that sooner or later they too would be swept away by the raging flood. But at least you could catch your breath. In the few hours that it was possible to go outside, people filled the streets to find out what had happened to relatives and friends and whether they were still in their previous workplaces and apartments. Or whether they were there at all.

I was still in the kitchen at Leszno 40, and my apartment at Leszno 66, where I lived with my relatives, was still within the confines of the ghetto. In early August we had the "privilege" of being taken over by the Toebbens firm, which requisitioned all of Leszno from Karmelicka to Żelazna. Our well-organized and technically well-equipped soup kitchen also had the "good fortune" of becoming a Toebbens shop kitchen. The only problem was that Toebbens' Jewish director of provisioning installed a clique of his own people and then brutally discharged me along with eighteen others who had organized the kitchen and had worked there the whole time.

On that first day of the pause in deportations, Yekhiel Lerer paid me a visit. The next day, very early in the morning, as the labor contingents began their daily trek to their workplaces on the Aryan side, the director Adam Furmanski and composer Yisroel Glatshteyn came to say goodbye. They were leaving the ghetto and hoping to find some hiding place on the other side.

That same day after lunch Yosef Kirman suddenly appeared. He was dressed like a laborer; a bread bag tied to a belt dangled from his waist. We had already served the daily meal. The new bosses had left for home. The girls in the kitchen were scrubbing the vats. The sun was shining through all the windows of the large hall. Even the piano, where in the afternoons Glatshteyn would teach young people some satiric ditty about the Judenrat, was still there on the podium. No one had stolen it yet. The white oilcloths shone on the freshly scrubbed long tables. Everything looked just as if this were a routine day.

But something was missing: the throngs of hungry people. At this hour they used to crowd the back entrance to the kitchen hoping to scrounge some scrapings from the pots. And what happened to the warbling beggars we used to hear from the street below? And the children, who sang as they begged: Where were they?

As the weeks passed you could feel summer fading away and could not help but notice that the days were becoming shorter and shorter.

It was about half past four in the afternoon. Groups of "platzuvkazhes"[6] were returning from work carrying bunches of summer vegetables, which they were allowed to take with them.

Kirman wanted to see if I was still in the ghetto. He also wanted to show me that he was one of the lucky ones who were "gainfully employed." His workplace was thought to be one of the "safest": the Ostbahn![7] But he did not want to live in a work camp outside the ghetto.

He wasn't carrying any green onions and carrots. He stuck his hand into his bread bag and handed me a present: a bunch of sour cherries, still attached to their stalks, which he had torn from a tree.

Suddenly something caught in my throat as I remembered the sour cherries from our garden in Lanowitz. Jars of preserves, flasks on the shelf, cherries that my mother used to distill into Passover wishniak, fresh sour cherries like the red sweet smile of a toddler's little lips . . .

"Eat!" Kirman said to me as he passed me the bunch, and I devoured the sour cherries in one go, so as not to start crying if I gazed at them.

I told him about what was going on in my kitchen, about the antics of the new boss.

"Your kitchen! Your kitchen!" he responded, grumbling reproachfully. "Don't you know what's going on all around us? Spare your nerves. Don't think about that scoundrel."

The lawyer Graf came into the kitchen along with his wife, Stefa, and Dr. Boczko, a refugee from Lodz who, before the Great Deportation, had been on our staff as a medical supervisor. Graf had been the secretary of the retail merchants association, which had owned the building where the kitchen was located. He told me that some members of the kitchen administration had collected several sewing machines and were negotiating to set up a Toebbens shop in the main dining hall. He also informed me that they were ready, gratis, to include me on the employment rolls. The doctor also had a proposal for me. He called me over to a corner and wanted to stick a cyanide capsule in my apron pocket, which I could carry around "just in case." This was the kind of present many people in those days could only dream about.

Kirman overheard both proposals. When I walked him to the door, he shook his head and wagged his finger, an unmistakable signal that meant *no*.

"Say no to both! As soon as you're able, find yourself a hiding place!"

>—<

That's exactly what I did. I survived that major selection in the "cauldron" only because I did not go. I hunkered down with some people in a coke cellar that was underneath my cousin Reuven Feldshuh's apartment at Leszno 66. After the Great Deportation, I hung around Leszno for a few weeks, like a wandering zombie of the netherworld. Then the surviving activists in the central ghetto found out I was still alive and brought me there.

>———<

After I arrived at the artificial honey factory at Franciszkańska 30 I met the three writers who were already registered there: Yoshue Perle, Y. Y. Propus, and Kirman.[9]

Officially, we each had a particular job. Perle was employed in the accounting department, Kirman worked with the large vats, and I packed the little candies. The sweets were made in a large hall in enclosed vats where the ersatz sweeteners were cooked. Then the mixture was placed on high tables, where the thick, half-cooled concoction was kneaded and shaped into various confections.

Yosef Kirman worked at one of those tables. He wore a small hat and was wrapped in a waterproof apron that reached to his armpits. As he carefully kneaded the warm dough he resembled a pious Jew baking matzos. Another time I saw him standing on top of a small bench, using a long shovel to mix a brownish "honey" liquid based on beet molasses, which was prepared according to a German recipe.

Our boss and supervisor was Grinberg, the prewar Danzig correspondent of the *Folkstsaytung*. He was a wonderful man who treated us warmly. We received brown sugar for our tea and an extra ration of bread, which we could smear with as much "honey" as we wished. We were together with people who were close and familiar. Despite the sadness and the sense of overwhelming loss that we all felt, despite the dangers and the daily alarms and horrors, we nonetheless were able, to some extent, to pull ourselves together.

>———<

On one of those first Sundays, when we only worked until noon, Kirman walked me home to the honey factory workers' quarters at Nalewki 37. He told me what he went through during the recent weeks of the Great Deportation and how he survived the selection.

One day when the Jewish police were given their quota of "heads" to catch, two scoundrels apprehended him in a courtyard and forcibly dragged him to the Umschlagplatz. He fought them, swore at them, but they called a third policeman for help and delivered him to the holding pen. That's how he came to see, with his own eyes, that horrifying scene of Jewish suffering and humiliation. But he was able to send out a note to Yitshak Giterman, and within a few hours he was able to leave.[10]

He could not forget what he went through when those "Polish-speaking renegades" grabbed him. As he told the story he became frighteningly agitated. "We should never have allowed this to happen," he shouted as he banged the table with his fist. "Nothing could be worse than what has taken place. We should have set fire to everything. We could have dispersed the Jewish police..."

What he said about setting the ghetto alight as soon as the Great Deportation started stuck deep in my memory, not least because I heard those same words often, both then and after the war. "*Borei me'orei ha'esh*"[11] became the slogan of the Jewish resistance. We see those words again and again in eyewitness accounts of revolts and resistance, especially in the camps and in small provincial towns.

Another time Kirman told me how he survived the mass selection in the "cauldron" by staying with a friend for more than a week in a hideout, with nothing to eat but raw groats and a few pieces of hard sugar. They drank standing rainwater caught in a rusty tin can.

>———<

Perle not only worked at Franciszkańska 30 but lived there as well. Once, hearing that he was sick, I went to visit him during the lunch break. One entered after giving a prearranged sign. I found him in bed writing, using the cover of an account book as a backstop.

From time to time, Shmuel Winter would give me a nod and I would also "get sick," stay away from the factory, and continue writing down the exhaustive testimony I had been hearing in the evenings from Abraham (Yakov) Krzepicki, the escapee from Treblinka. Krzepicki also lived in the collective residence at Nalewki 37.

It was only because of a hint dropped by Winter that I learned Kirman was also writing. Kirman himself did not read me anything he wrote then. Once I tried asking him about the poems he had read for me on Leszno and whether he should entrust someone to hide them. He answered that he'd left those poems in a bundle of his other possessions on Dzielna Street that he could no longer retrieve.[12]

>——<

One day as I was ready to go home Kirman approached me and asked me to remain in the factory to help him arrange a telephone call with some town in the provinces. I don't remember the name of the place. It was the town where he had sent his wife and children. I do remember the name of the Pole Kirman asked me to summon to the post office for the telephone call. Perhaps it was the same Pole whose address he used to send letters and packages to his family before the Great Deportation. Once we ordered the call, we waited perhaps an hour until the post office called to tell us that the person we asked for had arrived. Kirman was pale as a ghost. He rushed to the receiver and began to stammer:

"Hello! Hello! Pan Wozniak? Panie Wozniak? How are Marysia and the children? What about the children? What? What? Louder! I can't hear, Pan Wozniak, I can't hear . . ."

Marysia was probably the Polish name they had agreed to call his wife. It was clear that he could not take in what he was hearing. He grasped the receiver with both hands, screamed louder and louder that he couldn't hear, and kept repeating nonstop: "What? What?" As I looked at him, I too was about to start trembling with agitation. I didn't understand what the gentile said that Kirman was not able to grasp. Maybe the Pole didn't understand what Kirman was yelling into the receiver. It was too loud, too rapid, all said in a state of extreme agitation.

"Marysia! Marysia! Where is Marysia?" he yelled again, and I began to realize that he was losing his self-control. I quickly moved a bench toward him and all but ripped the receiver out of his grasp.

"Error! Error! You are requested to disconnect this call!" I heard some distant and angry voice say. Perhaps the Pole became frightened that someone might betray him? Or perhaps he wanted to walk away because he had no good news for the father? Maybe they had already deported his wife and child some time ago and the Pole didn't want to break the news?

"Hang up! Hang up! Hang up immediately!" I heard another voice call, probably the post office official's. I took one look at Kirman and hung up immediately.

I led him to the tall table and gave him a glass of water. He was unsteady on his feet and his forehead was covered with thick beads of sweat. He drank some water and sat for a while with his head in his hands, leaning on the edge of the table and not saying a word. He finally got up and in a flat voice urged me to go home because curfew was approaching. As we reached the gate, just before we got to the street, he told me something that was so strange it seemed as if he was hallucinating.

"I heard how they were calling me: 'Yosef, Yosef!'" he said. "I heard how they were calling my name . . ."

I didn't want to say that all I heard was their order to hang up the telephone, that he had been mistaken.

We reached Nalewki and went our separate ways. We did not discuss that telephone call ever again. That was one of our last meetings. But more than once I returned to that bizarre incident and tried to learn from him what had happened to his family.

They were probably no longer alive when Kirman made that call. By the end of 1942 there was hardly one Jewish settlement that had not endured either a deportation or a total liquidation. Perhaps Kirman's wife had tried to escape with her children to Wozniak's, who might well have been frightened at that critical moment and ordered them to leave his house or barn. Or perhaps she was never able to reach him? Maybe she did not want to separate from her family? Or perhaps when it happened, the absence of her husband had thrown her into a state of total apathy?

I do not know, and I will certainly never know which of these conjectures describes what happened or the true story of how this woman with the golden freckles and brown eyes, along with her two children, met her doom.

Or perhaps—it's a thought that comes to me even now—Kirman was not hallucinating when he heard her calling his name? Maybe that sound wandered for days and months in the empty space above the killing field, that sound that cried out in the final seconds before the very end, as the three of them yearned for him and cried for him with all their souls, longed to see him one more time, to say a final goodbye, to join him as one as they took their last breaths. And it was precisely at that moment, just when he was overcome with anguish, when his love for them made him so eager to hear the slightest word from them and about them—at that instant their abandoned, wandering voices found a way to reach him, voices that were intended only for him.

It is as if a torrent of voices pulsates through the ether, ranges over hundreds and thousands of miles, and without any direct wire link or intermediary finally reaches its intended recipient because that person is tuned to precisely that wavelength, ready to hear that particular signal.

Yes, he did hear their call. He would indeed share their fate and reunite with them. But not just yet.

>——<

The interrupted phone call that evening broke his heart. At first he did not want to admit they were no longer alive and if he was to ever see them again and hear their voices it would be *there* and not *here*. It happened sometime in early January 1943, and I saw him only once after that.

I was planning to leave for the Aryan side in another week or two. The last time we met I asked him to tell me the names of the Poles whom he worked with in the rubber factory in Praga before the war. I didn't know myself how I would manage on "that side," but I told him that perhaps I would be able to find them and get them to arrange a hiding place for him or a job protected by safe documents. I also added that maybe it might make sense to persuade one of those Poles to visit the shtetl where his wife and children had been.

As soon as I said this he raised his head and fixed me with a stern, piercing stare. Maybe he wanted to gauge, from the expression on my face, whether I was serious or just saying something to give him false hope. And then his expression once again became depressed and silent. Maybe he had heard something since we last met and did not want to tell anybody.

"Godspeed and good luck!" he finally wished me just before we said goodbye. Even though I left the ghetto only one and a half months later, that was the last time I saw Kirman. That talk happened just before the sudden German assault on the ghetto, the so-called second *aktion*, which lasted from January 18 to January 22 and threw all our lives into confusion and further uncertainty.

When I emerged from the hideout at Nalewki 37 I moved over to Muranowska. I finished taking down the Treblinka testimony, handed over my last manuscripts to the secret archive, and got ready to leave the ghetto.

I went to Franciszkańska just one more time, to say goodbye. I didn't find Kirman there and no one could tell me where he was. Perhaps during the panic and confusion of the January *aktion* he moved over to the Toebbens shops and stayed there until the outbreak of the uprising. Or maybe he left the ghetto with an earlier convoy of Toebbens workers. I only received further news about Kirman half a year later.

>——<

It was the end of July 1943. Emissaries from the Jewish National Committee[13] on the Aryan side had managed to free the Left Labor Zionist activist Pola Elster from the Poniatowa camp. She told me that, along with several other Warsaw Jews I knew, Kirman was in the camp. I asked her whether it would be possible to free him as well. Pola knew Kirman as a party sympathizer from before the war and promised me that she would discuss the matter with other members of the committee. I also spoke to Basia Berman and pointed out that Kirman was one of the very last surviving writers from the Warsaw Ghetto. She assured me that they would try their best, although getting him out of the camp was far from easy.

Time passed. They sent money to the underground organization in the camp, and Kirman probably benefited from this as well. But then the envoys to the camp began to run into problems. In early November they set out for Poniatowa with a large sum of money and were planning to take some people out, perhaps Kirman as well. They came too late.

>——<

It happened on November 3, 1943, and became known in the history of the German mass murders as Operation Harvest Festival.[14]

The Third of November—this is what the Kiev Jewish artist Zinovy Tolkachev, who came to Poland in January 1945 as a soldier in the Red Army, called his cycle of drawings. *The Third of November.*

Nine months had passed since the German defeat at Stalingrad, three months since the overthrow of Mussolini and the capitulation of the Italian army. The front line began to move closer. The Lublin district, the district in all of Nazi-occupied Europe with the second-highest number of murdered Jews, became the scene of armed resistance along the German lines of communication. More and more partisan groups, including Jews, appeared in the forests. Armed revolts, followed by mass escapes, broke out in two death camps: Treblinka in August and Sobibor in October. In a dispatch to his top SS commander in Krakow, Himmler wrote that the "Jewish problem has reached dangerous proportions."[15]

Telegrams and messages began to stream back and forth between Berlin and Lublin. The topic was the murder of 40,000 Jews, mostly deportees from the Warsaw Ghetto during the uprising who had been sent to labor camps in the area. Had this been one year earlier, killing such a number would have presented no problem. But now the gas chambers were no longer working. The Germans had to fall back on their tried-and-true method: bullets.

Twelve thousand Jews in Trawniki, thirteen thousand in Majdanek, and fourteen thousand in Poniatowa. The third of November. Operation Harvest Festival. A page of photographs in a picture album: the epilogue, the postscript to the destruction of Warsaw Jewry.

>——<

From the Nazi point of view, one of the drawbacks of mass shootings was the remaining witnesses: those who had been wounded and not killed, those who would crawl out of the killing pits at night, after the bodies had been partly buried, who somehow survived the countless horrors, who managed to find some clothing, some water to wash away the blood, some people who still had a trace of mercy and empathy and were prepared to help them regain the image of a human being.

By 1945 we had accounts of these survivors of the mass shootings, including those at Poniatowa.[16] One such survivor was Esther Rubinstein-Winderbaum, today a resident of Givatayim, who gave her testimony about the third of November to the Jewish Historical Commission in Lodz.

A few days before the massacre the Germans organized groups of men with shovels and long rods to dig "anti-Soviet tank ditches." The morning of November 3 they led those same groups of strong men to work, then took away their shovels and shot them. There is reason to believe that the 47-year-old Yosef Kirman was in this group of men and died in this first salvo.

Not only Jewish witnesses were able to relate what happened that November day. More than two years ago two gentlemen in their sixties, who took part in Operation Harvest Festival, appeared before a German court in Wiesbaden. One of them, Gotthart Schumann—yes, the same name as the well-known German composer—mentioned a detail in his affidavit that had somehow lodged in his memory.

"During the shooting various melodies were played on loudspeakers. The volume was turned as high as it would go. After the records were played, they would start from the beginning."

A Polish witness, a former inmate in Majdanek, gave the Polish commission investigating German crimes in Poland some more details about the musical accompaniment to the events of November 3. There were no record players with loudspeakers in Majdanek. But there was an orchestra made up of inmates that was placed close to the shooting pits, and as the salvoes echoed they played Odilo Glubocnik's favorite waltz, "An der schonen blauen Donau," by Johann Strauss Jr. Glubocnik was Himmler's right-hand man in the destruction of European Jewry and the higher SS and police leader of the Lublin district. When they finished playing the waltz they repeated it from the beginning. Glubocnik was raised and educated in Vienna.[17]

>——◄

Yosef Kirman might have had some chance, albeit small, to survive on the Aryan side, but he showed no interest. I don't mean that he did not want to stay alive; I do not even want to imply that he didn't try because he knew, or he guessed, that his nearest and dearest were already dead. Nonetheless, like some other Jewish writers in those days, he was driven by certain subconscious forces he could not control. He felt so much a part of the Jewish masses, so bound to their fate and lives, that perhaps he found it unthinkable to save himself and thus escape their plight.

He joined those who let that powerful tide sweep them away so they could die together with their people.

THE TWO GLATSHTEYNS

Just behind the parcel of land at Tlomackie 5, whose front side contained the synagogue and the Judaic Institute, there was another building that had belonged to the Warsaw Jewish Community Council: an apartment block for employees affiliated with the synagogue and the institute. The same entryway where David Eisenstadt lived had also housed Moshe Koussevitzky, the chief cantor of the Tlomackie synagogue. When the Germans marched in, the fabulous cantor with the phenomenal tenor voice fled to the Soviet zone, and a refugee from Germany, the composer Yisroel Glatshteyn, moved into his apartment.

Having spent twenty years in Germany, when Hitler came to power Glatshteyn returned to Poland, where he still had many friends and colleagues from his days in the musical world of Lodz.

Either before or during the First World War Glatshteyn had composed the melody to Yitshak Katzenelson's poem "The Sun Goes Down in Flames." The song became so popular and was sung so often that people thought it was a folk song. He wrote other melodies for poems that were sung by Jews all over the world. Glatshteyn maintained his ties with the Jewish public even when he was living in Germany and was working there as a professional musician. Now and then he would compose tunes for the Jewish ensembles that would tour before Hitler took power.

After he was forced to come back to Poland he renewed his contacts. When the Germans attacked, Glatshteyn stayed put and did not run. During the first winter of the occupation, when a revue was performed in the Scala Theater, it was Glatshteyn who arranged the musical accompaniment.

If I'm not mistaken he also wrote the melody to Nachum Sternheim's poem "Sorele," which became a major hit when it was sung by Diana Blumenfeld; soon everybody picked it up. Even in those tragic days between the September pause in the Great Deportation and the

January *aktion* of 1943, I remember how my neighbor, who had escaped from Treblinka, whistled and sang that song.

When Glatshteyn conducted that revue he also created and trained a very good revelers' choir.[1] He was a methodical worker, and in addition to his own talent, his systematic approach to musical training reflected the very highest European standards.

After Tlomackie was excluded from the ghetto, Glatshteyn lost his room and piano in Koussevitzky's old apartment. But he was able to find a new piano in the apartment of Hersh-Leyb Zhitnitski, the former editor of *Haynt*'s literary supplement, who was in Lwow at the time with his son. In the autumn of 1941, after Zhitnitski's wife and other child left for the provinces, Glatshteyn transferred his studio to our kitchen at Leszno 40. That happened by chance. There was a big stage in the large hall of the retail merchants union, which had now become our main dining space. Before the war that stage had been used for artistic performances. After the Germans removed Tlomackie from the ghetto, the excellent piano that had been in the main reading room of the looted library of the Judaic Institute was moved to that stage.

That's when Glatshteyn once again began to organize a revelers' choir. One of the members was David Birnbaum, whom I had known before the war when he was an actor in the Vilna Troupe. Rehearsals soon began in our kitchen for Y. Shaynkind's satiric song "Reb Abba undzer gabbai."[2] The choir rehearsed mostly in the afternoons, after we had finished serving the midday meal.

As our staff washed the dishes, mopped the floors, weighed out food for the next day's meal, and prepared the account sheet to hand over to the kitchen directorate, I kept hearing the same song being played and sung repeatedly, in different variations. The young girls working in our kitchen—Stella, Dina, and Dora—together with our young janitor Joseph Erlich soon began to belt out their own versions. The obsessive attention lavished on this one song struck them as hilarious, and they loved to make fun of it. After all, they did not think that learning one new song should be such a big deal. But they were young, they had a job, and they had enough to eat, relatively speaking. Despite all the dangers and troubles that afflicted us, they could still let loose and laugh. And besides, they still had their lives ahead of them: all six months' worth . . .

Even I began to wonder why they were devoting so much effort and attention to just one song. But Glatshteyn was a pedant and a perfectionist. For him it wasn't about that one number. He tried to transform those four amateur singers into a genuine revelers' choir.

I emphasize the word *tried*. He was no optimist, and he did not like to talk about future plans.

After the murderous rampage on the night of April 17-18, 1942, the rehearsals stopped. But Glatshteyn would still stop by, have a soup, and exchange a few words. At the beginning of the Great Deportation, when the kitchen became part of the Toebbens firm and acquired a new administration, I would still see Glatshteyn almost every day at Leszno 40, now in the company of the conductor Adam Furmanski. I knew Furmanski mainly because he had been one of the most important musical mentors of my little cousin, the 11-year-old pianist Josima Feldshuh, who lived in the same apartment as I did. When Josima made her concert debut as a soloist in the early winter of 1941 with a performance of Mozart's Piano Concerto in C Major, it was Furmanski who directed the orchestra.

I would often discuss our prospects with Glatshteyn, who had lived for many years in Germany and had even stayed a while after Hitler took power. He was sober and pessimistic. He didn't have the slightest illusions about what the Germans planned to do to the Jews. After the roundups began he showed a lot of self-control and a determination to survive. He too tried to save himself.

There was yet another Glatshteyn in the ghetto—Yankev, who directed the people's choir. Compared to David Eisenstadt he had far lower expectations of his choir, which consisted of working-class kids. They were boys and girls who came from the poorest strata of Warsaw Jewry. He was happy to share with the wider public the modest results he managed to achieve. A couple of singers did have fine voices. But the poor conditions in which they lived often kept them from singing at all. The pianist who accompanied the choir, Liliana Warm, told me that before rehearsals began they had to give each member of the choir a piece of bread topped with marmalade and a cup of ersatz coffee. Only then, after they had eaten something, could they start to rehearse.

I can see him now, this other Glatshteyn. He was small and curly haired. There he is, standing on that stage on Tlomackie, about to conduct the choir. The boys and girls are lined up just so, all wearing, as much as it was possible, identical outfits. They were poor and exhausted but also young and full of life. Some were dark eyed, with a shining glint. There were others with dreamy eyes of blue or green. One fiery redhead stood out among the many singers with big locks of dark, curly hair. All these young people from poor homes shared a yearning for something better, for beauty and culture. They found it when they sang "Dreams of Infinitely Superior Nature" in one of Handel's early oratorios. When the Germans arranged the streets and walls of the ghetto, they tried so hard to deprive these young people of the chance to see a green blade of grass or a tree that changed its colors twice a year. These kids had younger brothers and sisters who had never seen a flower in their lives and who had to ask, "Mommy, what's a flower?"

Even this did not sate the sadistic thirst of the German killers. It was such a short interval between that stage and the gas chambers.

The beloved teacher Yankev Glatshteyn perished along with his singers, the very person who had brought a spark of beauty and splendor into their short lives.

33. Wax Candles

I knew Yekhiel Lerer before the war in a casual way, like I knew so many other writers at Tlomackie 13. In those days our literary family was very large. I don't remember if he lived in Warsaw or if he would come into the city from his native Żelechow. At that time a lot of young men influenced by I. M. Vaysenberg began to appear in our literary milieu. People knew that Lerer had talent; his poems were emotionally rich, original, and garnered respect in the literary circles of the 1930s. His was a new voice and perhaps the very last that evoked the authentic landscape and deep context of Jewish life on Polish soil. Many writers had written poems and stories on this theme, but Lerer added something else. The PEN club awarded him its literary prize for his poem "Mayn heym,"[1] and he won recognition as one of the most talented of the up-and-coming writers on the Yiddish literary scene.

When the war began Lerer did not flee east. Or perhaps he did but returned. I don't know which was the case. But this I do know: when the wanderings of 1939–1940 stopped and we found ourselves locked into a closed ghetto on November 15, 1940, Lerer was one of the writers who stayed in Warsaw.

>——<

The writers in the Warsaw Ghetto did not abandon their craft. After the shock of the September battles, after the wave of repressions and the depression that bore down on us after the arrival of the Germans, there came a time when people began to adjust to the new terrible reality and to find a focus for their remaining strength. The wide-reaching and large-scale Jewish welfare and self-help activity took shape and in turn offered a convenient cloak for the political and cultural life of the Jewish community. The soup kitchen I ran at Leszno 40 was a central location, where many friends, including writers and artists, would visit me.

This is what I wrote about Lerer in the memoirs that I composed on the Aryan side in the winter of 1943–44:

> At various times Lerer was an "eater"—officially or off the books—in our kitchen. Along with Yosef Kirman and Shlomo Gilbert he would drop by to see me in the afternoons. Lunch had been served, and the clients who took their soup home in pots had left. The hangers-on waiting in the corridor and on the steps had licked the last spoonfuls of leftovers in the vats. The shouting, pleading, and arguments about "just one more bit of the thick stuff" or one more potato had ended for the day. The staff was busy cleaning, scrubbing the vats, weighing produce in the storeroom, and preparing the meal for the next day. Once I finished with the accounts and the daily report to the central board I had some time on my hands. So we would sit in the small office between the sacks of weighed products, bundles of rinsed vegetables, and containers full of oil and talk about literary matters. Gilbert would pull some papers from his pocket and start to read a new scene from his long dramatic poem about arguments between the people and God. It was full of symbolic characters, opaque and dense verses about the fantastic world of departed souls. He was trying to find some explanation for what was happening now.

Here is another excerpt from what I wrote in those days:

> During the second or third week of the Great Deportation, and without much ado, Gilbert was swept away to Treblinka along with Yekhiel Lerer. Lately I have been thinking about his lyric-elegiac poem about Jewish provincial life. It was so full of love for his home and for that place where the lives of ordinary Jews were filled with a passionate, determined struggle to endure and perse-

vere. Even now, even as Jews are being murdered, we read poisonous articles in the Polish underground press that repeat the old canard that Jews do not love their Polish fatherland. We should have those Poles read Lerer's poetry. It is true that the Polish Jew did not have a fatherland but rather a step-fatherland, evidenced by how the Polish government treated him. But it was also true that deep in his heart the Polish Jew loved the land and the Polish soil where he was born, where he grew up, and where his kin were buried. What better proof of this than Lerer's poems! Yes, one can imagine a king without a country, but you can't imagine a writer without a country, even if he is part of a homeless people.

>——<

Lerer worked as a clerk in the Judenrat. I had written that he worked in the evidentiary bureau while Ringelblum noted that he was employed in the post office. But whatever the case was, he had a job and at least a minimal livelihood. Aside from the visits he made with Kirman and Gilbert, on days when the kitchen didn't serve meals he would come see me at my place at Leszno 66. He was very interested in politics and the military situation, would read the German press, and tried to tease out the truth from between the lines.

Lerer came to see me for the last time during the Great Deportation. That day there were no blockades. The murderers were busy liquidating the Jews in the Otwock region. At the beginning of the blockades Lerer had procured a place in Schultz's shop on Nowolipie Street. His religious father, who had nine children, was a scholar and a respected person. He had been working as a trustee and bookkeeper for some businessmen from Żelechow. Such a person would not have had any artisans in his family. Nevertheless, at the beginning of the Great Deportation Lerer registered as a maker of fur hats in the workshops of Georg Schultz. Of course it was absolutely clear that his hat-making skills, real or bogus, would not save him for very long.

Although there were no blockades that day, there was no letup in the general mood of hysteria and nightmarish panic. The memory of my last meeting with Lerer comes back to me as if floating in a thick, yellowish haze. Here is more from what I wrote in 1943:

> His face was pale and drawn, like a corpse. His gray eyes glistened with tears. He looked much smaller than usual and his frame seemed broken, as if it had been cut down. But his heart still blazed like the waxen Yom Kippur candle that once burned in his home, a candle made of interwoven strands, each a memory of a departed dear one, a name lovingly evoked on his mother's lips. The words he said to me then were like the waxen droppings of the memorial candles on the Day of Judgment.[2]
>
> "Jewish police! Shops! Betrayal!" He sputtered about what was going on in the ghetto, about the general mood of *"sauve qui peut"*—save your own skin and by any means necessary. But he was thinking about those who were not able to save themselves.
>
> That was the last time I saw Lerer. After that it seems that he made no effort to save himself. His soul full of despair, this loyal son of the Jewish people went together with the common folk to their death.

Later I received a present from Rosa Grossman. It was a part of Moshe Grossman's inheritance, a nicely produced volume of Lerer's beautiful idyll "My Home." It was published, with Arieh Merzer's illustrations, by the Argentine Union of Polish Jews, and it reflected the respect in which Lerer was held. The first edition of "My Home" appeared in 1937 and on the eve of the war it was already an elegy for the past, for the world of his parents that was gone forever.

That poem expressed so much deep love and respect for his father, a devout Jew who was tied to the old traditions, who was disturbed and troubled by a son and daughter who made other choices. His children joined unions and went on *hakhshara*.[3] They rejected their father's authority. And what was worse, they left his shtetl, his home, his world.

Lerer's parents might well have thought that all the love and devotion they had given their children was wasted. Little could they have known, in their loneliness and yearning, that some of their children made choices that enabled them to survive. And might they not have derived some comfort from this?

Thanks to the *hakhshara* that attracted Lerer's brothers and sisters, Moshe Tsadok, Lerer's brother and later a high-ranking officer in the IDF, settled in Israel. He died not long ago, but thanks to him the family line continues. The youngest sister lives in Costa Rica and visits Israel often. There is another family member, Elimelech Ram, who became an important figure in Israeli radio and the Israeli diplomatic service.

>—<

In his book *Di umgekumene shrayber fun di getos un lagern un zeyere verk* (*The Lost Jewish Writers in the Ghettos and Camps and Their Works*) Ber Mark published a fragment of a poem of Lerer's that was found in the Ringelblum archive. It reads like a postscript, a continuation of "My Home":

> And just now a terrible hateful rumor has been spreading
> That my parents were driven out of their life-long home
> They are now with strangers, and walk unknown streets
> Is my mother still waiting for God to pull out the sun
> From her butter churn
> And brighten the world with his most brilliant and
>   holiest light?
> And drive away the thick shadows that are so huge and so
>   dark in our Jewish homes?
> Or maybe she is not hoping for anything at all. For nothing.
> My dear friends my heart is so heavy, so oppressed
> When I think about my mother and I want to ask you,
> Maybe you know something, maybe you've heard news
>   about her?
> And if you have, please tell me right away, and give me
>   some comfort.
>
> My old and gray mother is searching and awaiting a
> springtime, a young spring, in full bloom, with colors
> of rose and blue, a spring as powerful as a stream in full

flood, that breaks through all the levees and spreads everywhere, everywhere: over all the lands, all the seas;
that carries all the scattered and dispersed children to
their mothers.

If it were up to me I would take these words written by a murdered Jewish poet and set them up in little electric lights overlooking
the airport where the planes that carry dispersed children to Israel
land. Let those words be a memorial for the murdered children and
the murdered parents who never had the chance to see each other
again.

JOSIMA

Had she lived she would now be forty-three. Her name would be a household word among Jews everywhere. She would have been the darling of hundreds of thousands worldwide.

Josima Feldshuh a wunderkind? That eleven-year-old pianist in the Warsaw Ghetto? I hesitate to bring up an overused word. But she was endowed with all the gifts necessary to transform a musical talent into an exuberantly assertive mastery and an artistic bounty of beauty and power. The only gift she lacked was time.

She had an amazing ear, an excellent musical memory, a rare degree of artistic intuition, and a high level of technical proficiency. She was also beginning to show the first signs of inner maturity. You could sense her ardent love of life and her emotional depth.

Josima's many natural virtues, however, did not include an inborn work ethic. That was imposed by her strong-willed mother, who was herself musically talented and knowledgeable. When Josima was only five years old her mother sat her down at the piano and began to teach her. Soon she found other teachers. Before the war began, she had already begun to attract the attention of respected musical experts such as Professors Zhuravlev, Wojtowicz, Hermalin, and Sztampko. In the ghetto she took lessons with the virtuoso Hanka Dickstein and would practice four, six, even eight hours a day.

Although her hands were small they were quite strong. Her long fingers covered a wide range, and the level of technical proficiency she achieved was amazing. The most difficult études by Czerny and Moszkowicz were child's play for her.

Her mother allowed her neither real toys nor a chance to just sit back and sing a song or play a tango or even ad-lib some fantasy tune on the piano. Josima was only allowed to play important, serious classical music. She not only mastered the piano and learned entire works by heart, but she was able to *interpret* Chopin, Mendelssohn, Tchaikovsky, and above all Mozart. In 1942 she began to play Beethoven and became quite proficient with Bach. It was the performance of the Mozart Piano Concerto in C Major that she gave a year before, in 1941, that brought her to the attention of the serious music aficionados in the ghetto.

>——<

That must have been in the autumn of 1941, the peak season for hunger and plague, just a year after the establishment of the ghetto. Anyone not familiar with the real history of the Warsaw Ghetto might well wonder how it was possible to arrange a wealth of artistic performances in this isolated place that resembled one big jail. I have often wondered about that myself.

The Germans drove many famous musicians into the ghetto who few people had suspected of being Jewish before the war. A unique musical life sprang up. In the ghetto courtyards an opera singer from Vienna sang the arias of Traviata and Tosca. On the corner of Karmelicka and Nowolipki a brilliant violinist performed while his wife collected coins. You could go into the dingiest places and hear wonderful chamber music. Above all there was an excellent symphony orchestra that in the early days of the ghetto would give concerts in the hall of the Melody Palace on Rymarska Street.

That Mozart Piano Concerto in C Major, which was played twice under the baton of conductor Adam Furmanski, made a big impression in musical circles. Many former musicians of the Warsaw Philharmonic and Opera played in that orchestra. I remember one of them, an old, musically accomplished flutist with a big belly. After he and other musicians in the orchestra heard Josima rehearse for the first time they were absolutely dazzled by her talent. They literally lifted her in the air, embraced and kissed her, and jostled each other to be able to hold her. They passed the hat around and bought her a present to mark her concert debut: a prewar chocolate bar and a big bouquet of white lilacs smuggled in from the Aryan side.

Josima might well have gotten by without rehearsing at all. Any false note made her instinctively recoil, as if she had been bitten by a snake. She knew not only her own part but the whole piece by heart, and she had an unerring sense of when to come in. She showed no nervousness during either the rehearsals or the concert. Perhaps the fact that she was still a child spared her the jitters, hypersensitivity, and fears that afflict more mature performers. Just as at home, she had to sit on piles of musical scores to reach the keyboard. Totally immersed in her playing, she took no notice of the large audience and swayed and moved to the rhythm of the music. As she gave herself over to the exuberant and playful texture of Mozart's genius, her face radiated a wonderful charm that told everybody just how perfectly the music of that great composer attracted a youthful soul so eager to embrace life.

The apartment at Leszno 66, where Josima's parents lived and where I moved in the winter of 1940, was number 18. Josima's mother believed that the number 18, whose Hebrew letters were "chai" ("life"), would protect them from all kinds of evil. And it really seemed that we could thank a lucky charm: when the Germans were busy looting furniture throughout the city they failed to notice our apartment and did not remove the old Vienna piano.

After that concert our apartment became even more of a musical enclave than it had been before. Musicians came to visit Josima the wunderkind, and they surrounded her with an aura of respect and affection. This strengthened the warm mood with which we tried to shield the young pianist from the horrid darkness of ghetto life. Enveloped by understanding and love and happiness in her music, Josima lived quite removed from the tragic abyss. She even had the strength to make others forget that terrible *now*, even as the dark clouds gathered, becoming thicker and more threatening.

Josima would have liked to do other things besides play the piano night and day. For example, she loved to string beads and make bracelets and brooches, tastefully arranging the colors and handing them out as presents for those close to her. She loved to receive guests and to do something special for her parents' birthdays or wedding anniversary. She did these things with a disarming combination of childlike seriousness and mature charm.

Without any hint of exaggeration I must say that I thought Josima to be, despite her age, one of the most interesting and creative personalities in the Warsaw Ghetto. I regard those many enchanted hours when I listened to great music after returning from a day of hard work and awful experiences in the soup kitchen as some of my most cherished memories. A special kind of intimacy developed between us. Compared to her mother's strict and overbearing supervision, my lenient ways seemed to her like a blessed relief. When her mother would leave she and I would enjoy hours of light music. I would teach her Yiddish songs. She would learn the melody right away and would accompany me as I sang them. Other times she would accompany herself as she sang sweet Polish folk songs and prewar hits. She also sang Polish lyrics set to a tune from Schubert's *Unfinished Symphony* as well as a melody from Moniuszko's opera *Halka* with the following words:

> If I could be the sun just for a moment
> Then I would shine only for you.
> Not over valleys and mountains
> But for all time
> I would shine over your house
> And just for you
> If I could be the sun for just a moment.
>
> If I could become a bird just for a moment
> Then I would never sing in some far-off land
> Or in valleys and mountains
> But for all time
> I would sing under your window and just for you
> If I could become a bird for just a moment!

Today when I start to sing that song I feel a spark that brings back those days and that atmosphere, when Josima still lived in this frightful world. It seems that I have already lived another life; in a sense I died when she did. That song reverberates in my ears like an echo from that time.

I imagine her with me now, happy, bursting with life. There she is, sitting at that nonexistent piano inside that nonexistent apartment, playing and singing in a beautiful coloratura voice, each word expressing the total devotion of a young woman in love.

Now, suddenly, I hear other sounds. I peek through the half-open door. Once again, her strict mother has gone out. There sits Josima, pale, her lips skewed and half open, totally lost in herself as she begins to compose a new melody. Her fingers wander over the keyboard and the spirit of God hovers over her young head.

>———<

Indeed, a time came when Josima began to make up melodies. "Make up" isn't really the right word to describe it. She was already mature enough to compose in a creative way. It was funny to hear her proclaim, with a solemnity that seemed amusing coming from such a young girl, that she wanted to become a composer. She wanted to show the world that women could not just play somebody else's compositions but could create music themselves.

Her mother looked at this idea with a jaundiced eye. She believed that Josima was too young to be thinking about composing. But that didn't keep her from transcribing her daughter's short compositions in a notebook.

Josima wanted to present everyone with some gift. Her gift to me was a melody that she composed and called "Sadness at the Banks of a Little River."

Here are the titles of some of her other compositions: "A Bird Tells a Story," "The Birds' Dance Ball," and "The Melody of a Drop of Water."

Say what you will, you couldn't accuse her of any plagiaristic pretense or a desire to make of these songs anything more than what they were.

There were other tunes: some mazurkas, a kujawiak, a waltz, and above all five melodies that Josima "thought up" and were based on Jewish Sabbath songs, religious chants, and tunes that she heard in various Jewish homes. Her mother named these compositions "Sabbath motifs." An important musicologist in Israel told me that they were an original contribution to that genre.

>———<

Josima sang lullabies and love songs, played the works of great composers, and composed her own music. Multiply the world a thousandfold and she could have embraced its full measure. In the meantime she could only look at that world from a distance.

She wanted a lot of everything: a lot of beads, a lot of flowers, a lot of affection, a double, threefold portion of love and attention. Her young arms were stretched wide, ready to welcome the coming years in their embrace. She happily sensed the new longings and changes that were welling up inside of her; she was eager to feel the winds that blew from far-off deserts, oceans, and steppes.

We did not know that the prelude would be all that there was. Those light motifs, trills like the flutter of a little sparrow, that begin a great symphony and that promise so much became the finale.

There would be nothing more. The beginning was also the end. How hard I find it to accept the fact that it all happened. That Josima is not with us.

>——<

The situation in the ghetto became more and more threatening, and the tension became ever more palpable. Just a couple of weeks before the beginning of the Great Deportation there were some offers to take Josima out of the ghetto. A Pole from Radzymin, where the Feldshuhs had devoted friends and party comrades, suggested that Josima come live with him. He would tell people that she was his sister's daughter whom he had engaged to teach his daughter the piano. But Josima's mother insisted that he also take her and her husband. She had a habit of asking people to do the impossible. Or maybe she just couldn't bring herself to part from Josima.

After the Great Deportation began her mother became a total bundle of nerves. Her endless obsessive need to protect Josima from any danger expressed itself in a determination to keep her daughter "from catching cold." As they crouched in hideouts and ran from one place to another she smothered Josima with sweaters, scarves, and woolen dresses. She was doing this in July, August, and early September 1942, when the weather was very hot. Josima's body became overheated, and she developed a lung infection.

She recovered, but nobody suspected that the infection had left dangerous scars in her lungs. The first *aktion* passed. The family also survived the second *aktion* in January 1943. A few weeks later the three of them passed over to the Aryan side and found a hideout in the village of Pustelnik on the Radzymin railroad line. When I left the ghetto in March 1943 I spent the first couple of nights in that same place. I met

Josima and her father in some house, and it was the last time I saw her. She had clearly grown since I had last seen her, with a pale, oddly elongated face and a pointed nose. By then we all looked bad—the ordeals of the last six months had left their mark. So was it any wonder that Josima looked the way she did? She had lost everything that made her life worthwhile: her home, her piano, that tiny bit of freedom that she once had. By the time we realized that there was a special reason for Josima's bad appearance and constant cough—by the time we sent her to Warsaw, accompanied by a Polish girl, to see a doctor—her lungs were already infected with an advanced case of tuberculosis.

>—<

I was one of those Jewish "Aryans" who moved freely around Warsaw. Fate would have it that I was the one who had to inquire about Josima's condition. I had already developed a lot of contacts on the Aryan side, and we could have sent Josima to a sanatorium for people with lung diseases. I made up my mind to spare no effort to save her.

It was Saturday, April 17, 1943, the eve of Passover, of Easter, and of the Warsaw Ghetto Uprising. That day I took Josima to see a woman pulmonary specialist who was also the director of a sanatorium in Otwock. Her verdict was clear and concise: there was nothing left to save. Josima's lungs were like a sieve, and her days were numbered. She might last another week, or not.

I returned to the city sunk in a trance of pain. With an aching heart I stopped along the way and looked at the Easter show windows. Cute little baskets stuffed with miniature hens made of featherdown were placed next to shoddy wartime merchandise. There were little white lambs made of sugar and plaster with red ribbons around their necks, and clumps of real green grass placed in small glass vases. Blue ribbons tied little bunnies to enormous Easter eggs made from Bakelite and to stuffed childrens' toys. There were bouquets of fresh violets everywhere.

Josima had such a love of pretty little things!

Our dearest, our most beautiful Josima!

>—<

The traumatic scenes, when the parents said goodbye to their only daughter, took place behind locked doors and drawn curtains. Josima understood that she was dying. She spoke like a grown-up, thanked her parents, said farewell. There were other Jews who were sharing the Feldshuh's hideout. No one could make a loud sound, or cry, or move around.

It was only at night, when darkness came, that they could carry out Josima's body. The owners of the house demanded that they carry her to a nearby swamp, weigh her body down with a heavy stone, and let it sink. But the Jews managed to convince them to let them bury her.

They buried Josima in a little coffin in the dead of night in the garden behind the house, in a narrow hole under a tree. She was dressed in pajamas. It reminded me of how children bury a beloved cat or a dead bird.

All the dirges and funeral marches that mourned dead children seemed to fill the space over that grave, except that nobody actually heard them.

>—<

Josima died Wednesday, April 21, the second day of Passover and the third day of the ghetto uprising. I heard the news amidst the thick smoke of the burning ghetto, the rumble and shaking of explosions and shooting. Even though Josima died in the village of Pustelnik, for me her death was inseparable from the many young people who were dying over there, behind the bloody fog of the ghetto walls.

Her mother, whose sole purpose in life was Josima and her music, could not remain alive after what happened. She kept blaming herself for Josima's death.

I could no longer go to Pustelnik. I had no illusions as to what was happening there and was not surprised to hear that Josima's mother suffered a total breakdown. She began to scream, to speak in Yiddish, and became a danger to everyone else in the hideout. How could she not have broken down? It came as no surprise when a short time later I heard that she died.

They buried her the same way they buried Josima.

34. A Tree in the Ghetto

Maybe this happened in the spring or early summer of 1941. It was the peak time for hunger and typhus, for swarms of beggars, hucksters, and street singers. Hershele had already died. I could not forgive myself for not having tried sooner to feed him up a little in my soup kitchen. So when I ran into Yisroel Shtern in some office I called him aside and told him to come each day to Leszno 40 to get a soup. His first question was whether the kitchen was kosher.

"And how could it not be kosher?" I replied. "It's not dairy. It's not meat. We season the food with oil—so it's pareve."

A few days later he came to the kitchen and then started to come almost every day. As soon as my assistant Halina would see him, she would—as I instructed her—give him a bowl of soup without a ticket. Both she and the regular overseer of our kitchen, Abraham Beldiger, were used to seeing such "literary" visitors. They regarded him as just another one of my "helpless protégés." The one thing they could not accept was why I made him come to the kitchen instead of sending the food to where he lived.

And it's true. Why deny it? Even among the clientele of the kitchen, which consisted mostly of declassed and exhausted refugees from the provinces, Shtern's frighteningly unkempt appearance made him stick out like a sore thumb.

The bottom of his overcoat was ragged and torn, with holes poking through the lining of the sleeves and above the elbows. He hardly ever took off his greasy black hat. His cheeks were unshaven and bristly, like a stubbly field full of jutting weeds. I don't think there was any jacket under his coat, but his stomach still seemed very swollen.

I asked Kirman the reason for this, and he explained: since the pockets are torn, Shtern stuffs what he needs into the front of his coat—a book that he's reading and a little jug to rinse his hands before eating, as required by the *Shulhan Arukh*.[1] It was like that old saying about the wise man who carried all his worldly goods along with him.

Before the war we knew that Shtern was a Breslover, one of the "dead Hasidim."[2] Still, I had no idea he was so observant.

><

In January 1942 the kitchen was turned into a convalescent kitchen and began to serve nourishing and fatty soups, mostly for those recovering from typhus. People needed a special pass to eat there and they could do so for only one month. Oversight commissions constantly visited, but I could still finagle exceptions. Our friends—writers, artists, and musicians—now showed a lot of interest in the nourishing meals our kitchen provided. But for Shtern, keeping kosher was more important than anything else. So I had to tell him that from now on the meals would be cooked with nonkosher fats and would contain horse bones. From that day on Shtern disappeared from the kitchen.

I did not see him for a couple of months. It was just before Passover 1942 that Kirman came to Leszno 40 and told me that Shtern was in terrible condition, on the brink of death, and that we had to try to save him.

I dropped everything and we both went to visit. A middle-class Hasidic family lived in a basement apartment on the corner of Smocza and Pawia, where Shtern slept in a corner. A tiny ray of thin light crept in through the wire-covered window under the ceiling. Two tall beds covered in red down quilts were along the walls. There was an old bookcase just by the door. Before we went in we looked through the windows from the street.

Shtern was sitting at the table in the middle of the room. It was absolutely frightening to see how he had changed. His feet and his whole body were swollen. His puffy face was covered with an unkempt beard, like a mourner.

The couple who lived there were making excuses for the fact that by the looks of it, Shtern's bed had not been slept in. "If he does not want to lie down," they said, "what can we do?"

Shtern overheard our conversation. It looked as if he too had become distressed by how much he had gone to seed, and he seemed ready to agree with whatever we decided. But he warned us that there was no way he would travel on a rickshaw, the carriages in the ghetto that were pulled by people.[3]

I don't remember how we managed to conjure up a horse and wagon. At that time there were no droshkies to be found in the ghetto. We took Shtern to the offices of the TOZ[4] on Gęsia, whose administrative director, Yitshak Feld, was someone we could rely on to help us.

We got Shtern a shave, a haircut, a bath, and dressed him head to toe in a new set of clothes from the TOZ warehouse. After that we had a doctor examine him who did not wait for the test results to come back before injecting him with a big dose of glucose solution. We then took Shtern to the refugee center, which was located at Leszno 14.

We alerted Itsik Giterman and Emanuel Ringelblum, the leaders of the Aleynhilf, about Shtern's condition. The "top brass" ordered the directors of the refugee center to place a bed in one of the offices so Shtern could have a room to himself. He received special packages of uncooked food products from the Aleynhilf storehouses. We hired a lady to clean, cook, and serve him and procured medicines and money for additional meals that would be rich in vitamins. It was Yosef Kirman who doled out the funds. Everyone knew about Shtern's small-town, peasantlike stinginess when it came to spending money. Kirman knew Shtern inside out and was totally devoted to him. He looked after him lovingly and put up with all his foibles.

Once or twice a week Kirman would give me some money and I would go to the bazaar at Leszno 42—two doors down from my kitchen—and buy Shtern a bit of cheese or butter or some of the early vegetables and greens that had been smuggled from the Aryan side.

That's how we looked after Shtern and helped him get better. Our efforts were successful. The swelling slowly abated; Shtern got out of bed. By the end of June he was able to go out into the street.

Saving him from terminal hunger edema cost a few thousand złotys. I mention this because there were tens of thousands of people in the ghetto who suffered from the same condition. When the swelling reached a certain level death was all but certain. At that point the soups from the public kitchens actually did more harm than good. It goes without saying that the Aleynhilf was not able to spend 2,000 złotys for each person afflicted with hunger edema.

>——<

It happened in early summer 1942, during the nightly Gestapo kill-ings on the streets, a prelude of terror that preceded the Great De-portation. The portents were becoming steadily more ominous, the mood in the ghetto ever more anxious.

Shtern stayed alone in his room, thinking, reading poetry. We spared him the news about what was going on in the ghetto, and we did not let him see the newspapers full of news about German victo-ries. I think that Shtern was living a serene idyll on the eve of death.

I once paid Shtern a visit in that room and we had a conversation. I brought him some fresh strawberries in a paper bag along with a jar of berry compote that we cooked privately in our kitchen.

The offices of the refugee center were on the second floor of the left wing of the building. Right next door was the Evangelical church that had ended up in the ghetto, its front gate firmly locked. Shtern's window looked out on interlacing towers and little spires, as well as the stone facades typical of Christian architecture. Right up against the window was a high and wide chestnut tree, which was now cov-ered in white blossoms. It resembled a Christmas tree adorned in white lights and yellow candles. There were bird nests lodged in the cornices of the church, where chicks had hatched and where their parents kept arriving with bits of food in their beaks to feed them. They chirped and hovered over their nests. It's as if they had abso-lutely no idea that they were in a ghetto where all the Jews had been sentenced to death.

It was quiet there, set off from everything else. You would not have known that just a few steps away there was a street trembling with the fear of death, or that we had any idea of what was about to happen.

In the shadow of the "old cathedral" we spoke about the less-er-known romantic side of Zola, as reflected in his story "The Dream," about a youthful love affair between the illegitimate son of a bishop and the daughter of the organ player.

"There is no such thing as a great writer who was never a lyricist, at least at some point in his career," Shtern observed. He asked me to read aloud to him a poem by Stefan George, which he had trouble reading in the dim twilight.

"It would be better if you read me one of your own poems," I replied. "Write a poem about this tree that is blooming in the middle of the ghetto."

Before I left, Shtern asked me about the news. Although I tried my best not to tell him about the terrible happenings in the ghetto, and about the even worse rumors that were going around, I sensed that I could not fool him completely.

"The German is strong. The German is strong," he mumbled when we spoke about what was happening on the front. There was no shortage of optimists in the ghetto who seized on each glimmer of news to predict the imminent collapse of the Germans. Yisroel Shtern paid no attention to these optimists. He had no illusions about what the future held in store for the Warsaw Ghetto. He didn't want to take refuge in Pollyannaish stories. He didn't believe in them. Or maybe he did believe in them, just a little bit?

><

After the Great Deportation began, I didn't see Shtern again. I heard from others that Shtern tried to survive, even as he was sucked into the satanic whirlpool of people vainly fighting for life. Someone from the ghetto labor department, perhaps the journalist Ptakowski, got Shtern a spot in a German workshop.[5] Ringelblum thought it was Hoffman's shop. For a time in the early mornings, before the daily blockades began, you could see Shtern marching with the other workers to their workplaces outside the ghetto.

Shtern was already in his fifties. But like many others he tried to look healthy and strong. I heard that he had acquired a new light blue smock, wore a cap, draped a silk bread pouch around his shoulders, and marched in step with his group.

The masquerade did not last long. He did not survive the large general selection of September 6–12 that took place in the so-called "cauldron." He embarked on the journey taken by all the Jews: the march to the Umschlagplatz, the sealed wagon, the trip of the condemned to that last station in the pine forest, where he died in one of the Treblinka gas chambers.

><

Yisroel Shtern was one of the most significant poets to have appeared in our literature after the First World War. His cycle *Hospital Songs*, which appeared in the 1920s, won him recognition as one of the world's leading Yiddish poets.

An inner glow, a hidden light that was both deeply religious and totally serious, defined him. Each line he wrote radiated the intense energy of a soul that simultaneously embraced Jewish learning and modern thought.

Jewish poets had a particularly difficult row to hoe, and all poets, Jewish or not, have to deal with countless inner struggles and external conflicts. This helped explain why Shtern was simultaneously so helpless in everyday life and a true titan in spiritual matters. His impracticality was so serious that friends could not get him to take the necessary steps to publish even one collection of his poetry.[6]

That's the kind of person he was until the war began. So what happened to him during the Holocaust? Aside from what I've already written, I would like to add something about the spiritual transformation that Shtern underwent in the ghetto.

Somebody once remarked that in the ghetto Shtern the recluse, who had spent so many years alone, now revealed himself to be a different person. He became more approachable, more active in social affairs. Surrounded by human suffering, by the omnipresent sense of Jewish destiny hanging in the balance, Shtern, now in his natural element, found true inspiration.

>———<

From one end of Poland to the other piles of corpses lined the roads along which deported Jews marched and suffered.

Death stalked the streets in broad daylight. It was dressed in a green uniform. The helmet of a German policeman rested on its head. It hovered at the walls, guarded the gates, fired bullets into small children on streets crowded with starving people, streets engulfed in a cacophony of singing beggars and the shouts of peddlers and hucksters.

Scraps ripped from paper bags covered the corpses that sprawled along the edges of the sidewalks. The epidemic was raging. The gravedigger and the ghetto fool had already performed their assigned roles. Wasn't it only fair that a poet might also have a turn?

The days—those Jewish days that Markish once called "days of blood and honey"—became steadily darker. They gripped the heart in a vise and opened the lips of the Jewish poet.

So it happened that in the last weeks of his life Yisroel Shtern became yet another anonymous soul who, after a night of German killing, walked through the courtyards and stood on street corners offering words and poems of consolation and reassurance.

The tragic and grotesque, the fantastic and bizarre, all came together to disturb and confuse the soul, to tear it down to the very last layer.

>——<

In the chapter I wrote about Hershele I described the literary afternoon teas that used to take place in Y. M. Apelbaum's kitchen at Leszno 14.

There was a table on the podium, covered by a white tablecloth with two brass Sabbath candlesticks. The walls were decorated with stylized images of Hasidim, a nod to Peretz's legacy, which had by now become routine. In those late afternoon hours Yisroel Shtern would take a seat on the podium, stay still for a while lost in his own thoughts, and then he would begin to speak, unleashing a torrent of blazing sounds that rolled through the entire room. Everybody listened spellbound to his poetic Torah, his lofty philosophical reflections on whatever topic he happened to choose. His words were pure poetry in a sheath of fiery light.

Yisroel Shtern had lost his front teeth, so it was hard to understand his speech as he mumbled and roared the words that filled the hall. No matter. The audience grasped what he was saying. More and more people came to hear his Saturday afternoon talks.

Once he read one of his new poems, a poem about what we faced. I remember a fragment and a theme from one of those readings. The poem was called "A Letter to America." It was a paraphrase of a well-known song, a dirge, a message from the Jews who were sentenced to death to those Jews sitting in distant lands who would someday mourn their murder.

Perhaps we didn't fully grasp the meaning of that poem when we first heard it. Maybe Shtern himself didn't fully understand what he was trying to say. But he had a premonition, a hunch, which he expressed with a wonderful sense of poetic prophecy.

>———<

When Shtern took his final journey, all the poems he wrote in those last years vanished with him. And those were the poems that had more depth, more meaning, than anything he had written before.

How beautiful that last gleam of twilight just before death, how intense the inner glow of yearning as it burns the heart at that last moment before the final parting.

If I ever get the chance to see the authentic documents from the second cache of the Ringelblum archive, I might be able to identify one of Yisroel Shtern's poems that I handed over to the archive about thirty years ago, along with some of my own papers.[7]

There was a poem about the blooming chestnut tree in the middle of the ghetto, jotted down along the left margin of a blank order form of a ghetto laundry. That was the poem I had "ordered" from him a month before the Great Deportation. He sent it to me to read, and I was never able to return it.

35. Scattered Pearls

I knew Yoshue Perle before the war. When his autobiographical novel *Yidn fun a gants yor* (*Ordinary Jews*) appeared in 1935 I liked it so much that I wrote a long review article, which was published in two installments in the *Literarishe bleter*.

Perle began writing in the Peretz era. But his literary style and his treatment of Jewish themes marked him as a member of the literary generation that emerged after the First World War. In Perle's writing the world of the Jewish masses in Slavic lands, or the ongoing problematics of Jewish survival, were more background than central themes. What fascinated him was the individual human being in all his complexity, the basic drives and instincts—albeit in Jewish variations—that come to the surface. Sex, jealousy, the dramatic struggle between different members of the same family, the clash of psychological complexes, the struggle waged between a mother and a father for the soul—and within the soul—of a son.

Perle's characters did not talk very much. Nor did he go on at length about their thoughts and feelings. Instead they sprang to life through half-drawn sketches and seemingly irrelevant remarks.

Most of the Jewish writers of the late nineteenth century and during the first twenty or thirty years of the twentieth century drew their inspiration from the great Russian novelists. But Perle looked to modern Polish realist literature, which even before Poland had regained its independence sought to distance itself from the national themes that had dominated Polish writing from Mickiewicz to Wyspiański to Żeromski and was largely incomprehensible to non-Polish readers.

The great challenge that Yiddish literature faced was two-fold. How could it leave behind the well-worn tendency to depict Jewish life through a prism of ethnographical exoticism? And how could it free itself from the outsized influence of ideological controversies?

Yoshue Perle was deeply rooted in the authentic soil of Jewish reality. But the obvious differences that set apart the Jewish world from its non-Jewish surroundings didn't interest him much. What he really cared about was what all people had in common. He took on new themes and explored new areas of human experience.

>——<

Perle was born in Radom in 1888. His early years were difficult. There was little money in the house. His father had children from a previous wife and his mother brought children from a previous husband. At fourteen he had to leave home for Warsaw, where he did physical labor and finally worked his way up to the "comfort" of a bank clerk. His writing developed in fits and starts until he finally found his real voice and began to mature as an author.

While I don't think it necessary to provide a bibliography of Perle's writings, I do want to say that he was very productive and diligent. Despite the fact that he always had a day job, he still managed to finish many new books, including collections of short stories and novels. Thousands of Jewish readers throughout Poland couldn't wait to read new installments of the page-turners that he serialized in the Yiddish press.

From time to time Perle published essays about literature and art, and he also did translations, such as Janusz Korczak's *Moyshelekh, Yoselekh, Yisroliklekh*; a Siberian novel written by Wacław Sieroszewski; and more. He developed a style that was full-blooded and evocative. He mastered the technique of deftly depicting a rich interplay of characters, incidents, and feelings. Before the war his crowning work was *Ordinary Jews*, where his prose attained a high degree of creative maturity.

It's all the more heartbreaking to remember that he was cut down just when he had reached an unprecedented level of creativity, insight, and talent.

He was fifty-five years old.

>——<

After the war began I had no contact with Perle. I did not hear that he had left Warsaw. As news reached me about what was happening in the Soviet zone, I learned that he had settled in Lemberg. In the fall of 1941, a few months after the Germans occupied the city, Perle returned to Warsaw with his son and daughter-in-law, who were both engineers. He paid a visit to Bentsiyon Chilinowicz at Nowolipie 22. I was among the very first who rushed to see him and to find out what was happening with my friends and associates in Lemberg.

The tidings that Perle brought from Lemberg were horrendous. The scale and viciousness of the persecutions that engulfed the Galician Jews almost two years after they hit us far exceeded what we had endured in central and western Poland. The attack on the Soviet Union and the German advance eastward swept away all previous obstacles that had delayed the long-prepared plans for "solving the Jewish problem." In addition, the Nazis found a new partner in these occupied territories: Ukrainian fascists, who had been waiting for these "liberators" for a long time in order to help carry out the mass murder of the Jewish population.

Perle brought us these tidings of Job about the terrible killings that claimed many victims from our literary circle. He described how a frenzied Ukrainian mob was given carte blanche to take "revenge" on the Jews for all the real and imagined crimes of the Communist regime—crimes whose victims had included many Jews.

Just before the Soviets retreated, the NKVD sadists brutally murdered the political prisoners held in the jails of most of the larger towns in East Galicia, mostly Jews along with some Poles.[1] The Ukrainian militia herded together large groups of Jewish men to collect and bury the corpses of the victims. When the Jews got there, they were met by a mob of semi-depraved and totally debauched criminals armed with sticks, iron bars, and rods who beat and tortured them until the majority died on the spot.

The victims of this mass lynching included my first editor, Henryk Heszeles, chief editor of *Chwila,* who was murdered in the courtyard of the Brigidka prison—even as the roll of those killed there by the NKVD included his colleague and proxy, Leon Weinstock, who had been arrested for Zionist activity.

Ber Horowitz, a Ukrainophile and translator of Ukrainian literature, was murdered by a Ukrainian mob in Stanislaw. Alter Kacyzne was beaten to death by Ukrainian killers in Tarnopol.[2]

>——<

Those of us who had been isolated in the ghetto gained many rich insights about literary life in the Soviet zone after Perle returned to Warsaw. Lemberg, the capital of "Western Ukraine," was transformed into a trilingual center composed of three different national groups. The Communists, of course, were the bosses in each of these groups, although not necessarily the same Communists who had spent time in Polish jails.

The attractive palace of a Polish prince on Kopernikus Street, confiscated by the authorities, served as the headquarters of this tri-national literary club. The troubles began when it came time to turn the club into a professional literary union. Each writer who was up for membership had to go through a vetting process and then pass muster at a general meeting of all the members.

This was the opportunity for knives to come out. If what we heard is true, it was the Jewish section that saw the worst and most despicable incidents. Perle told us about what he had to endure from young, callow Communist writers who accused him of being a supporter of the Bund just because he had written for some Bundist literary journals before the war. The whole business was no joke. Characteristically, it was the Polish Communist writer Elżbieta Szemplińska who intervened on Perle's behalf. It was she, who hadn't read one word of Perle's writings, who publicly rescued him from the Jewish fanatics.

Someone else who did not have an easy time was Shmuel Yankev Imber, the essayist and translator who served as a link between Yiddish and Hebrew and between English and Polish. He was very erudite, a publicist and a polemicist, all in all a cultural figure of the highest class. Who was it that stepped forward as his accuser, who warned against admitting him to the Lemberg literary union, who accused him of being a Zionist and disloyal to the Soviet Union? I was absolutely astounded to learn that this was none other than David Koenigsberg, who had served as the official (but not actual) editor of our journal *Tsushtayer*. Imber had been his teacher and editor and had smoothed his path to becoming a Yiddish poet.

Imber had no choice but to apply. He needed an income, a residence permit, some minimal guarantee of material security, not to mention some protection against the wave of deportations and persecutions that had already begun in eastern Galicia. Koenigsberg's accusations were therefore not only stupid but also malicious and irresponsible. Imber's friends and relatives tried to get Koenigsberg to retract or at least soften his charges. But he refused to compromise.

Matters remained unresolved, and Imber couldn't escape the consequences of that great shock. That's how things stood until the German invasion. Perhaps he might have tried to escape to the Soviet Union, notwithstanding his negative attitude toward the Soviets. After all, he was the sharpest critic of Hitlerism in Poland and edited anti-Nazi publications in Polish. But he was now shut off from both worlds and had lost his self-confidence. He didn't have it in him to hit the road and flee. He left for the provinces. In the summer of 1942 they dragged him out of a bunker in Zloczow and shot him, not because he was Sh. Y. Imber, the fiery anti-Nazi journalist, but simply because he was a Jew.

After the war I learned of two other younger Yiddish poets who fell victim to their Communist colleagues: the genuine proletarian poet and member of our *Tsushtayer* circle Yankev Shudrich and the extremely talented poet Moshe-Maurycy Szymel, who wrote in both Yiddish and Polish. A certain scoundrel, jealous of Shudrich's talent, declared that he was a Trotskyite. Szymel was accused of harboring "petit-bourgeois" tendencies. Shudrich defended himself and was admitted, while Szymel, bothered by hypochondria and various phobias, just left the room. Because of these accusations, both were stranded in Lwow and were murdered by the Germans. Shudrich was killed, weapon in hand, on his way to join a partisan group in the Brztchowica forest.

David Koenigberg also did not live to see the end of the war. He suffered a vicious beating in the Gestapo prison on Lancki Street. Already close to death, he was taken to the Jewish hospital. The young French Jewish writer Piotr Rawicz saw him die and mentions him, although not by name, in his book *Blood from the Sky*.

Why did this fervent Soviet patriot not try to take his family and escape to the Soviet Union? That's as hard to figure out as the reason for his bizarre behavior toward his teacher and friend, Shmuel

Yankev Imber.

In Tania Fuch's postwar memoir, *A Journey through the Occupied Lands,* there is a photograph of Perets Markish surrounded by the Yiddish writers who were in Lemberg during the first year and a half of the war. Among them was Yoshue Perle and Alter Kacyzne. I saw the same photograph when I visited Perle in 1941. He told us about visits the Soviet Yiddish writers made to the newly occupied areas. After so many years of forced isolation the Soviet and Polish Yiddish writers were anxious to get to know each other. In addition to Markish also present were Itsik Fefer, Dovid Hofshteyn, a commander of the border guards, a Yiddish poet named Shike Driz, and others.

Markish came to Lemberg in connection with the premiere of his play *The Dinner* at the newly opened Yiddish state theater. Both sides were happy to be in contact once again. The Soviet visitors wanted to hear all about the new literary talents that had emerged in the past ten or fifteen years in Poland, Romania, and across the Atlantic. They eagerly read their works and were happy (not openly of course) to see for themselves the creative energy that coursed through Jewish communities that until now had been closed off to them.

You could sense that they felt a shared identity with fellow Jews across the world. Ten years later they paid for it with their lives.

After the Moscow Yiddish writers visited Lemberg, Yiddish writers from Lemberg went to Moscow. The delegation included Rokhl Korn, Alter Kacyzne, and Ber Shnaper. The Moscow writers invited Perle to send his writings. A Moscow journal published his reportage, in a Russian translation entitled "The Road," of his odyssey eastward in September 1939 along Polish roads jammed with escaping refugees. The Soviet Yiddish publishing house began to publish a new edition of *Ordinary Jews* in Soviet Yiddish orthography.

Perle never got to see the final product. Before the edition was completed, Germany invaded the Soviet Union.

>——<

A new chapter of Perle's life began, a chapter I witnessed myself. In my section on Yosef Kirman I mentioned that I was registered as part of the Jewish supply department at Franciszkańska 30. After the Great Deportation, in addition to Kirman and myself, Yoshue Perle and Y. Y. Propus also found refuge there. All of us managed to catch our breath and recuperate a bit after the horrible experiences of the roundups. Each of us received an official position and we all set out to write down our experiences for the secret ghetto archive.

Perle not only worked at Franciszkańska as a bookkeeper but also lived there with his son. Between the first and the second *aktions*, Perle wrote his description of the Great Deportation, which was found in the second cache of the Ringelblum archive after the war. It was published under the title *Khurbn varshe* (*The Destruction of Warsaw*).

Perle's little apartment, on the ground floor of the left wing of Franciszkańska 30, was right next to the honey and candy factory where I worked. Every now and then, on my way home, I would stop in to see him. Once he told me that just before the war began he had finished a second volume of *Ordinary Jews*, which had been ready to appear in print that fall. Before he fled Warsaw he left a copy of the manuscript with friends and after he returned from Lemberg he retrieved it.

"So where is it?" I asked.

"You want to see it?" Perle bent down and pulled a suitcase from under the bed, gave me a hefty folder, and invited me to read it.

I carried the typescript home with me to Nalewki 37 and was very eager to begin reading. It turned out to be an autobiographical sequel to the first volume, in a work which was to appear in three volumes. It covered Perle's years of transition, after he had left the provinces and arrived in Warsaw. I could not spend too much time reading the manuscript because I had to spend my evenings working for the secret archive, interviewing my neighbor who had escaped from Treblinka. And suddenly we were faced with the second *aktion* of January 18–22. The pages, unread, remained in my apartment. I hid it along with my own manuscripts. After the *aktion* ended I sent it as soon as I could to Franciszkańska 30. When my messenger, Krzepicki, did not find Perle there, he gave the packet to Winter.

Then the disaster happened.

When the *aktion* ended, we heard a rumor that the Germans intended to reduce the size of the ghetto and force the Jews to move to Niska and Stawki streets—right next to the Umschlagplatz. Winter's children and Perle's son relocated to the Toebbens shop on Leszno Street. Winter sent along their baggage and packed Perle's manuscript in a roll of bedding. But two days later we learned that the size of the central ghetto would not change. After Toebbens ordered all the workers of his shops to be transferred to the labor camp in Poniatowa, a wild scramble began to return to the central ghetto. During the rush someone stole the bundle of bedding belonging to Winter's children, which contained Perle's manuscript.

That's how the sequel to Perle's masterpiece was lost. I remember how distraught Winter was. For weeks he tried to ransom the manuscript through his contacts with the Jewish and German police. But the writings were never found. The anguish that Winter and I both felt almost drove us mad.

Perle, on the other hand, reacted stoically. He returned from Toebbens to Franciszkańska and I saw him there one more time—the last time. Neither Winter nor I heard one word of reproach from him. He regarded it as just one minor episode in the vast catastrophe that had engulfed us.

Another change of scenery. Up to now the story of Perle's life unfolded chapter by chapter. And finally, the very last chapter—that last-ditch effort to cheat fate.

As so often happens in a person's life, he made his most disastrous mistake just when he was making a superhuman effort to save the most precious and most beloved person in his life—his son.

Somebody from Warsaw who knew the younger Perle very well told me recently that after Perle's wife died her tragic death in 1926, he became obsessed with a morbid fear that some tragedy might befall his seven-year-old son.[3] This phobia kept him in its grip until the very end. He didn't let his son out of his sight, even after the boy married. He took the young couple into his apartment, and during the war he and his son were always together.

One winter night at the beginning of 1944, in one of the notebooks I kept on the Aryan side, I wrote this about Perle:

Some weeks after I left the ghetto, I learned that Perle and his son also went to the Aryan side in March. It turned out that the son had Christian friends who provided them with their first documents and rooms. The father went by the name "Pan Stefan." Soon they made other contacts. So it seems they were protected more or

less, and they would still be here now had it not been for
the terrible "dead souls" affair in the Hotel Polski. They
too fell into the trap and sought to buy the Latin American passports issued to Jews, long since murdered in
Treblinka, which had accumulated after the end of the
Great Deportation. In July they traveled under guard to
an internment camp not far from Hanover. They were
told that the camp was under the protection of the Red
Cross and that they would be exchanged for Germans interned in Allied countries.

A few months later we heard that all the "Latin
Americans" from the Hotel Polski were no longer alive.
They were all murdered in a death camp not far from
Auschwitz.[4] I cannot understand and I cannot accept that
an intelligent Jew like Perle could let himself be tricked
the way he was. He was already halfway free and willingly
reentered the devil's trap.

>——<

After the war I had the chance to learn more details about Perle's
murder and about the fate of many other important Jewish figures,
like Yitshak Katzenelson, who also fell for the deception and chased
the mirage of rescue. Katzenelson, who entered the Hotel Royal on
Chmielna Street, was put on a transport similar to Perle's in May
1943. He and his son were confined to an internment camp in the
French vacation resort Vittel and got help from the Red Cross, but in
the end he too had only taken the first step on a final journey to doom.

The "camp near Hanover" was Bergen-Belsen, which was not
formally regarded as an internment camp for foreign nationals. The
Jews who had arrived from Warsaw could neither receive nor send
mail and were strictly isolated from the outside world.[5] They were
not made to do forced labor and did not suffer brutal treatment at the
hands of the overseers. But their living conditions were not that much
better than those of ordinary concentration camp inmates, and it did
not take long for them to realize that they had fallen into a trap. But
there was no way for them to escape. They too fell into that madden-
ing kaleidoscope whirling between hope and despair, fully realizing

what lay before them. The only advantage they enjoyed over the Jews in Vittel was that their mental torture ended quickly. Three months after they arrived the Germans dispatched them on a transport that took them to Birkenau, the death station of Auschwitz.

>——<

There were no survivors from that group of Latin American passport holders in Bergen-Belsen. But there was another contingent from Warsaw who arrived with them and who had been registered as candidates for emigration certificates to Palestine. As it turned out, that group—whose status seemed the least secure—remained in Belsen almost until the very end of the war. And it was they—who had already suffered, and who then endured for one and a half more years—who survived to be the only witnesses to the tragic story of their "Latin American" compatriots from Warsaw.

We looked for these witnesses and we found them. A woman named Slava Citrinik told us in Yad Vashem about the mood of the Warsaw group when they learned that the "Latin Americans" were leaving on a transport. At first they were sure this was the long-awaited transport to Switzerland for a prisoner exchange. Those who prepared to leave on the transport were seized by a certain euphoria, a kind of ecstatic happiness that sometimes occurs with certain ailments just before death. Many of the "Palestinians" were ready to part with their most precious possessions in exchange for passports from those about to leave. One girl, who did not want to be separated from the group that was staying, actually agreed to such an exchange. The deal succeeded and the girl survived. At the very last moment the Jews on the transport began to smell a rat. But it was too late. They were already locked into the wagons and had begun their journey. The cries and the hysteria in the wagons probably began as the passengers began to read the signs on the stations they passed. They realized they were returning to Poland, and what that meant.

>——<

Lately I started looking again for some traces in the mountains of ash. I kept searching for people who might have known Perle in Bergen-Belsen. In the Radom memorial book, which was edited by Yit-shak Perlov and published in 1962, a great deal of space was devoted to Perle. I read an excerpt from *Ordinary Jews* and verified that the impact his prose made on me had not diminished one bit from when I first wrote that review article thirty-five years before. I also read in that same memorial book a very fine short essay by Yehoshua Lender entitled "Perle, Painter of the Polish Landscape." He wrote, "I heard from someone who returned from 'there' that he saw Perle in Bergen-Belsen a weeping, broken man." The author of those lines died in Paris some time ago. So I had no way to find the person who saw Perle in Bergen-Belsen.

I feel a deep sense of pity when I think about what Perle must have gone through during the last weeks and months of his life. Those tears sear me, those tears he must have shed in front of his compatriot, the tears of a father who realized that with his own hands he had brought his son to the sacrificial altar. Although with ever diminishing hope he waited for a miracle to happen, no miracle came. He gazed at the white clouds in the sky and hoped to see an angel. Perhaps that angel would come at the last moment and stay the hand that held the sharpened knife.

Many angels flew with iron wings and liberated the surviving Jews in Bergen-Belsen, surrounded by heaps of corpses. But that happened long after Shiye Perle and his son, and Yitshak Katzenelson and his son, flew to the heavens in the chimney smoke of Birkenau.

Ivan the Father and Ivan the Son

My family and relatives, the Jews in the village of Lanowitz, used to joke about "Ivan the father and Ivan the son." It seemed funny to them, being so different from the Jewish custom (or was it a religious law?) that a father and son should not have the same name.

When I was living on the Aryan side I often recalled that Lanowitz saying. But now the Ukrainian Ivan had turned into the Polish Jan. By some coincidence I was always dealing with Jans.

When I think back to my days as an "Aryan" I remember that I brought a Jan into the family even before I left the ghetto. The first time I had to choose an alias and a cover story for my new life I saw an image of the tall, imposing figure of a Jan: Jan Dobrucki, who had been the oldest son of our Lanowitz neighbor, the Polish blacksmith Szczepan Dobrucki. My inspiration turned out to be amazingly successful. Having decided to call myself Aniela Dobrucka, who had been the youngest daughter of Szczepan and Domicela, I knew immediately who the new "me" really was. When I left for the Aryan side I took along their family pictures, the pictures of their children, of their sons-in-law and daughters-in-law, along with a picture of their first grandchild, Franek. But the most important member of that family had been, and remained, Jan, my first teacher in the Lanowitz elementary school. That tall teacher with the clever smile inspired and encouraged me to study further. All those Dobrucki names figured in my first fake document, which was not all that good. But they stood me in good stead when I applied for the much safer *kennkarte*,[1] and they became a natural part of my new identity.

How did I survive on the Aryan side when hundreds of other Jews perished? It certainly was not because I was smarter. What helped me were my early years growing up in a village. Those close ties with non-Jews left a mark on my personality. What rubbed off on me was that rural Slavic temperament: easygoing, phlegmatic, somewhat gullible. And if my strategy succeeded it was because I had been close to the Dobrucki family. I never doubted that if I reached out to them they would certainly have helped me and might even have tried to rescue members of my brother's family in Lemberg. Just before the big roundups began I would stay awake at night and try as hard as I could to remember the address of the youngest son, Filka Dobrucki, who in the 1920s moved somewhere near Puszcza Czerwona, when the Polish government settled landowners from the Podolia region on large estates after the First World War.

Filka, the most refined and the least talkative member of the family, liked to play the mandolin and to make colored copies of pictures from illustrated magazines. After the war I learned that of all the members of the family it was he whom the Germans sent to Auschwitz, where he perished.

Of the sisters in the family my real friend was Wladzia. But I took the name Aniela, because the vowels A-I-A matched my three-syllable name Rachela.

It wasn't enough to live an independent life, or to acquire a Polish surname, often artificially made up. (Many of our "Aryans" made the mistake of simply translating their Jewish surnames into Polish.) You could not just appear as if you came from nowhere. You had to be able to talk about your family's home and be ready to explain the main details of your past and present. Thanks to the Dobruckis I was able to spin many stories, replete with episodes and noteworthy details. Four daughters. Four sons. One of those sons was the sailor Rudalko, who was a real globetrotter. Then there was Tonko, who emigrated to Canada. Above all there was the pride of the entire family, "Professor Jas."

It just turned out that as soon as I immersed myself in this new Aryan life I kept encountering new Jans everywhere I went. And each of them contributed in some way to my survival.

The First Jan Was Janina

My first Warsaw Jan was called Janina—Mrs. Janina Buchholc-Bukals-ka—and it was through her that I came to know most of the other Jans. These were her friends, colleagues, associates—people she met before the war and during the occupation. She recruited all of them for the dangerous and complicated task of saving Jews. I already wrote about one of them, Jan Żabiński, in the introduction to my book *Warsaw Testament*. Żabiński did not have to wait for Janina's call to start helping Jews.

Then there was Jan Gaszyński—a second Jan. He was a Nordic type—a tall, silent, rather depressed-looking giant with a long, bare skull. His nickname was Gacek. It turned out that this Jan had married late, and during the war was the father of a sweet, blond, four- or five-year-old boy called Jas.

I once heard a story from big Jan about little Jas.

The family lived on Nowy Świat. In October 1943, at a time of growing German terror, Nowy Świat became notorious as the site where the Germans publicly executed people they rounded up on the streets. They would bring them in groups of twenty or thirty from the Pawiak prison, cordon off a part of the street, line them up against a building, stuff their mouths so they could not shout anything before they died, and murder them with machine guns. This would be in retaliation for the killing of a German gendarme or a collaborationist policeman by the Polish underground.

After each massacre the Germans would post a list of hostages who would be shot next if the Polish underground mounted another assassination.

Right after the massacre the Germans would quickly take away the bodies, dismantle their guardhouse, and reopen the street. People who had relatives on the hostage list and who expected their execution would suddenly appear out of nowhere. Weeping, they prostrated themselves on the bloodstained stones, caressed the congealed pools of blood, lit candles, and left flowers by the bullet-riddled walls. Heart-rending wails of women and children filled the air. People who lived on Nowy Świat, whose windows faced the street, would peek through drawn curtains and hear the cries. Little Jas heard them too and asked why they were crying. His parents told him the reason. When they explained it to him for the second time, he asked: "What do little flies do? Do they cry when people kill their parents?"

Pani Janina was also married to a Jan. Her husband was Professor Jan Buchholc, who was descended from an old German family that had been Polonized for many generations. He refused to change his family name. Why should he? he thought. His loyalty to Poland was there for all to see. In fact, it was a lot more dangerous to have a German surname and refuse to sign the Volksliste than it was to have an ordinary Polish name.[1] Trying to convince him to change his surname to something more Polish-sounding was out of the question.

There was an even knottier question, which I discovered only after the war. It turns out that Janina was also the granddaughter of a Jan. Her father, Henryk Bloch, was the son of the famous assimilationist and philanthropist Jan Bogumił Bloch, the same person who sent I. L. Peretz to tour the provinces and collect information on the economic condition of shtetl Jews. He also hired the young Nahum Sokolow to work on the same project.

So it was hardly surprising that Jan Buchholc was less than over-joyed by his wife's efforts to help Jews during the occupation. He feared that these activities might attract unwelcome attention to her own "mixed" ancestry, since she was a quarter Jewish and could find herself subject to the Nuremberg laws. Afraid of her husband's reaction, Pani Janina would not bring any of the many Jewish women she was helping into her own home, even in an emergency.

I learned after the war that Jan Buchholc ironically knew a lot more about Jewish culture than his wife did. He knew the Hebrew alphabet and could even sing a few Yiddish songs, which he learned when he lived next to a big Jewish bakery as a student and listened to the bakery apprentices sing as they kneaded dough and baked rolls.

After the war I forgave Professor Buchholc for his reluctance to let me sublet a room in his apartment on the western part of Leszno. My friendship with Janina Buchholc survived the occupation. After the war her husband and I became friends, and we became a tight trio. I would visit them in Lodz in their apartment near the university at Żeromskiego 115; those were my most enjoyable times in postwar Poland.

As if I did not know enough Jans during the occupation, it was through the Buchholcs that I got to know Jan Sztaudynger, the well-known writer of epigrams, who also had more than a drop of Jewish blood in his veins. I'm not sure how Poles or, for that matter, religious Jews will react to what I'm about to say. But it's a fact that many of the individuals who took part in Żegota were the grandchildren and great-grandchildren of mixed marriages.[2] Despite the double danger that these people faced, they still felt some spark of Jewish solidarity.

>—<

To any outside observer Jan Rybczyński's translation bureau at Miodowa 11 functioned like any other agency that specialized in translating documents into German, as well as various requests and petitions addressed to German authorities. As was often the case in such offices, the tables, shelves, desk drawers, and cabinets were loaded with piles of paper. But suppose a Gestapo agent took a closer look at all those blank forms, certificates, school transcripts, and the many other personal documents that filled the office. If he only had the slightest idea of what was really going on there, he would have had an apoplectic fit!

This translation bureau was in fact a central agency that provided Jews with Aryan documents, helped them find apartments, and distributed money. When Jews escaped from the ghetto they left a note at the bureau alerting friends and relatives that they were on the Aryan side. Then they would return to the bureau to pick up instructions telling them where to go.

Mr. Rybczyński was tall and thickset, and he dressed like a prince of the old school. He hailed from Galicia and as a young man had ambitions of becoming an opera singer. He mastered the German language under the Habsburgs and before the war worked in the German embassy as a German-Polish translator. So when the Germans marched in, he didn't think twice and became an interpreter for the German occupation authorities. Later he worked on, and perhaps even edited, the illustrated Sunday supplement to the *Kurier Warszawski*, the Polish-language daily put out by the Germans and nicknamed the *Szmatławiec* (*The Rag*) and the *Gadzinówka* (*Reptile*).

Pani Janina Buchholc was also an interpreter before the war, specializing in medical publications requiring an expertise in Latin pharmacological and medical terminology. In addition to her knowledge of Latin and Greek, she was a true polyglot. She was almost as fluent in written and spoken French as she was in Polish, and she knew English, Italian, and Russian. Since she had studied in Krakow she had an expertise in German that one rarely saw in Congress Poland. During the occupation one could say that she became Rybczyński's partner in the translation bureau. Before the war she had gotten to know Rybczyński not only as a fellow member of the Interpreters Union but also through a shared interest in the occult.

This must have happened three weeks after I left the ghetto. I had already begun to learn how to live in my new surroundings. My first stop was a temporary lodging at Rogowska 18 in Praga, one of the many addresses I got from Adolf Berman. The next step was to register, find a permanent place to live, and become a legal resident of Warsaw. Meanwhile the Bermans thought it over and decided that the time had come to put me to work, although this was not work in the normal sense of the word.

Things were difficult at the translation bureau. Janina had an errand boy, some kid of thirteen or fourteen. She could send him anywhere she wished but in no circumstances could she allow him to enter the head office, which was the destination for Jews who had just left the ghetto. She needed somebody she could trust with the other side of her "business."

That's why one early afternoon I showed up at Miodowa to try out for the job of an assistant interpreter. I went in through the first door on the right, entered a long corridor, knocked, and walked into the first room on the right. A tall aristocratic lady dressed in black got up from behind her desk as I entered. When I told her that I came at the suggestion of Pani Basia she broke out in a broad smile and extended her hand with a sincerity that warmed the very depths of my soul.

It had been so long since anybody had smiled at me like that. Neither the Jews nor the Christians that I saw in those days felt much like smiling.

It was almost twelve o'clock. "Lunch break," Pani Janina announced. Then she locked the office and walked me out into the street. At the first left off Miodowa we turned into a small street, right by the big building of the land records office. The second or third door from the corner led into a small restaurant. Like all Polish restaurants it was required to serve, by order of the city administration, a cheap and filling portion of soup cooked with meat bones. That day they were serving a version of *żurek* with barley and potatoes, cooked in pickle oil. Pani Janina ordered two servings, took two large, fresh rolls from her handbag, and ordered me to start eating right away since she herself was hungry. I was so pleased with the soup, and even more with the person sitting across the table from me, that to this day I remember the entire menu and each word that we exchanged during that first, fateful meeting. She was one of the most extraordinary people I ever met.

It turned out Pani Janina and Adolf Berman were both acquainted with Professor Władysław Witwicki, which is what brought them together. I had been a student in Witwicki's conservatory thanks to the two years I had spent in Professor Twardowski's seminar in Lemberg. Suddenly Pani Janina became very sad as she mentioned Romana Wiśniacka. Romana had been a friend and a frequent visitor to their apartment. Pani Janina and her husband called their younger friend "Otuszka" ("Inspiration"). I immediately understood the sorrow I saw on her face.

My job on Miodowa Street began that same week, right after I moved into a place at 14 Próżna Street. I have more to say about my experiences in that apartment, which I shared with the special-needs teacher Helena Merenholc (now named Stasia Królikowska). From there it was only a ten- or fifteen-minute walk to Miodowa. I began my work in Janina's office full of hope and curiosity.

My official responsibilities included filling out enormous forms, nicknamed "blankets," that the land records office used to register in German all transactions completed during the occupation. The land records office would assign these "blankets" to various translation of-fices based on a fixed schedule, thus allowing each of them an easy and stable, albeit modest, income. At first Pani Janina would go pick up our share herself; then she informed the director that she would send her "assistant." The very friendly director would hand over the forms and give me a receipt, which I signed as Aniela Dobrucka in big letters. Unlike Pani Janina I was unable to fill out the blanks in the requisite number of copies on a typewriter for the simple reason that I did not know how to type. To make myself useful I would spoil one of the "blan-kets" and write in the blank spaces German translations of the informa-tion provided by Polish lawyers and notaries who dealt with real estate transactions. That was the sum of my help; my real function was to make it easier for Janina to move around and leave the office. Nonethe-less, she came in one day with a beat-up portable typewriter and tried to teach me how to type, insisting that such a skill could come in very handy given my situation. Half a year later I realized how right she was.

It was not easy to learn how to type while I was in the office. But no matter what I did there, the time I spent in that office was the best part of the day. And perhaps not just then. The feeling of security that I gained from being in the company of such a good and wise human be-ing as Pani Janina was like a convalescence after the traumas and losses I experienced during the deportations in the ghetto. A great and true friendship began between us that only deepened in the coming years.

Janina's actual specialty in the field of psychology was "psycho-hy-giene." For the first few years after the end of the war she ran a psy-cho-hygienic consultation clinic in Lodz. As I think back from the per-spective of many years I realize that her warm and caring manner, her pragmatic approach to people suffering from psychological problems, was already apparent in the way she related to Jews.

Of the Poles I got to know on Miodowa I particularly remember a Pani Jadwiga, an elderly spinster of very neat appearance with a great sense of humor. She liked to look on the bright side and loved passing on political rumors and anti-Hitler jokes. Her brother worked in a bank and helped Jews with various financial matters, including foreign cur-rency and gold—all in exchange for a normal banking commission.

Among those who knew what was really going on in Pani Janina's translation bureau was a Pan Władysław Wąsowski, who worked in Chelmicki's notary office, which occupied most of the adjoining building. The typist in that office was a nasty old hag who gossiped to the other employees, and Pan Władysław took special care to remember everything she said. He came from Lublin, had a lot of contacts in the provinces, and it was from him that I first learned about the Polish (and Jewish) partisan movement in the Lublin forests. He too encouraged and reassured Janina's Jewish clients. But his main job was to keep tabs on what people in the building were saying about the many people coming and going in the adjacent corridors. It was largely because of Pan Władysław's constant vigilance that Pani Janina, Basia Berman, and the entire "Jewish staff" who assembled there every few days were never arrested. And he never let on to our "clients" that anything worried him. His sense of humor kept Pani Janina in a good mood, and that too was no small feat.

Another frequent visitor was Pani Jadwiga Zawirska, a teacher who was always impeccably dressed. I think she was of Jewish descent. Her job was to help Jews get a job or find a rented room in an emergency. Later, as the Russians advanced closer to Warsaw, I would go to her place almost every day to read the secret news bulletins.

During my time on Miodowa I got to know a certain Pani Sylwia. She was a Jehovah's Witness, wore bast sandals, and had her own approach when it came to rescuing Jews: she preached a theory of overcoming fear. There was no way one could eliminate the constant danger, but she believed that it was entirely possible to conquer fear. "Fear is not something that God gave us," she would say. "It contradicts the honor of a human being, his sense of inner freedom." I took her into my confidence and told her that I was looking for a way to establish contact with my nephew Mundek in Lemberg and needed a return address to mail him a message. Pani Sylwia immediately volunteered her own address on Nowy Zjazd near the Kierbedź bridge. "Write him right away, and may God help you bring him here." It turned out that Pani Sylwia had made a vow never to refuse a request from any Jew so long as Jews lived in fear of being murdered because of who they were.

This must have happened in May or June 1943, right after the ghetto uprising. Using Sylwia's return address I sent a letter to Jozefa Sobejko, the former janitor of our old house at Marcina 26 in Lemberg. After the war I learned that Mundek got the letter and then tried, along with a friend, to get to Warsaw. But a Jewish policeman detained them at the railroad station and forced them to return to the ghetto.

>—<

There's yet another of Janina's friends that I'd like to mention: Bernard Kowalski, a somewhat old-fashioned Catholic young man who would later die, together with his father and two brothers, in the street executions. There are those who think that he was denounced by a Czech. In those days Czech collaborators felt that they could lord it over the Poles.

>—<

My official work on Miodowa did not last very long. After the ghetto uprising began in the second half of April 1943, Pan Władysław put out the word that it would be better if I came to the office less frequently. Basia, who had the final say on what went on there, ordered me to stay away. Although my job was over, until the outbreak of the Polish uprising in August 1944 I would still meet Pani Janina, sometimes on Miodowa, sometimes in other places.

An Attic in Praga

After some time I became a genuine veteran of the Aryan side. Having left the ghetto on March 9, 1943, I was now an officially registered Pole and was living in a rented apartment on Próżna Street with a friend. But before I was able to live in such a place I spent two weeks in a tiny first-floor flat recommended by Basia and Adolf Berman on Rogowska, a little suburban type of street located next to the Praga Jewish cemetery on Brudno.

The landlady of this place, together with her friend Sewek and her adolescent daughter Marysia, made money by hiding Jews who paid a good price for each day, night, and every "favor" they received.

The minute I was able to register as a Pole and hide the traces of my previous identity I lost no time in saying goodbye to my landlords on Rogowska and left with the firm resolve never to show my face in that neighborhood again.

As fate would have it, within two months I became a frequent visitor to that place. Pola Elster, my former colleague from the soup kitchens who ran the kitchen of the Left Labor Zionists, was sent there right after she was smuggled out of the Poniatowa labor camp. She shared that room with Hersh Berlinski, who was brought in from the Wyszkow forests. Hersh Wasser and his wife, Bluma, were in the same hideout after being taken there from another hideout. Marysia went to Lemberg, where she helped Natan Buchsbaum, his wife, Basia, and their daughter Mirele escape from the Janowska labor camp and brought them back to Rogowska. Doctor Rosenbaum, a young man whose pseudonym was "Stepan," was also in that group. He was a relative of Dr. Ringelblum's.

>———<

The weeks went by. It was probably the middle of June 1943—that fateful year. The fires of the uprising had died out, and the dos and don'ts for helping Jews hiding on the Aryan side were falling into place. Rogowska had become a stable safe house for the Jewish underground committee. They built a secret room in the attic with a hidden entrance using two false wooden walls. Somebody always stood watch through the tiny peephole. At the slightest sign of danger everybody would remove anything that could betray their presence and hide behind the wooden wall. There was also a night watchman whose main job was to wake any sleeper who was making too much noise.

For many months that hideout worked well. It even survived an incident where a denunciation led agents to swoop down and search every corner of the house, the courtyard in the front, and the attic. But they failed to find the hidden Jews. This happened in October 1943. The next day everybody had to leave, and the "base" was closed.

Until then, during that summer and early autumn, everything seemed to be going "normally." The one constant threat was the neighbor who raised doves and spent his spare time on the ladder that led to the dovecote. Occasionally he would even climb onto the roof of Rogowska 18 while he was chasing some recalcitrant bird.

It went without saying that the landlords would not make even the slightest complaint. Instead they pretended to be very interested in his hobby and joined him on their roof in order to give him a hand. Of course, the Jews in the attic were not thrilled.

The first time I went back there was to see Pan Antoni, that is, Natan Buchsbaum, whom I knew before the war. I hoped that he could give me some news about my nephew Mundek. Just before I left the ghetto I had learned that he was in the Janowska labor camp.

That first time the landlords did not allow me to go up into the attic. They called Buchsbaum to come down. For over an hour he told me frightening details about the destruction of Lemberg Jewry. He promised to write to his friends who were still in Lemberg about my nephew and to tell me what he learned.

But a short time later Buchsbaum let himself be fooled by the Hotel Polski affair and the false hope of survival.[1] Along with his family he went to Bergen-Belsen and then, along with the other "Latin Americans," was sent to Auschwitz and murdered. He never gave me the information that he promised to get from Lemberg, and I'm not sure that he even sent a letter.

As soon as I learned that the Buchsbaums had vacated their place,

I spoke to the landlords and asked Jozia Ziemian to get Bolek out of the labor site at the Warsaw-West railroad station and bring him in. Bolek had been my fellow tenant at Leszno 66 and had been an expert at smuggling people out of the ghetto. I survived the ghetto roundups thanks to him. He was also the one who helped me leave the ghetto.

The next day Jozia learned what happened just one hour after he helped Bolek escape. The two hundred Jews at the Warsaw-West work site, who had all survived the burning ghetto, were herded onto trucks and taken to Treblinka. A little later Jozia began to help a certain writer from Lodz, Miedziński, who had escaped from the transport. Miedziński told him that all the Jews from the labor site were furious with him and Bolek because they believed that the two of them had prior knowledge of the impending liquidation of the camp and, rather than warn them, preferred to save their own necks.

Just a few days before he rescued Bolek, Jozia extracted his younger brother from that same site. But neither that brother nor Bolek nor Miedziński, who had escaped from the Treblinka-bound transport, survived the war.

That's how things were in the summer of 1943.

>——<

When I returned to Rogowska 18 to see what I could do to help the new "guest" I had recommended, the landlords allowed me to climb up to the attic to meet the entire group gathered there.

On tiptoes and in whispers I had my first meeting after all the horrors with people I knew: Hersh and Bluma Wasser, Bolek, Pola. I also met new friends: Hersh Berlinski and Stepan. They all had stories to tell, but above all they wanted to hear what I had to say. What was going on in Warsaw? What was the clandestine Polish press writing? What was the Polish underground doing? What news of fresh defeats could one glean from the German press?

Five months had passed since the victory at Stalingrad, two months since the Allies had destroyed the last German armies in North Africa. As one little island after another fell in the Mediterranean, we imagined them on a map like a row of small electric lights, edging ever closer to the Italian coast, inspiring our dreams of freedom, of liberation, of living to see the day when Hitler croaked. I still remember the name of one of those islands, those little lights of hope: Pantelleria.

After the group discussion I began to talk with Pola Elster, my former colleague from the soup kitchens in the ghetto.

She was the total opposite of her light-blonde sister Wanda, Basia's fiery collaborator, whom I got to know on the Aryan side. So different from her sister and at the same time so alike.

It was only now that I began to really notice how Pola looked and what that meant. Her eyes and eyebrows, that dark mole more conspicuous than ever on her sunken cheeks, and her facial features gave her a distinct "southern" look. It was obvious that somebody with that face should not even think of walking around Warsaw.

I wanted her to give me some news about mutual friends and acquaintances who were still in the Poniatowa labor camp. I learned from her that the poet Yosef Kirman was still there.

Speaking concisely, she described what went on in the burning ghetto. She talked about the living conditions in Poniatowa, which made the attic on Rogowska look like a holiday resort.

It was in that attic at Rogowska 18 that I first spoke with Hersh Berlinski, who commanded the fighting group of the Left Labor Zionists on the terrain of the brushmakers shop. He gave me details about the fate of my former neighbor Avrom Yankev Krzepicki, the escapee from Treblinka. He was also a member of the Jewish combat organization, fighting in the detachment of Hanoar Hatzioni (Zionist Youth). Berlinski knew him well and told me that he was wounded in the leg when the Germans shot up the brushmakers shop. His comrades left him in a cellar along with others who could not move when the detachment abandoned the burning shop and retreated to the area of Franciszkanska. There were no illusions about the fate of those left behind.

I also had a long talk with my close acquaintances Hersh and Bluma Wasser. I met both a few times between the January and April *aktions*, first at Aleksander Landau's carpentry shop on Gęsia and later in the central ghetto, where they lived with Eliyahu Gutkowski.

No matter how strange it seemed given the circumstances, they raised the question of continuing the work of our archive by recording events and personal experiences.

I learned that both Hershes were writing reports about the resistance organization in the ghetto before the outbreak of the uprising.[2]

The first assignment that this group in the attic gave me was to get them notebooks and writing materials.

I had to meet Wanda in the city and work out a schedule of when to visit Rogowska.

It was not easy to go into Polish homes where the landlords knew that your Aryan identity was fake and have to deal with them when their main reason for risking death hiding Jews was money. Even though these landlords had a hard time procuring the large quantities of food that were required to feed their charges, they resented any efforts by others to buy provisions at normal prices to help feed their "cats," especially when those others were themselves compromised. The comings and goings of unknown people put them in danger, so not all landlords were willing to tolerate it. Needless to say, these "nonkosher" visitors were also risking their lives.

Nevertheless, one had to go there. For Wanda, who was one of the chief couriers of the Jewish National Committee, this had become a daily routine, and she didn't just make those trips to help her sister. To give herself better cover Wanda made a point of befriending the landlady's daughter Marysia and let all the neighbors know that she was her cousin and good buddy. It didn't hurt that blonde Wanda looked more like a "shiksa" than Marysia herself. In these matters I was still a rank amateur, and when I had to visit hidden Jews I would play the part of a declassed provincial schoolteacher who supported herself by selling socks and soap. When I would leave the little house at Rogowska 18, walk through the front garden, and open the metal gate leading onto the main street, the landlady would shout: "I have to do laundry early next week. Bring me two bars of soap!"

A story in itself—a very sad story at that—was the psychological state of the people who had to sit locked up and semiclothed in the hideout. It was hard for a Jew who could freely walk the streets—if that's the term you're willing to use—to observe the psychological dependence of people whose landlords knew them to be Jews. They were paralyzed with anxiety and totally dependent on the whims and moods of their Polish "hosts."

In this hideout—and not just in this one—it helped them emotionally when they were asked to do a specific task, such as writing an account of what they had gone through.

For the group at Rogowska this was simply a continuation of what they had been doing in the ghetto at the behest of Dr. Ringelblum. They were all the more eager to do so after they learned that he had returned from Trawniki and was sitting in his hideout and writing.[3] It was Wanda herself who would take his writings and bring them to our common base, Pani Janina's translation bureau at Miodowa 11, where his notes would be typed up and sent to a hiding place arranged by the Bermans. There they survived the war. The same conduit transferred the writings of others, both members of the original archive and those who had just begun to write. Most of these materials also survived, despite the new violence that would soon befall all of us in Warsaw.

In time, asking Jews in hiding to keep diaries and write about their experiences became a general practice, thanks to which we have many important, rich documents fully reflecting the pain and searing reality of that period.

Here are some of the documents written in the attic on Rogowska and in subsequent hideouts. I have already mentioned the reports of Hersh Wasser and Hersh Berlinski. Wasser's notes were included in the first report that was sent abroad during the war, in November 1943, with the help of Polish couriers. Some of Berlinski's notes became widely known only later, at the commemoration of the twentieth anniversary of the ghetto uprising. They were published in Hebrew in *Davar ha-Shavua* and were included in the Hebrew-language volume of documents on the ghetto uprising edited by Dr. Joseph Kermish and Nachman Blumenthal, which was published by Yad Vashem.[4]

I need to mention what I persuaded Bolek W. to write: "Smuggling through the Ghetto Gates," "Befehlstelle Zelazna 103," and "Niska-Prosta." Only the last two works survived, as well as a supplement entitled "Child Smugglers." The essay on smuggling, which was given to Pan Mikolaj (Dr. Leon Feiner of the Bund), burned during the Polish uprising of 1944 along with many other important materials that the Bund had gathered on the Aryan side. There was also a provisional list of workers who were taken to the Warsaw-West railroad worksite after the uprising. It was given to Kozaczyńska, the mother of the landlady, and along with the two surviving works mentioned above is now in the possession of Yad Vashem.

Pola Elster wrote what she experienced and endured before she left the burning ghetto and during her incarceration in the Poniatowa camp. Some of her writings were published in Poland in 1966 as well as in the book *Dray*, edited by Shlomo Schweitzer and published by the Ringelblum circle in Tel Aviv. Here in Israel her sister Wanda showed me charred, moldy pages covered in Pola's handwriting, which she retrieved after the liberation. She found them alongside the corpses of Pola, Hersh Berlinski, and Eliyahu Erlich in the ruins of their last hideout.[5] She holds them close as a keepsake, a last surviving link. Until now they have not been entirely deciphered.

I particularly remember one time I visited Rogowska. I can even remember the exact date, which entered the annals of the history of the Second World War.

It was during the hottest days of the Polish summer. The sun burned without letup, and it was far from easy to sit just underneath the hot shingles of that roof. The group lay around half naked, their necks covered with wet handkerchiefs. They looked as sunburned as if they had been on a beach. That day when I climbed the ladder with my heavy bag, preparing to treat them to juicy sour cherries, I realized that they were all worried and agitated.

It turned out that the Mr. Chief and Mrs. Chief—what hidden Jews usually called their landlords—had been fighting with each other since early morning. Now Mr. Chief was quite drunk, and he aimed his fury at them, the "cats." What did he get from them? Nothing! Absolutely nothing!

He began to shout confused accusations against his woman friend, her daughter, and above all against the entire "shaggy crew" that did whatever they pleased and thought they were living in some vacation resort—while he had to serve them, carry out their shit, and risk his neck. But if they thought he was just their lackey, their useful fool, well, he'd see about that . . .

Shortly after I arrived, he started in on me. He leaned on the ladder that led up to the attic and began to bombard me with insults.

"Oh, just look at that 'Polish lady,' look at the way she moseys through the city as if she owns the place! See how she pretends to be this poor little thing without a penny to her name, even though she's probably rolling in money, like all those other mangy cats. But it's not only people that she's fooling. She's pretending to be a Christian—she's deceiving the Christian God!"

As they heard the taunts and insults, my friends in the attic kept giving me signs that I should leave immediately, as soon as it was possible to get down the ladder and go through the door of the anteroom.

But I strongly felt that, given the circumstances, to leave right then would be a big mistake. As was always the case when I faced real danger, a strange feeling of composure took hold of me. Who knew the harm that this lowlife character could cause not only the Jews but also, out of sheer spite, his woman friend and her daughter? And who else could I turn to? Who could I bring here to fix the breach and cover the abyss that suddenly threatened our "base"?

Sewek went into the courtyard for a while. I quickly left the attic, but I had no intention of leaving. I gave the landlady a wink and signaled that I needed to speak with them both. Even though Sewek came back and declared that "they should drag me by my hair" and "deliver me to you-know-where," I stood my ground and signaled them to follow me into the alcove behind the kitchen, the same place I slept for the two weeks when I lived there. I was happy to see that they followed and sat down with me on the bed that was there.

The alcove was relatively cool, but I felt a strange onrush of feverish heat. Words began to pour out of my mouth, words that surprised even me.

I began to describe for Sewek what the future would be like. I flattered him. I talked about honor. I threatened with all the forces of heaven, earth, and hell. I appealed to their sense of humanity and decency and warned them not to ruin everything they had accomplished until now, having provided a refuge for human beings who were being hunted like wild animals in a forest.

I began to draw for Sewek an image of what would come, when people would shower him with honors. The war would be over, Germany vanquished, Poland free, the world normal, everything back in its place. Jewish survivors would regain their rights, and they would certainly know how to repay all those who helped them in their hour of need. All over the world, humanity would single out and recognize all the courageous people who saved Jews.

I believed what I was saying. I had no way of knowing that after the war was over and Germany surrendered, Sewek and people like him would find themselves in danger from fellow Poles who wondered why they helped Jews survive.

As I got carried away with my description of the coming "messianic age," I even told him that people would make no distinction between those who rescued Jews for money and those who did so for purely altruistic and humanitarian reasons. After all, whatever their motives happened to be, all rescuers lived in mortal fear and risked not only their lives but the lives of their children as well.

Just when I was making that point in my exhortation, I snuck a peek at the couple and a stone lifted from my heart. The landlady had probably cursed herself a hundred times for letting herself get involved in such a dangerous business. It made her dependent on the kindness or malevolence of any neighbor she quarreled with and put her at the mercy not only of any German or policeman but also of her "friend," whom she had to keep happy. Now I saw that she was crying. She clearly realized just how deeply she yearned for the day when she would no longer have to fear a neighbor or a German.

I don't know what was going on in Sewek's imagination as I spoke. Maybe he was sobering up a little from the home brew or shaking off the effects of the depressive moral rot that the Germans had set loose in his unhappy homeland. Whatever the case was, I saw a tear in his foggy eyes.

"As long as I am here, not a hair will fall from their heads!" he began to spout, as he banged his chest with his fist.

I realized that I had made my point and shouldn't press my luck any further. It was time to leave, and fast.

I extended my hand, blurted out a loud and assertive goodbye, making sure that those in the attic would hear it, and left the house, the courtyard, and the street next to the Jewish cemetery as quickly as I could. As I ran to the tram stop, trying to get out of Praga as soon as possible, I remembered that I had a meeting in the city that day.

➤—◄

Then I had another bizarre experience. When I reached Targowa Street I saw little Polish kids running around waving the new edition of the collaborationist *Kurier Warszawski*, which the Poles called the *Szmat-*

lowiec (*The Rag*). What we read was old news already rationalized by the German propagandists. But the triumphant tones of those newspaper boys conveyed the fateful, sensational importance of what had just happened. The kids yelled at the top of their voices: "Revolution in Italy! Mussolini arrested! Marshal Badoglio now in power!"

It was Monday, July 26, 1943. I bought a copy for double the regular price, and my first thought was to run back to Rogowska and be the first person to tell this news to my unhappy, humiliated, and depressed friends who had just endured such a painful confrontation with their landlords. I would show Sewek that the wonderful moment I had just been describing to him was indeed approaching quickly.

I remembered the newspaper article "Without Mussolini, No Hitler" that I read in some Vienna newspaper before the Anschluss.

The axis of the machine that had carried millions of Jews and non-Jews to their deaths had collapsed! After Stalingrad, North Africa, and the landings in southern Italy, this was surely a new, powerful, and decisive blow to Nazi power in occupied Europe.

I wanted to soar, to run, to fly. I yearned to share this colossal piece of news with others. I was seething with energy, yearning to comment on what I heard, looking for some outlet for my excitement.

I did not run very far. Ten times I stopped and had second thoughts. Should I go there or not? Who knows how the landlords at Rogowska 18 would react after we had already reconciled? What if the neighbors saw me with that newspaper? Maybe they would run to hear the news and then I would have to deal with them face to face?

In the end I did not go there. I did not have the privilege to gladden and encourage those suffering souls who were so eager and anxious to see and hear, to experience, this moment: Pola and Hersh, the Wassers, Bolek, and Stepan. I did not have the chance to fan the flame of hope in their hearts, to instill confidence that the day for which they yearned with such fervor was getting closer.

Later I learned that they got the news the next day. But endless troubles and great dangers and misfortunes were still in store for us.

I never returned to the little house at Rogowska 18. My Polish and Jewish superiors did not allow me to go there anymore.

Among the "Cats" in the Zoo

Now for a long digression. Or to be more precise a parallel story that also features a Jan and a second place on the Aryan side where I did my clandestine work and made contacts.

This must have been at the end of July or beginning of August 1943. It was when some of the euphoria sparked by the news of Mussolini's downfall had worn off, even though big crowds still gathered around the "growlers"—the public loudspeakers that carried German newscasts. Included in those crowds were those who were most desperate to hear good news: Jews.

For the two "Polish teachers" (me and Helena Merenholc) who lived at Próżna 14, the nearest loudspeaker was on Płac Grzybowski, which we could get to from a second exit in our building. I hoped to hear that Marshal Badoglio's new Italian government had capitulated but came away disappointed.[1]

Around 9 a.m. I returned to the apartment on the second floor with a quart of milk and a loaf of bread. Right away I sensed that something was wrong. My roommate Stasia Królikowska (actually Helena Merenholc) was running around the two rooms grabbing her things and stuffing them into a suitcase. As soon as she saw me, she began saying over and over, "Get out of here. Run! Now!" Breathlessly she told me that just a minute ago a messenger came from our landlady's relative and partner who lived on Grójecka Street. He said that the Germans had arrested the landlady near Majdanek as she was trying to deliver a package for her sister who was imprisoned there. The package contained foreign currency. The boy warned us that since the Germans now had her address, the Gestapo or Kripo[2] might arrive any minute to search the apartment. We were really frightened. They might come here to look for dollars and then start asking questions about us. As one Polish policeman once said about a similar situation, "We came looking for apples and we found pears." We didn't even want to meet her relatives, who would now surely try to take over the apartment. After a quick discussion we decided to leave one of our house keys with the janitor, telling him that we were both going off to the country for a vacation.

The trouble was that Stasia could go to the hideout where her mother, sister, and sister's child were living. She would be able to spend the night there and wait until the situation became clearer or until somebody found a new apartment for her. I, on the other hand, had nowhere to go even for a night. My only address was the translation office at Miodowa 11. So there I went with my little bag and imposed myself on my protector, Pani Janina Buchholc. She scratched her head, thought for a while, and then declared: "There's no other choice. We'll have to send you to the zoo!"

While I certainly didn't feel like laughing, I tried to make a joke of what she said.

"Oh, that's great! But zoos are not for ordinary cats." In those days "cats" was the most widely used slang term for fugitive Jews.

"Actually, yes," replied Pani Janina. "When there are no regular animals at the zoo, cats fit the bill."

There were still many hours left until nightfall. It just so happened that Pani Janina was scheduled to meet Antonina Żabińska, the zookeeper's wife, that very day. She could arrange the transfer of a new "animal." Even before the meeting took place she gave me the necessary information.

After the office on Miodowa closed I went to Praga, crossed the Kierbedź bridge, turned left, and descended the steps that led to the city park bordering the zoo on the east bank of the Vistula.

The spacious grounds of the zoo contained cages and other buildings meant to house various four-legged and two-legged creatures, as well as birds and reptiles from different parts of the world. Now most of those buildings stood empty. In September 1939 the army command ordered all the potentially dangerous animals shot, since they could endanger the population if their cages were bombed and they escaped. After Warsaw surrendered the Germans sent the surviving animals to various German zoos. The only animals that remained were a group of silver foxes and nutria, looked after by an attendant named Wróblewski. The chief watchman and some former employees lived in one of the residential buildings. The spacious home of the head zookeeper also survived, barely damaged during the siege. He still lived there along with his family.

If you assumed that the other buildings in the zoo stood empty, you would be wrong.

><

Following Janina's instructions I made myself look as carefree and relaxed as possible as I walked through the park. Mothers, grandmothers, and nursemaids sat on benches along the lanes and watched sleeping infants in baby carriages or toddlers as they ran around. On other benches gray-haired gentlemen sat absorbed reading the *Gadzinówka* (*The Reptile*) or *Szmatlowiec* (*The Little Rag*), as the collaborationist newspaper was called. Some also followed the subtle shifts in the German newspaper, which was called the *Warschauer* for short. I had also brought along a copy of the *Little Rag* that I had already read. But I sat down on a bench and pretended to be totally engrossed in every word of the newspaper.

The afternoon scene in the park felt as if I had stepped back in time to prewar days. There was even some guy in a uniform trying to pick up a young babysitter wheeling a pram. Given the circumstances, that uniform did not seem too dangerous. More dangerous, no doubt, would be the blue uniform of a Polish policeman. But I did not see one here. As I walked down from the bridge I noticed for the first time the guard post of the river police.

Pani Janina instructed me to wait until quarter to eight, when people would start going home. I would also pretend to leave but instead would carefully make my way toward the zoo. I did this but became very worried when I noticed that some other people were doing the exact same thing. As I approached the villa, I noticed a couple of individuals loitering by the trees, waiting near the house like me for the daytime employees to leave.

As I approached and entered the villa, I saw a tall blonde woman I recognized from the office on Miodowa. She gave me a friendly nod of the head and a few minutes later showed me a corner under a window just where the staircase curved upward toward the second floor. She handed me an old overcoat that I could use as a blanket as I slept on the children's mattress on the floor.

"Tomorrow I'll get you a folding chair, since one woman won't be returning," she told me.

There were about ten people there who, like me, suddenly found themselves forced out of their "burned" apartments. The same scene, with ten or so people, repeated itself the following evening: armchairs in the hall, rugs on the floor, chairs on the terrace, all turned into makeshift beds. People who had spent a terrible day facing danger in the streets claimed a corner and plunked themselves on whatever resembled a place to lie down. Watched over by courageous, clever, and decent people, they immediately fell asleep.

We were not the only people who found refuge in this asylum. What I saw was only a minor aspect of a much larger picture, which I came to know only later.

I was homeless for the next month. During that time things happened in the world so compelling that they kept me from thinking too much about my personal situation. One day I managed to buy a bogus issue of the *Kurier Warszawski*,[3] between whose pages the Polish underground had inserted entire sheets of news based on foreign radio reports and commentaries. The whole day's run was sold out in a half hour. The newspaper boys were able to get two złotys for the last copies left. That night I took the newspaper, which I had practically memorized, to the zoo. I was so pleased with myself that after I overheard somebody's joke I couldn't resist calling Pani Antonina a couple of days later to tell her that "the macaroni is cooked." That meant Marshal Badoglio had finally authorized Italy's capitulation. But I jumped the gun; the capitulation had not yet happened, and I was happy that nobody teased me about bringing noodles to dinner.

Despite this setback I kept a close watch on every possible source of information. As I wandered around the city on foot and in trams, without any place of my own, I carefully noted the locations of all the loudspeakers. Even though I faced the danger of being scooped up in the street dragnets that sent people to forced labor in Germany, I still joined the crowds of people that gathered to listen to the belated and distorted German military communiques. The crowds took particular pleasure in hearing about the "planned retreats": "German military forces successfully withdrew after destroying all objects of military significance." These phrases, delivered in a deep bass voice and with perfect diction by the collaborationist Polish-language announcer, always mentioned some important new point on the eastern front, to the enormous delight of the crowd. With each passing day Germany's defeat seemed more certain, and final redemption appeared to be a lot closer than it was. Some elderly lady, as she heard the loudspeaker through the window of the tram, commented mordantly: "Sralis, maxgalis, referendis, dupcis."[4] The tram slowed down and waited at the stop to give the passengers, the driver, and the conductor enough time to hear what the loudspeaker was spitting out. For us Jews-in-hiding this was like a wonderful shot in the arm that helped keep our spirits up and gave us strength to resist the evil winds assailing us from all directions.

Needless to say, this was a time when the rules governing mutual relations between friends, relatives, or acquaintances did not allow you to just relax and focus on yourself or on one other person. One day, because the maid did not show up for work, Pani Antonina Żabińska asked me to stay at the zoo and help her air out and dust off the books and papers in the large library. This is a chore that is always the bane of housekeepers, no matter where in the world they are.

I too hated this job with every fiber of my being, but I couldn't say no to Pani Tola. So I took a clothes brush and began to beat and dust the piles of books and paper that covered the whole width of the terrace. While I was doing this I allowed myself now and then to admire the beautiful colored illustrations in the foreign journals that kept arriving, even in wartime, from various neutral countries.

At that time, when I still barely knew Jan Żabiński, the director, I suddenly heard echoes of a small argument between the couple. Pani Antonina was defending herself as her husband grumbled that she was lazy, saddling me with a chore she should have done herself.

I don't think Pan Jan was upset by the fact that Pani Tola kept me at the zoo during the day, thus putting the entire household in more danger. I believe that what bothered him was a matter of principle, the absolute refusal to gain any personal benefit from protecting people who were facing death. Later, I heard about a Pole from Vilna who had sheltered a Jewish family in a hideout. After the war he sold their home for them and absolutely refused to accept their offer of an extra sum of money, declaring that he did not want to sell his good deed for money since he wanted to get his reward in the world to come.

I don't know if Żabiński was motivated by the possible rewards that awaited him, either on this earth or in the world to come. But as time went on I noticed something else. He was born to give orders and commands, be it with animals or humans. (People would call him in jest "the commander of women and animals.") So he was quite demanding of his close family and relatives. During the occupation he also commanded a unit of the underground Home Army.

Yet when he met helpless and depressed Jews who depended on him for empathy and help he couldn't have been kinder. Having been a pedagogue since his earliest days he saw it as a personal obligation to care about the psychological health of his Jewish clients. He didn't give them only concrete help. He also knew how to bring back people who were totally broken and restore their sense of self-respect.

IN FRAU KRAUZE'S HOUSE

In the meantime I finally found myself a room. There was a certain Pani Renzdner, a friend of Janina Buchholc's, who had taken in the sculptress Magdalena Gross, a prewar friend of the Żabińskis. She learned that her half-German cousin, Frau Krauze, had a small room for rent in her five-room apartment on Smolna Street. Pani Renzdner agreed to recommend me as a reliable tenant who could pay the rent and, most important, as a Polish lady of impeccable descent.

All washed and ironed, made presentable by Pani Janina after all the nights sleeping at the zoo, one early morning I went to Smolna 24. I made a good impression, paid three months' rent in advance—a modest sum of 135 złotys a month—and moved in the next morning.

One great advantage of my new place was that I could eat a good and filling lunch prepared by the landlady for a very reasonable price. But the best part of my new living arrangement was that my little room was somewhat isolated from the rest of the apartment. Because of this I could resume what I had begun doing for the Ringelblum archive: writing about the ghetto and what I saw there. Working every night from midnight until five in the morning between October 1943 and April 1944 I wrote two major works, including the first version of this book.

After I managed to find a new place to live I still stayed in touch with the "enchanted garden" of the Żabiński family, which is what Pani Janina called the villa in the zoo. With a fixed address and a cover story for my Aryan identity, I became a welcome guest and a daily visitor. Since I had now become just another respectable tenant of Frau Krauze's, who thought I was some teacher from East Galicia that had turned up in Warsaw, it was important for me to find an alibi to explain what I did all day, how I earned my money, and where I got my personal contacts. In those days most of the declassed Polish intelligentsia survived by engaging in some form of trade. So Pani Janina provided me with a large carry bag, very modern by the standards of those days. It was made of

THE LAST JOURNEY

dense layers of woven paper and shaped like a trapezoid topped by two planed and polished panels, through which ran a handle of thick colored rope. Two Jewish women in hiding produced these bags, which all of Pani Janina's "buddies" used to buy things and trade.

It was from Janina Buchholc that I got my first goods to sell. The first article was a kind of refined spirit that two engineers concocted out of a sweet potato brew. One of the engineers was her husband, Jan Buchholc, and the second was her son-in-law, a fellow named George. I would carry that 90 percent spirit in 10-liter jars based on orders I received from Jan Gaszyński, the one called Gacek. When news came about Mussolini's fall from power we had a real field day. Warsaw went on a drunken bender that lasted three days and nights. One guy who owned a restaurant on Wspólna Street took 10-liter jars off my hands and paid in cash, even though he had not ordered them beforehand.

Once I learned the recipe I began to use that spirit to make a 45 percent liqueur, a trick that came in handy when it was decided that I had to throw a party in Frau Krauze's place to celebrate my "name day." With the help of a kilo of sugar, a liter of water, and some green syrup, I prepared 2 liters of "zubrówka," bought a big package of wartime cakes, and spent a whole day receiving congratulations on the telephone from my "Aryan" friends. I was careful to give each one of my fellow tenants, along with specially invited guests, a glass of the home brew. According to the calendar, that was the day of Saint Aniela. Only after the war did I learn that the real Anielas celebrate their name day on the holiday of Our Lady of Angels.[1] Fortunately, both the landlady and her servant were Evangelicals and were therefore not up to speed on Catholic customs.

In my carry bag I lugged laundry detergent, bottles of cooking oil, and white rolls that I would pick up at a bakery in the western part of Leszno Street on the corner of Wronia, almost across the street from where Jan and Janina Buchholc lived. Those round, braided rolls with a brownish crust, baked according to an old Jewish recipe, gave me the perfect opportunity to renew my daily visits to the zoo. No sooner did I pull out one of those rolls for Pani Tola then she asked me to bring twenty-five to the zoo each day, it being understood that I would get there between seven and eight in the morning. That order was not just a convenient pretext but gave me an actual reason to get up quite early, get to the bakery on Wronia, pick up the rolls, and then take them to Praga.

320

>——◂

Once I arrived at the zoo, Pan Paweł Zieliński, who slept on the first floor, would let me into the villa. He was a delicate man, not very tall, who came from Lemberg and had been a friend of the sculptress Magdalena Gross. Before the war she used to visit the zoo to study and sculpt models of animals. After the establishment of the ghetto she stayed with the Żabińskis and eventually brought in her future husband.

When I had been sleeping at the zoo I did not know Pan Zieliński, and I was unaware of the lawyer Levi-Krzyżanowski, who lived there legally with his wife and two daughters. Only now did I gradually come to learn about other Jewish tenants and visitors, who received help and support in various ways. After the war I found out that not every secret had been revealed to me. From the memoir *People and Animals* that Pani Antonina published in Warsaw in 1965, as well as the two visits that the Żabińskis made to Israel, when they gave testimonies in the Tel Aviv branch of Yad Vashem, I learned many new facts. For example, it never occurred to me that there was a large cellar and attic in the villa. Nor did I know about Żabiński's "enterprise" in the city. When I published an article in 1945 about Janina Buchholc, I wrote about an engineer named Cywiński who had sheltered more than ten Jews at his place. Most of them were referred to him by Żabiński.

Cywiński came to Israel along with Jan Żabiński, and Yad Vashem awarded him the title "Righteous among the Nations." Regina Sobol-Kenigswein, whom they had saved along with her husband and children, told us more details about both.

>——◂

I would like to return to Paweł Zieliński, whose real name was Doctor Maurycy Frenkel. It sufficed for me to know that he came from Lemberg, that we had acquaintances in common, and that we were bound by a common fate. Director Żabiński explicitly ordered me to stay away from depressing subjects when I met him: I was only to discuss positive and upbeat matters that would make him feel better. This was about paying attention to the psychological state of people living in hiding, an issue I understood quite well; the visits I made once or twice a week to Jews in hiding gave me first-hand experience.

How wonderful it is to be young. In those days I did my clandestine writing between midnight and five in the morning. At six I would get up, run around the city for hours on end, ride on overcrowded trams, go to secret meetings, trade, arrange matters for people, make things happen—and I managed to show up when I had to and do what needed to be done.

>——<

I have very pleasant memories of those early morning meetings with Pan Paweł. Apart from my now-rare visits to Miodowa, those were opportunities to take off my mask and to return, if only for a short time, to my real identity. When I would arrive at the zoo the water would already be boiling in a pot on the alcohol cooker. Paweł would pour us two cups of ersatz tea sweetened with real sugar. We would share one of the rolls I brought and get to talking, mostly about war news. He was better informed than I was, not only because he read the German paper every day but also because he received the secret bulletins of the Polish underground that Żabiński brought from the city.

The news kept getting better. The Americans and the British were bombing German cities night and day, as more and more islands and ports in the Mediterranean fell to the Allied fleets. Paweł would deliver exhaustive commentaries, but his conclusion was always the same: "Yes, it's all great, but when will it finally end?"

>——<

Our talks would usually break off around eight. I would give Paweł all kinds of messages from the Żegota and monthly allowances for the people hiding at the zoo. A few days later he would hand me receipts and replies to the messages. Occasionally he would give me items to sell, which I would take over to Miodowa. Once, for example, he gave me a silver service for twenty-four people. It was not an easy job to pack all that, with separate boxes for the utensil cases and my usual wares. Although we had settled into a stable routine, issues like this made it necessary for me to meet with the owners of this "house of enchanted wonders." Pani Madzia called it "the house under the crazy star." I learned that in addition to the "nocturnal ghosts," a group that had recently included myself, there were also legal residents, including the lawyer Levi, his wife, and two daughters. His wife was suffering from menopausal depression with symptoms that were quite problematic. But the Żabińskis believed that this was just another reason to keep her there. After all, "Who would be willing to hide her in such a condition?"

One day the Żabińskis came down from their floor earlier than usual. They greeted me with good-natured laughter, teased me that I was flirting with Paweł, and made me join them for a breakfast "with all the trimmings," including a soft-boiled egg. Half an hour later, when I was getting up to leave, Żabiński interjected that he was also going into the city and that we should travel together. This put me in an uncomfortable situation. My outfit made it inappropriate for me to be seen strolling along the riverbank in the company of the most prominent citizen of the neighborhood. In addition, a bottle of oil had turned over in my carry bag, which now had a conspicuous stain on the front. To make matters worse he took the carry bag from me, looped it over his arm, began to swing it up and down along with his leather briefcase, and motioned for me to walk on his right side. What worried me most was that we would have to walk past the guard post of the river police.

"Mr. Director," I tried to argue, "why should you take a risk? I might put you in danger."

"Don't talk nonsense," he replied. "I'm the one who is endangering you, not the other way around. Don't you see what I look like?"

This was funny, but I realized he was right. Despite a bald spot he still had plenty of brown hair along with a very suspicious-looking nose. Once he had actually been detained in some distant part of the city. But I realized that he had no worries at all about the river police.

After the war I read in his wife's memoir that he had been the commander of the Vistula unit of the Home Army, which included most of the river police. The unit underwent military training on the grounds of the zoo, so I understood that he had no worries about them. Of course, in those days Żabiński couldn't let me in on that secret.

I still remember some of our discussion during that long walk. As we got to the bridge and went up to the tram stop on Nowy Zjazd we began to talk about how constant exposure to danger and the unceasing need to deal with new emergencies affected the human organism. What about people who were forced to spend all their time in hideouts, completely powerless, face-to-face with the constant fear of death? Did these experiences enable them to develop new mental resources and greater psychological resilience?

"As a biologist you can evaluate the degree to which new capabilities that people acquire in such circumstances can help them deal with dangerous developments and unexpected changes. For example, let's take the new skills that people learn in German camps. Couldn't we say that the skills used to survive and stay healthy might also help them later? Maybe those skills will help them make a new start, live longer, make up for lost time?"

"Oh my, you've really gotten ahead of yourself!" he answered. "There is no simple answer to the questions you are raising. I see biology as a particular science with its own rules. Although one should look for analogies between people and animals, finding them is not so easy. But I think that the need to expend extra energy now leads to a shorter rather than a longer life-span. The unrelenting tension of living in constant danger can allow a person to access incredible resources. But later, after the danger is past, he can fall apart."

What he said was right. In the collection of testimonies gathered at Yad Vashem there are hundreds of examples of people who overcame the greatest dangers and difficulties to stay alive and help others survive, only to die because of minor problems after liberation.

Trouble and a Silver Lining

About going to the zoo to sell things: it was not all one way. I also took items from there to sell in the city. For example, Pani Tola told Pan Wróblewski, the caretaker of the silver foxes, to give me two gorgeous fox pelts to peddle. I was able to sell one of those luxury items to Miss Saska, a fellow tenant in our apartment. She was the daughter of a pharmacist from Ostrowiec Kielecki and came to Warsaw to take a special wartime pharmacy course. Although I did not walk away from that deal with a big profit, I still thought it would be good for my landlady, Frau Krauze, to see that I was a serious trader. But nothing is as simple as it appears to be. Frau Krauze came from a Polish aristocratic family on her mother's side and was especially proud that one of her uncles had been a bishop; his portrait hung right in the middle of the dining room wall. Mrs. Renzdner, who had recommended me to Frau Krauze, told Pani Janina that Frau Krauze was not at all pleased to hear of my wheeling and dealing. As soon as Pani Janina told me this I imagined the awful possibility that Frau Krauze would tell me to get out, leaving me homeless once again. I began to feverishly think through how I could give up trading and do something else. It just so happened that a happy coincidence gave me yet another chance to survive.

It was already autumn. The parks and tree-lined squares sparkled with the gold and crimson hues of fallen leaves. When a gust of wind blew the leaves around, the word "October"—scrawled on sidewalks in chalk or coal—became clearly visible. The wider public did not know what it was supposed to mean. We heard that the same inscription appeared in other occupied countries. Although Germany was suffering defeat after defeat, the oppressive occupation showed no signs of abating. My God! October 1943! In Warsaw the terror grew only worse with each passing day.

The wave of public street executions had begun, something I have already described. After each act of sabotage, after each assassina-

325

tion of a gendarme on some distant street, they would take dozens of prisoners from the Pawiak prison, stuff their mouths with clay to prevent them from crying out, and gun them down on one of the major thoroughfares. They would then post an announcement with a list of new hostages who would be shot if there was another "provocation." To guarantee a steady supply of victims in the prison, the Germans would suddenly swoop down with blockades and street roundups.

I too got caught up in an "incident." It happened when I was on my way to the zoo. My large carry bag was stuffed even more than usual. Along with the usual supply of rolls I was carrying a new bottle of cooking oil, a large bottle of Jan Buchholc's home brew, three long sticks of laundry detergent, and, at the very bottom, a letter to Pan Mikolaj, the Bundist representative on the Coordinating Committee. Just one sentence was enough to show that a Jewish woman who was in contact with the underground had written it. Suddenly, as the tram was in the middle of the bridge, we heard an order: "Halt!" The tram stopped.

Somebody next to me whispered: "We're surrounded. They're taking people off." I instantly went numb. I went to the conductress and tried to get her to hide my bag. She assumed a stony expression, and I saw the first green uniform enter the tram. I stuffed the carry bag under the seat and pulled out my ID card wrapped in cellophane. Then I made a second mistake. As I was standing in a long line along a barrier on the bridge waiting for the document check, a German appeared waving my bag over his head. In a friendly, jocular tone he asked who had forgotten it, as if he were planning to return it to the owner.

Once again I did something dumb. "It's my bag," I whispered to the woman standing next to me. "I don't know what to do."

That lady, who was smarter than I was, fixed me with a look of amazement. "It depends on what's in the bag," she blurted out. I stopped looking at the bag, moved forward, and went through the document check with the others. As I moved along I noticed two men kneeling on the concrete abutment facing the river. A truck, its bed covered with a large tarp, was ready to take them away.

>—<

I lost everything. When I took out my ID I neglected to take along my purse with the few złotys I had. I arrived at the director's villa at the zoo at 8:30. Everybody was already seated around the table and were finishing their breakfast. Even before I arrived they had heard about the blockade.

"Oh my, did they clean you out!" the director exclaimed when I stammered my explanation of what happened. To make me feel better, he treated it as a laughing matter.

"Maybe you got up late today," Pan Paweł remarked, and he was not entirely wrong. "The Germans never start doing things before eight in the morning. So, because you chose to be a sleepyhead, we had to do without our rolls this morning."

"Oh, that reminds me!" Żabiński interjected. "Had this not happened, it would have totally slipped my mind. I have a wonderful job for you."

Job? What was he talking about? But he already had the telephone receiver in his hand and was talking to somebody. "Yes, I have just the person for you. You were looking for someone to work in the office who knows German? I have an excellent candidate. She comes from Lemberg and knows German fluently. What else? Can she type? I don't know. You'll teach her. Right now you won't find anybody better."

He was talking with the former prefect of Wadowice. He had settled in Warsaw after 1939 and either leased or bought a business that made paper bags, which the Germans needed to allocate rations. The factory was located on the east side of the Vistula but far from the river. The proprietor's apartment and office were located on one of the more modern built-up streets, to the left of the Eastern Station.

Mr. Rudzinski employed eighteen workers, paying them just a little more than the official wage. His problem was that he could not supplement their earnings with extra food allotments or, and this was even more serious, personal labor cards. It was perfectly understandable that as a high official of the former Polish government he wanted to keep a low profile and therefore rarely left his apartment. He also placed a small "v" before his last name to make German officials think he was an ethnic German prewar aristocrat. But he had not been able to do much for his employees and he very much needed a factotum who could fill out forms, write requests, and knew how to deal with German agencies. The German offices had hired many people with an even minimal knowledge of German, making it difficult for private employers to find qualified people.

Our first interview was enough for him to realize that my office skills were modest, at best. That did not bother him much. What really mattered was that I knew German. Despite his Silesian background, his own German was very weak. So he hired me for a trial period and even paid me an advance. As for typing, filling out forms, and payroll lists, he said that he would teach me. After a couple of weeks I had already reached a certain level of proficiency.

So my knowledge of German, which people advised me to conceal when living on the Aryan side (and which I would like to forget forever), enabled me to improve my living conditions and to get by, something that was difficult even for native Poles.

Pan R. began to send me to different German offices every day, and I managed to get everything done. The first thing was to register all the employees of the factory, including myself, with the labor bureau. Pan R. told me to find a certain Polish clerk and give him the application with a góral (500-złoty note) stuffed inside. The clerk gave me a pile of forms, and I filled them out on the spot, using a list of employees' names that I had with me. In a week I received labor cards for each of the employees in the factory including one for Aniela Dobrucka, complete with the stamp of the paper bag factory. I still have that card.

My new position as an employee of Pan R.'s factory turned out to be the foundation of all my subsequent achievements. The employees were now able to get extra food allocations, which they had not been until then. For cigarettes and alcohol they had to go to Inflancka Street, where a high fence bordered the Umschlagplatz. Once I tried to peek behind the fence and was almost shot. A badly dressed Polish kid pulled me by the hem of my dress and pointed out a German guard who had just taken his rifle from his shoulder.

"Do you want them to shoot you?" he asked me.

Now, all the things I managed to get done for others I also accomplished for myself. I could also make up little packages from the allotments and give them to friends and to my landlady, Frau Krauze, who accepted them with a smile.

>——<

Two trips I made for my boss remain particularly etched in my memory. One had to do with getting permission for employees to move around at night; there was access to electricity mainly after dark. To get it I had to go to the notorious Gestapo headquarters on Aleja Szucha. This building was to the right of the corner of Ujazdowskie, not to the left, where the infamous torture of Jews and Poles took place.

The second trip was a visit to a high official in Governor Fischer's office near the intersection of Krakowskie Przedmieście and Nowy Świat. The official had the ugly name Henker,[1] but he was quite gracious to me. It seemed that he believed it very important to convince himself that he treated Poles decently. I learned that my boss had already invited him to a nocturnal get-together with alcohol.

As soon as he heard my request for an allocation of coal for the factory from the Department of Trade and Industry, he started dictating a letter in my presence to a German typist. The letter began: "Ich bitte sie recht sehr" ("I am kindly asking you please"). The typist piped up: "either recht or sehr." She objected to an exaggerated and unseemly show of politeness toward a member of a subject people. Or maybe she felt in her bones the tremor of the inevitable German retreat . . .

Each month my boss would give me an envelope stuffed with górals to take to a Polish address in Praga. That was his contribution to the Home Army. I reckon that his acquaintanceship with Żabiński also had something to do with the Polish underground movement.

As soon as I transformed from a trader to an office employee my standing with Frau Krauze greatly improved. After the period of the street executions and the underground retaliation killing of SS and police leader Kutschera, which cost the Polish population of Warsaw a collective fine of 100 million złotys, the now uneasy and worried occupiers began to try and frighten the Poles with placards and rumors about a deportation to the provinces of all Varsovians who were not employed in essential war production.[2]

The Poles—who, ever since the "resettlement" of the Jews to Treblinka, had reacted with hypersensitivity to all such rumors—became very frightened. The leadership of the underground reacted in its time-tested manner and organized an assassination attempt on the chief of the housing department in the General Government, somebody named Braun. The Germans then ceased talking about deportations.

Had the Germans carried out their plans, my new position would have enabled me to shield the other tenants of the apartment on Smolna.

My new job in Praga also enabled me to put on some weight for the first time since I left the ghetto. For many months I had not been able to gain even a decagram, despite the improvement in my living conditions. It was only after I started working for Pan R. that my nutrition improved both in quality and quantity. Pani Marysia, a lifelong single woman who was the housekeeper and friend of the boss, always gave me a second helping of delicious soup.

If It Wasn't for Pani Maria

Nevertheless, I soon realized that in times like these it was better not to get too optimistic. Around the middle of April 1944 a new danger suddenly hung over my head. Pani Janina believed that even in this case "my guardian angel was watching over me," as she always liked to say. Had those angels not been doing their job, or to be more precise, had a Jan not helped me, then what happened might have led if not to total catastrophe then at least to the loss of my room.

It happened a few days before Easter. The ethnic German maid got up before dawn with the praiseworthy intention of decorating the large front window of the big empty room next to mine. Two country girls studying medicine rented that room, but they only came to Warsaw during exam time. Between midnight and 5 a.m. I would sit by a small nightlight and write about what happened in the ghetto. Totally absorbed in my writing, I did not hear the maid's soft steps. The old lady noticed the light coming through the keyhole and, it turned out, happened to be one of those women who see nothing wrong with taking a little peek.

Totally unaware of what was going on, I went to work like every day. I followed my daily routine: I washed, dressed, and hid the notebooks. Just before I locked my room I turned around and checked to see that no notes, pieces of paper, or random cards remained on the table, chair, or floor near the wall. Although written in Polish, they could easily and unmistakably betray who I was. The journals filled with my notes were in an open drawer of an old dresser, shoved between two thick wads of brown paper that served as a false bottom. To hide them better I covered the paper with apples, pears, bags of barley meal, rye flour, or other articles Poles could buy with their ration cards in the grocery stores. That's what I did for concealment. I had no key to lock the drawer since the dresser itself had no locks, and I could not install one without raising the suspicions of the landlady and the maid.

Since I had already said that I would be working in the office in the afternoon as well, after work in Praga I went to Towarowa 8 for the weekly visit to "my" hidden Jews. By the time I finally returned to Smolna it was half an hour before curfew. When she heard me on the stairs, Miss Marysia, the tenant who rented the room to my left, motioned me with her finger to come into her place.

She told me that earlier that day the landlady declared, in a bombastic tone of voice, "Dobrucka has the mind of a trader. She writes! What is she writing? Why does she do that at night?"

I had little time to think or to figure out what the old landlady and her devoted servant must be thinking. Who knows whether they used all those hours of my absence to rummage through my room? They might be asking themselves why there was nothing in the desk drawer. Or perhaps they had already figured out the secret and emptied out the dresser?

Without another word I left Pani Marysia's and hurried into my room. The notebooks were in their proper place! Within two minutes I had stuffed the contraband into my old shopping bag. It was twenty minutes to eight and there was still some light outside. Within a few minutes I hurried along Smolna, took a right turn on Nowy Świat, and, totally out of breath, leaned on the second-floor door of Jan Gaszyński. This was the same Jan, Janina's friend, with whom I would sell Jan Buchholc's home brew. Jan was at home.

"My notebooks," I stammered. He took the package from my hands and without saying a word shoved them through a hole in the deep cotton-straw stuffing of an old armchair. After the war he told me that it was all the same to him. He was hiding so much dangerous stuff in his apartment that if the Germans had come to search, the Jewish materials would have been the least of his troubles.

During the occupation three of the most dangerous things to hide were Jews, home brew, and weapons. And he had them all.

BIGOS AND HOME BREW IN THE PHEASANT CAGE

I can't even begin to describe all that Jan Żabiński did in those days, when the most difficult challenge was to act like a decent person. So I'll just relate one story.

This must have happened sometime in November 1943. The hideout that sheltered seven Jews, located in the attic of the building at Rogowska 18 right next to the Jewish cemetery, was suddenly "burned." One of those Jews had been my neighbor at Leszno 66.[1] He had helped save me during the roundups and later to cross over to the Aryan side. Our roles reversed after he fled the ghetto during the uprising, leaving his forced labor group at the railroad just one hour before the Germans liquidated all the workers. He was young, courageous, and smart. But he had a Jewish nose.

Somebody informed the Gestapo, and that night they raided the attic. They banged and searched everywhere but were unable to find the hideout, which was in a concealed room flanked by boards. The next day six people went to a new hideout. My "client" remained alone in the attic, and the landlords threatened that they would drop him off that very night and leave him in the ghetto ruins. I got the alarming news in the early morning and did not go to work that day, spending hour after hour talking to every possible contact. I did everything I could but without success. At about two in the afternoon, as I was losing all hope, I showed up on Chocimska Street, in the hygiene institute where Jan Żabiński worked. He had given me that address when I was trying to help "Aniela number two," a friend of mine. He was able to find her a rather peculiar job feeding lice that were being used to produce typhus vaccine. It was exactly what she needed.

I said little, but his experience with animals made him quite adept at telepathy. Now he understood my despair, and he also realized that I was turning to him only because I had exhausted every other possibility. He curtly told me to bring the man over that night. I have written elsewhere about how difficult it was to "pilot" a Jew with a Jewish nose through the streets, someone who had been sitting in a hideout for many months and was now outside for the first time. Now I want to repeat what this person later told me after he left the zoo and got to a new hideout.

After I brought Bolek to the zoo I had to leave immediately in order to make it to Smolna before the curfew. As she did with other Jews in similar circumstances, Pani Żabińska led him into the former pheasant cage. It was open, but there was a far corner where he could hide.

My charge was draped in the cotton padded jacket he had brought with him from the ghetto, and his teeth were chattering from the cold. He was depressed; now and then he fell into a semi-sleep full of nightmares. In the middle of the night, when everything became quiet and the lights went out, he suddenly heard approaching steps. It was Jan Żabiński, who came with a big sheep pelt and a full basket: a loaf of bread, a bottle of alcohol, salami, and a bowl of hot *bigos*. They drank, ate, and the director stayed with the young man until it was almost dawn. They spoke about politics and sports. Żabiński gave him back his self-respect, his hope, and the resolve to renew the struggle to survive.

The Notebooks in Glass Jars Survived

Occasionally, after I had taken Bolek out of the zoo, the Żabińskis would ask me how the "pheasant" was doing. Later, when Żabiński visited Israel in 1965 and 1967 and I mentioned the "pheasant," he did not remember who I was talking about. Based on what I read in Antonina Żabińska's memoir *People and Animals,* as well as the testimony that Mrs. Regina Kenigswein gave to Yad Vashem, I learned that Regina's husband, who had been a well-known Warsaw boxer, also hid out for a time in the pheasant cage and that Jan Żabiński also visited him at night with some vodka and warm *bigos.* Mrs. Kenigswein was the daughter of a Praga vegetable merchant from whom the zoo used to buy animal feed. It turned out that those nightly visits with hot food and a warm pelt to lift the spirits of the "cats" hiding in the pheasant cage were almost routine. So that moniker "pheasant" applied to more than one hidden Jew.

>———<

In June or July 1944, as the war moved to a close and we awaited the big Soviet offensive, I once again appeared at the zoo.

Using a glass pen, Bolek Warm had made clean copies of my notes and writings. Through Pani Janina the Bermans received one copy and put it in their archive; other copies went to "Pan Mikołaj" (Dr. Leon Feiner). The agronomist Hela Rajcher, also known as "Aniela number two" and "Aniela Makarewicz," buried another cache in a tin container in Pani Janina's garden plot in the Mokotow fields. These documents included more of my drafts as well as other materials, including the memoirs of Elisha Landau, who came from Lemberg. Landau and his daughter were in the same hideout as Bolek for a time, and he wrote his memoirs according to my instructions and direction.

After talking it over with Żabiński, I brought the most important

documents to the zoo: my original text, my testament, and the addresses of people who were to receive my writings in the event of my death. I
also took along a big vacuum jar with a hermetic glass seal and handed
it all over to Pan Paweł, just as I had done with other deliveries in the
past.

I saw my documents once again in April 1945. I later found out that
Żabiński's twelve-year-old son Ryszard (Rysia) had helped his father
seal the vacuum jar using large pliers.

>———<

Occupied Warsaw's final drama, the tragic and heroic finale of the bitter struggle that sealed her fate, played out in stages. When Jan Żabiński heard the siren wail at 11 a.m. on August 1, 1944, he, along with tens of
thousands of other fighters, moved to their assigned combat stations.
His wife Antonina together with their boy Rysia and their newborn
daughter Teresa—just a few weeks old—endured the first phase of the
uprising in their own home, only leaving when the Germans evacuated
the farm where the silver foxes were raised and finally being sent on a
German transport to Lowicz. It was there that she, together with her
two children as well as Lola and Antosha, the two daughters of the Jewish lawyer Levi-Krzyzanowski, saw the Germans make their final retreat
and the Red Army arrive. Wounded and miraculously rescued under
fire, Jan Żabiński sat out those final days of the war in a German POW
camp and later, until the fall of 1945, in an American hospital.

>———<

Having been caught up in the mass expulsion after the defeat of the
uprising, I returned to Warsaw from the small town of Konsk in March
1945. The whole city on the western bank of the Vistula lay in ruins
under a cover of snow. A Jewish committee was already functioning
in Praga, on the eastern bank. I ran into people I knew from the time
of the occupation and found Pani Janina in Praga. Żabiński's wife was
living on Florianska Street along with the children, in the home of their
former housekeeper's relatives. After the mud had dried a little, I set
off one day in April for the zoo. The destruction was worse than in September 1939. But Pani Tola had already started to visit the premises,

giving orders and directions and trying to put back together whatever had survived the carnage.

Rysia had no hesitation whatsoever about where to dig up my treasure. Among the trenches and fallen trees he recognized a stone that had been close to the entrance of the now-destroyed villa. He started to dig, threw away several shovelfuls of earth, knelt over the hole, and pulled out the vacuum jar. My seven notebooks were all there, dry and clean. They contained the first drafts of the two books I wrote during those nights at Frau Krauze's place in the winter of 1943–1944: *They Called It Resettlement* and *Together with the People.*

It is thanks to that courageous and noble knight of the Polish nation, Jan Żabiński, who was buried in the earth of Poland's fighting capital in 1974, that I owe not only my own personal survival but the survival of my one remaining possession: that history in which I wrote, full of pain and sorrow, about the creative works and martyrdom of the last Jewish writers and artists in Warsaw.

POSTSCRIPT

My unforgettable, devoted, motherly friend Janina Buchholc-Bukolska died in Lodz in 1968. Since I left Poland in January 1950, she sent me dozens of witty, clever, captivating, and emotional letters constantly begging me to come visit: "Let's be together and make each other happy." But I kept postponing my trip, too distracted by the constant challenges of my work at Yad Vashem. Even worse, I didn't have the sense or energy to follow the example of many other Jews in Israel who survived on the Aryan side and invite Pani Janina and her husband to visit Israel. Yes, I had ready-made excuses: her health, her obesity, my fear that she could not tolerate our hot weather.

In 1966 I finally decided to see her in Poland. I would go there from France where, in connection with the Steiner-Hachette controversy, I was fighting to get Steiner and the publishing house to excise falsifications that he had knowingly put in his book after I had let him see my materials on Treblinka that I had brought with me from Poland.[1] But I was refused a Polish entry visa. This was after Yad Vashem had warmly welcomed dozens of delegates of sister institutions in Poland, including many from the Auschwitz Museum, who were involved in the study of the occupation period. It seems that this was not about me personally but was a harbinger of the shift in Poland's relationship with Israel, which began even before the Six-Day War. Perhaps had I made a private visa application, rather than going through the channels of the Jewish Historical Institute, I would have succeeded. But by the time I realized that it was too late. The Polish consul in Tel Aviv, who had received many invitations to Yad Vashem and who had given us many richly illustrated albums and interesting Polish publications, was himself surprised. But neither he nor his colleague in Paris were able to change the decision.

Alarmed by a telegram that I had sent her from Paris, Pani Janina immediately went to Warsaw to try to get advice and help from old friends.

Then the misfortune happened. She had first turned to Jan (Gacek) Gaszyński, her trusted old friend from the occupation days. It was early evening. Since there was nobody home Janina turned to leave and, walking down from the second floor, slipped and fell on the stairs, breaking her hip. She never recovered. In May 1967 my colleague and friend from Yad Vashem, Miriam Peleg-Marianski, visited Poland and, at my request, went to see Pani Janina in Lodz.

Miriam found Janina in a very bad way. Pani Janina had spent the entire winter in the hospital but was now back home. Nothing could cheer her up: not the box of oranges, nor material for a new black dress, nor the ample vial of excellent French perfume that she used to love so much. She did not react to the warm regards I sent or to my gifts. I later received one more letter from her. Frightened, I asked Antonina Żabińska if she had heard any news from Lodz. Then I got the terrible news.

I wrote a letter of condolence to Professor Buchholc, who was a pensioner. He did not answer my letter, which was returned with the inscription "addressee deceased." I believed then and still believe that he wrote that himself. He could never forgive me for what happened and blamed me for hastening the death of his life companion, the mother of his only daughter and the grandmother of his grandchildren.

I cannot forgive myself for having put off seeing Janina for so long. It was a chance that was lost forever, and neither she nor I can feel the joy of meeting each other one more time.

May her memory be blessed.

Notes

Introduction

1   The Oyneg Shabes (Oneg Shabbat in Hebrew) was Yiddish for "Joy of the Sabbath." It was a code word that Ringelblum chose for the archive, emphasizing the importance of keeping the project secret. Perhaps the name was chosen because the executive committee of the archive met on Friday nights or Saturday afternoons.

2   Leora Bilsky underscores how important it was for Auerbach, in preparing her testimony for the Eichmann trial, to highlight the importance of "cultural genocide." See Leora Bilsky, "Rachel Auerbach and the Eichmann Trial: A New Conception of Victims' Testimonies," *The Journal of Holocaust Research*, 36:4, 327-345, 2022. See also Leora Bilsky and Rachel Klagsbrun, "The Return of Cultural Genocide?", *European Journal of International Law*, Volume 29, 2, May 2018.

3   See Efrat Gal-Ed, *Niemandsprache: Itzik Manger-ein europäischer dichter* (Berlin: Jüdischer Verlag im Suhrkamp Verlag, 2016), 310.

4   Alexander Donat, *The Holocaust Kingdom* (New York: Holt Rinehart and Winston, 1965), 211, quoted in Alvin Rosenfeld, *A Double Dying* (Bloomington and London: Indiana University Press, 1980), 37–38.

5   Ruta Sakowska, *Ludzie z dzielnicy zamkniętej* (Warsaw: PWN, 1993); Israel Gutman, Ina Friedman trans., *The Jews of Warsaw, 1939–1943: Ghetto, Underground, Revolt* (Bloomington: Indiana University Press, 1983); Havi Dreifuss (Ben-Sasson), *We Polish Jews: The Relations between Poles and Jews during the Holocaust* (Hebrew) (Jerusalem: Yad Vashem, 2009); Barbara Engelking and Jacek Leociak, Emma Harris trans., *The Warsaw Ghetto: A Guide to the Perished City* (London and New Haven: Yale University Press, 2009); Katarzyna Person, *Assimilated Jews in the Warsaw Ghetto, 1940–1943* (Syracuse: Syracuse University Press, 2014); Leah Preiss, *Displaced Persons at Home: Refugees*

in the Fabric of Jewish Life in Warsaw (Jerusalem: Yad Vashem, 2015); Gunnar S. Paulsson, *Secret City: The Hidden Jews of Warsaw* (London and New Haven: Yale University Press, 2002).

6 Mendel Mann, "Rokhl Auerbach tsu ir bazukh in Pariz," *Unzer Vort*, August 6, 1966.

7 "Okupatsiye bikher fun mekhabrim yidn," Yad Vashem Archive, P16/23.

8 Auerbach did publish a book after the war about the 1943 ghetto uprising. See Rokhl Auerbach, *Der yidisher oyfshtand* (Warsaw: 1948).

9 Quoted in Boaz Cohen, "Rachel Auerbach, Yad Vashem and Israeli Holocaust Memory," ibid. See also Rokhl Auerbach, "Sifrei Zikaron," *Davar*, January 12, 1958.

10 While Auerbach had many difficulties in her new home, she never wavered in her conviction that after the Holocaust Israel had become the vital center of the Jewish people. For those who read Yiddish I highly recommend her book *In land yisroel*, a collection of reportage from the early 1950s that revealed her devotion to the new state as well as her empathy for the struggles of Jewish immigrants from the Middle East and North Africa. See Rokhl Auerbach, *In land yisroel: reportazhn, eseyen, dertseylungen* (Tel Aviv: Y. L. Peretz Farlag, 1964).

11 Annette Wieviorka, *The Era of the Witness* (Ithaca: Cornell University Press, 2006); Rachel Auerbach, "Edim v'eduyot b'mishpat Eichman," *Yediot Yad Vashem,* December 1961.

12 See Rokhl Auerbach, "Eduyot," *Davar*, November 4, 1955.

13 The conference organized at Yale University on November 3–4, 2019, "Rokhl Oyerbach: The Bridge between Wartime and Postwar Testimony," serves as a welcome reminder that Auerbach's legacy is finally gaining more recognition.

14 See Rokhl Auerbach, "Arkhiv 'Hemshekh' oyf der arisher zayt" in Yad Vashem Archives, Rokhl Auerbach Collection, 16–32.

15 The meeting decided that if the buried materials surfaced after the war, they should become the property of the YIVO Institute for Jewish Research in New York. In the event, both caches of the

Ringelblum archive remained in the Jewish Historical Institute in Warsaw, although Hersh Wasser surreptitiously sent many materials to the YIVO, where they form the Hersh Wasser collection. By the time the second cache of the archive was discovered, in December 1950, Auerbach was already in Israel, and she failed to gain access to most of those materials. However, some were published by the Jewish Historical Institute.

16 ARI/655

17 *Behutsot Varsha*, 7.

18 *Baym letstn veg*, 301. The best scholarly treatment of Auerbach's ghetto diary can be found in Karolina Szymaniak's annotated edition. Karolina Szymaniak and Anna Ciałowicz, *Pisma z getta Warszawskiego* (Warsaw: 2016).

19 *Behutsot Varsha*, 8. I have used Boaz Cohen's translation here. See Boaz Cohen, "Rachel Auerbach, Yad Vashem, and Israel Holocaust Memory," *Polin*, No. 20, 198.

20 *Behutsot Varsha* (Tel Aviv: 1954); *Varshever tsavoes* (Tel Aviv: 1974); *Baym letstn veg* (Tel Aviv: 1977).

21 See the obituary written by Joseph Kermish after Auerbach's death: "Ha za'akah gavra al kavanti," *Davar*, July 23, 1976.

22 On the Yad Vashem website Auerbach's date of birth is given as 1903. This is the date that Auerbach always used and was accepted by most researchers. She was required to retire from Yad Vashem in 1968 when she turned 65, or so it was thought. But Karolina Szymaniak, in her research in local archives in Ukraine, discovered a birth record that lists Auerbach being born in 1899. The reasons for this discrepancy are unknown. On the question of the birthdate see Karolina Szymaniak, "On the Ice Floe: Rachel Auerbach—The Life of a Yiddishist Intellectual in Early Twentieth Century Poland," in Ferenc Laczó and Joachim von Puttkamer (eds.), *Catastrophe and Utopia: Jewish Intellectuals in Central and Eastern Europe in the 1930s and 1940s* (Berlin–Boston: De Gruyter, 2018).

23 Lemberg was the German name for the beautiful multinational city that was called Lemberik in Yiddish, Lwow in Polish, and Lviv in Ukrainian. When Auerbach lived and studied in Lwow,

the city had over 300,000 inhabitants, of whom about a third were Jewish, 60 percent Polish, and the rest largely Ukrainian. Today Lviv is an almost entirely Ukrainian city.

24 From this volume, page 293.

25 She graduated from the Adam Mickiewicz Gymnasium in Lwow in 1921 and then enrolled at the Jan Kazimierz University in Lwow to study philosophy, psychology, and history. She left the university in 1925 without a degree, perhaps, as Karolina Szymaniak speculates, because the death of her father left her in straitened financial circumstances. She resumed her studies when she moved to Warsaw but never, it seems, earned a formal degree, although she completed her course work and passed the state exams to become a history teacher. See Karolina Szymaniak, "On the Ice Floe," 308–311.

26 Rachel Auerbach, "Nisht oysgeshpunene fedem," *Di goldene keyt*, 1964, No. 50. Karolina Szymaniak offers the best discussion of Auerbach's literary and intellectual development before the war in "On the Ice Floe."

27 For Auerbach's own reminiscences of *Tsushtayer* and her friendship with Vogel and Schulz, see "Nisht oysgeshpunene fedem." In recent years several scholars have begun to write about *Tsushtayer*. Some of these articles include Anastasiya Lyubas, "Gender, Language and Territory: The Tsushtayer Literary Journal in Galicia and the Contributions of Yiddish Women Writers," *Nashim: A Journal of Jewish Women's Studies and Gender Issues*, Fall 2020, No. 37; Karolina Szymaniak, *Rozdwojony język, „Cusztajer" i galicyjskie jidyszowe środowisko artystyczne, „Midrasz"* 2006, no. 7–8; Carrie Friedman-Cohen, "Kevutsat *Tsushtayer* beGalitsyah, 1929–1933˙ (The *Tsushtayer* group in Galicia, 1929–1932)," *Khulyot*, 10 (2007).

28 Ironically, most of Auerbach's wartime writings—in the ghetto and on the Aryan side—were originally written in Polish, rather than Yiddish. There is no clear explanation why this is the case. For more on this see Szymaniak, "On the Ice Floe," and Karolina Szymaniak and Anna Cialowicz, *Pisma z Getta Warszawskiego* (Warsaw: 2016), 63–65. See also footnote 8 for chapter 18.

29 Friedman-Cohen, "Kevutsat Tsushtayer," 164.

30 On her often abusive and dysfunctional relationship with Manger see Efrat Gal-Ed, *Niemandsprache: Itzik Manger-ein europäischer dichter*.

31 Rokhl Auerbach, "Dos yidishe galitsiye," *Literarishe bleter,* July 1, 1932.

32 There are many memoirs about Tlomackie 13. See, for example, Zusman Segalowicz, *Tlomackie 13: fun farbrentn nekhtn* (Buenos Aires: 1946) and Ber Rozen, *Tlomackie 13* (Buenos Aires: 1950). For the best scholarly study see Nathan Cohen, *Sefer, Sofer ve-Iton: Merkaz ha-Tarbut Ha-yehudit be-Varsha* (Jerusalem: Magnes Press, 2003).

33 On this last, tumultuous meeting with Manger see Gal-ed, *Niemandsprache,* 506–508.

34 On the Aleynhilf, which in fact operated legally under different names, see Samuel Kassow, *Who Will Write Our History: Rediscovering a Secret Archive from the Warsaw Ghetto* (Bloomington: Indiana University Press, 2007), and Barbara Engelking and Jacek Leociak, *The Warsaw Ghetto: A Guide to the Perished City* (New Haven: Yale University Press, 2009). The American-based Joint Distribution Committee played a major role in financing the Aleynhilf. This bought the Aleynhilf a certain degree of legitimacy in the eyes of the German authorities. After Germany's declaration of war against the United States in December 1941, the Aleynhilf faced growing problems obtaining money and resources and lost some of its autonomy to the Judenrat.

35 In a talk she gave for Yiddish journalists in Lodz in October 1947, Auerbach described how in the Aleynhilf radical leftists befriended leaders of the religious Agudas Yisroel such as Zysha Frydman. See Yad Vashem Archive, P16/58. This talk was an impassioned plea for Jewish unity.

36 In a diary entry of May 26, 1942, Ringelblum wrote, "The [Aleynhilf] . . . does not solve the problem [of hunger], it only saves people for a short time, and then they will die anyway. The [soup kitchens] prolong the suffering but cannot bring salvation [because there is not enough money]. It is an absolute fact that the clients of the soup kitchens will die if they eat only the soup they get there, and the bread they get on their ration cards."

37 On February 28, 1942, she was even more pessimistic: "I have been slowly concluding that the whole balance of this self-help activity is simply that people die more slowly (*śmierć na raty*). We must finally admit to ourselves that we can save nobody from death, we don't have the means to do it. We can only put it off, regulate it, but we can't prevent it. In all my experience in the soup kitchen, I have not been able to rescue anybody, nobody! And nobody could accuse me of caring less than the directors of other soup kitchens." It should be noted, however, that after the war Auerbach looked back and realized that her efforts in the soup kitchen were not a total failure. While those who relied solely on the soup kitchens eventually starved, Jews who had a secondary source of food benefited from them.

38 In her diary Auerbach gave free rein to her growing fear of death as reports of mass executions in the provinces streamed into the Oyneg Shabes. In the past, she wrote on March 6, 1942, Jews had gone to their deaths knowing that they could have saved themselves had they only chosen to renounce their faith. Now, Polish Jewry did not have the comfort of kiddush Hashem, of dying to sanctify God's name. Like a convict on an American death row, they were waiting for their date with the executioner. In her diary, Auerbach betrayed her uncertainty and dread as her thoughts flitted back and forth between despair and hope. "How will our ordinary Jew get the strength to meet such a death, what will hold up his spirit as he waits week after week for his execution?" she wrote. ". . . I am sure that our age-old spiritual capital, this golden pillar of our community, has not been totally shattered."

39 In 1947 Auerbach published a book based on visits to the camp with survivors, *Oyf di felder fun treblinke* (Warsaw: 1947). In the mid-1960s, when the French Jewish author Jean-François Steiner published his *Treblinka: The Revolt of an Extermination Camp*, an indignant Auerbach led a widely publicized campaign against the author and his fictionalized account of the Treblinka Uprising. Steiner, she claimed, had abused her trust and that of the Treblinka survivors whom he interviewed. On the Steiner controversy and Auerbach's role in it see Samuel Moyn, *A Holocaust Controversy: The Treblinka Affair in Postwar France* (Hanover, NH: Brandeis University Press, 2005).

40 Some of what follows is taken from a previously published article, "The Warsaw Ghetto in the Writings of Rokhl Auerbach," Glenn Dynner and Antony Polonsky, eds., *Warsaw the Jewish Metropolis: Essays in Honor of the 75th Birthday of Professor Antony Polonsky*, (Leiden: Brill, 2015).

41 Anita Norich, *Discovering Exile: Yiddish and American Jewish Culture during the Holocaust* (Stanford: Stanford University Press, 2007), 135.

42 Leo Finkelstein, "Iber un ariber varshever yidishe gasn," in Melech Ravitch, ed., *Dos amolike yidishe varshe* (Montreal: Farband fun varshever yidn in montreal, 1966), 585.

43 Antony Polonsky, ed., Abraham Lewin, *A Cup of Tears: A Diary of the Warsaw Ghetto* (Oxford and New York: Basil Blackwell, 1988), entry for December 29, 1942.

44 A case in point was her blistering attack on Wanda Melcer's "Czarny Ląd" ("Dark Continent"), a series of articles that appeared in the *Wiadomości Literackie*. The weekly newspaper was one of the most prestigious pillars of Polish high culture, and many of its editors, writers, and readers were Jewish. The "Dark Continent" was actually the Jewish neighborhoods of north Warsaw, which Melcer described in terms not that different from an anthropological report on central Africa or the Amazon: bizarre rites of circumcision, ritual baths, boys hunched over books in exotic heders. Auerbach accused Melcer, and by extension the entire *Wiadomości Literackie* crowd, of pretentious arrogance. Ironically, *Wiadomości Literackie* was also one of the few bastions of tolerance and liberalism in interwar Poland. But as Jewish writers often complained, it was more likely to publish an obscure Senegalese poet than a Yiddish writer from Warsaw. The relationship between this liberal and urbane tribune of high culture and the Jewish intelligentsia was very complex. See Magdalena Opalska, *"Wiadomości Literackie: Polemics on the Jewish Question, 1924–1939,"* in Yisrael Gutman et al. (eds.), *The Jews of Poland Between the Two World Wars* (Hanover, NH: 1989), 434–53. For more on the Melcer controversy see the excellent study by Katrin Steffen, *Jüdische Polonität* (Göttingen: 2004), 160–61. On Auerbach's rejection of Melcer, see *Baym letstn veg*, 48.

45 From this volume, page 6.

46 The title *Yizkor* is taken from a prayer for the dead recited on certain Jewish holidays.

47 *Yizkor* was translated by Leonard Wolf and appeared in David Roskies, ed., *The Literature of Destruction: Jewish Responses to Catastrophe* (Philadelphia-New York-Jerusalem: The Jewish Publication Society, 1989), 461–464. Translations that appear below from *Yizkor* are taken from this source.

48 David Roskies, *The Jewish Search for a Usable Past* (Bloomington: Indiana University Press, 1999), 23–24, 38–39.

49 That Auerbach needed little convincing on this score can be seen from a suggestive book review of Yoshue Perle's *Yidn fun a gants yor* (*Ordinary Jews*) that she published in *Literarishe bleter,* a leading Yiddish literary journal. At a time when so many Jewish writers wrote about national and political issues, Perle focused on human relationships, adolescent sexuality, and family dysfunction. In her review Auerbach lambasted a prudish Bundist critic for looking askance at the sexual themes in the book. See Rokhl Auerbach, "Y Perle's *Yidn fun a gants yor,*" *Literarishe bleter*, 49, November 1935; 50, December 1935.

50 David Roskies, ed., *The Literature of Destruction*, 461–464.

51 See Havi Dreifuss (Ben-Sasson), *We Polish Jews: The Relations between Poles and Jews during the Holocaust* (Hebrew) (Jerusalem: Yad Vashem, 2009).

52 Emanuel Ringelblum wrote that the September 1939 siege, during which Poles and Jews stood side by side, reminded him of the brief period of Polish-Jewish "brotherhood" during the 1863 rebellion against Russia.

53 From this volume, page 22.

54 *Oyf di felder fun treblinke* (Warsaw: 1947); *Der yidisher oyfshtand* (Warsaw: 1948).

55 By 1965 Auerbach had collected more than three thousand testimonies in fifteen different languages. Cohen, "Rachel Auerbach, Yad Vashem and Israeli Holocaust Memory," 202.

56 As Boaz Cohen points out, her department, located in Tel Aviv

away from Yad Vashem's main building in Jerusalem, became a "stepchild." Her request for tape recorders met with a lukewarm response. By 1967 recorded testimonies were only 20 percent of the total. Ibid., 202.

57 Rachel Auerbach, "Edim ve'eduyot b'mishpat Eichmann," *Yediot Yad Vashem*, December 1961. Here Auerbach outlines her thoughts about the trial and her collaboration with chief prosecutor Gideon Hausner. As Leora Bilsky notes, there were still critical differences between Hausner and Auerbach. "Both wanted to give voice to the victims, but Auerbach sought to promote a more collaborative conception of the trial in which Holocaust survivors would be considered equal partners to the prosecution. In her view, the trial would become a victim-centered trial not only because of the survivors' testimonies, but also because it would recognize their initiative and agency in promoting a new conception of testimony." Bilsky, "Rachel Auerbach and the Eichmann Trial: A New Conception of Victims' Testimonies," *The Journal of Holocaust Research*, Volume 26, 2022, Issue 4, 330.

58 Letter to Aryeh Kubovy, no date, quoted in Boaz Cohen, "Auerbach ... ," 218.

59 Cohen, "Auerbach . . ." 218. Letter to Jacob Robinson, n.d. Yad Vashem Archive P16/59.

60 Ibid.

Foreword

1 Ethnic German.

2 In the south part of Warsaw.

3 *Dos poylishe yidntum (Polish Jewry)*, a series edited by Mark Turkow and dedicated to the memory of Polish Jewry. By 1955 over 150 volumes had appeared.

4 The first cache of the Ringelblum archive was discovered on September 18, 1946, under the ruins of Nowolipki 68 in the former Warsaw Ghetto.

5 *Ulica Graniczna (The Border Street)* was a 1948 Polish film about the Warsaw Ghetto directed by Aleksander Ford. It won the Gran

Prix at the 1948 Venice Film Festival.

6   The second cache of the Ringelblum archive was unexpectedly discovered by Polish construction workers in December 1950. By then Auerbach was in Israel.

Chapter 1: Blades in the Sky

1   The Polish-language *Nasz Przegląd* (*Our Review*) was one of the most popular Jewish daily newspapers in interwar Poland. Auerbach was a frequent contributor.

2   In October 1938 the Polish government decreed that all Polish citizens living abroad would lose their citizenship unless they acquired a special stamp at a Polish consulate. Determined to get rid of potentially stateless Jews, on the night of October 27, SS, SA, and German police arrested 17,000 Polish Jews living in Germany and literally dumped them at various spots on the Polish border. Of these about 9,000 ended up in Zbąszyn, where after Polish border guards refused to let them cross the frontier, they languished under open skies in mud, rain, and cold. The Poles eventually let Jewish relief agencies set up a refugee camp. Emanuel Ringelblum, who worked for the Joint Distribution Committee, played a major role in the relief effort.

3   This refers to Kristallnacht when, on November 9–10, 1938, mobs burned synagogues, smashed Jewish shops, and murdered at least ninety-one Jews all over Germany. German authorities then sent 30,000 Jewish men to concentration camps.

4   Short for *Obrona Przeciwlotnicza*, or air defense.

5   Tlomackie 13 was one of the most celebrated and best-known addresses in prewar Jewish Poland. It served as a gathering place for Jewish writers and journalists and sponsored lectures, cultural events, dances, and musical evenings. Many memoirs describe the special atmosphere of that locale.

6   Natan Szwalbe and Saul Wagman were journalists affiliated with *Nasz Przegląd*. The Bug River became the demarcation line at the end of September 1939 between the German and Soviet zones of occupied Poland.

7   The Germans occupied Lwow on June 30, 1941.

Chapter 2: Candles at Twilight

1   Auerbach is referring primarily to the growing use of the Polish language within the Jewish community. This was especially true in Galicia, among middle class Jews in central Poland, and among the younger generation, most of whom were receiving their elementary education in Polish public schools. Yiddishists were very alarmed by these developments.

2   The Jewish Landkentenish Society was founded in 1926 in order to promote "engaged tourism." This included visits to museums, excursions throughout Poland (including by kayak), the writing of local history, and the study of Jewish architecture and material culture. The purpose of such activities was to remind Polish Jews of their centuries-old connection with Polish lands and to counter antisemitic propaganda that portrayed Jews as harmful aliens with no right to live in Poland.

3   The Yidisher Visnshaftlekher Institut (Yiddish Scientific Institute), or YIVO, was founded in Vilna in 1925 to promote Jewish scholarship in the Yiddish language. It created a community of scholars and ordinary Jews dedicated to studying the language, literature, art, psychology, folklore, and history of East European Jewry as a living community.

4   Between 1941 and 1944 the Germans murdered about 70,000 Jews from Vilna and its surrounding towns in the nearby Ponary forest.

5   Lemberg was the German name for the multinational city that was called Lemberik in Yiddish, Lwow in Polish, and Lviv in Ukrainian. When Auerbach lived and studied in Lwow the city had over 300,000 residents, of whom about a third were Jewish, 60 percent were Polish, and the rest were largely Ukrainian. Today Lviv is almost entirely Ukrainian.

6   *Chwiła* was a Jewish daily newspaper in the Polish language. It was published in Lwow between 1919 and 1939.

7   Founder of the Sasov Hasidic dynasty.

Chapter 3: My Last Time at Tlomackie 13

1   *Haynt* was a Zionist-leaning Yiddish daily and the most widely read Yiddish newspaper in prewar Poland.

Chapter 4: September Neighbors

1   Both Ararat and Azazel were Yiddish theaters based on *kleyn-kunst*, or popular cabaret, characterized by a playful interplay of folklore, ditties, and Jewish tunes interspersed with satire and criticism. Azazel was organized in Warsaw in 1925, while Ararat began in Lodz in 1927. These theaters brought together poets, artists, and writers, as well as popular comedians and actors.

2   Auerbach is repeating a popular myth that is actually false. The Polish air force was not destroyed on the ground and fought back against superior German air power, destroying at least 126 enemy planes.

3   Here again Auerbach is repeating a myth. The Polish cavalry did not engage in "suicidal charges" against the Germans. It fought as dismounted infantry and often inflicted heavy losses.

4   Auerbach is mistaken about Warsaw being an undefended "open city"; it was defended by the Polish military. In contrast, Paris was declared an "open city" by the retreating French army in 1940.

5   On September 15, 2014, the Instytut Pamięci Narodowej (Institute of National Remembrance) issued the results of its investigation into when Starzyński died. It concluded that the Gestapo shot him sometime between December 21 and December 23, 1939, after he refused to collaborate.

6   A *narciarka* was a hat favored by skiers. It had a visor and cloth flaps that could cover the ears or button together under the beard, thus concealing at least a part of the nose. This hat became very popular with Jews in the early days of the occupation, and "narciarz" became a derisive nickname for a Jew.

Chapter 5: Sunday "Five O'Clocks" at Mrs. Cecilia Slepak's

1   The Żydowskie Towarzystwo Opieki Społecznej (Jewish Social Welfare Association), or ZTOS, was more widely known by its Yiddish name, the Aleynhilf. What distinguished the Aleynhilf from similar organizations in other ghettos was its degree of autonomy and the far-ranging scope of its activities, which included soup kitchens, schools, refugee shelters, day-care centers, and a social base of 1,200 house committees. Because of its close affiliation with the U.S.-based Joint Distribution Committee, the Aleynhilf benefited from American neutrality until December 1941. Its leaders included Yitshak Giterman and Emanuel Ringelblum, whose secret archive was "folded into the Aleynhilf." The Aleynhilf provided perfect camouflage for the operations of the archive.

2   The Centralne Towarzystwo Opieki nad Sierotami (Central Society for the Care of Orphans), or CENTOS, was the leading organization dealing with childcare in interwar Poland. Originally organized to look after orphans and heavily supported by the Joint Distribution Committee, it developed a far-flung network of clinics and camps.

3   The Germans invaded Norway in April 1940.

4   Slepak's essay on Jewish women under Nazi occupation was found in the first cache of the Ringelblum archive, which was buried in August 1942 and uncovered in September 1946.

Chapter 6: The Kitchen at Leszno 40

1   The victory parade actually took place on October 5, 1939.

2   While the Aleynhilf fought to maintain its independence from the Judenrat, seeing itself as the true representative of the Jewish public in the Warsaw Ghetto, by the spring of 1942 shortages of products and the cutoff of U.S. aid whittled away its independence.

3   Ashkenazi Jews do not eat legumes on Passover. Sephardi Jews do.

4   Agudas Yisroel was the political party of Orthodox Jews in prewar Poland, where it ran an extensive network of schools and newspapers.

Chapter 7: Hunger

1   Auerbach is referring to the 1918–20 war between the Poles and Ukrainians over control of eastern Galicia, a conflict that was won by the Poles.

2   This analysis of the psychological condition of those swollen with hunger is based on the author's own observations. Medical circles in the Warsaw Ghetto devoted a lot of attention to the phenomenon of hunger and its effects on the human body. Doctors in the Jewish hospital on Czysta Street organized a medical group whose members studied the physiological impact of extreme hunger. Their notes were stored on the Aryan side of the city and were published after the war with the help of the Joint Distribution Committee. Symptoms of the effects of extreme hunger were also observed in the German concentration camps, where the starved, exhausted, and totally apathetic prisoners were called "Muselmans." This name probably stemmed from the fact that the symptoms first appeared en masse among Soviet prisoners of war, many of whom were Muslims. In the Lodz Ghetto people who had reached this state were called *klepsydras*, after the Polish word for a funeral announcement. The symptoms of apathy and passive hysteria so pervasive among those suffering the effects of advanced hunger disprove the assertions of certain ignorant writers that "Jews who were swollen from hunger" started the ghetto revolt. [Auerbach's note.]

3   As of July 1942.

4   In the reportage that I would send each week to the archive I often wrote enthusiastically about the smuggling, which provided the ghetto with an essential food supply. This was an extraordinary achievement, precise and expertly managed. It was especially true of what was called "big smuggling"—bringing dozens of trucks into the ghetto filled with flour, grain, potatoes, meat, and even live horses for slaughter. There were often great losses and many Jewish victims, but the smuggling did not stop. That was our chief weapon, without which we could not have survived. Even the collaborationist chief of the Jewish police understood how important this was for the Jews and offered some of his most skilled policemen, called *graykes*, or "players." They knew how to

bribe, or "stuff," the German police at the ghetto gates. This profession developed its own terminology. A couple of weeks before the start of the Great Deportation ten "players" and a hundred smaller smugglers were shot on the same day. In order not to repeat myself I refer the reader to my reportage in the first part of *Behutsot Varsha*, published in Tel Aviv by Am Oved in 1954. An essay by a former policeman, M. Passenstein, was found in the Ringelblum archive and appeared in the *Biuletyn Żydowskiego Instytutu Historycznego*. See M. Passentein, "Szmugiel w getcie warszawskim," BZIH, No. 26, 1958. [Auerbach's note.]

Chapter 8: Adolf As In Hitler. Bund As In *Felkerbund*

1   League of Nations.

2   Gentleman.

Chapter 10: People and Pots

1   "Two Years in the Ghetto" was a major project of the Oyneg Shabes archive to study Jewish society in Poland under Nazi occupation. The archive identified eighty different topics, all headed by a team leader, and hoped to collect the material in a book of 1,600 pages. Because of the liquidation of the Warsaw Ghetto in 1943 this ambitious project was never completed.

2   Praga was a predominantly working-class suburb of Warsaw on the east bank of the Vistula.

3   After the ghetto was established many Jewish lawyers or engineers became janitors and were quite happy with this job, which gave them a place to live as well as various "payments in kind." Nokhem Neufeld, among his other functions, relayed and commented on the news that he heard from a secret radio, which he hid in a different place each evening. To this day I can't remember all the names and locations on the maps that traced the movement of the frontlines over the weeks and months of the early war years. He knew them like the back of his hand. His father was an important rabbi in the refugee community in Warsaw. [Auerbach's note.]

4   Literally, the person who says the prayer over the wine on the Sabbath and holidays.

5   In other words, she would subtract the weight of the containers from the weight of the food twice.

6   Presumably in exchange for the potatoes.

Chapter 11: Instructors

1   The Umschlagplatz was the loading point from which Jews were sent from the ghetto to Treblinka.

2   Emanuel Ringelblum, *Shriftn fun geto vol. 2* (Warsaw: Yidish Bukh, 1963). [Auerbach's note.]

Chapter 12: The Kitchen Staff

1   Besides the Beldigers, Józef Kalasiński, a Polish refugee from Rypin, also helped other Jewish families from that town. The Rypin *landsmanshaft* in Israel invited him for a visit in 1961, and he was recognized by Yad Vashem as a Righteous Among the Nations. A tree was planted in his honor on Har Hazikaron in Jerusalem. The testimonies department of Yad Vashem recorded his account of the help he gave Jews during the war. See testimony k/15/2487. [Auerbach's note.]

2   Young squire.

3   Convalescent kitchens fed people recovering from typhus and other severe illnesses.

4   The notorious selection known as the "cauldron" took place September 6–12, 1942. All Jews remaining in the ghetto, about 100,000, had to gather and pass through an SS selection in which they either received work numbers or boarded trains to Treblinka. At the end only 32,000 Jews had the legal right to stay in the ghetto, while a similar number—the so-called "wild" Jews—remained without documents.

5   See my book *Behutsot Varsha*, chapter 5, p. 25. [Auerbach's note.]

Chapter 13: The Blue Overalls

1   The Warthegau was the section of western Poland annexed to the Third Reich in 1939.

2   The first deportations to the Nazi death camp Chelmno began from the Warthegau in December 1941. Many postcards from that area, containing coded references to the deportations, arrived in the Warsaw Ghetto and were deposited in the Oyneg Shabes archive.

3   Hebrew for "We are in great danger."

4   Chelmno was the first Nazi killing center. It killed Jews in gas vans and began operations on December 8, 1941. At least 250,000 Jews and Roma died there. In the Warthegau the Germans often forced Jews to buy their "train tickets" in advance.

5   The village of Chelmno in the district of Kolo entered the annals of the Jewish catastrophe as the first death camp on the territory of occupied Poland. The operation to murder the Jews began in a small palace in December 1941. They were killed by carbon monoxide injected into a truck compartment after they had been told that they were being driven to a disinfection facility. See Władysław Bednarz, *Obóz straceń w Chełmnie nad Nerem* (*The Extermination Camp of Chelmno on the Ner*) (Warsaw: Państwowy Instytut Wydawniczy, 1946). [Auerbach's note.]

6   Many Jews were fooled by the illusion of security granted by German documents. This meant that the best way to stay alive was to ignore those German documents and hide.

7   A left-wing Zionist youth group.

8   The Sonderkommandos were special units of the SS, in this case in charge of the deportation of Warsaw Jewry in 1942.

9   A *sheytl* is a wig worn by Orthodox married women. *Yidene* is Yiddish for an old Jewish lady.

10 On January 18, 1943, the Germans entered the ghetto with plans to deport eight thousand Jews. They were met with armed resistance and left the ghetto four days later, having managed to deport only around five thousand. This second *aktion* saw the first armed resistance against the Germans and encouraged the

remaining Jews to build hundreds of underground bunkers and hideouts, which would play a key role during the April uprising.

11 *Himmelstrasse*, or "Road to Heaven," was what the Germans jestingly called the narrow path along which Jews had to run to the gas chambers in Treblinka.

Chapter 14: They'll Take You Too

1 As a result of the Great Deportation, 300,000 Jews, about 80 percent of the ghetto population, were deported and murdered in the gas chambers of Treblinka. In the so-called "cauldron," the general selection that took place in the square bounded by Gęsia, Smocza, Niska, and Zamenhof streets during the week of September 6–12, a certain number of workers in various enterprises received "life numbers." I learned that the kitchen at Leszno 40, which at the time was serving thousands of soups each day for the Toebbens shop, received forty numbers. But none of the eighteen workers who started the kitchen and who worked in it until that last moment got one. Five or six numbers were given to a well-connected family from Posen and the rest went to the relatives of the director and his lover. Of all the previous employees only two young girls—Stella and Dora—returned from the selection. That was thanks to the whim of a German guard, who let them out of the fenced-off enclosure because he admired their pretty, radiant faces. [Auerbach's note.]

2 This is a mordant and sarcastic commentary on the initials of Walther C. Toebbens, worn by Toebbens workers, which supposedly protected them from deportation.

3 See Chapter 29 and Chapter 30. [Auerbach's note.]

4 The *Żydowska Organizacja Bojowa* (Jewish Fighting Organization), or ZOB, was organized in August 1942 by Hashomer Hatzair and Dror and later expanded to include the Bund, the Communists, the Labor Zionists, and other groups. It was one of two major fighting groups in the ghetto, the other being the Revisionist *Związek Żydowski Wojskowy* (Jewish Fighting Union). The ZOB was the larger group. In addition to preparing for a military uprising, the ZOB executed Jewish collaborators

and extorted large sums of cash from wealthy Jews in order to buy weapons.

Chapter 15: The Death of a Righteous Man

1   *Zamler* is a Yiddish word meaning a collector or someone who gathers documents or snippets of folklore. Before World War II it was widely used by the YIVO to refer to the hundreds of Jews who gathered documents, wrote down stories and proverbs, collected folklore and tombstone etchings, and took photographs of Jewish architectural landmarks such as old synagogues. In short, it underscored the fact that these archives were a national mission and reflected a grassroots effort.

2   As far as I know the material that Lehman gathered on the topic of Polish-Jewish relations included expressions and sayings, words expressing mutual hostility and contempt, but also expressions and folklore reflecting neighborly familiarity. Dr. Emanuel Ringelblum researched the same topic, which is hardly surprising given the friendship between him and Lehman. On the Aryan side he wrote a major work on this topic that survived in the Berman archive. It appeared, translated by Ber Mark, in the second volume of Ringelblum's *Ksovim fun geto*. This year Yad Vashem published the work in an English translation, edited by Joseph Kermish and Shmuel Krakowski. Ringelblum's book deals with, along with other matters, the economic cooperation between Jews and Poles during the occupation as seen in smuggling and illegal trade, as well as the issue of hiding Jews on the Aryan side. [Auerbach's note.] [Ed. note: The book was published in English as *Polish-Jewish Relations in the Second World War* (Evanston: Northwestern UP, 1992).]

3   Unfortunately this hope turned out to be false. [Auerbach's note.]

4   The *Nayer morgn* (*New Morning*) was a Yiddish daily newspaper.

5   Since ordinary yeast is forbidden on Passover Auerbach probably uses this expression to convey the subversive and ironic nature of this rich lode of folklore that she was helping Lehman retrieve.

6   Victor Henkin was an artist who was part of the Russian variety

ensemble The Blue Bird that toured Europe in the 1920s. His solo routine included Jewish songs like *"Di alte kashe."* [Auerbach's note.]

7   *Literarishe bleter (Literary Pages)*, edited by Nakhmen Mayzel, was published in Warsaw between 1925 and 1939. It was a high-quality weekly devoted to Yiddish culture and the arts.

8   I remember how Adler used to behave at such events. He would get angry at me when I would remove bottles of liquor from the table. His main contribution to these little happy occasions would be a Hebrew "lecture," where he would imitate the tone and rhythm of a Hebrew orator and convince the audience that he was speaking Hebrew when in fact he did not use one real Hebrew word. [Auerbach's note.]

9   A teacher in a *heder*, or religious elementary school.

10   Umiastowski's radio address had called on all men of military age to leave Warsaw and go east to help man a new Polish defense line. See chapter 4.

11   One of those who returned was the intelligent, communist-leaning writer Menachem Mendel Gelenberg. After the war I read the account of his sufferings along the Soviet-German demarcation line, which was deposited in the Ringelblum archive. I know nothing about his fate. [Auerbach's note.]

12   Auerbach is not correct here. The assassination attempt that took place on November 8, 1939, was quite real. Georg Elser planted a bomb in the Munich beer hall, timed to go off while Hitler was making his annual speech to the party faithful. Hitler left early, and the bomb went off thirteen minutes later, killing eight people. Elser died in a concentration camp in 1945.

13   After I was expelled from Warsaw in 1944 and arrived in Konsk, I observed similar hostility on the part of the local Polish population toward the Warsaw refugees. Despite the efforts of a young priest and the relief activities of the RGO [a Polish relief organization sanctioned by the Germans] the local Poles related to the heroic survivors and victims of the Warsaw uprising with indifference, if not outright hostility. At a certain moment a rumor began that a Warsaw refugee had killed a local woman, the mother of seven

children. The story was totally groundless. [Auerbach's note.]

14 For more on IKOR see chapter 28.

15 Auerbach is referring to the bowdlerized 1963 edition published by the Jewish Historical Institute in Warsaw.

16 In the first four-volume edition of the *Leksikon* of Yiddish literature, press, and philology.

17 In 1960, knowing that Lehman's archive was lost, I spent weeks with the late Uriel Weinreich and informed him about the ethnography and folklore of Jewish Podolia. He was then a visiting professor at the Hebrew University and was recording interviews about Yiddish dialects. He also wrote down my extensive memories and explanations of the customs and sayings of the Jews of Podolia, including specific dishes and baked goods. He told me then that he had conducted extensive interviews with Daniel Leibel, the poet and philologist, who gave him considerable information about Jewish ethnography and folklore in West Galicia. I hope that the tapes he made of our conversations survived. [Auerbach's note.]

Chapter 16: A Remembrance for Menakhem Kipnis

1 The Hazamir chorus was organized in Warsaw by I. L. Peretz in the early 1900s. Under conductors such as Matisyahu Bensman and Leo Low, Hazamir became a major locus for Yiddish secular culture in Warsaw, gaining fame for its choral performances of Yiddish songs.

2 Daniel Guzik and Yitshak Giterman, the major leaders of the JDC in German-occupied Warsaw, asked wealthy Jews for cash loans that would be repaid after the war. This was illegal, especially after the German declaration of war against the United States in December 1941. When money transfers from the United States ceased, this became a critical source of JDC social welfare funding in the ghetto.

3 Auerbach is specifically referring to Ber Mark, the Communist director of the Jewish Historical Institute in Warsaw. The book *The Lost Jewish Writers in the Ghettos and Camps and Their Works* was

published by the official publishing house Yidish Bukh in Warsaw in 1954. Mark edited the book and wrote the introduction, in which he blamed the indifference and malice of the Jewish bourgeoisie and its institutions for the deaths of those Jewish writers.

4   My thoughts and reflections on Abraham Gancwajch are contained in an essay "The Jewish National-Socialist," which will appear in a forthcoming volume of my writings. [Auerbach's note.]

5   A prayer for the dead recited at funerals and other memorial occasions.

6   In Warsaw there were many other widows who, because of a misplaced sense of protectiveness of their late husbands' writings, stymied the efforts of Dr. Emanuel Ringelblum to rescue these cultural treasures, the fruit of many years of intense effort. As I have already written, what happened with Kipnis's musical works also explained the loss of Shmuel Lehman's archive, the sum total of thirty years of activity, which had already been partially cataloged and classified. [Auerbach's note.]

Father and Daughter

1   *Bible Poems* (1935).

2   Morris Bassin (1889–1963) published the two-volume *Antologiye finf hundert yor yidishe poeziye* (*Five Hundred Years of Yiddish Poetry*) in New York in 1917, with an introduction by the Labor Zionist theorist and Yiddish philologist Ber Borochov.

Chapter 17: The Mission and Fate of Emanuel Ringelblum

1   Nowy Sącz in Polish.

2   During the siege of Warsaw in September 1939 the Polish authorities recognized a Jewish section of the citywide relief committee and gave it a share of the overall relief budget.

3   There were more than 1,200 "house committees" organized in the Warsaw Ghetto, grouped together in an Aleynhilf "parliament" headed by Ringelblum.

4   "Joy of the Sabbath" in Yiddish. *Oneg Shabbat* in Hebrew.

5   In 1964 the well-known West German literary critic Marcel Ranicki visited Israel. I used this opportunity to interview him about his activities as a secretary who helped handle Judenrat chairman Adam Czerniaków's correspondence with the German authorities. He told us about Ringelblum's attempts to get copies of this correspondence, not only of replies sent by Czerniaków to the Germans but also of the letters, directives, and orders sent by Dr. Heinz Auerswald, the commissioner of the Jewish Residential District, as well as from Gestapo agents who handled Jewish affairs. Ranicki convinced Czerniaków that it was important to make copies of all incoming and outgoing correspondence, which he then handed over to Ringelblum. Ringelblum would come in person to get them. The Polish Jewish writer Gustawa Jarecka, who made the copies, was also in on the secret. [Auerbach's note.]

6   The General Government, or Generalgouvernement, was the official German name for that part of occupied Poland in 1939 that had not been annexed to the Reich and had not been taken over by the Soviets. Located in the central part of prewar Poland, it included Warsaw, Krakow, Lublin, and, after June 1941, Lwow. It was ruled by Hans Frank, who set himself up in royal style in the Wawel Castle in Krakow.

7   Dr. Joseph Kermish published an article describing this questionnaire in the *Goldene keyt*. It was entitled "The Testament of the Warsaw Ghetto." The article also appeared in Hebrew in a brochure entitled "Conference dedicated to the memory of Dr. Emanuel Ringelblum." Jerusalem, 12 Nissan, 5724 [March 25, 1964]. [Auerbach's note.]

8   For more on Perle see chapter 35.

9   Rina Opper-Opoczynski, *Gezamelte shriftn mit a biografiye* (New York: 1951). See also Peretz Opoczynski, *Reshimot* (Tel Aviv: Beit Lokhamei Ha'getaot Kibbutz Ha-Meukhad, 1970). [Auerbach's note.]

10   A selection of Opoczynski's reportage from the Warsaw Ghetto has recently been published in Samuel Kassow, ed., David Suchoff, trans., *In Those Nightmarish Days: The Ghetto Reportage of Peretz Opoczynski and Joseph Zelkowicz* (New Haven: Yale

University Press, 2015).

11 Harav Shimon Huberband, *Kiddush Hashem: K'tavim Meyimei Ha'shoah* (Tel Aviv: Ho'tsaat Yizkor, 5228/1969). [Auerbach's note.]

12 On the evening of April 17–18 groups of uniformed SS with lists in hand went through the ghetto and systematically murdered fifty-two people. They shot their victims in front of their buildings and left their corpses on the street. This was a harbinger of intensified terror. The Jews called this incident "Bartholomew's Night" or "The Night of Blood."

13 Emanuel Ringelblum, *Shriftn fun geto* vols. 1–2 (Warsaw: Yidish Bukh, 1961–1963). [Auerbach's note.]

14 The Ringelblum year took place in 1964. The participants of the symposium included professor Ben-Zion Dinur, professor Rafael Mahler, magister Hersh Wasser, Dr. Joseph Kermish, Dr. Shaul Esh, and Dr. Aryeh L. Kubovy. During that year various memorial meetings took place in Israel and in other countries. Various cities in Israel named streets after Ringelblum. [Auerbach's note.]

Chapter 18: Personal Encounters

1 For some reason Auerbach is omitting Wasser's wife Bluma, the third member of the secret archive to survive.

2 I am attaching here an incomplete list of my works about Treblinka.

A. Abraham Krzepicki. "18 teg in Treblinke (8/25–9/13)" ("18 Days in Treblinka"), *Bleter far geshikhte*, nos. 1–2 (Warsaw: 1956)

B. Historical Reportage: "Oyf di felder fun Treblinke" ("On the Fields of Treblinka") (Lodz: Jewish Historical Commission, 1947)

C. A radio play entitled *Di letste yidn* (*The Last Jews*), broadcast in Yiddish and Hebrew on Kol Yisrael

D. Manuscript of a screenplay titled *Di meride* (*The Revolt*)

E. Article "Treblinka," *Encyclopedia Judaica*, pp. 1365–1372 (Jerusalem: 1972) [Auerbach's note.]

3   This book itself is a response, you might say, to Ringelblum's proposal during our first conversation about the archive. [Auerbach's note.]

4   I never heard that any of Kave's works were found in the recovered sections of the Oyneg Shabes. Perle wrote a report about the Soviet occupation of Lemberg. He also wrote a description of the Great Deportation, "Khurbn varshe" ("The Destruction of Warsaw"), after the first phase of the *aktion* ended in September 1942. Perle also wrote a satire of the shops, "4580." See chapter 35 of this book, "Scattered Pearls." [Auerbach's note.]

5   "Sanctification of the name," or the willingness to suffer martyrdom. This term was used to describe Jews during the time of the Crusades who suffered death rather than convert to Christianity.

6   This was the section of the ghetto south of the bridge that spanned Chlodna Street.

7   This is a reference to Franz Werfel's 1933 novel *The Forty Days of Musa Dagh,* about Armenian resistance to the Turks during the Armenian genocide. The novel was widely read in the Warsaw Ghetto.

8   Auerbach's explanation of why she chose to write in Polish is, on the face of it, unconvincing. There are probably deeper reasons why such a dedicated Yiddishist like Auerbach would compose most of her ghetto writings in Polish. Karolina Szymaniak believes that writing in Polish afforded her the possibility of greater emotional distance and that the Polish language, simultaneously close and distant, was a better medium to describe the strange interplay of familiarity and strangeness in the ghetto experience. See Karolina Szymaniak and Anna Cialowicz, *Pisma z Getta Warszawskiego* (Warsaw: 2016), 63–65. One could also surmise that Auerbach's formal education was in Polish, not Yiddish, and that in many cases it was easier for her to express herself in Polish, especially after a grueling day in the ghetto.

9   The Yung-teater, led by Michał Weichert, was a leading Yiddish avant-garde theater in Warsaw between 1932 and 1939. Supported by the Bundist Kultur-lige (Culture League), it staged many plays that carried a political message. Though constantly hounded by the Polish authorities, the Yung-teater and its actors, most-

ly workers who rehearsed in the evenings, toured all over Poland. In 1939 it won special recognition for its performance of Shakespeare's *The Tempest*.

10   The archive contains a copy of Auerbach's prewar review article on *Wozzeck*, but Bruno Frank's drama seems to be missing.

11   This bulletin was called *Wiadomości* (*Messages*). Four issues appeared. The bulletin publicized German atrocities and pleaded with Jews not to be taken in by false promises.

Chapter 19: Testaments

1   See note 2 to chapter 5.

2   Auerbach is not correct when she says that Hariton was the first person in the United States to recognize Singer's talent. Many others did as well, including the literary critic Shmuel Niger and Abraham Cahan, editor of the *Jewish Daily Forward*, who published many of his writings.

3   The Stalingrad pocket originally contained about 300,000 German and Romanian troops.

4   At this point Toebbens and other German shop owners were trying to persuade the Jews to move to labor camps in the Lublin area. There they would be under direct SS control. Heinrich Himmler was especially insistent on moving the shops out of the Warsaw Ghetto.

5   The Sunday before the ghetto uprising was April 18. Ringelblum mistakenly gave the date as April 17. He was writing on the Aryan side and did not have easy access to a calendar. [Auerbach's note.]

Chapter 20: One Last Conversation

1   Trawniki was a labor camp in the Lublin region.

2   This is the only time that Auerbach mentions she was in this camp. Perhaps this is a misprint since elsewhere she gives a detailed timeline of her whereabouts after she left the ghetto and does not refer to Pelcowizna.

3   The Council to Aid Jews with the Government Delegation for Poland, or Żegota, was first organized in September 1942 by members of the Polish Catholic resistance, including the writer Zofia Kossak-Szczucka. It eventually became a formal part of the Polish Underground State and included Polish representatives from the Socialist Party (PPS-WRN) and the People's Party (SL), as well as Jewish representatives. It helped a few thousand Jews, especially in big cities like Warsaw and Krakow, by distributing forged documents and money sent to Poland by foreign Jewish organizations.

4   The organization Auerbach is referring to is the clandestine Jewish National Committee, among whose leaders was Ringelblum's close friend Adolf Berman.

5   "Kein Hitler ohne Mussolini." I think that the author of the article was the Austrian socialist Julius Adler. [Auerbach's note.]

Chapter 21: The Martyr's Crown

1   Judyta was her name in Polish, with Juzia the shortened and familiar version. Yehudis is the Yiddish name. Auerbach uses these names interchangeably.

2   The person who moved into the place in Izabelin was the Right Labor Zionist activist and high school teacher Jozef Sak, together with his family. [Auerbach's note.]

3   Y. Hirszhaut, *Finstere nekht in Paviak: zikhroynes, geshtaltn, bilder* (Buenos Aires: Central Union of Polish Jews in Argentina, 1948). [Auerbach's note.]

Chapter 22: Old Man Zaks

1   Saxon Square was the historical name for the large space in front of the Bruhl Palace, the home of Minister Henryk Brühl, who administered the country under King Augustus II during the Saxon dynasty. Between the two world wars it was called Pilsudski Square. During the occupation it became Adolf Hitler Square. [Auerbach's note.]

Chapter 23: Hershele

1 "Holiday Pages."

2 As opposed to the more formal *ir*.

3 Dry products were not cooked. They were not soup. The packages of dry products that the Aleynhilf handed out included flour or bread, sugar, fats, or any kind of products that might have been in the storehouse. [Auerbach's note.]

4 For more on Yisroel Shtern see chapter 34. [Auerbach's note.]

Chapter 25: Our Gandhi

1 "Be well."

Chapter 26: The Holy, the Worldly, and the Polished Boots

1 *Together with the People*, an early version of this book.

Chapter 27: The Self-Taught Scholar

1 See Chapter 12. [Auerbach's note.]

2 See Chapter 34. [Auerbach's note.]

Chapter 28: The Organizer

1 Kabtsansk ("Beggarville") and Glupsk ("Stupid Town") were caustic sobriquets used by the Yiddish writer Sholem Yankev Abramovitsh (1836–1917) to criticize the backwardness and obscurantism of traditional Jewish society in the Pale of Settlement. Abramovitsh is widely known by his pen name, Mendele Moykher-Sforim (Mendele the Book Seller). He wrote in both Yiddish and Hebrew.

2 Ringelblum's essay on Linder can be found in Emanuel Ringelblum, *Kosvim fun geto* vol. 2, 164–168. This is the edition edited by Joseph Kermish and published by the I. L. Peretz Farlag in Tel

Aviv in 1985. Auerbach is referring to an earlier and somewhat bowdlerized edition of Ringelblum's ghetto writings published by the Jewish Historical Institute in Warsaw in 1963.

3   Auerbach uses Lemberg University. Between the wars it was called the Jan Kazimierz University in Lwow.

4   *Jewish Economics.*

5   I got my information about Linder from Ringelblum's biographical essay published in the second volume of *Shriftn fun geto.* In Israel, besides Linder's sister-in-law Zehava Linder, I also spoke with several of his personal friends from Sniatyn. One of them was Yonah Metzger, the sister-in-law of the writer Itche Metzger, who was the author of "On My Grandfather's Fields" about Lanowitz, the village in which we both grew up. Yonah gave me many names of long-settled Galitsianers in Israel, where Linder too would have made his home if he only had the chance. Unfortunately, I did not have the opportunity to gather more biographical information about this young, first-rate scholar and communal activist whose life was brutally cut short. So I would like to express my hope that somebody will write about him. There are students and master's candidates who study the Holocaust, and Menakhem Linder would make an excellent thesis topic. [Auerbach's note.]

6   My connection with the Warsaw branch of the YIVO happened because I had been a board member of the Friends of the YIVO in Lemberg, which was headed by Dr. Leib Landau. [Auerbach's note.]

7   See note 5 to chapter 18.

8   On that infamous night of April 17–18, 1942, murder squads drove around the ghetto, one of which came to look for Linder in our kitchen. I described this search in Chapter 18. [Auerbach's note.]

The Mousetrap at Mylna 9

1   "*Afera, kombinacja, lipa*" in Polish.

2   Instead of "*Deutschland siegt an allen fronten,*" they would change the *s* to an *l*: "*Deutschland liegt an allen fronten.*"

3   The policeman "P." is most likely Marek Passenstein (1900–

1944). Passenstein, who earned a law degree from Warsaw University before the war, served in the Jewish police in the ghetto but also earned the trust of Emanuel Ringelblum, with whom he shared a hiding place on the Aryan side. Ringelblum encouraged him to write an essay on smuggling in the ghetto, which survived. His nephew was the Polish political writer Daniel Passent, who survived the war as a hidden child.

4   Rubinstein was a famous jester and street performer in the tradition of the Jewish *badkhn* who roamed the streets of the Warsaw Ghetto entertaining crowds with his extravagant gestures, humorous ditties, satiric verses, and mordant prophecies. One of his best-known lines was *"ale glaykh, urem un raykh"*—"everyone is equal, rich and poor"—implying perhaps that everyone would meet the same fate. No one actually knew his first name. The late professor Israel Gutman, who survived the Warsaw Ghetto, recalled that only his last name, Rubinstein, was known. Gutman wrote, "He moved quickly, catlike, in the crowd, choosing his victims from within it . . . He latched on to only the few people who were well-dressed, clerks of the Judenrat and the leaders of the ghetto . . . Rubinstein's exploits became well-known in the ghetto." See Ofer Aderet, "Cabaret of Death," *Haaretz*, March 9, 2015.

5   Richard Strauss's 1894–95 tone poem "Till Eulenspiegels Lustige Streiche" ("Till Eulenspiegel's Merry Pranks") was about a zany German peasant folk hero.

Chapter 29: The Lecturers

1   Traditional Jewish study hall.

2   Mazo's former wife and Auerbach's friend.

3   Pola Altuska was the original name of Miriam Orleska. [Auerbach's note.]

Chapter 30: The Librarians

1   This was the clandestine Jewish National Committee that worked

on the Aryan side. It was led by Adolf Berman, Yitshak Zuckerman, and others. Because the Bund would not formally join the committee, its delegate, Mikolaj Feiner, worked with the others under the formal template of a "Coordinating Committee."

2   The TSEKABE was an organization affiliated with the Joint Distribution Committee. As a response to Polish economic antisemitism it sponsored various initiatives of economic self-defense in the 1930s, such as free loan societies. Emanuel Ringelblum edited its monthly journal, *Folkshilf.*

3   This was a library associated with the Bundist Kultur-lige (Culture League) and was one of the largest Jewish libraries in Warsaw. Its librarian was Herman Kruk, who later headed the library in the Vilna Ghetto and was murdered in Klooga, Estonia, in September 1944.

4   This song, written by the American Yiddish poet H. Rozenblat, became very popular in the Warsaw Ghetto thanks to a certain woman singer who would sing it at all of her concerts. [Auerbach's note.]

5   The *parówki* were disinfection centers where people had to wait naked for hours to take a shower and hand over their clothes to be deloused. More often than not they either lost their clothing or found them ruined. The Polish and Jewish officials who supervised the *parówki* collected fat bribes in exchange for exemptions from a procedure that was humiliating and, more often than not, ineffective.

6   Brest-Litovsk.

7   This was the 12-year-old son of the Revisionist leader, A. Lipman, who at that time was lying sick in the hospital of the ghetto jail. His mother, who could no longer do anything to help her husband, let herself be deceived by the announcement that those who reported voluntarily for "resettlement" would not be separated from their families and would receive the "privilege" of an allotment of three kilograms of bread and a big jar of honey or marmalade. She believed that in this way she would be able to reach her family in Brisk. No longer having anything to live on, she hoped that she might at least be able to save her child. [Auerbach's note.]

Pani Basia

1   *Szmalcownik* was the term for the Polish blackmailers of Jews trying to survive on the Aryan side.

2   Auerbach is doubtless referring here to such figures as Zofia Kossak-Szczucka, a leading Catholic writer who called for the exclusion of Jews from Polish life. During the war she expressed hope that Jewish survivors would leave Poland. But as long as Jews were in mortal danger she believed that Catholics had a religious obligation to help them.

3   While Polish delegates to Żegota came from the Front for the Rebirth of Poland (a Catholic organization), the socialist PPS, the Democratic Party, and the Peasant Party there were few Communists who played any leading role. The main nationalist party, the Stronnictwo Narodowe (National Party), was conspicuous by its absence in Żegota.

4   This diary was published in English as *City Within a City* (New York: IP Books, 2013).

5   Auerbach is referring to one of the many Jewish informers that the Gestapo used to ferret out Jews trying to survive on the Aryan side. These agents were promised their lives in exchange for their collaboration.

Chapter 31: The Supplier

1   Like Emanuel Ringelblum, Auerbach has a harsh opinion of the Judenrat and sees the Aleynhilf as the true representative of the Jewish masses. The truth was more complicated.

2   After September 1942 what had been the Warsaw Ghetto was broken up into noncontiguous enclaves, the largest being the so-called central ghetto. The spaces between these enclaves were called "wild." Anyone found there without proper documents could be shot on sight.

3   The *Folkstsaytung* was the prewar daily organ of the Jewish Labor Bund. It was published in Warsaw.

4   The Schupo, or Schutzpolizei, were the uniformed German police.

5   On Yom Kippur 1942, ten days after the pause in deportations began, the Germans suddenly staged an unexpected one-day roundup.

6   Carbide was used to light small lamps, as electricity was unreliable.

7   My neighbor Krzepicki, who escaped from Treblinka and whose account of his eighteen days in that death camp I wrote down, had been a German prisoner of war during the battles of September 1939. After a few weeks he was able to escape to occupied Warsaw. According to the personal details that I learned from him, his first name was Abraham. That's what I wrote on the testimony and on the photograph that he gave me, on which he wrote greetings to his family in Mauritius. His family had been part of a group of Jews who planned to immigrate illegally to the Land of Israel in 1940 on a wretched ship down the Danube, then across the Black Sea to the port of Haifa. But they were deported by the British Mandatory authorities to Mauritius.

After the war, whenever I wrote about Treblinka, I would mention that first witness I had interviewed, Krzepicki. It surprised me that no member of his family ever contacted me to learn details about his fate. In 1956 Krzepicki's testimony was published in the Warsaw *Bleter far geshikhte* (*History Pages*). In Israel I published long excerpts from the testimony in *Al Ha-Mishmar*. And still no one contacted the editors, either in Warsaw or in Israel.

This puzzle was solved only in 1967 with the arrest of the former commandant of Treblinka, Franz Stangl. After this sensational arrest Noah Kliger, a correspondent for *Yediot Ahronot*, visited the Tel Aviv branch of Yad Vashem to gather material. I gave him a few excerpts from Krzepicki's testimony, and after they were published in that newspaper Krzepicki's brother and sister contacted me. It turned out that his real name was Yakov and Abraham was the name of their father, who had died long before. After he escaped from the German POW camp he used his father's papers that had been sent to Warsaw, and from that time on began to use the name Abraham whenever he would register. After I learned this, I began to use both names whenever I wrote about him, *Yakov* because it was his true name and *Abraham* because that's how he was called in the literature about the Holocaust, both as an early and precise witness and as a fighter who perished in the Warsaw Ghetto Uprising. So I feel obligated to preserve his identity and memory.

Krzepicki's brother Menahem and I wrote a page of testimony about Abraham-Yakov as well as about the experiences of his family and the other families who had been exiled by the British to Mauritius. He also gave me some photographs, including a copy of the same picture which I had attached to the original testimony. The testimony along with the photograph is located in the Jewish Historical Institute in Warsaw. See "Witness Declaration of Menahem Krzepicki" in the Tel Aviv Branch of Yad Vashem, k. 2759/130.

In a future essay, "An Attic in Praga," I will describe Krzepicki's participation in the Warsaw Ghetto Uprising, where he fought on the terrain of the brushmakers shop in the Hanoar Hatzioni unit commanded by Yakov Praszkier. [Auerbach's note.] See pages 303–312.

8 About a week after I arrived on the Aryan side I called Ringelblum at the telephone number of the Bernard Hallmann shop that he had given me. When he next met Berman, he arranged for me to meet him in a small place on Wileńska Street in Praga. Thanks to that contact I was able to stay on the Aryan side. [Auerbach's note.]

9 Czesław Klarner was a top Polish government official in the interwar period. He organized chambers of commerce and industry in the major regions of Poland and served as a minister of commerce and industry in several governments. [Auerbach's note.]

10 The name *Zimowski*, a Polish word similar to *Winter*, was an example of a common mistake Jews made on the Aryan side. If one sought a real Polish name that was similar to *Winter*, *Zimiński* would have been the natural choice. Unfortunately matters never got to the point where that mistake made any difference. [Auerbach's note.]

11 See Rokhl Auerbach, *Mered Geto Varsha*, chapter 20, 105 (Meno-

rah Press, 1963). [Auerbach's note.]

12 These half-burned, half-rotten pages of Winter's diary were partially deciphered and published along with a commentary by Ber Mark in the third volume of *Bleter far geshikhte*, Nos. 1–2, 29–48 (Warsaw: 1950). [Auerbach's note.]

13 This was also the site where Hersh Wasser said the third cache of the Ringelblum archive was buried just a week before the outbreak of the ghetto uprising. If Auerbach is correct, Polish scavengers probably found that cache and discarded it as well.

Chapter 32: The Father

1 *Tsushtayer* was a journal that appeared in Lwow between 1929 and 1931, devoted to the promotion of Yiddish culture in Galicia, where the Jewish intelligentsia was largely Polish speaking. Auerbach was one of its editors.

2 The *Khalyastre* (The Gang) was an avant-garde movement in Yiddish literature and the arts in Poland between 1919 and 1924.

3 This was a suburban train line linking many summer resorts and dachas, ringed by pine forests, that were popular with Warsaw Jews.

4 See note 7 to chapter 18.

5 The Rollkommando were the SS killers of Operation Reinhardt, the 1942 project to murder the Jews of the General Government.

6 Jews employed outside the ghetto.

7 This referred to the German railway network in occupied Poland.

9 See Chapter 31. [Auerbach's note.]

10 That note to Giterman was published in Ber Mark's *Di umgekumene shrayber fun di getos un lagern un zeyere verk* (Warsaw: Yiddish Bukh, 1954). [Auerbach's note.]

11 "The creator of the lights of the flames," a prayer said during the Havdalah ceremony at the end of the Sabbath.

12 In 1972 the poet Abraham Zak and his wife Fanya Rems visited Israel. Fanya had lived in Warsaw before the war, and she lived

through the ghetto and the deportations. I learned that she and her first husband had owned the Rigavar rubber and galoshes factory where Kirman worked before the war. They were in touch with him during the occupation, and Fanya told me certain details. She corroborated my hunch that Kirman continued to write between the end of the Great Deportation in September 1942 and the second *aktion* in January 1943, and told me that Kirman would read his poetry to his friends. It's possible that he was referring to them when he told me that he had left the ghetto poems written before the Great Deportation somewhere on Dzielna. Kirman's younger sister-in-law had lived with them before the war. But Miss Fanya did not remember where Kirman's wife and children had gone after the ghetto was closed. [Auerbach's note.]

13 See note 1 to chapter 30.

14 Operation Harvest Festival was probably the single largest mass shooting of World War II.

15 See David Silberklang, *Gates of Tears: The Holocaust in the Lublin District* (Jerusalem: Yad Vashem, 2013), and Yitzhak Arad, *The Operation Reinhard Death Camps, expanded and revised edition* (Bloomington: Indiana University Press, 2013).

16 See N. Blumenthal, ed., *Obozy, Dokumenty I Materiały* (Lodz: Żydowska Komisja Historyczna, 1946). See also the testimony of Esther Winderbaum-Rubinstein, Yad Vashem archive in Tel Aviv, 118/2209. [Auerbach's note.]

17 Stanisław Piotrowski, "Misja Odyla Globocnika" (Warsaw: Państwowy Instytut Wydawniczy, 1949). Each time the debate reemerges on Israeli radio or in the press about whether or not to allow the playing of Richard Strauss, I think about the musical accompaniment to November 3, 1943. [Auerbach's note.]

The Two Glatshteyns

1 A revelers' choir was an expanded barbershop quartet that was popular in Europe during the interwar period.

2 "Reb Abba, the Warden of our Synagogue."

Chapter 33: Wax Candles

1   "My Home."

2   In Galician Podolia, where I came from, during the Ten Days of Repentance, and perhaps beginning with the month of Elul, the mothers of the family would come together to make wicks for ritual candles. To do this my mother and aunts would leave our village of Lanowitz and go to Ozerian, the nearest shtetl, where the village Jews would bury their dead. Each mother would bring two containers of white cotton string: one for the candle of the living, which would be taken to the synagogue on the eve of Yom Kippur, and the second for the memorial candle, which would be placed inside a pot of sand and would burn in the house the entire day of Yom Kippur.

I saw this ceremony once when I was a child. A speaker sat in the middle and the women repeated the words after her, fervently crying and praying for their families. As they took the wicks meant for the living they would say the following words: "This wick for my husband, this wick for his livelihood, may he live long, may he be strong and well," etc.

As they prepared cotton for the candles for the dead, they did not use the word *kneytl* (wick) but *fodem* (thread). For example: "My father's thread, the thread for my father's earthly work, may he have a beautiful rest in the Garden of Eden, may he be an intercessor for us," etc.

As they pronounced each phrase they would measure and wrap a bit of cotton cord. They would then take these cotton cords—properly blessed and sanctified—to old Aunt Frume, who would plait them into two long fragrant candles made of yellow beeswax. The candles for the dead were smaller and were called memorial candles.

I remember that in our village, when people would say, "They're already carrying the yellow candles," it meant that it was late, it was Yom Kippur eve, and one had to hurry to the synagogue. This is the source of the folk saying "add a wick" (*tsuleygen a kneytl*), which refers to someone praising or criticizing an interlocutor while seemingly talking about an absent person. [Auerbach's note.]

3   Young Jewish men and women in prewar Poland went to special farms and quarries where they lived in collective poverty, performed hard labor, and toughened themselves for a pioneering life in Palestine. This was called *hakhshara*, or "preparation."

Chapter 34: A Tree in the Ghetto

1   The *Shulhan Arukh* is a widely used compilation of Jewish law authored by Joseph Karo in Safed in the mid-sixteenth century.

2   This was a Hasidic sect that followed the teachings of Nahman of Bratslav (1772–1811). Because they did not follow a living rebbe they were called the "dead Hasidim."

3   There was a strange epilogue to my conversation with Shtern. After the war and after Ber Mark returned from the Soviet Union, I let him look at my wartime notebooks. He read about how Shtern, when I saw him at Leszno 14, gave me a poem that he had written on the left side of a blank order form for some ghetto laundry. When Mark's book about the murdered ghetto writers was published in Poland in 1954, I saw that poem on page 57:

> The sky is so blue
> In this world
> I have no space
> A forest full of trees
> I look around
> Am I happy?
> Or unhappy.
> I must live
> I want to die a natural death.

I want to explain the backstory of this poem. During the winter of 1942–43, as I was transcribing Krzepicki's testimony, there were times when I would hear an interesting turn of phrase. So I would turn over the page and write down his exact words in the left margin. About the text that Mark cites in his book: I wrote those words down when Krzepicki was trying to describe how he felt when he had escaped from Treblinka, hiding in a boxcar bound for Germany under bundles of clothing taken from the murdered

Jews. Then he jumped from the boxcar before dawn in an uninhabited area and felt free. But at the same time, he realized that he had no idea where to go or what to do next.

The words "am I happy or unhappy" are authentic. There was another expression that stuck in my imagination, "such a beautiful, green world." But I can't be 100 percent sure. My Treblinka manuscript was found in the second cache of the Ringelbum archive, which consisted of two hermetically sealed aluminum milk cans and was accidentally discovered during the construction of the foundation of a building. When that happened I was already in Israel. Mark sent me a congratulatory letter about the new find, which included more of my writings, and he advised me which Polish authorities I should contact for permission to receive copies.

Sometime later I received a microfilm copy of the Treblinka manuscript. Unfortunately, because of the way it was copied, I did not receive what was in the left-hand margin, including Krzepicki's expressions and other notes I made.

So I am warning literary historians not to make a mistake with these lines and not to regard them as part of a Holocaust poem by Yisroel Shtern. [Auerbach's note.]

4   The Towarzystwo Ochrony Zdrowia Ludności Żydowskiej (Society for Safeguarding the Health of the Jewish Population), or TOZ, was the major organization dedicated to improving the health of the Jewish population through the sponsorship of hospitals, sanatoriums, children's colonies, and the dissemination of information on proper diet and sanitation. It continued its activities in the Warsaw Ghetto.

5   Ptakowski-Podkowiński helped many Jewish writers and artists get work documents. He survived on the Aryan side along with his wife and daughter. In the latter part of the war I would visit them as part of my activities with the aid committee. They lived in a distant part of south Warsaw. One day, before the outbreak of the Polish uprising, when no trollies were running, I walked to their place and brought them their monthly allowance for August. This helped them during the uprising and after, when they were able to reach a suburb and survive there until the liberation. After the war Ptakowski became well known for his reportage on

the Nuremberg trials, which appeared in many Polish journals under the name Marian Podkowiński. For many years he used the same name to publish articles in the Krakow weekly *Przekrój*, which was edited by another talented journalist of Jewish origin, Marian Eile. [Auerbach's note.]

6   After the war, in 1955, a selection of Yisroel Shtern's poems and essays was published by CYCO in New York. [Auerbach's note.]

7   While many of Auerbach's writings were retrieved from the secret archive, there is no indication of any works by Shtern.

Chapter 35: Scattered Pearls

1   Ukrainian nationalist mobs blamed Jews for the killings and used them as an excuse to engage in large-scale pogroms. One of the worst began in Lwow on June 30, 1941. While there were doubtless many Jews among the prisoners murdered by the Soviet secret police, Auerbach's assertion that most of the victims were Jews cannot be verified.

2   In July 1945, on the fourth anniversary of Kacyzne's death, a memorial meeting took place in the newly organized Jewish literary union in Lodz with the participation of Kacyzne's daughter Shulamis. The newspaper *Dos naye lebn* (*This New Life*) published Nachman Blitz's shocking article "Alter Kacyzne's Final Journey." [Auerbach's note.]

3   Perle's wife committed suicide. Perle found her body hanging in the closet.

4   Since Auerbach is writing this in 1944, she might not be aware that the camp was called Birkenau.

5   Further details on the deaths of Yitshak Katzenelson and Yoshue Perle, along with their sons, can be learned from the following works of Dr. Nathan Eck: "Nisyonot Hatsala Be'ezrat Darkonim V'teudot Shel Ezrakhei Aratzot America Ha-latinit," *Kovetz Mekhkarim Yad Vashem,* 1, Jerusalem, 1957. "Yehudim Tmurat Germanim," *Dapim le'Kheker ha'Shoah* (Tel Aviv: Katzenelson, Ho'tza'at Kibbutz ha-Meukhad, 1973). See also the work of Dr. Eberhard Kolb, *Bergen-Belsen* (Hanover: 1962). Among the pa-

pers that I brought from Poland I found a memoir written by Mrs. Esther Bauman about Yoshue Perle's last months in Bergen-Belsen, which appeared in *Dos naye lebn,* Lodz, Number 16 (185), 1948. [Auerbach's note.]

Ivan the Father and Ivan the Son

1   The official German identity card.

The First Jan Was Janina

1   Signing the Volksliste meant that a Polish citizen of German descent declared his status as a Volksdeutsche, or ethnic German, with all the privileges such status conferred, including being drafted for military service.

2   Żegota, founded in 1942, was the Polish Council to Aid Jews. It was affiliated with the Polish Underground State and included both Polish and Jewish representatives, although no Poles from the nationalist right wing served. For more on Żegota see note 3 to chapter 20.

An Attic in Praga

1   This was a trick by the Gestapo to trap Jews in hiding. They were told that they could buy the ownerless Latin American passports that had been sent to Jews who had since been murdered. Those who fell for the trick paid good money, were housed in good conditions in the Hotel Polski in Warsaw, and were then sent to Bergen-Belsen and Vittel. From there most of these "Latin Americans" were sent to the gas chambers of Auschwitz. See chapter 35.

2   Hersh Berlinski's memoirs of preparations for the ghetto uprising were published in Israel in *Dray: an ondenkbukh* (Tel Aviv: Ringelblum Institute, 1966).

3   Emanuel Ringelblum escaped from Trawniki in August 1943 and joined his wife and son in a hideout on Grójecka Street in Warsaw, where he resumed his writing. Wanda Elster would come once a week, take his notes, and give him fresh ink and paper. The Ringelblums, the other thirty-four Jews in the hideout, and two

Poles who helped them were all murdered in March 1944. For more on these events see chapter 21.

4   They appeared in Yiddish in the volume *Dray: an ondenkbukh* (Tel Aviv: Ringelblum Institute, 1966).

5   They were all killed in Żoliborz in September 1944, during the Polish uprising. Hersh and Bluma Wasser, who were in the same hideout, survived.

Among the "Cats" in the Zoo

1   After the fall of Mussolini in July 1943 General Pietro Badoglio (1871–1956) became the Italian prime minister. He began secret negotiations with the Allies to take Italy out of the war and signed an armistice with the United States and Britain on September 3. He did not inform the Italian armed forces, however, who were taken by surprise when the Germans quickly occupied the country and disarmed the Italian military.

2   The Kripo, or Kriminalpolizei, were the German criminal police.

3   The official collaborationist newspaper.

4   This is a pun based on Polish obscenities and an equivalent of Pig Latin. Something like, "These solemn words are like shit running through your ass."

In Frau Krauze's House

1   Celebrated on August 2.

Trouble and a Silver Lining

1   "Hangman" in German.

2   On February 1, 1944, the Polish Home Army mounted a complex operation that assassinated Franz Kutschera, who was SS police chief in Warsaw and had a well-earned reputation as a ruthless killer. In retaliation, the Germans shot three hundred Polish

civilians the next day and levied a 100-million-złoty fine on the Polish population of Warsaw.

Bigos and Home Brew in the Pheasant Cage

1   Auerbach is referring to Ber Warm, aka "Bolek." He had been in the Jewish police and probably perished during the Polish uprising in 1944.

Postscript

1   A good treatment of this controversy, including Auerbach's campaign against Jean-François Steiner and his book *Treblinka: The Revolt of an Extermination Camp*, is Samuel Moyn, *A Holocaust Controversy: The Treblinka Affair in Post-War France* (Waltham, MA: Brandeis University Press, 2005). Auerbach was outraged by what she considered Steiner's deliberate distortions of the testimony that she heard from Treblinka survivors.

BIOGRAPHICAL NOTES

Adolf Berman (1906–1978) received a doctorate in psychology from Warsaw University, and was active in the Left Labor Zionist party, where he became a good friend of Emanuel Ringelblum. In the Warsaw Ghetto he helped run the Central Society for the Care of Orphans (CENTOS) while his wife, Basia, organized a children's library. The couple left the Warsaw Ghetto in September 1942 and became key figures in the Jewish underground on the Aryan side of the city. The Bermans left Poland for Israel in 1950. Adolf Berman was the younger brother of Polish Communist Party boss Jakub Berman (1901–1984), who was ousted from power in 1956.

Eliezer Lipe Bloch (1888–1944) was a member of the executive committee of the Oyneg Shabes and a leading Zionist activist before the war.

Jan Bloch (1836–1902) was a famous entrepreneur who played an instrumental role in the construction of railroads in Poland. Though he converted to the Evangelical faith, he was a generous contributor to Jewish causes and did his best to defend Jewish interests in the Russian Empire. Yiddish writer I. L. Peretz wrote one of his earliest masterpieces, *Scenes from a Provincial Journey,* based on the statistical materials he collected for Bloch, who wanted to use them to forestall anti-Jewish legislation.

Nokhum Bomze (1906–1954), a Yiddish poet and journalist from Sasow, Galicia, survived the war in the USSR before immigrating to the United States.

Moyshe Broderzon (1890–1956) was a Yiddish poet and theater director based in Lodz, who helped found the literary group Yung-yidish. He spent the war in the USSR, was arrested by the Soviets in 1950, and was freed in 1954. He died shortly after his return to Poland.

Yehoshua (Shiye) Broyde (1898–1942) was born in Lodz and played an active role in Yiddish education and the YIVO before the war. He translated Plato's dialogues into Yiddish. Suffering from severe lung disease, he committed suicide in 1942.

Natan Buchsbaum (1890–1943) was a leader of the Left Labor Zionists in Poland and of the Central Yiddish School Organization (CYSHO). Like Yoshue Perle and Yitshak Katzenelson, Buchsbaum fell victim to the Hotel Polski scam, bought a Latin American passport, and was murdered in Auschwitz in October 1943.

Shmuel Niger, pen name of **Shmuel Charney** (1883–1955), was a prominent Yiddish literary critic and journalist. His brother, Baruch Charney Vladeck, became a well-known activist in the American Jewish labor movement and the managing editor of the *Jewish Daily Forward*. Another brother, Daniel, became a Yiddish poet and journalist.

Bentsiyon Chilinowicz (1889–1942) was a journalist on the staff of *The Moment*. He was murdered in Treblinka in 1942.

Hersz Cyna (1911–1942) had been a member of Tsukunft, the youth movement of the Bund. He studied in the Academy of Fine Arts in Warsaw and designed posters and political art in the 1930s.

Adolf Dygasiński (1839–1902) was a Polish novelist and educator.

Aaron Einhorn (1884–1942) was a leading journalist for the Zionist Warsaw Yiddish daily *Haynt*. He was murdered in Otwock in 1942.

Wanda Elster–Rotenberg (1924–2008), the sister of Pola Elster, was a member of the Left Labor Zionists and the Jewish Fighting Organization (ZOB). In 1943 and 1944, thanks to her excellent Polish and "Aryan" appearance, she served as a courier for the Jewish National Committee and regularly visited Emanuel Ringelblum to pick up his finished manuscripts and supply him with fresh paper and ink.

Reuven Ben-Shem Feldshuh (1900–1980) was born in Buczacz. He was a journalist and an activist in the Zionist Revisionist movement, and he kept a diary in Hebrew of his experiences in the Warsaw Ghetto. His only daughter, Josima, was a musical prodigy whose concerts in the ghetto made a deep impression on its inhabitants.

Leon Feiner, a.k.a. Pan Mikołaj (1885–1945), was one of the leaders of the Bund during the German occupation. He played a leading role in the underground Jewish Coordinating Committee (ZKK) and in The Council to Aid Jews with the Government Delegation for Poland, or Żegota.

Ludwig Fischer (1905–1947) was the Nazi governor of the Warsaw District of the General Government. He was hanged by the Poles for war crimes in 1947.

Zysha Frydman (1897–1943) was an important Agudas Yisroel activist in prewar Warsaw and in the ghetto.

Adam Furmanski (1883–1943) was a conductor who led various ensembles and orchestras in the Warsaw Ghetto.

Bogusia, whose real name was **Klima Fuswerk–Krymko** (1909–2006), worked in childrens' theater in the Warsaw Ghetto and postwar Poland.

Abraham Gancwajch (c. 1903–1943), a talented prewar speaker and journalist, was a Gestapo agent in the Warsaw Ghetto and the head of a group called the Thirteen. Officially it administered first aid and combated speculation and price gouging. Unofficially it was a lucrative extortion racket that provided services in exchange for hefty bribes. Gancwajch tried to burnish his reputation by providing financial support to Jewish intellectuals and rabbis. For a time the Thirteen competed for power with the Judenrat. Gancwajch disappeared under mysterious circumstances in 1943, and was likely murdered by the Gestapo.

Mordkhe Gebirtig (1877–1942) was a Yiddish poet and an exceptionally popular songwriter. He is best known for such songs as "Es brent" ("It's Burning"), "Reyzele," and "Kinder yorn" ("Childhood Years"). He was shot in the Krakow Ghetto in 1942.

Abraham Gepner (1872–1943) was one of the wealthiest Jewish industrialists in Poland. He had a reputation for honesty and integrity and was an important figure in the Judenrat. In the ghetto he worked tirelessly to help children and orphans. He was murdered in 1943.

Yitshak Giterman (1889–1943) was the prewar director of the Joint Distribution Committee in Poland and later in the Warsaw Ghetto. A key leader of the Aleynhilf and the Oyneg Shabes archive, he was one of Ringelblum's most important mentors. Giterman was shot by the Germans in January 1943.

Moshe Grossman (1904–1961) was a Yiddish writer who worked in the administration of *Haynt*, Poland's largest Yiddish daily, and wrote various literary works, including a biographical novel about

Rosa Luxemburg. He was arrested by Soviet authorities in 1939 and spent the war in labor camps and then in Soviet Central Asia. His two-volume account of his wartime experiences, *In farkisheftn land fun legendarn Dzhugashvili* (*In the Enchanted Land of the Legendary Dzhugashvili*) was a superb memoir of Soviet reality and a helpful corrective to the idealization of Stalin common in certain left-wing circles. In 1950 he immigrated to Israel.

Maria Grzegorzewska (1888–1967) was a pioneering educator of children with special needs. During the war she was active in Żegota and in the Polish resistance movement. She designed the curriculum for the State Institute of Special Education, which she directed from its founding until her death.

Eliyahu Gutkowski (1900–1943) was a key member of the Oyneg Shabes archive. Before the war he taught in Lodz and was a member of the Right Labor Zionists. In 1940 he and Yitshak Zuckerman compiled an anthology, *Payn un gvure* (*Pain and Heroism*), which collected accounts of past Jewish heroism and martyrdom. It served as an important text for the seminars organized by youth movements in the Warsaw Ghetto.

David Guzik (1890–1946) was one of the leaders of the Joint Distribution Committee in the Warsaw Ghetto. He helped raise money through clandestine means to finance self-help activities and to purchase weapons. He survived the war in hiding and died in a plane crash in 1946.

Bernard Hallmann was the German proprietor of a woodworking shop at Nowolipki 59. Many members of the Oyneg Shabes, including Emanuel Ringelblum, found temporary refuge there during the Great Deportation.

Bentsion Hariton was a Yiddish cultural activist who lived in Schenectady, New York. He visited Poland in 1938.

Moyshe-Leyb Halpern (1886–1932) was a Yiddish modernist poet and a leading member of *Di Yunge* (The Youth) literary movement in New York.

Ber Horowitz (1895–1942) was a Galician Yiddish poet, writer, and artist.

Moshe Indelman–Yinnon (1895–1977) was a Hebrew and Yiddish journalist as well as a Zionist activist. In 1940 he was able to leave Warsaw for Palestine. For many years he was on the editorial board of the Yiddish newspaper *Haynt*.

Alter Kacyzne (1885–1941) was a Yiddish author, literary critic, and photographer. He was best known for his two-volume novel *Shtarke un shvakhe* (*The Strong and the Weak*) and plays such as *Dukus*. A close friend of S. An-sky, Kacyzne wrote the screenplay for the 1937 film *The Dybbuk*. He was murdered by Ukrainian nationalists in Tarnopol while he was fleeing the German invasion in 1941. Many of his photographs of Jewish life in Poland were published in *Poyln: Jewish Life in the Old Country* (New York: Metropolitan Books, 1999).

Froym Kaganovsky (1893–1958) was a Yiddish writer who won acclaim for his short stories about Jewish life in the poor neighborhoods of Warsaw. He spent the war in the USSR, returned to Poland in 1946, and settled in Paris in 1949.

Joseph Kamien (1900–1943) was one of the founders of the renowned Vilna Troupe. Before he became involved with Nadia Kareny he had been married to the popular Yiddish actress Dina Kenig. He and Kareny fled to the Soviet occupation zone, where he died in Uralsk in 1943.

Yitshak Katzenelson (1886–1944) was a Hebrew poet, dramatist, teacher, and the principal of a well-known Hebrew gymnasium in Lodz. After the German invasion he moved to Warsaw, where he worked closely with the Dror-Frayhayt youth movement and wrote searing, emotional poems and plays in Yiddish. After his wife and two sons were deported to Treblinka, Katzenelson bought Latin American passports for himself and his surviving son. While interned at the Vittel camp in France, Katzenelson wrote one of his most important works, *The Song of the Murdered Jewish People.* He also kept a diary in Hebrew, which was published after the war. Katzenelson and his son Ben-Tsion were gassed in Auschwitz in early May 1944.

Shloyme-Leyb Kave (c. 1889–c. 1942) was a Yiddish essayist, satirist, and critic, and had been a close associate of I. L. Peretz.

Yosef Kirman (1896–1943) was a Yiddish poet from a poor, working-class Warsaw background. He published one collection of poetry before the war; some of his poems from the Warsaw Ghetto were preserved in the Ringelblum archive. He was murdered in the Poniatowa concentration camp.

Menakhem Mendel Kon (1881–1943) was the treasurer of the Oyneg Shabes and a member of its executive board. Before the war he had been a wealthy merchant and had extensive contacts within Orthodox circles. He died during the ghetto uprising.

Moritz Kon and **Zelig Heller** were refugees from Lodz who prospered in the Warsaw Ghetto through various business dealings, including ghetto streetcars and smuggling people in and out of the ghetto. They had an unsavory reputation and were said to be Gestapo collaborators. But they showed a special solicitude for rabbis and tried to help them survive. They were both murdered by the Germans when they were no longer useful.

Moyshe Kulbak (1896–1937) was a Yiddish poet and writer best known for his 1932 novel *Zelmenyaner* and for poem cycles including *Raysn* (*Belorussia*, 1922) and *Disner tshayld–harold* (Childe Harold from Disna, 1932). He also wrote "Vilna," a 1926 poem celebrating the unique Jewish character of that city. After spending time in Weimar Berlin and Vilna he returned to the Soviet Union in 1928, where he fell victim to Stalin's purges.

Aleksander Landau (?–1943), an engineer by training and the wealthy proprietor of a lumber factory before the war, was a member of the Oyneg Shabes executive committee. During the Great Deportation many members of the archive found temporary refuge in the woodworking shop he ran for the Germans. He perished in Auschwitz in 1944.

Yekhiel Lerer (1910–1943) was a Yiddish poet who gained special acclaim for his long poem "Mayn heym" ("My Home"). In the Warsaw Ghetto he played an active role in the Yiddish Culture Organization (IKOR). He was murdered in Treblinka in 1943.

Jakob Lestschinsky (1876–1966) published many books and articles about Jewish demography, sociology, economic issues, and Holocaust research. After being expelled from Germany in 1933, Lestschinsky moved to Poland and then immigrated to the United States in 1938.

Vita Levin ran a school in Vilna for mentally challenged children.

Luba Levitska (1917–1942) was a beloved soprano in Vilna, gaining fame with her performance of Violetta in a 1938 Yiddish production of *La Traviata*. She gave memorable concerts in the Vilna Ghetto until she was beaten and then murdered in 1942.

Mani Leyb (1883–1953) was a Yiddish poet known for his creative use of alliteration and rhyme. Born in Nezhin, he immigrated to New York when he was 22, where he became a key member of *Di Yunge* (The Youth) literary group.

Kalman Lis (1903–1942) was born in Kowel. From 1937 until his death he ran the CENTOS institution for children with special needs in Otwock. The institution was bombed on the first day of the war, a number of children were killed, and Lis was wounded. He was murdered in 1942.

Maxim Litvinov, born Meir Henoch Wallach (1876–1951), was a Soviet diplomat who served as foreign minister between 1930 and 1939, as well as ambassador to the United States during World War II. Against all odds, he died a natural death in 1951.

Dov Ber Malkin (1901–1966) was a Yiddish journalist and essayist who was active in the Bund and later in the Labor Zionist movement. He immigrated to Palestine from Warsaw in 1934.

Itsik Manger (1902–1969) was a Yiddish poet, playwright, prose writer, and essayist. Born in Czernowitz, Romania (now Chernivtsi, Ukraine), he moved to Warsaw in 1927, where he lived and wrote for the next decade. After being forced out of Poland in 1938, he made his way to Paris, England, New York, and eventually Israel, where he spent the last decade of his life. As a writer for both literary and popular audiences, often on biblical themes, Manger became one of the most beloved Yiddish poets of the twentieth century.

Perets Markish (1895–1952) was a Yiddish modernist poet who settled in the Soviet Union in 1926 and fell victim to Stalin's purge of Yiddish cultural activists. His 1921 poem "Di Kupe" ("The Heap"), about Jews murdered in Ukrainian pogroms, was one of the most powerful evocations of a tragedy that claimed 100,000 Jewish lives.

Mordecai Mazo (1880–1943) was a director of the Vilna Troupe and played a leading role in the development of Yiddish theater in Eastern Europe. In the Warsaw Ghetto he was active in the

Yiddish Culture Organization (IKOR), and directed the kitchen department of the Aleynhilf.

Helena Merenholc (1907–1997) was born into a middle class Jewish family in Warsaw, earned a psychology degree from Warsaw University, and was a psychiatry resident in the city's Jewish hospital before the war. In the Warsaw Ghetto she helped needy children in the CENTOS. After escaping to the Aryan side in March 1943 she procured false documents (her nickname was Mrs. Stasia) and worked as a courier for Żegota and the ZKN. For a time she shared a flat with Auerbach on Próżna Street. After the war she helped direct children's programming on Polish radio and participated in the oppositional Worker's Defence Committee (KOR) in the 1970s, which was a precursor to Solidarity.

Israel Milejkowski (1887–1943) was a well-known Jewish physician. He played a key role in the health department of the Judenrat and participated in a clandestine medical study on the effects of hunger in the Warsaw Ghetto.

Miriam Orleska (1900–1943) was an actress famous for her roles in the Vilna Troupe, especially her performance as Leah in S. An–sky's *The Dybbuk*. In the Warsaw Ghetto she worked in the Aleynhilf self-help organization in addition to acting.

Stanisław Ossowski (1897–1963) was a Polish sociologist known for his humanism and opposition to chauvinistic nationalism. After the war he was a professor at Warsaw University. He was married to Maria Ossowska.

Maria Ossowska (1896–1974) was a sociologist, social philosopher, and professor at Warsaw University. Between 1952 and 1962 she directed the Institute of the History and Theory of Ethics at the Polish Academy of Sciences. In 1964 she signed the "Letter of 34," a protest of leading intellectuals against state censorship.

Abraham Ostrzega (1889–1942) was a leading Jewish sculptor in Warsaw who specialized in designing tombstones, including the famous Ohel Peretz in the Warsaw Jewish cemetery.

Yankev Pat (1890–1966) was a Bundist activist who played a major role in the secular Yiddish school movement in interwar Poland. He survived the war in the United States, where he took an active role in Yiddish cultural life and advocated for Holocaust survivors until his death in 1966.

Yoshue Perle (1888–1943) was a leading member of prewar Warsaw literary society. He is best known for his 1937 novel *Yidn fun a gants yor* (*Ordinary Jews*) and its two sequels.

Y. Y. Propus (1880–1943) was a poet, journalist, and editorial board member of *The Moment*. He died in a bunker in 1943 during the Warsaw Ghetto Uprising.

Noah Prylucki (1882–1941) was a leading Jewish folklorist, expert on the Yiddish language, and a leader of the Jewish People's Party (Folkspartey). He was very active in the Warsaw branch of the YIVO. He was murdered by the Germans in Vilna in 1941.

Hersz Rabinowicz (1900–1942) was a painter specializing in landscapes, still lifes, and portraits in oils and watercolors. Critics noted his deft use of color.

Yehoshua (Shiye) Rabinowicz (1888–1943), a scion of a prominent Hasidic family who joined the Bund, was a key member of the Oyneg Shabes executive committee. The successful owner of a roofing tile business, he was a supporter of the YIVO and in the ghetto was active in the Aleynhilf. He was murdered in Auschwitz in October 1943.

Melech Ravitch (1893–1976), the pen name of Zekharye Khone Bergner, was a Yiddish writer and poet. He was born in Redem, East Galicia, and had a literary career that spanned continents. He was a member of the literary group *Di Khalyastre* (The Gang), secretary of Tlomackie 13, and one of the founders of the journal *Literarishe bleter* (*Literary Pages*). After leaving Poland in 1935 he lived in Australia, Mexico, Israel, and the United States before finally settling in Montreal, Canada, where he headed the city's Jewish Public Library and played a leading role in Yiddish cultural activities.

Mendel Reif (1910–1942) was a Jewish artist and illustrator. He perished in Belzec in 1942.

Avrom Reyzen (1876–1953) was a popular Yiddish poet, writer, and editor.

Zalmen Reyzen (1887–1941), younger brother of Avrom Reyzen, was a leading Yiddishist, a founder of the YIVO, and between 1918 and 1939 the editor of the *Vilner tog* (*Vilna Day*), a leading Yiddish newspaper. He collected biographical materials on Yiddish writers, journalists, and scholars, which were published in four volumes between 1926 and 1929 as the *Leksikon fun der yidisher literatur, prese un filologiye* (*Biographical Dictionary of Yiddish Literature, Press, and Philology*). This became a standard reference work. He was murdered by Soviet secret police in 1941.

Ber Rozen (1899–1954) was a Yiddish writer who was close to the Bund. He spent the war in Shanghai and then emigrated to Melbourne, where he was active in Yiddish cultural life. He wrote a memoir about Tlomackie 13.

Roman Rozental (1897–1942), best known for his watercolor landscapes, was secretary of the Association of Jewish Artists in Poland. Originally from Lodz, he was also a theater director.

Irena Sawicka (1890–1944) was a Polish archaeologist and educator who was a member of the outlawed Polish Communist Party (KKP). She played an active role in Żegota as well as in the left-wing Armia Ludowa (People's Army). She was killed during the 1944 Warsaw uprising.

Leon Schiller (1887–1954) was one of Poland's most important theater directors. Before the war he took an interest in Jewish theater and worked with the Warsaw Yung-teater as well as others. He collaborated with Michał Weichert when he staged Shakespeare's *The Tempest* in Yiddish in 1939.

Moses Schorr (1874–1941) was a major figure in the prewar world of Polish Jewry. He was a respected scholar of Jewish and Assyrian history; the rabbi, from 1923 until 1939, of Warsaw's Tlomackie synagogue; a member of the Polish senate and one of the founders of the Institute of Judaic Studies in Warsaw. He died in a Soviet prison camp in 1941.

Maurice Schwartz (1890–1960) was a well-known Yiddish actor and theater impresario.

Klara Segalowicz (1897–1943) was a popular Yiddish stage and film actress who starred in such films as *In Poylishe velder* (*In Polish Forests*) and *Al khet* (*For Our Sins*). For a short time she was married to the Yiddish writer Zusman Segalowicz.

Zusman Segalowicz (1884–1949) was a popular Yiddish writer in Poland who fled Warsaw in 1939 and spent the war in Palestine. Although his books were best–sellers, he lacked the respect of other Yiddish writers, who regarded him as a middlebrow author. After the war he gave voice in poetry and prose to his profound grief over the murder of Polish Jewry.

Ber Shnaper (1906–1942), a Galician Yiddish poet, was Rokhl Auerbach's first husband.

Moshe Shneour (1885–1942) was born in Kherson and came to Warsaw around 1900, where he studied music with Gustaw Nossakowski. He joined the circle of young writers and intellectuals surrounding I. L. Peretz, and soon found his calling, making music an essential part of Yiddish secular culture. After leading the Bund's Grosser Choir, he took over the Hazamir Choir in 1908. Over time Hazamir became the Jewish People's Choir, and Shneour conducted it until 1939. Shneour led a bohemian lifestyle. He never married and spent his free time at Tlomackie 13, where he could always be found at the piano. After the Germans invaded Poland in 1939, he fled to Bialystok and in 1941 to the interior of the Soviet Union. He died of hunger and disease in Uzbekistan in 1942.

Zalman Shneour (1886–1959) was a Hebrew and Yiddish poet and novelist who became especially popular for his Yiddish novels about the Jews of his native Belarus.

Yisroel Shtern (1894–1942) was a celebrated Yiddish poet and literary critic who led a traditionally religious lifestyle. His work often concerned the economic and existential suffering of everyday Jews. He was murdered at Treblinka in 1942.

Genia Silkes (1914–1984) was a graduate of the Jewish Teachers Seminary in Vilna and taught in Jewish schools in prewar Warsaw and in the ghetto. After jumping from a train bound for Treblinka she survived the rest of the war in hiding. After 1945 she worked for the Jewish Historical Institute in Poland and later for the YIVO Institute for Jewish Research. Her papers in the YIVO archive are a valuable historical resource.

Cecilia Slepak (1900–1942) came from the Russian–speaking Jewish intelligentsia and settled in Warsaw, where she became a journalist and translator, best known for translating Simon Dubnow's *World History of the Jewish People* from Russian into Polish. In the Warsaw Ghetto she undertook a study of Jewish women under Nazi occupation at the request of Emanuel Ringelblum. She and her daughter were probably murdered in Treblinka in 1942. Her husband, an engineer, survived the war.

Józef Sliwniak (1899–1942) was an artist and sculptor who specialized in religious themes. He also helped design stage sets for the Azazel theater.

Shaul Stupnicki (1876–1942) was a Warsaw-based Jewish journalist who wrote in Yiddish and Polish and was active in the Folkspartey.

Walther Caspar Toebbens was a German businessman who established factories in the Warsaw Ghetto to make uniforms and clothing. He made enormous profits from exploiting Jewish slave labor and evaded punishment after the war.

Simcha Trachter (1890–1942) studied in Krakow, Paris, and Vienna. He was an active member of the Jewish Society for the Propagation of the Arts. In the Warsaw Ghetto he was one of the artists that Adam Czerniaków engaged to decorate the walls of the Judenrat building. An exhibition of his work was shown in the Jewish Historical Institute in Warsaw in 2020.

Jonas Turkow (1898–1988) was a well-known Yiddish actor who survived the Holocaust along with his wife, the actress Diana Blumenfeld, and his daughter. He wrote an essay on theater in the Warsaw Ghetto for the Ringelblum archive and several postwar memoirs about his experiences, including *Azoy iz es geven* (*That's How It Was*), *In kamf farn lebn* (*The Struggle for Life*), and a two-volume book about murdered actors and actresses, *Farloshene shtern* (*Extinguished Stars*), published in Buenos Aires in 1953.

Kazimierz Twardowski (1866–1938) was a Polish philosopher and psychologist. He served as rector of the Jan Kazimierz University in Lwow.

Izrael Tykocinski (1895–1942) had several exhibits of his paintings in the 1930s and was also active in the Association of Jewish Artists in Poland. Especially renowned for his portraits of women, he also designed stage sets and posters.

Itshe Meyer Vaysenberg (1881–1938) was a Yiddish writer known for his naturalistic style and his descriptions of class conflicts and tensions within Jewish society. His masterpiece was the 1906 novella *A shtetl*, which focused on the tumultuous revolution of 1905.

Władysław Wajntraub (1891–1942) was an artist and writer who studied in Warsaw, Paris, and with Leon Bakst in Switzerland. Wajntraub participated in the modernist literary groups *Di Khalyastre* (The Gang) in Warsaw and *Yung-yidish* in Lodz. He designed the title page of the introductory edition of the avant–garde journal *Albatross*, as well as stage sets for the Azazel theater and for the Vilna Troupe. Wajntraub published art criticism in the *Literarishe bleter* as well as in *Nasz Przegląd*.

Hersh Wasser (1912–1980) was one of three survivors of the Ringelblum archive and a close collaborator of Emanuel Ringelblum.

Izrael Chaim Wilner, a.k.a. "Jurek" and "Arie" (1917–1943), was a member of the left-wing Zionist youth organization Hashomer Hatzair. After being sent by the Jewish Fighting Organization to negotiate with the Polish Home Army for weapons, he was captured by the Gestapo, brutally tortured, escaped, and later died in the ghetto uprising.

Romana Wiśniacka (1902–1942) played a pioneering role in the field of judicial psychology in Poland. She was murdered in Treblinka in 1942.

Władysław Witwicki (1879–1948) was a Polish psychologist who translated Plato into Polish and wrote extensively about secular ethics and the psychology of religion. He was one of the founders of the Polish Philosophical Society.

Shakhne Zagan (1892–1942) was the leader of the Left Labor Zionists in the Warsaw Ghetto, one of Ringelblum's key mentors, and a major figure in the Aleynhilf. He died in Treblinka in 1942.

Janina Zawirska was a Polish psychologist who helped Basia Berman and other Jews.

Hillel Zeitlin (1872–1942) was a scholar, religious thinker, and journalist. His sons Elkhonen and Arn also became well known Yiddish writers. Some reports say that Zeitlin put on his prayer shawl and phylacteries on his way to the Umschlagplatz in August 1942.

Chaim Zhitlowsky (1865–1943) was one of the major proponents of Yiddishism as a cornerstone of modern Jewish identity. He was a prolific writer, journalist, and social philosopher. Zhitlowsky spent the last three decades of his life in the United States, where he remained a controversial figure, partly because of his on-again, off-again support of Stalin's Soviet Union.

Józef Ziemian (Zysman) (1922–1971) was a member of the Jewish Fighting Organization (ZOB) and the clandestine Jewish National Committee (ZKN). He wrote *The Cigarette Sellers of Three Crosses Square*, a memoir about helping a gang of intrepid Jewish children trying to survive on the Aryan side.

Yitshak Zuckerman (1915–1981) was a leader of the Dror-Frayhayt youth movement and one of the founders of the Jewish Fighting Organization (ZOB) in the Warsaw Ghetto. During the uprising Zuckerman was on the Aryan side, trying to establish contacts and procure weapons from the Polish underground. He then played a major role in the clandestine Jewish National Committee in occupied Warsaw and fought in the 1944 Polish uprising. After the war he helped organize the Bricha, which smuggled Jews out of Poland to Palestine. Zuckerman and his wife, the ghetto fighter Zivia Lubetkin, helped organize Kibbutz Lohamei HaGeta'ot and played key roles in shaping Holocaust memory in Israel.

Reyzl Zychlinski (1910–2001) was a Yiddish poet known for her spare language and free verse. After leaving German-occupied Warsaw she survived the war in the USSR and emigrated to the United States with her husband and son in 1951. In 1976 she was awarded the Itzik Manger Prize for literature.

Selected Chronology

1899

Auerbach is born in Lanowitz (now Lanivitsi, Ukraine), a village in Polish Galicia. For unknown reasons she always claimed to be born in 1903.

1921

Auerbach graduates from the Adam Mickiewicz Gymnasium in Lwow and enrolls at Jan Kazimierz University to study philosophy, psychology, and history. At university she befriends poet Debora Vogel and writer and painter Bruno Schulz.

1925

Auerbach leaves Jan Kazimierz University without receiving a degree. The same year she makes her first visit to Warsaw.

1929

With Vogel and others, Auerbach founds *Tsushtayer*, a literary journal that tries to bring the Polish-speaking Galician Jewish intelligentsia closer to Yiddish.

1932

Tsushtayer folds after three issues. The same year, Auerbach moves to Warsaw, where she works as a freelancer for Yiddish and Polish-Jewish publications, enters the city's Yiddish journalistic and literary community, and becomes the partner of Yiddish poet Itsik Manger.

October 1938

The Polish government decrees that all Polish citizens living abroad will lose their citizenship unless they acquire a special stamp at a Polish consulate. On the night of October 27, SS, SA, and German police arrest 17,000 Polish Jews living in Germany and leave them along the Polish border. Of these, about 9,000 end up in Zbąszyn where, after Polish border guards refused to let them cross the frontier, they languish under open skies in mud, rain, and cold. The Poles eventually let Jewish relief agencies set up a refugee camp. Emanuel Ringelblum, who works for the Joint Distribution Committee, plays a major role in the relief effort.

September 1, 1939

Germany invades Poland, starting World War II.

September 5, 1939

Auerbach receives word of Warsaw's imminent capitulation and considers leaving on a train reserved for journalists.

September 17, 1939

The Soviet Union invades Poland from the east.

September 28, 1939

Warsaw capitulates to the invading German army.

October 1, 1939

On Emanuel Ringelblum's instructions, Auerbach organizes a kitchen for writers at Leszno 40, former headquarters of the retail merchants association and the Hazamir Society.

Winter 1939–1940

Emanuel Ringelblum begins to organize the secret Oyneg Shabes archive at meetings held on Friday nights or Saturday afternoons.

April 30, 1940

German occupation authorities establish the Lodz Ghetto, leading to an influx into Warsaw of Jewish refugees from Lodz.

October 16, 1940

German Governor-General Hans Frank announces the creation of the Warsaw Ghetto. The Ghetto is closed a month later, on November 15, with more than 400,000 Jews imprisoned behind its walls.

Winter 1940

Auerbach moves into the apartment of her cousins, the Feld-shuhs, at Leszno 66.

June 22, 1941

Germany launches Operation Barbarossa, a surprise attack against the Soviet Union.

June 30, 1941

The German army occupies Lwow, where much of Auerbach's family lives.

Spring–Summer 1941

Auerbach becomes involved with the Oyneg Shabes, when Emanuel Ringelblum enlists her to write an essay about the soup kitchen at Leszno 40.

Summer 1941

Artists in the Warsaw Ghetto organize a garden where music and theatrical performances take place.

August 4, 1941

Auerbach finishes her first piece for the Ringelblum archive.

Early Fall 1941

Writer, singer, and ethnographer Menakhem Kipnis dies in the Warsaw Ghetto and is buried in the Gęsia cemetery.

October 23, 1941

Folklorist Shmuel Lehman dies in the Warsaw Ghetto.

Late 1941

Writer Yoshue Perle returns to Warsaw from Lwow.

January 1942

Auerbach's kitchen at Lezsno 40 is reorganized as a "model convalescent kitchen."

April 17–18, 1942

The SS carries out a nocturnal murder spree in the ghetto, killing members of the underground press and other cultural figures.

July 22, 1942

The Great Deportation, or *Grossaktion* Warsaw, begins, in which hundreds of thousands of Jews are deported from the Warsaw Ghetto to be murdered at Treblinka. Around this time the kitchen at Leszno 40 is taken over by the W. C. Toebbens shop.

August 3, 1942

The first cache of the Oyneg Shabes archive is buried.

End of August 1942

The Karl-Heinz Müller workshop is liquidated, and its artist-workers sent to Treblinka.

September 5, 1942

Adolf and Basia Berman escape the ghetto for the Aryan side of Warsaw.

September 6–12, 1942

The remaining 100,000 Jews in the ghetto are forced to pass through an SS selection in which they receive work numbers or are sent to Treblinka. At the end of the "cauldron," about 32,000 Jews are legally allowed to stay, while a similar number remain without documents.

September 21, 1942

The first phase of the Great Deportation ends.

End of September 1942

Shmuel Winter, a sympathetic member of the Judenrat, arranges for Auerbach to move to the central ghetto, where she works at an artificial honey and candy factory alongside Yoshue Perle and Yosef Kirman. At the same time, he and Ringelbum task her with interviewing Abraham Krzepicki, an escapee from Treblinka.

January 18–22, 1943

The Germans enter the ghetto planning to deport eight thousand Jews. This time they are met with armed resistance and leave the ghetto four days later. This second *aktion* encourages the remaining Jews to build hundreds of underground bunkers and hideouts, which will play a key role during the April uprising.

March 9, 1943

Auerbach escapes the ghetto for the Aryan side. She moves into Próżna 14, where she shares a room with teacher Helena Merenholc.

April 19, 1943

Several thousand Nazi troops enter the ghetto, and the Warsaw Ghetto Uprising begins.

April 21, 1943

Auerbach's cousin, the musical prodigy Josima Feldshuh, dies of tuberculosis.

Summer 1943

Auerbach flees Próżna 14 after her landlady is arrested. About a month later she moves in with Mrs. Krauze at Smolna 24.

Fall and Winter 1943–44

Writing secretly at night, Auerbach completes two works: *Together with the People* and *They Called it Resettlement*.

March 1, 1944

Emanuel Ringelblum and Adolf Berman complete a report about cultural life in the Warsaw Ghetto, which is smuggled out through the Polish underground.

March 7, 1944

Ringelblum's hiding place at Grojecka 81 is discovered and its inhabitants sent to Pawiak prison. Ringelblum is murdered around three days later, on March 10.

August 1, 1944

The Warsaw uprising begins. After the capitulation of Polish forces on October 2, the remaining civilian population is expelled and the city is almost completely destroyed.

January 17, 1945

Warsaw is liberated by the Red Army and the First Polish Army.

September 18, 1946

The first cache of the Ringelbum archive is discovered in Warsaw.

1948

Auerbach publishes a book about the Warsaw Ghetto Uprising, *Der yidisher oyfshtand (The Jewish Uprising)*, in Warsaw.

January 1950

Auerbach immigrates to Israel.

December 1, 1950

The second cache of the Ringelblum archive is discovered.

August 19, 1953

Yad Vashem is established by the Israeli Knesset. In March 1954 Auerbach becomes director of its Department for the Collection of Witness Testimony.

October 1958

Auerbach publishes an attack on Yad Vashem leadership, notably its director, Ben–Zion Dinur.

April 11–August 15, 1961

Adolf Eichmann is tried for crimes against humanity and the Jewish people in Jerusalem. Auerbach testifies at the trial, emphasizing the role of cultural resistance during the Holocaust.

1968

Auerbach retires at the insistence of the Yad Vashem directorate.

1972

Auerbach is diagnosed with breast cancer.

1974

Varshever tsavoes (*Warsaw Testament*) is published.

May 31, 1976

Auerbach dies in Israel.

1977

Baym letsn veg (*The Last Journey*) is published posthumously.

Rokhl Auerbach (1899–1976) was born in a small Podolian village in the Habsburg Empire and received her higher education in Lwow, where she studied psychology. A fervent supporter of Yiddish culture, Auerbach wrote for the Yiddish- and Polish-language Jewish press in both Lwow and, after 1932, in Warsaw. In the Warsaw Ghetto she ran a soup kitchen and began to write for Emanuel Ringelblum's secret archive. After she left the ghetto in 1943 she survived using forged Polish papers, becoming a courier for the Jewish underground and writing the first installment of her memoirs. One of only three survivors of the Ringelblum archive collective, Auerbach worked as a Holocaust researcher and journalist in postwar Poland until her emigration to Israel in 1950. Auerbach founded the witness testimony department at Yad Vashem and played an important role in the preparation of the Eichmann trial. She died in 1976.

Samuel Kassow is the Northam Professor of History at Trinity College and holds a Ph.D from Princeton University. He has been a visiting professor at many institutions and was on the team of scholars that planned the POLIN Museum of the History of Polish Jews in Warsaw. Among his various publications are *Students, Professors, and the State in Tsarist Russia* (University of California Press, 1989) and *Who Will Write Our History? Emanuel Ringelblum, the Warsaw Ghetto, and the Oyneg Shabes Archive* (Indiana University Press, 2007), which was translated into eight languages. Along with David Roskies he edited volume 9 of the *Posen Anthology of Jewish Culture*. Kassow was on the team of scholars chosen by Yad Vashem to write a one-volume history of the Holocaust in Poland. A child of Holocaust survivors, Professor Kassow spent his earliest years in a displaced-persons camp in Germany.

About White Goat Press

White Goat Press, the Yiddish Book Center's imprint, is committed to bringing newly translated work to the widest readership possible. We publish work in all genres—novels, short stories, drama, poetry, memoirs, essays, reportage, children's literature, plays, and popular fiction, including romance and detective stories.

whitegoatpress.org
The Yiddish Book Center's imprint